THE CONTEMPORARY SCIENCE SERIES.

EDITED BY HAVELOCK ELLIS.

MAN AND WOMAN.

MAN AND WOMAN:

A STUDY OF HUMAN SECONDARY
SEXUAL CHARACTERS.

BY

HAVELOCK ELLIS.

FOURTH EDITION, REVISED AND ENLARGED.

ILLUSTRATED.

THE WALTER SCOTT PUBLISHING CO., LTD.,
PATERNOSTER SQUARE, LONDON, E.C.
CHARLES SCRIBNER'S SONS,
153-157 FIFTH AVENUE, NEW YORK.
1904.

Havelock Ellis.

PREFACE TO THE FOURTH EDITION.

————•◆•————

THIS book was written ten years ago as a study of human secondary sexual characters. It was at the same time intended as an introduction to a more elaborate study of the primary phenomena of sex on the psychological side. As such the book was in the first place undertaken for my own help and instruction, more than for that of others, simply as a necessary piece of pioneering work at the approach to a difficult and confused field. It has been a satisfaction to me to find that various distinguished workers in anthropology and psychology have found my little book helpful; while it also appears to have commended itself to a wider public both in English and in the translations which have been made into various languages. I do not myself know how many translations are in existence, for it has more than once happened that, with a touching faith in the impersonal and disinterested character of my work, translators have not thought it necessary to communicate the honour they have paid me; in this way, I understand, it has come about that in at least one country (Poland) two translations of the book have appeared simultaneously.

Although it is only ten years since the book was published, during this brief interval has appeared much accurate and valuable specialist work in which the question of sexual differences has been investigated. More than ever before, there has been a tendency to take note of the existence of such differences. To some extent the present book may have stimulated that tendency; but, in any case, it was inevitable. The result has been that to cover this field has become both more easy and more difficult; more easy because the material is now copious and of better quality, more difficult because of its increasing extent and complexity. I have the satisfaction of knowing that my book has been the point of departure of various highly instructive investigations in various countries. Without mentioning living workers, I may refer especially to the late Professor Pfitzner of Strassburg, an anthropologist of admirable accuracy and thoroughness, whose too early death occurred last year. In the first edition of this book, when quoting certain results reached by Pfitzner, I pointed out that he had misinterpreted their significance. With his usual open-minded candour, Pfitzner took up the matter again on a much larger scale, and was thus started on a series of researches which have greatly contributed to our knowledge of sexual differences. So far as I am aware, only one investigation to some extent starting from my book has been brought forward in a hostile and destructive spirit. As this attack was seemingly supported by a ponderous amount of data, it has appeared to me to require an attention it would not otherwise have received, and I have devoted to it a special appendix.

For the reasons that I have named it has happened that in this new edition of my book the ground has perhaps been covered in a less complete fashion than was the case in the first edition. To embody all recent researches it would be necessary not only to re-write the book, but to enlarge it to an inconvenient extent. I trust, however, that in its revised form it will still be found a useful introduction to its subject. All the ground has been worked over again and much new material added. I am pleased to find that it has not been necessary to correct any of the main conclusions, and the last chapter is almost untouched. The only chapter in which it has been necessary to overturn some of the original conclusions is that on the senses; as originally written the chapter was based on a careful study of all the existing data, but those data were scanty; they are now more numerous, and in some respects they seem to point in a different direction.

A leading aim in this book, I may remind the reader, was the consideration of the question how far sexual differences are artificial, the result of tradition and environment, and how far they are really rooted in the actual constitution of the male and female organisms. That remained, and still remains, a question that cannot be decisively answered in any dogmatic manner. So far as we can answer it, our answer is not at most points one of very revolutionary character. If, however, we cannot always see our way beyond the opinions our fathers held, if we even learn to appreciate the wisdom of some of our remote ancestors, at all events it may be said that our opinions become more and more according to knowledge and less rooted in prejudice. In that, at all events, lies a real progress.

In these fields our knowledge is still very young. The sciences of human life have been the latest of all to gain self-consciousness. Anthropology is not two centuries old; scientific psychology is not half a century old. Men studied the stars, but their own souls and bodies seemed to them both too sacred and too shameful for study. It is but a few years since the great French ethnographist, Gabriel de Mortillet, inaugurated in Savoy methodical and precise methods of photographing to scale the unclothed ordinary population of Europe; and in the admirably illustrated books of the indefatigable Dr. Stratz we have, in a somewhat more popular and less scientific form, what is really the first attempt to look at the human body in a natural and wholesome way, and to set forth pictorially its variations according to sex, race, age, and individual development; while, on the psychological side, the contemporary endeavours of Professor Stanley Hall and his collaborators in America to explore on a wide basis the contents of the human mind in early life cannot even yet be said to be thoroughly systemised. Before this century has passed, it may safely be asserted, human knowledge in regard to all the subjects covered by this little book will be accurate and extensive to a degree we can now scarcely conceive, and the attempts of a pioneer to stumble across an uncultivated field will have been forgotten, or only passingly remembered as one of the milestones of progress.

HAVELOCK ELLIS.

February 1904,
    CARBIS WATER,
        LELANT, CORNWALL.

PREFACE TO THE FIRST EDITION
(1894).

----◆----

ABOUT twelve years ago, for my own instruction, I
began to collect definite data concerning the constitutional differences between men and women. I
was moved to do this because I realised that such
differences lie at the root of many social questions
in which I took great interest, and I knew of no
full and unprejudiced statement of the precise facts.
I have continued to collect, sift, and ponder over
my data for some years after I had satisfied myself
personally as to their general significance and drift,
because I believe that there are many men and
women who are in the same position as I was
twelve years ago, and who will welcome this book
as I should have welcomed it at that time. When
I look into newspapers and magazines, and observe
the reckless or ignorant statements that are still
made regarding these matters, I am strengthened
in my belief. To the best of my ability I have
here presented an anthropological and psychological
study of those secondary sexual differences which

recent investigation has shown to exist among civilised human races.

I have throughout sought the advice of acknowledged authorities in various countries on points of detail concerning which a specialist can alone give helpful advice; if I had not done this my work would have been even more imperfect than I am conscious that it is. I am indebted to the specialists in question for the courtesy and readiness with which they have in every case responded to my requests. I am also indebted to various friends, whose names are not mentioned in the text, for suggestions and help of a more general character.

H. E.

CONTENTS.

◆

CHAPTER I.

CHAPTER II.

CHAPTER III.

CHAPTER IV.

CHAPTER V.

CHAPTER VI.

CHAPTER VII.

CHAPTER VIII.

CHAPTER IX.

CHAPTER X.

CHAPTER XI.

CHAPTER XII.

CHAPTER XIII.

Abnormalities, Idiocy, Genius, etc.—The Primitive Racial Elements in a Population perhaps more clearly represented by Women—Women more disposed than Men to preserve Ancient Custom and Ancient Methods of Thought—The Organic Conservatism of Women — Advantages of this Sexual Difference.

CHAPTER XVII.

The Birth-rate of Males higher than of Females—Their Death-rate still higher—Causes of the greater Mortality among Males—The Resistance of Women to Disease—As Illustrated by Scarlet Fever, Small-pox, Influenza, etc.—Recent Improvements in the Death-rate have specially benefited Women—Greater Longevity of Women—The Characteristic Signs of Old Age less marked in Women—The greater Tendency to Sudden Death in Men—The greater Resistance of Women to Disease and Death perhaps a Zoological Fact.

CHAPTER XVIII.

The Knowledge we have gained does not enable us definitely to settle Special Problems—What it does enable us to do—Women are nearer to Children than are Men—But Woman is not Undeveloped Man—The Child represents a Higher Degree of Evolution than the Adult—The Progress of the Race has been a Progress in Youthfulness—In some respects it has been a Progress in Feminisation — Absurdity of Speaking of the Superiority of one Sex over another—The Sexes perfectly poised—But Social Readjustments may still be necessary—We may Face all such Readjustments with Equanimity.

MAN AND WOMAN.

———◆◆◆———

CHAPTER I.

INTRODUCTION.

THE PRIMITIVE SEXUAL DIVISION OF LABOUR—MAN CHIEFLY
MILITANT, WOMAN CHIEFLY INDUSTRIAL—AMONG SAV-
AGE RACES WOMEN NOT INFERIOR TO MEN — THE
INDUSTRIES OF WOMEN GRADUALLY SHARED AND
THEN MONOPOLISED BY MEN—THE STATUS OF WOMEN
IN BARBARISM—THE MEDIÆVAL ATTITUDE TOWARDS
WOMEN, AND ITS CAUSES—THE PHYSIOLOGICAL MYSTERY
OF WOMANHOOD—THE MODERN STATUS OF WOMAN.

"A MAN hunts, spears fish, fights, and sits about,"
said an Australian Kurnai once;[1] the rest is woman's
work. This may be accepted as a fair statement
of the sexual division of labour among very primitive
peoples. It is a division of labour which is altogether independent of race and climate. Among the
Eskimo, in their snow-houses on the opposite side of
the globe, there is the same division of labour as among
the Australians.[2] The tasks which demand a powerful
development of muscle and bone, and the resulting
capacity for intermittent spurts of energy, involving

[1] Fison and Howitt, *Kamilaroi and Kurnai*, Melbourne, 1880,
p. 206.
[2] See, for instance, II. H. Bancroft, *Native Races of the Pacific
States*, vol. i. p. 66.

I

corresponding periods of rest, fall to the man; the care of the children and all the very various industries which radiate from the hearth, and call for an expenditure of energy more continuous but at a lower tension, fall to the woman.

That is the general rule. In such matters the exceptions are very numerous. For example, among the Similkameen Indians of British Columbia, according to Mrs. Allison, who knows them well, formerly "the women were nearly as good hunters as the men," but being sensitive to the ridicule of the white settlers, they have given up hunting.[1] Among the Yahgan of Tierra del Fuego fishing is left entirely to the women;[2] among the Tasmanians, perhaps the lowest human race ever known, the women alone dived for fish; and among the Tasmanians also it was the women who performed the remarkable feat of climbing the lofty smooth-trunked gum-trees after opossums.[3] In all parts of the world, in Australia and Africa, as well as among the ancient Celts, Teutons, and Slavs, women have fought at need, and sometimes even habitually. But usually the perilous and fatiguing tasks of fighting and hunting, of such great moment in early culture, are left to the men. To these might for the most part be added dancing, which is more closely related to the others than is perhaps visible at first sight; it is at once a process of physical training and a mode of reaching the highly-wrought mental condition most favourable for war; the more even activities of primitive women would be impaired rather than assisted by powerful stimulants.

The Indians of Guiana, as studied by a very careful and sympathetic observer,[4] present us with a fairly

[1] Allison, "Similkameen Indians," *Journal Anthropological Institute*, Feb. 1892, p. 307.

[2] P. Hyades et J. Deniker, *Mission Scientifique du Cap Horn*, tome vii., Paris, 1891.

[3] Backhouse, quoted by Ling Roth, *Tasmanians*, p. 16.

[4] Everard im Thurn, *Among the Indians of Guiana*, 1883.

average picture of the sexual division of labour among a race which has yet made little progress in barbarism. Men's work is to hunt and to cut down trees when the cassava is to be planted. When the men have felled the trees and cleared the ground, the women plant the cassava and undertake all the subsequent operations; agriculture is entirely in their hands. They are little if at all weaker than the men, and they work all day while the men are often in their hammocks smoking. But there is no cruelty or oppression exercised by the men towards the women. Pottery is entirely in the hands of the women; the men are specially skilful in basket-making; while both men and women spin and weave. If we turn to the heart of another continent we find in East Central Africa a closely similar division of labour. "The work is done chiefly by the women; this is universal; they hoe the fields, sow the seed, and reap the harvest. To them, too, falls all the labour of house-building, grinding corn, brewing beer, cooking, washing, and caring for almost all the material interests of the community. The men tend the cattle, hunt, go to war;" they also do all the tailoring and spend much time sitting in council over the conduct of affairs.[1]

While the men among all primitive peoples are fitted for work involving violent and brief muscular effort, the women are usually much better able than

[1] James Macdonald, "East Central African Customs," *Journal Anthropological Institute*, August 1892, p. 102. And for another picture of the sexual division of labour among a primitive people see Prof. Haddon's interesting paper on the "Ethnography of the Western Tribes of Torres Straits," in the *Journal Anthropological Institute*, February 1890, p. 342. "The men fished, fought, built houses, did a little gardening, made fish-lines, fish-hooks, spears, and other implements, constructed dance-masks, head-dresses, and all the paraphernalia for the various ceremonies and dances. They performed all the rites and dances, and in addition did a good deal of strutting up and down, loafing, and 'yarning.' The women cooked and prepared the food, did most of the gardening, collected shell-fish and speared fish on the reefs, made petticoats, baskets, and mats."

the men to undergo prolonged and more passive exertion, and they are the universal primitive carriers. Thus, among the Andombies on the Congo, according to Sir H. H. Johnston, the women, though working very hard as carriers, and as labourers in general, lead an entirely happy existence; they are often stronger than the men and more finely developed, some of them, he tells us, having really splendid figures. And Parke, speaking of the Manyuema of the Arruwimi in the same region, says that they are fine animals, and the women very handsome; "they carry loads as heavy as those of the men, and do it quite as well."[1] In North America, again, an Indian chief said to Hearne, "Women were made for labour; one of them can carry, or haul, as much as two men can do."[2] Schellong, who has carefully studied the Papuans in the German protectorate of New Guinea from the anthropological point of view, considers that the women are more strongly built than the men.[3] In Central Australia, again, the men occasionally beat the women through jealousy, but on such occasions it is by no means rare for the woman, single-handed, to beat the man severely.[4] At Cuba, the women fought beside the men, and enjoyed great independence. Among some races of India, the Pueblos of North America, the Patagonians, the women are as large as the men. So among the Afghans, with whom the women in certain tribes enjoy a considerable amount of power. Even among the Arabs and Druses it has been noted that the women are nearly as large as the men. And among

[1] T. H. Parke, *Experiences in Equatorial Africa*, 1891, p. 344.

[2] Hearne, quoted by Bancroft, *Native Races*, etc., vol. i. p. 117. The chief added: "They also pitch our tents, make and mend our clothing, keep us warm at night; and in fact there is no such thing as travelling any considerable distance in this country without their assistance."

[3] Schellong, "Beiträge zur Anthropologie der Papuas," *Zeitschrift für Ethnologie*, heft iv., 1891, p. 173.

[4] *Journal Anthropological Institute*, August 1890, p. 61.

Russians the sexes are more alike than among the English or French.[1]

The militant side of primitive culture belongs to the men; the industrial belongs to women. The characteristic implement of women is not a weapon, but that knife called by the Eskimo the "ulu" or woman's knife, which is used primitively for all manner of industrial purposes, and which still survives among European women as the kitchen chopping knife.[2] The man undergoes the fatigue of hunting, and when he has thrown the game at a woman's feet his work is done; it is her part to carry it and to cook it, as well as to make the vessels in which the food is placed. The skins and the refuse are hers to utilise, and all the industries connected with clothing are chiefly in her hands.[3]

The domestication of animals is usually in women's hands. They are also usually the primitive architects; the hut in widely different parts of the world—among Kaffirs, Fuegians, Polynesians, Kamtschatdals—is built by women. Women are everywhere the primitive agriculturists, though the rougher and heavier work of making a clearing has usually fallen to men, and women hold their own in the fields even in the highly civilised Europe of to-day; thus in Italy, among eleven million women over nine years of age, more than three millions are employed in agriculture. Women have everywhere been the first potters; even

[1] H. Schaaffhausen, "Die beiden menschliche Geschlechte," *Anth. Studien*, Bonn, 1885.

[2] See an elaborate study by Prof. Otis T. Mason of "The Ulu, or Woman's Knife of the Eskimo," *Report of the United States National Museum*, 1890.

[3] There are, as ever, exceptions. In East Central Africa, for example, all the sewing for their own and the women's garments is done by the men, and very well done; "neater tailors than Africans it would be impossible to find anywhere," says Macdonald. Sewing is here so emphatically recognised as men's work, that a wife may obtain a divorce if she "can show a neglected rend in her petticoat." (Macdonald, "East Central African Customs," *Journal Anthropological Institute*, Aug. 1892, pp. 102-110.)

in Europe, almost up to the present day, girls in Jutland were brought up to make pots.[1] Becoming the first potters, women prepared the way for decorative art, but they never went beyond its rudiments; ornamentation, apart from use, seems usually to be peculiar to men.[2] Women seem to have prepared the first intoxicating liquors; whatever we may think of the obscure Hebrew myth which represents a woman as plucking the fermentable apple, in the north the ancient legends clearly represent woman as discovering ale.[3]

Women are sometimes the primitive doctors;[4] but this is by no means universal, probably because medicine-craft at an early period is not differentiated from priest-craft, which is always chiefly in the hands of men; their more stimulating life of alternate fasts and orgies amid wanderings far afield during the hazards of the chase or of war makes them more acquainted with morbid mental phenomena, and with the more " supernatural " aspects of nature.

It is worth while to quote from the picturesque generalised account of women's industries among primitive races given by Professor Otis T. Mason, Curator of the Department of Ethnology in the United States National Museum. He is writing more especially of the tribes of North America, the primitive races of whom our knowledge is most extensive (*American Antiquarian*, January 1889):—"Let us follow the savage woman through her daily cares, in order that we may comprehend the significance of her part in the play. The slain deer lying before her cave, or brush-shelter or wigwam, shall be the point of

---

[1] See evidence quoted by Hein, " Altpreussische Wirthschaftsgeschichte bis zur Ordenszeit," *Zeitschrift für Ethnologie*, 1890, heft v. p. 204. For an account of the primitive manufacture of pottery by women, see Man, " Nicobar Pottery," *Journal Anth. Institute*, August 1893.

[2] Im Thurn states that in Guiana, even though the women make all the pottery, yet the ornamentation is as often the work of men as of women.

[3] " Magic Songs of the Finns," *Folk-lore*, March 1892.

[4] Among the Kurds, for instance, Mrs. Bishop found that all the medical knowledge is in the hands of women, who are the hereditary hakims. (*Journeys in Persia and Kurdistan*, 1891. And see Max Bartels, *Medicin der Naturvölker*, Leipzig, 1893, pp. 52, 53.)

departure in the inquiry. She strikes off a sharp flake of flint for a knife. By that act she becomes the first cutler, the real founder of Sheffield. With this knife she carefully removes the skin, little dreaming that she is thereby making herself the patron-saint of all subsequent butchers. She rolls up the hide, then dresses it with brains, smokes it, curries it, breaks it with implements of stone and bone, with much toil and sweat, until she makes her reputation as the first currier and tanner. With fingers weary and worn, with needle of bone, and thread of sinew, and scissors of flint, she cuts and makes the clothing for her lord and her family; no sign is over the door, but within dwells the first tailor and dressmaker. From leather especially prepared she cuts and makes mocassins for her husband. . . . Out of little scraps of fur and feathers, supplemented with bits of coloured shell or stone or seeds, she dresses dolls for her children, makes head-dresses and toggery for the coming dance, adorns the walls of her squalid dwelling, creating at a single pass a dozen modern industries—at once toy-maker, milliner, modiste, hatter, upholsterer, and wall-decker. . . . She was at first, and is now, the universal cook, preserving food from decomposition and doubling the longevity of man. Of the bones at last she fabricates her needles and charms. . . . From the grasses around her cabin she constructs the floor-mat, the mattress, the screen, the wallet, the sail. She is the mother of all spinners, weavers, upholsterers, sail-makers. Counting and varying stitches, and adding bits of black, blue, red, and yellow on her textures, she becomes the first decorative artist; she invents the chevrons, herring-bones, frets and scrolls of all future art. To the field she goes with this basket or wallet strapped across her forehead. By the sweat of her face she earns her bread and becomes the first pack animal that ever bent under a burden in the world. . . . Home she comes with her load of acorns, roots, seeds, etc., and proceeds to crush them in a mortar or to roll them on a stone slab. Here she appears clearly as the primitive miller. Or, perchance, she lays her seeds in a flat tray, and by help of the wind or a hot stone removes the chaff. Here begins her first lesson in threshing. . . . Perhaps with a stick, hardened and pointed in the fire, she digs the roots from the earth, or cleans or tears away troublesome weeds from useful plants, or digs a hole and drops the seeds of pumpkins, gourds, or maize therein. While we watch her working we are looking at the first gardener, farmer, and nurseryman. It may be that on some lonely plain or alluvial river-bank there is no cave to shelter her and her babes. How long will it take this aforetime basket-maker and leather-worker to devise a shelter of grass or skin, and become the architect primeval? . . . The primeval woman was not a potter. It was not until near the polished stone age that she became the pristine plastic artist. This is true, however, that every form, decoration, and function of pottery were invented by women. . . . In the struggle for existence and exaltation which takes place among many occupations, as among individuals and species, militancy no longer demands all man's waking movements. The arts devised by woman are in the ascendency, and the man militant has glorified them by his co-operation. Her very ancient digging-stick is now a plough; her rude carrying-strap over her aching forehead is now the railroad train; her woman's boat, the ocean steamer; her stone hand-mill, the costly roller-mill; her simple scraper for softening hides, the great tanneries and shoe-factories; her distaff and weft-stick, the power-loom; her clay and smooth pebble, the potter's wheel; her sharpened stick and bundle of hairs are all the apparatus of the plastic and pictorial arts. . . . In the early history of art, language, social life, and religion, women were the industrial, elaborative, conservative half of society. All the peaceful arts of to-day were once woman's peculiar province. Along the lines of industrialism she was pioneer, inventor, author, originator."

As a more special detailed example of the primitive sexual division of labour we may take the Central Eskimo as described by Dr. Boas (F. Boas, "The Central Eskimo," *Annual Report Bureau of Ethnology*, 1884-85, pp. 579, 580). "The principal part of the man's work is to provide for his family by hunting, *i.e.*, for his wife and children and for his relatives who have no provider. He must drive the sledge in travelling, feed the dogs, build the house, and make and keep in order his hunting implements, the boat-cover and seal-floats excepted. The woman has to do the household work, the sewing, and the cooking. She must look after the lamps, make and mend the tent and boat-covers, prepare the skins, and bring up young dogs. It falls to her share to make the inner outfit of the hut, to smooth the platforms, line the snow-house, etc. On Davis Strait the men cut up all kinds of animals which they have caught; on Hudson Bay, however, the women cut up the seals. There the men prepare the deerskins, which is done by the women among the Eastern tribes. Everywhere the women have to do the rowing in the large boats while the man steers. Cripples who are unable to hunt do the same kind of work as women."

When the ethnographic knowledge of primitive races was less advanced than at present it was frequently stated that women are a source of weakness among savages, and that therefore their position is so degraded that they are almost in the position of slaves. Even at the present time, anthropological writers whose faith in the future leads them to be unjustly scornful of the past, have unintentionally misrepresented and distorted the facts of savage life. A more complete statement of the facts, and the deeper insight which we now possess regarding their interpretation, enable us to assert that while among many races women have been to a greater or less extent in subordination to their more powerful mates, on the whole the wider control which women have had over the means of production, as well as the skill of women in diplomacy,[1] have given them influence and even authority. To these results have contributed in many cases no doubt factors of a different order due to certain modes of marriage and filiation which have tended to give greater dignity to women.

M'Lennan, Lubbock, and Letourneau are probably the most prominent anthropologists who have argued, apparently from their knowledge of civilised women, that among savages women are a "source of weakness," and in consequence liable to oppression. But, as has often been pointed out by those who possess more than a second-hand acquaintance with savage life, although this is sometimes the case, it is not seldom the very reverse of the truth. Thus Fison and Howitt, who discuss this point, remark, in regard to Australian women: "In times of peace, as a general rule, they are the hardest workers and the most useful members of the community." In times of war, again, "they are perfectly capable of taking care of themselves at all times; and, so far from being an encumbrance on the warrior, they will fight, if need be, as bravely as the men, and with even greater ferocity" (Fison and Howitt, *Kamilaroi and Kurnai*, pp. 133-147, 358). Buckley, who lived for thirty-two years among Australian savages, mentions that when those he lived with were attacked by a numerous hostile party, "they raised a war-cry; on hearing this the women threw off their rugs and, each armed with a short club, flew to the assistance of

---

[1] Of the women of many races it may be said, as the Rev. C. Harrison says of the Haidas of the Queen Charlotte Islands, "The women are great diplomats, and generally contrive to have their own way, and it is a great mistake to imagine that they are treated as slaves" (*Journal Anthropological Institute*, May 1892, p. 472). Among the Australian Dieyerie, Curr (*Australian Races*) states that the women act as ambassadors to arrange treaties, and invariably succeed in their missions.

their husbands and brothers" (*Life and Adventures of William Buckley*, p. 43). "They who are accustomed to the ways of civilised women only," remarks Mr. Fison, "can hardly believe what savage women are capable of, even when they may well be supposed to be at their weakest. For instance, an Australian tribe on the march scarcely take the trouble to halt for so slight a performance as a childbirth. The newly-born infant is wrapped in skins, the march is resumed, and the mother trudges on with the rest. Moreover, as is well known, among many tribes elsewhere it is the father who is put to bed, while the mother goes about her work as if nothing had happened."

Man has been the most highly favoured and successful of all species, and, as Professor Mason well remarks, "If one half of this species, the maternal half, in addition to many natural weaknesses, had been from the first the victim of malicious imposition and persecution at the hands of the other and stronger half, humanity would not have survived" (Mason, "Woman's Share in Primitive Culture," *American Antiquarian*, Jan. 1889). Mr. Horatio Hale, another well-known American anthropologist, in a paper read at the annual meeting of the Royal Society of Canada in 1891 (and reprinted in the *Journal Anthropological Institute*, May 1892, p. 427), likewise observes, "The common opinion that women among savage tribes in general are treated with harshness, and are regarded as slaves, or at least as inferiors, is, like many common opinions, based on error, originating in too large and indiscriminate deduction from narrow premises. A wider experience shows that this depressed condition of women really exists, but only in certain regions and under special circumstances. . . . The wife of a Samoan landowner or a Navajo shepherd has no occasion, so far as her position in her family or among her people is concerned, to envy the wife of a German peasant." Mr. Hale goes on to argue that "it is entirely a question of physical comfort, and mainly of the abundance or lack of food," and illustrates this proposition by the difference between the position of the women among the northern sub-arctic Tinneh and among the southern Tinneh (or Navajos) in sunny and fruitful Arizona; among the former tribes "women are slaves: among the others they are queens;" women, he considers, are the comparatively weak members of the community, and are, therefore, the first to suffer under harsh conditions of life.

In a primitive and unstable state of existence, men are chiefly occupied in the absorbing duties of war and the chase. As the position of a tribe and its means of subsistence become more assured, the men are enabled to lay down their weapons and to take up women's implements, and specialise women's industries. Thus, as Professor Mason points out,[1] the primitive woman handed her ulu over to the saddler, teaching him, apparently, how to work in leather; the saddler of ancient Egypt, as depicted on monuments, used the ulu, and the saddler of to-day still uses it. It may thus have happened that, as we sometimes find still among races which have passed from savagery into the earlier stages of barbarism, and among whom war happens to occupy a small place, various industries are fairly divided between the sexes. Thus, among the Melanesians, a horticultural people who show great skill in such work, "the respective share of men and women in garden work is settled by local custom."[2] But an equality of this complete kind rarely seems to have been the rule. Women invented and exercised in common multifarious household occupations and industries. They were unable to specialise their work, and in consequence they could not develop it highly. Men, liberated more or less from the tasks of hunting and fighting, gradually took up the occupations of women, specialised them and developed them in an extraordinary degree. Why the division of labour should be a masculine and not a feminine characteristic, whether it is the result of physical and mental organisation, or merely due to social causes, is not quite obvious; probably it is due to both sets of causes. Maternity favours an undifferentiated condition of the various avocations that are grouped around it; it is possible that habits of war produced a sense of the advantages of specialised and subordinated work. In any case the fact itself is undoubted, and it has had immense results on civilisation.

To speak with assurance regarding the respective status of the sexes in savagery and the early stages

[1] "The Ulu," *Report U.S. National Museum*, 1890, p. 414.
[2] Codrington, *The Melanesians*, 1891, p. 304.

of barbarism is not easy. There are not many races in an uncontaminated stage of early barbarism; it is rare to find an observer who is sufficiently intelligent and sympathetic to be able to understand the conditions of such races; and it is difficult to estimate the disturbing influence of various conditions which deviate the circumstances of such races from the typical order. When we turn to races in a highly developed state of barbarism, such as we find in mediæval Europe, the difficulties are of another kind. The materials on which to found a judgment are so ample that it is impossible to generalise in a broad and unmodified manner. We have before us chronicles, romances, *fabliaux, contes, acta sanctorum*, codes, customaries, proverbs — altogether a vast amount of original documents—all throwing more or less unintentional light on the respective parts played by men and women in the developed barbarism of mediæval Europe. One who has only been able to dip here and there into this fascinating mass of literature cannot pretend to speak of any definite and assured result. But there are certain points that strike one again and again. The militant element ruled throughout mediæval Europe, and that meant the predominance of men. Thus if we examine the great French epic cycle as Krabbes has done,[1] we see such a state of society depicted the more veraciously because incidentally and unintentionally. The men were above all fighters, and even the women delighted in fighting; women had utter contempt for the man who was a coward in war, and at times took a subordinate part in war themselves, guarding prisoners for example. The entire absorption of the men in fighting had a marked effect on the passion of love. The women in these epic poems are usually the wooers; the men are generally indifferent, rarely

[1] Theodor Krabbes, *Die Frau im altfranzoesischen Karls-epos*, 1884. (Stengel's Series of *Ausgaben und Abhandlungen aus dem Gebiete der romanischen Philologie.*)

actively in love with the women to whom they yield;
they merely respond, and often not so warmly as the
women desire; the women openly embrace the men
who attract them, and only once do we read of a
woman who was ashamed to kiss in public, while men
are represented as decidedly less sensual than women.
But notwithstanding this freedom of initiative, when
the woman becomes a wife she is entirely in the
power of her husband, who may address her in terms
of the greatest contempt.

The beginnings of industrialism were not destructive of the militant spirit and its predominance.
Even in republican industrial towns it was frequently
necessary that the workers should also be fighters.
In early barbarous societies we see men gradually
taking up and specialising the industries originated
by women; in the developed barbarism of Europe
only a few simple household industries were on the
whole left to women. Even in the monasteries, where
men and women lived under similar conditions, it
cannot be said that the achievements of women in
any field rivalled those of men. For women there
was the home and, it must be added, the brothel;
while a vast stream of women for whom there was
no other outlet—a stream including the insane and
the hysterical, but certainly many who were neither
—fell under suspicion of sorcery and perished as
witches. This divergence of the paths of women
from the paths of men had two different classes of
effects: on the one hand, more marked sexual differences in physical development seem (we cannot speak
definitely) to have developed than are usually to be
found in savage societies; and on the other hand, the
attitudes of men towards women and of women
towards men were correspondingly wrought up to
pitches of emotional intensity before unknown.
When we look into this wonderful mediæval literature we never find men and women in the attitude of
comrades and fellow-workers, as we nearly every-

where find them in earlier stages of society. We find, instead, men, influenced to some extent doubtless by traditions of Christian asceticism, as well as by the actual facts of mediæval life, regarding women as the symbols of the sensual element in life, as the force that retards progress and growth, and at the same time—a more Pagan element perhaps coming in together with a tinge of mysticism—we find that women are regarded as the inspirers of men, the spiritual and refining elements of life. Partly, it seemed, women were good to play with, partly good to worship.[1] A large part of the real work of the world was women's to do—although under military as well as monastic conditions men and women were relatively independent of each other—but their work seems to have been regarded as little worth mention; work did not fit in with the mediæval theory of women.

An important origin of the element of mystery which women have aroused in men and even in themselves lies in the periodic menstrual function. This function, unlike any normal physiological function in men, has been an everlasting source of marvel and of profound repugnance among all primitive races. They have been singularly unanimous on this point, and even seem to show a certain amount of unanimity in their explanations. As has been shown by Ploss and Max Bartels, the snake (or occasionally some allied reptile, such as the crocodile or lizard) has been connected with this function or with its mythical origin; in New Guinea, in Guiana, in Portugal, in Germany, traces may be found of this connection, often seeming to indicate that a snake, whether from love or a hostile purpose, had bitten the sexual organs of woman and so caused the phenomena. I

---

[1] The comic literature of mediæval times—*farces, fabliaux, contes,* etc.—is impregnated with the feeling of suspicion and horror as regards women. The opposite and complementary tendency to glorify women may be found not only in the love-poetry of the epoch, but also in a large but now forgotten group of prose-literature. Thomas, in his *Essai sur le caractère, les mœurs, et l'esprit des Femmes,* gives an account of some portions of this literature. A contemporary picture of the fascination and duplicity of the mediæval woman, drawn with a psychologic subtlety altogether modern, is embodied in *Petit Jehan de Saintré.*

would add that in the Hebrew story of the Garden of Eden we trace a similar primitive connection between woman and the snake. This is still obscure, but there is no obscurity whatever with regard to the universal attitude of savage and barbarous races towards the menstrual function. Everywhere during the continuance of the flow the woman is regarded as more or less unclean. When this attitude is more clearly marked she must refrain from all household duties, especially from the preparation of food, and to approach her is often an offence. For the time she is in exactly the same position as the mediæval leper. She must wear a special garment (as in some parts of India), or call aloud to warn all who approach her that she is unclean (as in Surinam), or dwell apart either in a hut alone or in a house reserved as a common dwelling for women in the same condition (as in the Caucasus, Japan, the Caroline Islands, among the Hottentots, the North American Indians, and many other races). We are familiar through the Old Testament with the elaborate code of barbarous ritual which grew up among the Jews, while, according to some of the ancient Hindoo sacred writings, the menstruating woman was taught to regard herself as a pariah; by an early Council of the Western Church a woman was forbidden to enter a church during her period; and among the Christians of modern Greece she is not allowed to kiss the images in church, or to partake of the communion. (The ethnography of this subject is dealt with in detail by Ploss and Max Bartels, *Das Weib*, 7th edition, 1901, vol. i. chap. xiii.) As we approach the higher levels of barbarism the custom of making a marked social difference in the treatment of women at this period gradually disappears, but the feeling itself by no means disappears. Instead of being regarded as a being who at periodic intervals becomes the victim of a spell of impurity, the conception of impurity becomes amalgamated with the conception of woman. It was thus that a large number of the early Christian writers regarded woman; she is, as Tertullian puts it, *janua diaboli;* and this is the attitude which still persisted in mediæval days, though it should be added that ascetics impartially extended the idea of impurity to men also. At the same time the belief in the periodically recurring specific impurity of women has by no means died out even to-day. Among a very large section of women of the middle and lower classes in England and other countries it is firmly believed that the touch of a menstruating woman will contaminate food; only a few years since, in the course of a correspondence on this subject in the *British Medical Journal* (1878), even medical men were found to state from personal observation that they had no doubt whatever on this point. Thus one doctor, who expressed surprise that any doubt could be thrown on the point, wrote, after quoting cases of spoiled hams, etc., presumed to be due to this cause, which had come under his own personal observation:—" For two thousand years the Italians have had this idea of menstruating women. We English hold to it, the Americans have it, also the Australians. Now I should like to know the country where the evidence of any such observation is unknown." Women of every class preserve this belief, and still regard the periodic function—although it is frequently a factor of the very first importance in their personal and social life—as almost too shameful to be alluded to.

The effect on women of the militant mediæval organisation and its correlated conditions was peculiar, and may still be felt. Openly they tried to live up to the angelic ideals of men; secretly they played with men; unostentatiously they worked, either honestly in their homes, or by intrigue in public affairs. In the great centres of European life, during mediæval and later times, these conflicting ideals have produced very complex and attractive feminine personalities, often much more delightful and even more wholesome than the influences which moulded them would lead us to expect, but usually more or less profoundly tinged by the unavoidable duplicity of conflicting ideals.

Many of these sexual characteristics have doubtless persisted to modern times, but the conditions which gave rise to them have in large measure changed. The eighteenth century in Europe, and more especially in England and France, was marked by a widespread resolve to reason clearly concerning the nature and causes of things, so far as possible casting off prejudice, and it could not fail to touch the questions that concerned the status of women; such problems were no longer left to work themselves out in unobserved silence. At the same time an economic revolution was taking place which tended to withdraw women from their homes and men from their previously more independent and intermittent labour. A new industrial *régime* was emerging by which work became organised in large centres, and the introduction of machinery enabled men and women to work side by side at the same or closely allied occupations. This is still going on to-day. It is also being recognised as reasonable that both sexes should study side by side at the school and the college, and where not side by side, still in closely similar fashion, while the recreations of each sex are to some extent becoming common to both. Such conditions have tended to remove artificial sexual differences, and have largely obliterated the coarser signs of superiority which may before have been possessed by one sex over another. The process of transition is still in rapid progress. It began in the lower and more mechanical fields of labour; it is proceeding to the higher and more specialised forms. Women have entered, or are about to enter, the various learned professions, and are tending to acquire the same rights of citizenship as men.

As such social changes tend more and more to abolish artificial sexual differences, thus acting inversely to the well-marked tendency observed in passing from the lower to the higher races, we are brought face to face with the consideration of those differences which are not artificial, and which no equalisation of social conditions can entirely remove, the natural characters and predispositions which will always inevitably influence the sexual allotment of human activities. So long as women are unlike in the primary sexual characters and in reproductive function they can never be absolutely alike even in the highest psychic processes. What is the nature, so far as we can venture to tell it to-day, of these fundamental secondary sexual characters?

CHAPTER II.

HOW TO APPROACH THE PROBLEM.

THE DEFINITION OF SECONDARY SEXUAL CHARACTERS—
TERTIARY SEXUAL CHARACTERS—STANDARDS OF COM-
PARISON — THE INFANTILE AND THE SENILE — THE
HUMAN CHARACTERISTICS OF INFANT APES — THE
POSITION OF THE LOWER HUMAN RACES—FALLACIES
DUE TO INCOMPLETE DATA AND TO BIAS—INCOM-
PLETENESS OF OUR KNOWLEDGE.

THE term " secondary sexual character " was first
used by Hunter. He applied it to such a structure
as, for instance, the comb of the cock, but, so far as
I have been able to find, he does not anywhere define
precisely what he means by the term. Darwin, also,
who wrote one of his most important books, *The
Descent of Man, and Selection in Relation to Sex*,
chiefly on this subject, refrains from defining very
precisely what is to be included under the term
" secondary sexual characters," only remarking that
they graduate into the primary sexual organs, and
that " unless indeed we confine the term ' primary '
to the reproductive glands, it is scarcely possible to
decide which ought to be called primary and which
secondary." [1]

When we are dealing with Man it is perhaps most
convenient to set aside as primary the sexual glands
in each sex, and the organs for emission and reception
in immediate connection with these glands. That is

[1] *Descent of Man*, chap. viii.

to say, the primary sexual organs are those that may fairly be regarded as essential to reproduction. The breast, which is not necessary to reproduction, but is an auxiliary of the first importance in the propagation of the race, may be counted as the chief of the secondary sexual characters; or else (with Darwin) as occupying a borderland between the primary and secondary characters.

The difficulty lies not so much in determining the boundary between primary and secondary sexual characters as in limiting the extension of the latter characters. Perhaps the most marked human secondary sexual characters are the difference in the massing and arrangement of the hair, so that while the man's is largely concentrated on his face the woman's is chiefly massed on her head, and the difference in the larynx and voice by which a further degree of development forms a part of male evolution at puberty, while in woman there is comparatively little development. These are typical secondary sexual characters, and we may perhaps define a human secondary sexual character as one which, by more highly differentiating the sexes, helps to make them more attractive to each other, and so to promote the union of the sperm-cell with the ovum-cell. Other things being equal, a man is more attracted to a woman with luxuriant hair on her head than to one whose hair is sparse; other things being equal, a woman is more attracted to a man with deep vibrant voice than to a man with a shrill feminine voice. The sexes are not greatly attracted by any purely æsthetic qualities; it is the womanly qualities of the woman which are attractive to the man, the manly qualities of the man which are attractive to the woman.[1] The secondary sexual characters, as thus understood, are

[1] As Chateaubriand somewhere remarks: "On sait qu'instinctivement la nature porte la femme à préférer l'homme fort et vigoureux à l'être chétif et délicat, et j'ai lu que si on présente à une jeune fille un Adonis ou un Hercule, elle rougira, mais choisira Hercule."

those which indirectly favour reproduction and which might conceivably be developed by sexual selection as understood by Darwin, whether or not they actually are so developed.

There are, however, other sexual differences which do not so easily fall into this group. These differences are less obvious; many of them are relative, or only perceptible when we take averages into consideration; but they are very numerous. Thus we have, for instance, the much greater shallowness, proportionately, of the female skull; we have the greater size and activity of the thyroid gland in women and the smaller average proportion of red blood corpuscles; and we have a different average relationship of the parts of the brain to each other. These differences are probably related indirectly to primary and secondary sexual differences; they are not of great importance from the zoological point of view, but they are of considerable interest from the anthropological point of view, very often of interest from the pathological point of view, and occasionally of great interest from the social point of view. They cannot be easily put into the same group as the secondary sexual characters as usually understood; and perhaps it would be convenient if we were to agree to distinguish them as tertiary sexual characters.

It would be desirable to have a fairly definite classification of sexual characters into groups, but there is no distinct natural division between the groups which tend to merge into each other. Professor Charles Stewart defines secondary sexual characters as comprising those features by which we are enabled to distinguish the male from the female quite irrespective of the essential organs of reproduction, and which are not concerned either in the nourishment or in the reproduction of the young. This seems to me to give an inconveniently large extension to the primary group, while it allows no place for what I have called the tertiary sexual characters. Ultimately, if we take a sufficiently broad outlook, *all* sexual characters, as Weismann points out, are really secondary (in the sense in which I have defined such characters): "Just as the differentiation of cells into male and female reproductive elements is secondary," he remarks, "so is that of male and female individuals. All the numerous differences in form and function which characterise sex among the higher animals, all the so-called 'secondary sexual characters,' affecting even the highest mental qualities of mankind, are nothing but adaptations to bring about the union of the hereditary tendencies of two individuals." (A. Weismann, "Remarks on Certain Problems of the Day," 1890, in *Essays upon Heredity*, vol. ii. p. 91.)

It is with secondary sexual characters, or with secondary and tertiary sexual characters, as I have defined them, and more especially the latter, that we have here to deal. In order to estimate the significance of each character as it comes before us we must have certain standards against which to measure it. What are our standards of comparison for sexual characters in a man or in a woman?

The reader will soon perceive that there are two standards. The first is constituted by the child and its anatomical and physiological characteristics. The second is constituted by the characters of the ape, the savage, and the aged human creature. As each character in a man or in a woman comes before us for consideration we shall instinctively place it between the same characters as they appear associated with infantilism and with senility. When it is there placed we shall observe whether on the whole it tends to lean towards the one side or the other, towards infantilism or towards senility. Let me say at the outset that in pointing out that such and such a character in men or in women brings men or women near to children or the apes, I have no wish to disparage the sex in question. It is simply that thereby we may be helped to understand the significance of the particular masculine or feminine character before us. The larger question of the significance of infantilism and senility themselves in the evolutionary process will perhaps become clearer as our examination proceeds.

The reader will, however, perceive immediately that these two standards of infantilism and senility are of very unequal value. The standard offered by the child is comparatively simple and uncomplicated. The child with its relatively enormous head, its large protuberant abdomen — "all brain and belly," as

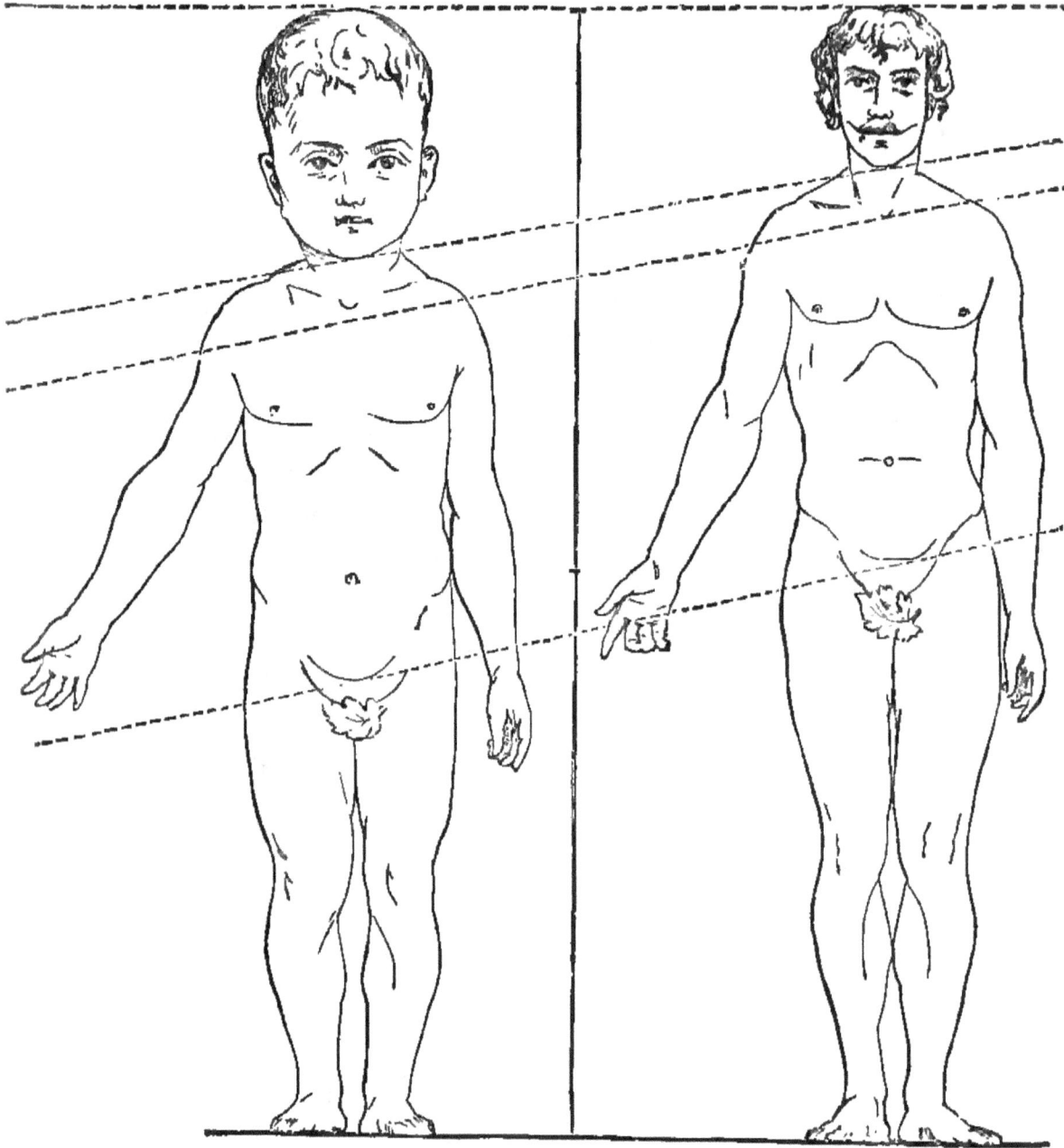

DIAGRAM SHOWING RELATIVE PROPORTIONS OF CHILD AND ADULT. (*Langer.*)

some one defines it—its small chest, short feeble legs, comparatively vigorous arms, smooth almost hairless skin, large liver, kidneys, thymus, and suprarenal capsules, presents us with a distinct anatomical picture; and the facts of the child's physiological and psychic life are also fairly clear. But the compound standard, on the other side, of simian, savage, and senile characters is much less clearly defined. We encounter, for instance, the fact that the anthropoid apes at an early period of life often present characters quite unlike those they exhibit in the adult form. The young anthropoid is comparatively human in character, the adult ape is comparatively bestial in character. The young ape has a smooth globular head and a relatively small face, as man has; the profile is more human, with little prognathism; the base of the skull also is formed in a more human way than in the adult ape; and, above all, the brain is relatively very much larger than in the adult.[1] If we take, for example, the gorilla, we find that the fœtus differs from the adult by having relatively a much larger head, a longer neck, a more slender trunk, shorter limbs, a longer thumb and great toe; while the head is more globular, the face less prognathous, and the hand more like man's.[2] In nearly all these characters the fœtal gorilla approaches Man. The adult male Ape has rapidly developed into a condition far removed from his early man-like state. The brain has become relatively very small, and his receding skull has become hideous with huge bony crests, sharp angles, and on its enormously enlarged facial portion prominent outstanding superciliary ridges, projecting jaws, and receding chin; while the dark hairy body has also become more bestial in character. The female Ape remains midway between the infantile and the adult male condition. So far as Man is ape-like, it is, on the whole, the infantile and not the adult Ape whom he resembles. Man also in

[1] See, for instance, Professor J. Ranke, "Ueber Beziehungen des Gehirns zum Schädelbau," at the Danzig meeting of the German Anthropological Society, August 1891.

[2] Deniker, "Recherches anatomiques et embryologiques sur les Singes anthropoides," *Archives de Zoologie expérimentale*, 1885-86.

the course of his life falls away more and more from the specifically human type of his early years, but the Ape in the course of his short life goes very much

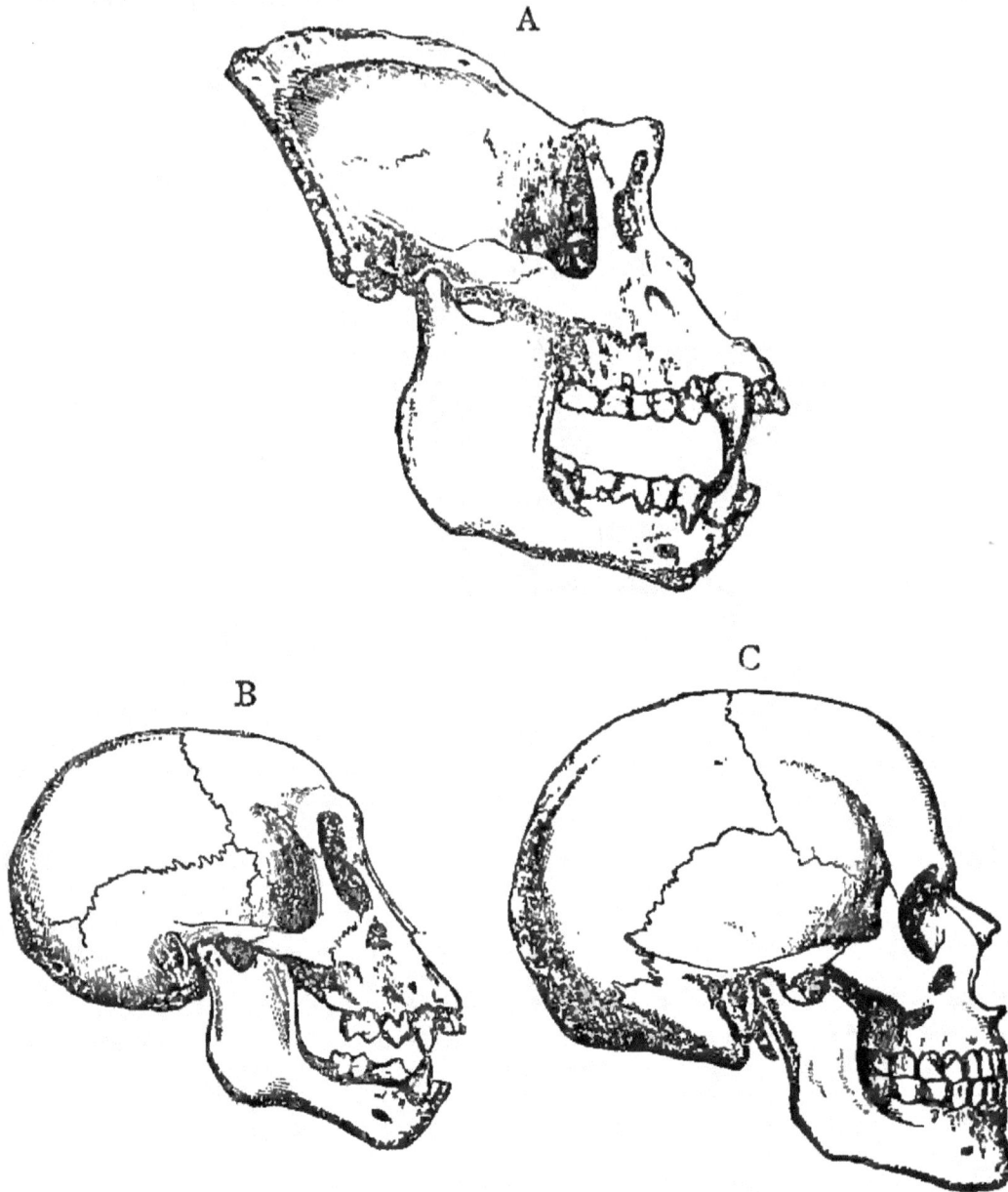

A

B   C

A. SKULL OF ADULT GORILLA.   B. SKULL OF YOUNG GORILLA.
C. SKULL OF MAN.
(*British Museum Guide to Mammalia.*)

farther along the road of degradation and premature senility. The Ape starts in life with a considerable human endowment, but in the course of life falls far away from it; Man starts in life with a still greater portion of human or ultra-human endowment, and to a less extent falls from it in adult life, approaching more and more to the Ape. It seems that up to birth, or shortly afterwards, in the higher mammals such as the Apes and Man, there is a rapid and vigorous movement along the line of upward zoological evolution, but that a time comes when this fœtal or infantile development ceases to be upward, but is so directed as to answer to the life-wants of the particular species, so that henceforth and through life there is chiefly a development of lower characters, a slow movement towards degeneration and senility, although a movement that is absolutely necessary to ensure the preservation and stability of the individual and the species. We might say that the fœtal evolution which takes place sheltered from the world is in an abstractly upward direction, but that after birth all further development is merely a concrete adaptation to the environment, without regard to upward zoological movement.

We see, therefore, that the infantile condition in both the Apes and Man is somewhat alike and approximates to the human condition; the adult condition of both also tends to be somewhat alike and approximates to the ape-like condition. The phenomena which we find among the lower human races are in harmony with those we find among the Apes and in Man generally, although the divergences are so wide that we cannot speak definitely. In some respects some of the black races may be said to be more highly evolved than the white European races. Thus the short body and long legs which we usually find among negroes are far removed from the simian condition, and equally far removed from the infantile condition. On the whole, it may be said that the yellow races are nearest to the infantile condition; Negroes and Australians are farthest removed from it, often although not always in the direction of the Ape; while the white races occupy an intermediate position.[1] In certain characters, however, the adult European is distinctly at the farthest remove as well from the simian and the savage as from the infantile condition; this is especially so as regards the nose, which only reaches full development in the adult white. In some other respects, as in the amount of hair on the body, the adult European recedes both from the specifically human and from the infantile condition, and remotely approaches the Ape.

The variations and uncertainties are so considerable that we can never assume that because a given character is simian or savage or senile, it belongs to all three groups; nor can we base arguments on any such assumed identity of the three groups. Practically, however, we do find that these three groups agree in various particulars to furnish characters which are removed to the farthest extremity from the child. Such characters are the comparatively small head, the large and fierce face, the long limbs, the general tendency to hairiness, the dark and wrinkled skin, the comparative absence, usually, of fat and the exaggeration of the muscular and bony systems, a general tendency to ossification, and on the nervous and mental side a general inclination to rigidity and routine. Such characters are usually, though not quite universally, simian, savage and senile. So that we have on the one side the group of immature characters, and on the other side the group of over-mature characters; and any characteristic of the male or female adult individual may lean in either of these directions.

Even, therefore, when the facts of secondary sexual differences are fairly established, there is sometimes a certain difficulty in arriving at the significance of the facts. It has to be added, as a further difficulty, that the facts themselves are in a

[1] See Professor J. Ranke, "Ueber das Mongolenauge," etc., at the Bonn meeting of the German Anthropological Society, 1888.

very large number of cases by no means well established. Few persons have made it their business to ascertain sexual differences; such differences have most usually come to light incidentally in the course of more general investigations. Again, nearly all those sexual differences which I have proposed to call tertiary are merely a matter of averages. In order to obtain reliable results, not only must the investigation be accurately and uniformly carried out, it must be extended to a very large number of individuals. By confining our observations to a small number of individuals we either reach results that are expected or that are unexpected; in the former case we accept them without question; in the latter case we suspect a fallacy and reject them. Thus, for example, Quetelet, an unreliable statistician but a man of genius who did much to open out new lines of investigation and to place the knowledge of man on a sure basis, used to draw his conclusions from a few selected cases which he regarded as typical. This was a thoroughly vicious method which could only lead to expected results. Thus he prepared a table to show the comparative height and weight of men and women at all ages; this table shows with beautiful uniformity that at no age are females taller or heavier than males. Subsequent investigation, on a more extensive scale and in a large number of countries, has shown that during certain years of development girls are distinctly heavier and taller than boys. This fact was not suspected in Quetelet's time, and it is evident that if in his group of cases of boys and girls at the age of thirteen he had found that the girls were heavier and taller than the boys, he would have said to himself: "This result is so extremely improbable and at variance with my other results, that I have evidently committed an error of judgment here." Then he would perhaps select a fresh series of cases, and if the result happened to reverse his previous questionable result he would be at once reassured in his error. Again, until quite recent times it has over and over again been emphatically stated by brain anatomists that the frontal region is relatively larger in men, the parietal in women. This conclusion is now beginning to be regarded as the reverse of the truth, but we have to recognise that it was inevitable. It was firmly believed that the frontal region is the seat of all the highest and most abstract intellectual processes, and if on examining a dozen or two brains an anatomist found himself landed in the conclusion that the frontal region is relatively larger in women, the probability is that he would feel he had reached a conclusion that was absurd. It may, indeed, be said that it is only since it has become known that the frontal region of the brain is of greater relative extent in the Ape than it is in Man, and has no special connection with the higher intellectual processes, that it has become possible to recognise the fact that that region is relatively more extensive in women. It is only in the case of observations which are carefully and methodically carried out on a large number of subjects, and without prepossession—as in the case of Broca's brain registers, which were not worked out until after his death—that results can be obtained which cannot be questioned.

We have to recognise, it will be seen, not merely the difficulties which come from too small a number of observations, where we have the resource of putting one series of observations against another, but also the more serious difficulty of inevitable bias in the investigator's mind. This bias has an unfortunate tendency to run on similar lines, so that we gain nothing by putting one observer's results against another observer's results. Or, again, the results obtained by two observers, each working in accordance with his own bias, may be so disparate that there is no comparison. Thus one conscientious investigator (like Manouvrier) may find that all the facts of anatomy and physiology point to the superiority of women; another, equally conscientious (like Delaunay), may find that they all point to the superiority of men.

I have endeavoured to set in the clearest light those facts of sexual difference which may be regarded as fairly well ascertained by a large number of observations in the hands of numerous competent investigators. So far as possible, I have ignored or placed in the background those facts which are still unsettled. In many cases I have been able to place side by side facts which, although by no means necessarily new, had not previously been placed in a juxtaposition which brought out their significance. In other cases I have found, after much trouble and inquiry, even on matters where precise knowledge seemed easily attainable, that the results so far reached are so contradictory or incomplete that nothing can be done with them. Occasionally I have noted such results in passing, merely to indicate how the matter in question at present stands. An incomplete or unsupported result may at least serve as the stimulus to a more conclusive investigation. With this thought I have willingly exposed the painfully barren tracts in our knowledge of secondary sexual characters.

While the present volume is, so far as I am aware, the only attempt to deal comprehensively with the question of human secondary sexual characters from the modern standpoint, there are several books of earlier date which must be mentioned in this connection. The first genuinely scientific effort in this direction with which I am acquainted is Ackermann's *Ueber die körperliche Verschiedenheit des Mannes vom Weibe ausser den Geschlechtstheilen* (Koblenz, 1788). Ackermann was a pupil of the famous anatomist Soemmering, and his book, though brief and bald (corresponding with the state of knowledge at that time), is commendably scientific and free from speculation. Then comes Burdach. In his great work on physiology (*Die Physiologie als Erfahrungswissenschaft*, 1826-40) that remarkable man dealt very fully with all the aspects of sexual difference which at that time it was possible to deal with. While his

statements are sometimes too bold and often require some
revision, his treatment of the question on the whole is astonish-
ingly accurate.   Burdach neglected some lines of scientific
advance which we now regard as valuable, and was too much
under the influence of philosophical conceptions, but he faces
this problem in the broadest and most genuinely scientific
manner, and anticipates very many of the results of subsequent
investigation.   Even up to the present day there has been no
better statement of this complex problem than that of the
inspired physiologist of Königsberg.   Burdach's results were
often a little ahead of his facts; inspiration is not a recognised
modern method of scientific research, and no biologist of
Burdach's immense range has since his time been able to treat
the problem in the same broad and assured manner.   Darwin
touched on human secondary sexual characters in his *Descent
of Man*, but only in so far as they illustrated his general theory
of sexual selection.   The great work of Ploss and Max Bartels,
Das Weib in der Natur- und Völkerkunde (7th edition, Leipzig,
1902), deals primarily with anthropological and ethnographic
differences among the lower human races; it is a valuable
treasure-house of facts, and is richly illustrated   *Woman's Share
in Primitive Culture* (1894), by Otis Mason, mainly founded on
the data of American ethnography, may be read with profit.   Dr.
Harry Campbell's *Differences in the Nervous Organisation of
Man and Woman: Physiological and Pathological* (London,
1891) is interesting though discursive.   Lombroso and Ferrero's
La Donna Delinquente, la Prostituta e la Donna Normale (Turin
and Rome, 1893) must also be mentioned, because, although its
chief subject is the criminal woman, the first part is devoted to
the investigation of the characteristics of the normal woman; it
is original and suggestive, though at many points questionable.
Mantegazza's *Fisiologia della Donna* (1893), though only in
part scientific, is of interest as embodying the most mature
conclusions of an anthropologist, traveller, and man of the world,
who seems always to have regarded woman as the chief study
of man.   Marro's *La Pubertà* (1898)—the work of an Italian of
very different type, a man of the laboratory, a cautious and
searching student—contains much original work bearing on the
problems we are here concerned with.

CHAPTER III.

THE GROWTH AND PROPORTIONS OF THE BODY.

GENERAL CHARACTERISTICS OF THE MALE AND FEMALE
FORMS — SIZE AT BIRTH — GREATER DEVELOPMENT
OF GIRLS AT PUBERTY — SEXUAL DIFFERENCES IN
HEIGHT OF ADULTS—WEIGHT COMPARATIVELY UN-
IMPORTANT—SEXUAL DIFFERENCES IN THE GROWTH
AND PROPORTIONS OF THE BODY—THE ABDOMEN—
THE BREASTS—THE CHEST—THE ARM—THE HAND—
THE INDEX FINGER — THE LEG — THE FOOT — THE
FUTURE OF THE LITTLE TOE—GENERAL CONCLUSIONS.

WHEN we contemplate the human figure—or, if we
prefer, those classic representations of it which we
owe to the genius of Greek sculptors—we note certain
obvious sexual differences in form and contour. The
man is larger, with a certain tendency to rugged
though not unbeautiful outline which conveys an
impression of energy; his bony prominences are
usually more conspicuous, and his muscles are everywhere more clearly defined. The woman is smaller
and more delicately made; the bony points are less
clearly seen, and the muscles, even although they
may be powerful, are softly encased in abundant
connective tissue which makes them less obvious.
The man's form is erect and closely knit; the woman's
is more uneven, with large hips and flowing protuberant curves of breast and abdomen and flanks.
While the man's form seems to be instinctively
seeking action, the woman's falls naturally into a

state of comparative repose, and seems to find satisfaction in an attitude of overthrow.

The sexual contrasts of this simple kind are fairly obvious, and they have their significance. A more precise knowledge of the sexual differences in the human form has only grown up during the past century. The old masters, like Leonardo and Dürer, seem to have possessed a considerable science of human proportion, but their science does not appear to have been based on a wide induction of facts, and they usually subordinated it to their art. During recent years anatomists and anthropologists have been engaged in building up a detailed knowledge of the growth and proportions of the human body according to age and to sex. They are yet far from having reached the end of their labours, but certain definite conclusions are becoming evident; and while it is here impossible to discuss fully a subject which has produced so large a mass of work, it will be possible to indicate some of the main results.

At birth male infants are already rather heavier than female infants, and somewhat taller (about one-fifth of an inch in England and Scotland, according to the Anthropometric Committee of the British Association), and their chest-girth is greater. During the early years of life the comparative growth of the sexes has not been very closely studied; both boys and girls grow rapidly during the first two years of life, and slowly during the third and fourth, the boys appearing to keep ahead, as they do also from the ages of five to nine or ten in England.[1] It was always supposed, until some thirty years ago, that this superiority of the male is maintained throughout the whole period of development; this conclusion agreed with *a priori* ideas on the subject, and was supported by a few observations made by Quetelet. In 1872 Bowditch began to collect and publish statistics of the height

[1] Report of the Anthropometric Committee of the British Association, 1883, p. 288.

and weight of nearly 14,000 boys and 11,000 girls in Boston and its neighbourhood. These investigations mark an epoch in our knowledge of human development; they were followed and confirmed in 1876 by those of Pagliani on a large number of Italian children; in 1883 by the Anthropometric Committee's Report on British children; in 1890 by Axel Key's observations on 15,000 boys and 3000 girls in Sweden; and in 1891 by Emil Schmidt's investigation of nearly 5000 boys and 5000 girls at Leipzig.

Bowditch's original tables were published in the *Boston Medical and Surgical Journal*, December 1872; his complete study, "On the Growth of Children," appeared in the *Eighth Annual Report of the State Board of Health of Massachusetts*, 1877; see also, for a summary of Bowditch's results and for the British results, C. Roberts, *Manual of Anthropometry*, 1878. Luigi Pagliani's first monograph, "Sopra alcuni Fattori dello Sviluppo Umano," appeared in the *Archivio per l'Antropologia*, 1876, vol. vi.; his complete investigations were published in the *Archivio di Statistica*, Ann. i., vol. iv., 1877. Professor Axel Key's paper, *Die Pubertätsentwickelung und das Verhaltniss derselben zu den Krankheitserscheinungen der Schuljugend*, was read at the International Medical Congress of Berlin, but was published separately, 1890. Schmidt's results are briefly stated in the *Correspondenz-blatt der deutschen Gesellschaft für Anthropologie*, April 1892; in the same paper will be found bibliographical references to some other investigations in the development of children. All the investigations I have named are important and instructive; perhaps Axel Key's pamphlet is as useful as any, as it is short and is also rich in diagrams and tables which set forth at a glance the results of other investigators as well as those of the author himself. Other interesting and extensive investigations in which the same sexual differences are brought out are those of Jastchinsky on Polish and Jewish children in Warsaw schools, and those of Geisler and Ulitzsch on 21,000 German children, both of which are summarised in the *Jahresberichte der Anat. und Phys.*, 1890; Dr. Sargent's investigation of 1600 American school children and students recorded by him in a paper on "The Physical Development of Women," *Scribner's Magazine*, 1889; Porter's inquiry in regard to American children at St. Louis, *Trans. Acad. Sci. St. Louis*, 1894; *Zt. f. Eth.*, 1893; *Pub. Amer. Statist. Assoc.*, 1894; Macdonald's observations on American children at Washington, *Education Report*, 1897-98;

Combe's observations on Swiss children at Lausanne, *Zt. f. Schulgesundheitspflege*, 1896. A useful summary of some of the above investigations, as well as of many others, together with a bibliography with over one hundred entries, will be found in an article by F. Burk, "Growth of Children in Height and Weight," *Am. Jour. Psych.*, April 1898.

There can now be no doubt that, for a period of several years during the development of puberty, girls of European race are both taller and heavier than boys of the same age. The amount of the difference, and the exact age at which this predominance of girls begins and ceases, vary in different races and under different conditions.

In Great Britain girls grow more rapidly than boys between the ages of 10 and 15; and at the ages of $11\frac{1}{2}$ to $14\frac{1}{2}$ they are actually taller, and between the ages of $12\frac{1}{2}$ and $15\frac{1}{2}$ actually heavier, than boys at the same age. The acceleration in the growth of girls seems to be coincident with a retardation in the growth of boys. At the age of 15 boys again take the lead, growing at first rapidly, and then more slowly, and their complete growth is attained, practically, about the age of 23. Girls, on the other hand, grow very slowly after the age of sixteen, and attain their full stature about the twentieth year. Both in Europe and the United States the year of most active growth appears in boys to be the sixteenth, in girls the thirteenth or (as in Sweden) the fourteenth. The period of active growth is preceded by a period of marked delay in growth, reaching a maximum in about the eleventh year in boys and the tenth in girls, in whom, however, it is less regular and conspicuous; this has been verified in America, England, Germany, Sweden, Denmark, and Italy. In the United States during the first twelve years of life boys are from one to two inches taller than girls of the same age; at about $12\frac{1}{2}$ years of age girls begin to grow faster than boys, and during the fourteenth year are about one inch taller than boys of the same age; during the

YEARLY INCREMENTS OF HEIGHT AND WEIGHT BETWEEN AGES OF
7 AND 20.   (*Axel Key.*)

sixteenth year boys again become taller. The English and American girls resemble each other on the whole more than the English and American boys, but the period of the developmental supremacy of the American girl is short and its degree is inconsiderable, while in Sweden it extends from the twelfth to half-way through the sixteenth year; in Germany it begins during the eleventh year and extends up to the six-teenth year;[1] in Italy, also, it covers the same period, and is well marked in degree. This comparatively slight preponderance of the American girl is no doubt due to the great developmental activity of the American boy during the whole period of puberty; from his thirteenth to his eighteenth year he is the tallest and heaviest boy, on the average, yet produced and measured; during all other years, before and after, the Swedish boy comes to the top. The Swedish girl keeps at the head of European and American girls throughout her whole evolution, except, as regards weight alone, during her fourteenth year, when she yields to her American sister. In Sweden puberty both for boys and girls is a year later in reaching completion than either in America or Italy. All these variations are but minor modifications of the general rule that the evolution of puberty is more precocious in girls than in boys, being both begun and completed at an earlier age.

Porter concluded from his investigations among St. Louis children that the tallest and heaviest children are the most intelligent. His results have, however, been criticised, and Gilbert found that among Iowa children, so far as there is any difference at all, it would appear that the taller and heavier the children the duller they are.

Axel Key pointed out that in Sweden the period of most rapid growth in boys is also the period of greatest freedom from disease, but found this relation between growth and resistance to disease less marked in girls, attributing the difference to the comparatively unhealthy conditions under which growing

---

[1] This is shown by Geisler and Ulitzsch's examination of 21,000 children belonging to Freiburg, in Saxony.

girls are placed; the same relation has been found in other countries, especially in America. Thus at Chicago Christopher found (*Jour. Am. Med. Ass.*, 14th Sept. 1901) that though there is a marked tendency to disease during the pubertal period, the mortality is low; and at Boston, as Hartwell showed ("Report of the Director of Physical Training," *School Documents, No. 8*, Boston, 1894, pp. 43 *et seq.*), during the period from ten to fifteen years, when increase in height and weight is most rapid, the fewest deaths occur. The year of lowest death-rates for boys Hartwell found to be the thirteenth, for girls the twelfth, so that pubertal resistance to disease runs parallel with growth, though in boys the maximum growth falls a little later than the minimum mortality. Hartwell (*ib.*, pp. 82 *et seq.*) has pointed out an interesting parallel between the prevalence of stuttering and pubertal development. The prevalence of stuttering varies at different ages, and the variation may be regarded as an indication of nervous balance. He found that boys of eight, thirteen, and sixteen, and girls of seven, twelve, and sixteen are specially apt to stammer, and concluded that the irritability of the nervous system of which stuttering is an expression is correlated with the most marked upward and downward fluctuations of the power of the organism to resist death-compelling influences.

It would appear that the more precocious development of the female is not a merely human but a widely spread zoological phenomenon. Among many animals it has been found that the females are ahead of the males in growth (H. de Varigny, art. "Croissance," *Dict. de Phys.*); thus, although the adult male giraffe is taller than the female, at puberty the female is taller.

The development of puberty is, however, considerably influenced by alimentation and hygiene—that is to say, by the social class to which the child belongs. But the influence of social condition seems to be strictly limited. Pagliani and Axel Key have given special attention to this point. In Italy the differences in development between well-nourished and ill-nourished children are very marked, but Pagliani has shown that though the development of the ill-nourished is slow, this is largely compensated by its prolongation, while the development of the well-nourished is rapid and precocious, but small in its later stages. (It is worth noting that in this respect girls follow the law of development of the well-nourished classes.) While alimentation enormously influences the rate of growth it has thus comparatively small influence on the final result, which is chiefly affected by race and sex. Axel Key does not find that the compensatory process takes place quite in the same manner observed by Pagliani; according to him the period of puberty is delayed in children of the poorer classes, but then takes place very rapidly, to be completed at the same period as in the well-

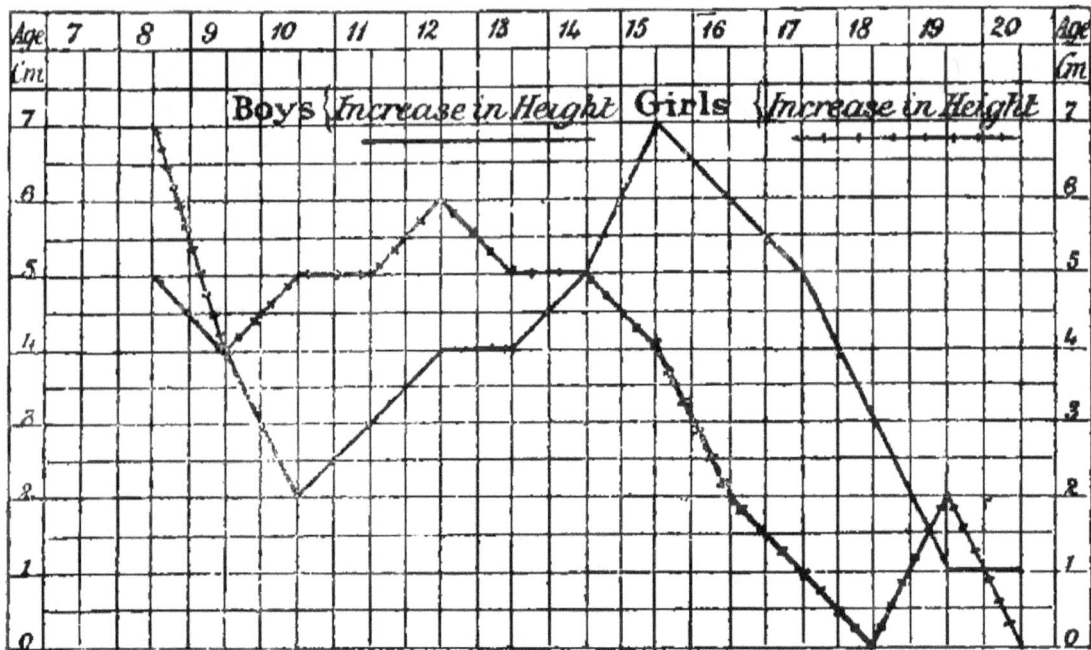

CHART SHOWING COMPARATIVE INCREASE IN HEIGHT OF SWEDISH
BOYS AND GIRLS.

(*Adapted from Axel Key.*)

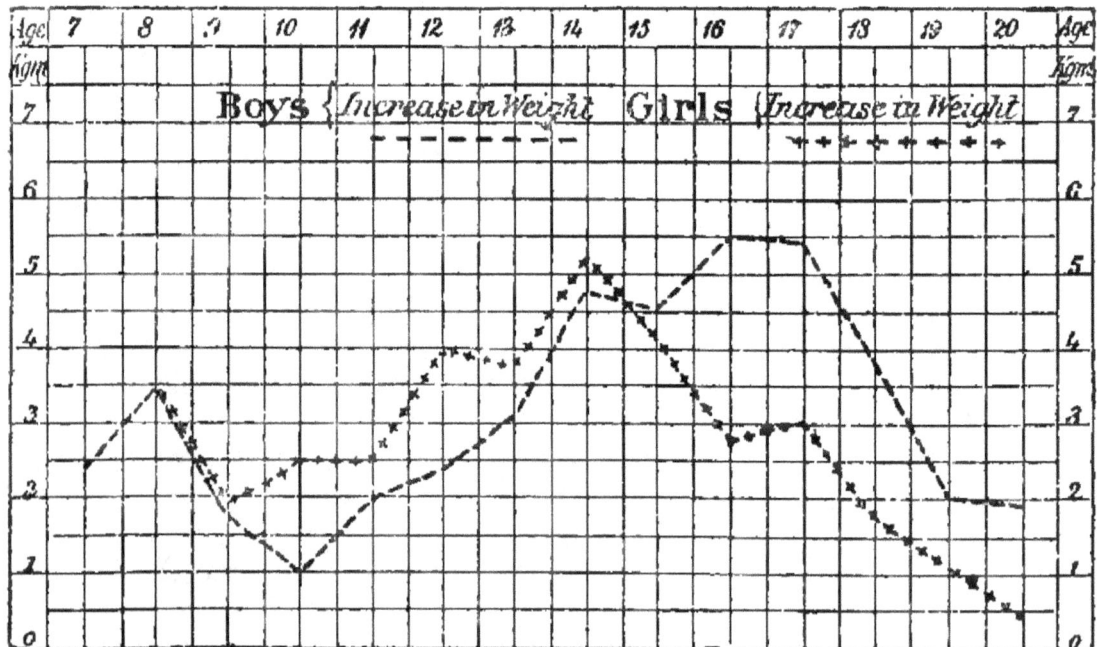

CHART SHOWING COMPARATIVE INCREASE IN WEIGHT OF SWEDISH
BOYS AND GIRLS.

(*Adapted from Axel Key.*)

to-do classes. He compares the development of the poor to a feather which can be strongly bent only to fly back rapidly when the pressure is removed; but if the pressure is too great or too prolonged the retractility may be largely lost. Quetelet, Pagliani, Bowditch, Broca, Dally, and Axel Key seem to agree that environment, alimentation, exercise, climate, altitude, occupation modify the rate of growth with more intensity the more removed the individual is from the final stage of development. The height finally attained depends chiefly on sex and race.

A woman may be said to have reached her full development at the age of twenty; a man continues to show a fair degree of development for some years after this age, especially under favourable conditions. Venn and Galton have shown by their investigations on Cambridge students that the student's head, for example, grows after the age of nineteen more than the average head.[1] It is well known that the upper classes in most European countries are taller than the lower classes, and although this may be, to some extent, as Lapouge supposes, a question of difference of race, it cannot be entirely so; Galton, also, considers that among the educated classes the average height is greater than it was some years ago. I am not acquainted with any elaborate investigation of women students, showing to what extent the physical development of women may be prolonged under favourable conditions. Under ordinary conditions it seems to be the general rule that physical precocity is greater in women than in men, and the lower the race, generally speaking, the earlier is the full stature attained; thus among the Nicobarese, according to Man, males reach their full height at about the age of eighteen, females a little earlier.[2]

The average height of adult males in England is about 1.700 m. (or 67.4 ins.), of adult females about 1.600 m. (or 62.7 ins.); the ratio of stature of men and women is in England 1 to 0.930, or as 16 to

[1] *Journal Anthropological Institute*, 1889, p. 140.
[2] E. H. Man, *Journal Anthropological Institute*, May 1889.

14.88.[1]   The mid-stature of the well-to-do male members of the British Association at Newcastle in 1889 was 1.715 m., of the female members 1.589 m. The sexual difference in stature in England, therefore, corresponds very closely with that found in neighbouring countries; in France, according to Topinard and Rollet, it is 12 centimetres; in Belgium, according to Quetelet, 10 centimetres; in the United States, according to Sargent, it is somewhat greater, being nearly 13 centimetres.   In America, while the sexual difference in weight is somewhat less than in England, the sexual difference in height and also in vital capacity is to a marked extent greater, the greater sexual differences being, it seems, due to the greater development of American men rather than to the less development of women.

Dr. Sargent prepared for the Chicago World's Fair two nude clay figures of man and woman, founded on the average measurements of several thousand students of Harvard and of various girls' colleges.   The general characteristics of the two statues are thus described in *Scribner's Magazine*, July 1893:—

"One admits that the young man is the finer figure of the two.   Standing squarely, clean-limbed, strong-necked, he looks rather like a runner than a rower; but there is nothing sordid, nothing warped, nothing to indicate the deterioration of a civilisation of too many wheels, the stunting, or the abnormal one-sided development, of the factory or of city life.   The pose, of course, must be the sculptor's, but the measures show: height, five feet eight; weight, one hundred and thirty-eight (the equivalent of one hundred and forty-nine, as we clothe ourselves); chest, thirty-four, to thirty-seven inflated.   It is reassuring that both in height and weight and strength as well, this statue far exceeds the average of any other nation, even England.

"When we come to the woman, we must—*glissons un peu*.   A prominent artist looked her over from a professional point of

---

[1] Report of Anthropometric Committee of British Association, 1883. As expressed by Galton (*Natural Inheritance*, 1889), about 12 to 13: "Consequently by adding to each observed female stature at the rate of one inch for every foot, we are enabled to compare their statures, so increased and transmuted, with the observed statures of males on equal terms."   In Belgium, where the race is much shorter, the ratio, according to Quetelet, is as 16 to 15.

view and refused to accept the statue as the ultimate model. Of course, said her creator; for that you would in fairness select a figure on the eighty or ninety per cent. line, not this, which meets exactly fifty per cent. of them all, and is half-way from the best to the worst; or, to put it more precisely, is only *the greatest good of the greatest number.* He then naïvely explained her inferiority to the boy on a ground one hardly dare whisper —namely, that women students in colleges came from a class not equal, socially or intellectually, to that which universally sends its boys. [Whether this is the case or not it could scarcely account for the facts in question; the woman of low social class, at all events in the country, is favourably situated so far as the attainment of a well-developed and beautiful body is concerned.] The figure has more fragility without a corresponding gain in grace; the lower half is better than the upper; it is not that tight-lacing has left evident traces (the waist is over twenty-four), but the inward curve of the back, the thinness of the body, lack strength and erectness of pose. The height is five feet three, the weight one hundred and fourteen, the chest measurement but thirty, and the feet ten inches long."

Differences in weight, although instructive as regards the individual's condition, are not of any great significance in the adult from our present point of view, and are in some respects fallacious. This is due to the tendency of women to develop exuberant fatty connective tissue. This tendency, while it is chiefly responsible for the charm and softness of the smoothly rounded feminine form, results in women possessing a larger amount than men of comparatively non-vital tissue and makes them appear larger than they really are. Bischoff once took the trouble to investigate the proportions of the various tissues in a man of thirty-three, a woman of twenty-two, and a boy of sixteen, who all died accidentally in good physical condition. He found the following relation between muscle and fat:—

	M.	W.	B.
Muscle	41.8	35.8	44.2
Fat	18.2	28.2	13.9

It is owing to this tendency to put on fat that, as Quetelet found, while man reaches his maximum weight at the age of forty, woman reaches hers only at fifty. The same tendency causes a liability to morbid obesity which all authorities agree to find more common in women; thus, for instance, of Bouchard's eighty-six cases, sixty-two were in women, and only twenty-four in men.

The preponderance of the adult man over the adult woman in total stature and bulk is fairly obvious and well established; the less obvious sexual differences in the growth and proportions of the various parts of the body are, however, more interesting and significant. Speaking generally, it may be said that, relatively to the total height, in women the head is longer than in men, the neck shorter, the trunk longer, and the legs and arms shorter.

Topinard found that, reckoning total height as 100, in 78 men of European race the trunk equalled 33.5, and in 30 women 34.0. E. Harless, at Munich, found that in 9 men and 7 women the trunk equalled 35.9 in the former and 37.8 in the latter. Quetelet obtained similar results in Belgium. Professor Riccardi (*Di alcune Correlazioni di Sviluppo*, Modena, 1891) has examined 1200 Bolognese and Modenese persons of all ages and both sexes with reference to the height of the seated body, and finds that in children under six there are no sexual differences; then comes a period of oscillation between the sexes, and finally the proportion of the height of the seated body to the total stature is in men as 52 to 100, and in women as 53 to 100; thus a woman, when seated, if we judge her by male standards, appears taller than she really is.

Ranke states unconditionally that relative shortness of trunk is a character of superiority, as it indicates an organism arrived at maturity.[1] If we compare the human adult with the human infant, or with the ape, this statement is perfectly justified. As Quetelet has pointed out,[2] while the adult head is only double the height of the head at birth, the trunk is nearly tripled in length, while the arms are nearly four times, and the legs as much as five times as long as they were at birth. This is one of those sexual differences which are simply the result of the total difference in bulk and stature due to the precocity and earlier arrest of growth in women. In fairly well-proportioned men, in whom growth has been arrested before they have reached the aduls male standard, we find the same proportions as in women. In a dwarf of the usual type, with his huge

[1] *Beiträge zur Urgeschichte Bayerns*, Bd. viii., Fasc. 1 and 2, 1888.
[2] *Anthropométrie*, pp. 194, 195.

head and diminutive legs, the same infantile type is seen in an exaggerated degree. In defective development, due to the influence of rickets, it has been found that the trunk is on the average only about one inch shorter than usual, the arms two and a half inches shorter, while the legs may be as much as ten and a half inches shorter, thus preserving the infantile type.[1] In giants, on the other hand, the increased stature is chiefly due to undue growth of the legs.

It is not, however, true that relative shortness of trunk is a mark of superiority if we compare together the adults of various human races. Thus, as Topinard shows,[2] negroes possess relatively the shortest bodies, the yellow races the longest, while the white races occupy an intermediate position.

From these differences in proportion there naturally results a difference in the position of the centre of the body according to age and sex. The old artists and authors who occupied themselves with the canons of proportion, following the lead of Vitruvius, regarded the navel as the centre of the body. This is not exactly the case. The more immature the human body is the lower the navel is, and the higher the centre of the body. At birth the middle point of the body closely coincides with the navel, or, rather, it is two or three centimetres above it, but as growth proceeds the centre of the body falls until ultimately it is a little below the symphisis pubis in men, remaining a little higher in women.

In women the distance between the navel and the pubes is greater than in men; that is to say that in women the abdomen is larger. This is the rule as stated by Manouvrier, and Professor Cunningham has found from the examination of numerous subjects that the various abdominal zones have the same average depth in women as in men; taking into

[1] Shaw, confirmed by Walter Pye, " Lectures on Growth Rates of the Body," *Lancet*, July 26 and August 16, 1890.
[2] *Anthropologie Générale*, pp. 1065 *et seq.*

account the greater size of the men, the relative size of the abdomen becomes thus distinctly greater in women.[1]   This character is in harmony with the reproductive functions of women, and in the artist's hands the full and firm abdomen is one of the beauties of woman's form, in contrast to man's comparatively flat and inconspicuous abdomen, but at the same time a large abdomen is both an infantile and a primitive character; it was, for example, very marked in the Fuegians who were in London a few years ago, and a Fuegian boy with his abdomen exposed bore a strong resemblance to a woman.

A still more obvious sexual distinction lies in the breasts, but from the present point of view they cannot be very profitably studied.   The only sexual difference worth mentioning here is the distance between the nipples.   This is often greater in men than in women; the reason for this is, as Brücke points out, that in its development the breast in women requires a large amount of skin for its increasingly convex surface, and as the skin on the side of the body yields more readily than that between the breasts, the nipples tend to approximate.[2]   "The breasts should always live at enmity," a sculptor once said to Brücke; "the right should look to the right, and the left to the left."   In well-developed individuals this is so, and in the careful measurements of artist's models given by Quetelet at the end of his *Anthropomètrie* the exceptional distance between the nipples is noteworthy, especially in the case of women belonging to Rome and Cadiz.

---

[1] "Delimitation of the Regions of the Abdomen," *Journal of Anatomy and Physiology*, Jan. 1893.

[2] E. Brücke, *The Human Form*, pp. 71, 72.   Chapter III. of this book is an interesting discussion of the artistic anatomy of the female breast.   From the anthropological point of view the breast has been fully studied in the great work of Ploss and Max Bartels, *Das Weib*, Bd. i., Ch. viii.   These writers recognise four different forms of breast: the bowl-shaped (like half a Tangerine orange), the hemispherical (like half or three-quarters of an apple), the conical, and the goat's udder shape.

With reference to the sexual differences in the thorax or chest itself, the most authoritative anatomists are at present singularly at variance. This is partly due to the fact that not many detailed investigations of a large number of subjects have yet been made, and partly to the fact that it is necessary to allow for the artificial deformation of the chest which is still very common among civilised women. It seems most probable that, as Gegenbaur asserts, the female thorax is relatively shorter and broader than the male. This is also suggested by the shortness of the dorsal region of the spinal column in women and the relative shortness of the breast-bone (as shown by Dwight, as well as by earlier anatomists), and also by the greater relative length of the clavicle in women (as shown by Broca and others). It also seems probable that the depth of the chest antero-posteriorly is less in women than in men. It was asserted by the old anatomists that while man has a large chest and small belly, woman has a small chest and large belly. While this conclusion, which is in harmony with the marked inferiority of the respiratory system in women, is no doubt true, sufficient allowance does not appear to have been made for the artificial constriction of the lower part of the chest in women.

Charpy has made a careful study of 200 subjects—male and female, short and tall, fair and dark—in the dissecting room, with special reference to the shape of the chest. He finds no notable sexual differences until the age of fifteen, and less well marked after this than many people imagine. He recognises three different types of the female chest, which are, however, more obvious to the artist than the anthropologist: (1) the *broad type*, square and full like that of a man, with well-spread shoulders, and breasts like expanded discs; it is the type of the ancient goddesses, of the women of Tuscany and Liguria, and the Roman women of Transtevere; (2) the *round type*, rarer and of more delicate and highly sexualised character; it is smaller and more folded in than the first type, with less antero-posterior diameter, and is the chest of the Venetian women; (3) the *long type*, with oblong lungs, though its capacity is probably by no means defective; it is the type of English women, and Arab women with their sloping shoulders and graceful carriage often have this form. (Adrien Charpy, " L'Angle xiphoïdien," *Revue d'Anthropologie*, 1884, p. 268.)

In women, generally speaking, while the trunk is relatively long, the limbs are relatively short. By her short arms woman approaches the infantile condition more closely than man, as Ranke points out, but it must be added that by the same character she is farther removed than man from the ape and the savage, among whom the forearm especially is very long.

The difference is usually trifling, but there is agreement upon the point among most of the chief authorities. It was found to hold good among various lower races examined during the voyage of the *Novara*, and by Weisbach for German women also; Topinard lays it down as a general rule (*Anthropologie Générale*, p. 1096); Sargent found that the forearms of American girls are decidedly shorter, the arms very slightly shorter than those of boys; and Ranke concludes as the result of his observations that women have shorter arms and forearms, thighs and legs, relatively to their short upper arms still shorter forearms, relatively to their short thighs still shorter legs, and relatively to the whole upper extremity a shorter lower extremity. (Ranke, " Beiträge zur physischen Anthropologie der Bayern," *Beiträge zur Urgeschichte Bayerns*, Bd. viii., Fasc. 1 and 2, 1888.) The arms of women are relatively more shortened than are the legs. (Pfitzner, *Zt. f. Morph.*, 1899, p. 375.) A long forearm, it may be added, as well as a long leg, are among the characters which indicate superiority when we compare the adult to the infant, but indicate inferiority when we compare the European to lower races, like the negro and the Australian, in whom the arms are especially long.

The male arm differs from the female by being flatter in youth and more highly moulded and less cylindrical in adult age; in women the arm in adult age develops in rotundity in consequence of the deposit of fat, and constitutes one of the chief beauties of adult womanhood; it is also often somewhat laterally compressed, and (as Brücke remarks) it is so depicted by Renaissance artists, in comparison with the broad shallow forearm. Artists have differed in their preferences with regard to boys' arms and girls' arms; thus, while Palma Giovane and many other artists have given their angels girls' arms, Andrea del Sarto preferred boys' arms.

Brücke has some sensible observations on the effects of exercise on the arms of girls:—" Many mothers are afraid of their daughters doing any exercises with their arms lest the latter should acquire a masculine shape. It is remarkable, however, that no apprehension is shown if these same daughters practise the piano for several hours every day, exerting certain muscles of the forearm in a violent and exclusive fashion in doing so. Yet there is, in general, no foundation for the fear. Bodily exercises only affect the form of the body disadvantageously under two conditions: either when they begin at too early an age, or when they are so excessive as to produce emaciation. Violent exercise may be taken without injury in this respect is proved by the well-known gymnast who, under the name of Leona Dare, displayed the beauty of her arms in all the great cities of the world." (E. Brücke, *The Human Figure*, pp. 48, 49.) As a more recent example I may refer to the beautifully developed arms of the gymnast Alcide Capitaine.

The study of the hand and the proportions of its various parts has received considerable attention from time to time, and was studied in great detail by Pfitzner at Strassburg. Europeans, speaking generally, have smaller hands than the black races, while the yellow races have the longest hands; the Javanese, for example, have peculiarly long hands, which are seen to great advantage in the characteristic Javanese dances in which the hand plays the chief part. As regards the relative size of the hand, Quetelet and Topinard considered that there are no sexual differences; Ranke, however, has more recently found that the hand is relatively somewhat shorter in women, and this seems to be confirmed by Pfitzner's investigations, but in any case the differences are slight.

Sexual differences in the comparative length of the different fingers have attracted some attention. Ecker found many years ago that while in anthropoid apes, and so also in nearly all negroes, the index-finger is shorter than the ring-finger, in women (including negresses) the index tends to be longer than the ring-finger more frequently than in men, thus giving the hand a more elegant shape.[1] Mantegazza examined a very large number of people with reference to this point, and found that while over 500 possessed a shorter index than ring-finger against under 100 with longer index-finger, among the former men were in a majority, and among the latter women were in a large majority; 77 per cent. of the men, against 63 per cent. of the women showed the longer ring-finger, but only 7 per cent. of the men against 21 per cent. of the women showed a longer index-

[1] *Arch. für Anthropologie*, Bd. vii., p. 65.

finger. Examining twelve very beautiful women from various parts of Italy, he found a longer index-finger in six—a proportion considerably above the average; he adds that he is not prepared to say that he finds the longer index-finger itself more beautiful.[1] Pfitzner confirmed the fact of the greater length of the index-finger in woman, and finds also that woman's thumb is relatively shorter than man's.[2] The latter characteristic goes with a comparatively low type of organism, but the long index-finger has its interest, bearing in mind the conservative morphological tendencies of women, because it indicates superior evolution.

Weissenberg supported these conclusions; he found the predominance of the index-finger unusually marked in Jews, and especially in Jewesses, and he noted that in Assyrian reliefs and Egyptian statues the ring-finger is generally longer than the index, and in the former case at all events, of beautiful type.[3] Féré, who has studied the proportions of the hands and the fingers both in men and women and in apes,[4] finds that, if we compare the length of the different fingers to the middle finger, while the thumb is shorter in women than in men the little finger is relatively still shorter, while in the ape the little finger is long though the thumb is short.

It is by his relatively long legs that the adult civilised man most conspicuously differs in proportion from the infant, although not necessarily from the savage, whose legs are sometimes very long; and the leg is that portion of the body which grows most rapidly and to the most variable extent; it is also

[1] P. Mantegazza, " Della lunghezza relativa dell' indice," *Arch. per l'Antropologia*, 1877, p. 22.

[2] W. Pfitzner, " Beiträge zur Kenntniss des menschlichen Extremitätenskeletts," and " Anthropologische Beziehungen der Hand- und Fussmasse," in Schwalbe's *Morphologische Arbeiten*, Bd. i.-ii., 1890-92.

[3] S. Weissenberg, " Die Formen der Hand und des Fusses," *Zt. f. Eth.*, 1895, heft 2.

[4] *Jour. de l'Anat. et de Phys.*, May-June, 1900.

that part of the body which is most affected by an early arrest of development, although in this the arm also largely participates.[1] The thigh grows with greatest rapidity, and shows also the most decided sexual differences. In women the thigh is markedly shorter than in men; it is larger, and is set at a different angle. As to the greater absolute and relative length of the thigh in men there seems to be no question, although the results of investigation do not show any similar marked difference for the leg, and according to some observers the leg is relatively very slightly longer in women. The greater circumference of the thigh in women is very well marked, and begins at a comparatively early age. It is indeed the only measurement of which we can safely say that it is from an early period of puberty onwards both absolutely and relatively always decidedly greater in both European and American women than in men; for although the diameter and still more the circumference of the hips are relatively greater in women than in men, the excess seems greater than it really is, and does not invariably exist, or at all events at so early an age, when we deal with absolute figures. According to the measurements of Quetelet on Belgians, the circumference of the top of the thigh becomes absolutely greater in girls of fourteen, and is relatively greater than in boys even after the age of twelve; while Dr. Sargent shows that the thigh of the American girl of fifteen is on the average, in absolute figures, two inches larger than that of the American boy of fifteen. Taking 400 male and female students (who in America fairly represent the average population), of the mean age of twenty, Sargent found that the girth of thigh in the women exceeds that in the men by $1\frac{1}{4}$ inches, and is the only measurement in which the women do absolutely exceed the men. Dr.

[1] Humphry, *Human Skeleton;* Topinard, *Anthropologie Générale,* pp. 1030-31; Roberts, *Anthropometry,* pp. 115-117.

Sargent suggests that the large thighs of women are due to impediment to the blood-stream caused by artificial constriction at the waist, but the opinion is unsupported and is highly improbable. In woman the thigh, though short, tapers rapidly, and at the lower part it is, absolutely, scarcely if at all larger than that of a man; so that while the masculine thigh tends to be columnar the feminine thigh tends to be conical. This characteristic imparts some appearance of instability to the female figure, and the effect is increased by the marked inward inclination of the thighs in women, resulting from the breadth of the pelvis, an inclination which, when it exists in a very marked degree, gives an appearance of knock-knee, and the inward inclination of the thigh is compensated by an outward inclination of the leg. There is an analogous obliquity of the upper extremity; the forearm is never in a straight line with the arm; and this obliquity is also emphasised in women. In 90 women Potter found that the angle of obliquity of the forearm with the upper-arm was 167.35 degrees; in 95 men the angle was 173.17 degrees.[1] But while the lack of straightness in the arm is inconspicuous and conflicts with no demand of the eye, since the arms are not normally called to support the weight of the body, it is not so with the legs. This obliquity of the legs is the most conspicuous æsthetic defect of the feminine form in the erect posture, while it unfits women for attitudes of energy, and compels them to run by alternate semi-circular rotations of the legs. In large-hipped civilised women the characteristic is much more obvious than in small-hipped savage women. Artists have adopted various devices to disguise it. It is minimised by toning down the hips and giving to women a comparatively masculine outline, or by the

[1] H. Percy Potter, "Obliquity of the Arm of the Female in Extension," *Journ. Anat. and Phys.*, July 1895; C. Langer, *Anatomie der äusseren Formen*, p. 269; E. Brücke, *Human Figure*, 1891, p. 83.

elongation of the thighs and legs; thus the long, straight, and beautiful legs which Tintoret gave to his women almost correspond to heroic canons of proportion which in nature are rarely found in women.

The foot has received even more study than the hand, and certain interesting sexual differences emerge. Pfitzner, who has studied the foot[1] with the same care as the hand, finds that there are two types of foot: the *elongated* type with long and well-developed middle phalanges, and the *abbreviated* type in which the middle phalanges are short and coarse. The first type is most common in men, the second in women. Which is the more primitive form? We are accustomed, he remarks, to regard women's forms as more primitive, but notwithstanding this he is inclined to look upon the abbreviated type common in women as a more recent acquisition of the race. At the same time he regards the abbreviated form as rather a retrogressive than a progressive evolution; "no one can look at a middle phalanx of the abbreviated type and not recognise that it is unworthy of any noble mammal, and only to be regarded as a *partie honteuse*." By their great toes, as well as their thumbs, women are less developed than men; a long great toe and a long thumb are recent acquirements of the race, and they are relatively longer in men.[2] Pfitzner has also made an interesting discovery with regard to the present position and probable future of the little toe. It is well known that while the fingers and toes generally are made up of three bones and are three-jointed, the thumb and great toe possess only two phalanges, and are therefore only two-jointed. Pfitzner finds that there is a tendency for the little toe also to possess only two joints, the

[1] Schwalbe's *Morphologische Arbeiten*, Bd. i., pp. 94 *et seq.*
[2] In harmony with its primitive nature, the long second toe is also a foetal character, as Braune has shown (quoted by Stratz, *Die Schönheit des Weiblichen Körpers*, 1903, p. 196).

middle and end phalanges being welded together. This result is not artificially produced, as it is nearly as common in the embryo and the child as in the adult. There appears, therefore, to be at the present time a progressive, or, as Pfitzner regarded it, retrogressive development of the little toe; though it should, perhaps, be added that in such a matter the degeneration only applies to the particular part and not to the organism generally. The course of higher evolution has always been accompanied by the disappearance or degeneration of particular organs and parts which are no longer needed. It is interesting to note that women seem to be leading this movement. Among 111 feet of men and women 41.5 per cent. of the women showed fusion of the joint, and only 31.0 per cent. of the men. But, as Pfitzner himself remarked, new investigations with a larger number of subjects are needed to confirm this sexual distinction.[1]

The relative length of the big toe and the second toe occupied the attention of Weissenberg when investigating the fingers (*Zt. f. Eth.*, 1895, heft 2, p. 95). He found that in more than half the cases observed (Greeks, Jews, etc.) the big toe was longer, but in Bashkirs the second toe tended to be longer. The Greek women had a longer big toe more often than the men, but Jewesses not so often as Jews. In England Park Harrison (*Jour. Anth. Inst.*, vol. xiii., 1884) found that the second toe tends to be longer in women, the big toe in men; in various groups the sexual difference was marked. Papillault found in Paris a very slight excess of women among individuals showing a longer second toe (18 per cent. as against 16 per cent. men), and considers that the best conformed foot has a long big toe. Stratz, on the other hand, believes that the best developed foot shows a long second toe, and there can be little doubt that this is the most beautiful form, as may be seen by an examination of the pictures in the National Gallery, or any other large collection. The tendency to the greater prevalence in women of a long index finger thus appears to be accompanied by a similar though less constant tendency to a long second toe. Weissenberg notes that ancient Greek statues usually show a

---

[1] W. Pfitzner, "Die kleine Zehe," *Archiv für Anat. und Phys.*, heft. i. and ii., 1890.

longer second toe, and there are, he observes, æsthetic reasons for such a preference. In Egyptian sculpture (though not in Egyptian statuettes) Weissenberg also found the second toe usually longer; in Assyrian reliefs the big toe is always longer. The Papuans, who tend especially to have a long second toe, would thus appear to approach the classic ideal much more than do modern Europeans. Lombroso at Turin has recently examined various groups of subjects, normal and abnormal, with reference to the point, and has found in every group that the women showed a larger proportion of shorter big toes than the men (*Arch. di Psich.*, 1901, p. 337). Lombroso's general conclusions on the significance of this variation are, however, faulty, since he is imperfectly acquainted with the results obtained by previous observers.

Ottolenghi and Carrara have examined the feet of a large number of persons—men and women, sane and insane, criminals and prostitutes—in order to find out the amount of space between the great toe and its neighbour, and so to estimate the extent to which the individual's foot approaches the primitive prehensile condition. Carefully examining 100 normal men and 62 normal women, they found that the space between the first two toes and the power of separating them are much more marked in women than in men; the proportion of well-marked cases being 28 per cent. among women and only 11 per cent. among men; although the tendency of women to cramp the feet would lead us to expect an opposite result. Among male criminals, prostitutes, epileptics, and idiots there was a still nearer approach to the prehensile condition which is frequent among lower races. (Ottolenghi e Carrara, "Il Piede prensile negli alienati e nei delinquenti," *Arch. di Psichiatria*, 1892, Fasc. iv., v.) I may add that it is probable that women in ordinary life use their toes more than do men. A lady who has written to me on this point demurs to the statement of Ottolenghi and Carrara that women's shoes, even with the pointed toe affected by women, really interfere greatly with their lateral movement of the toes, while the fact that they are thinner and more flexible than men's boots is also favourable to movement. She notes in herself when standing a tendency to turn the ankles slightly over outwards and to claw down with the toes in an instinctive effort to obtain greater stability. She believes this is common among women both in walking and standing, while women undoubtedly use their toes more than do men in dancing, and she has observed that the heels of women's shoes, especially among the lower class, are often worn down on the outside, but not so often men's. The greater prehensility and flexibility of women's toes may thus, it is possible, while involving the retention of a useful primitive characteristic, be a phenomenon analogous to the greater use of the fingers by women in gesticulation.

In the somewhat bird's-eye view we have obtained in this chapter over a very large field of anthropological investigation[1] it has been sufficiently evident that the differences between men and women extend not only to general proportions and laws of growth but to each part of the body taken separately; that, taken in the average, a man is a man even to his thumbs, and a woman is a woman down to her little toes. Three general conclusions clearly emerge: (1) women are more precocious than men; (2) in women there is an earlier arrest of development; (3) as a result of these two facts, the proportions of women tend to approach those of small men and of children. This greater youthfulness of physical type in women is a very radical characteristic, and its influence vibrates to the most remote psychic recesses. It is an important factor, but by no means the only factor, in the constitution of secondary sexual differences.

[1] Many further details may be found in Daffner, *Das Wachstum des Menschen*, Buschan, art. "Körpergewicht" (dealing both with the body as a whole and with its parts); *Real Encyclopädie der Gesammten Heilkunde*, 3rd ed., 1896; in Pfitzner, "Ein Beitrag zur Kenntniss der sekundären Geschlechtsunterschiede beim Menschen," *Morphologische Arbeiten*, 1896, Bd. vii.; and in the same author's elaborate "Sozial-Anthropologische Studien," published in the *Zeitschrift für Morphologie* from 1899 to 1902.

CHAPTER IV.

THE PELVIS.

THE MOST PROMINENT SECONDARY SEXUAL CHARACTER—
CONSTRUCTION OF THE PELVIS—THE PELVIS IN CHILD-
HOOD—THE PELVIS IN RELATION TO THE SPINAL
COLUMN—THE INFLUENCE OF THE ERECT POSTURE
IN MAN AND WOMAN — PELVIC INCLINATION — THE
SADDLE-BACK — THE EVOLUTION OF THE HUMAN
SPINAL COLUMN — DISADVANTAGES OF THE ERECT
POSTURE—WOMEN LEADING EVOLUTION IN RESPECT
TO THE PELVIS—THE EVOLUTION OF THE PELVIS IN
RELATION TO THE EVOLUTION OF SEXUAL EMOTION.

IN the brief sketch of the sexual differences in human growth and proportions presented in the foregoing chapter, no attention has been given to what we may regard, at all events from the present point of view, as the two most important parts of the body. Nothing has been said of the head or of the pelvis. The head is entitled to attention separately, not only as the most conspicuous and generally interesting portion of the body, and the seat of the chief nervous centres, but on account of the great amount of study devoted to it, an amount which to-day we are entitled to consider as even excessive. The pelvis is entitled to a chapter to itself because it constitutes the most undeniable, conspicuous, and unchangeable of all the bony human secondary sexual characters. Among numerous lower races, indeed, it is not well marked, and the women of several Central African peoples, for instance, when viewed from behind, can scarcely be distinguished from men; even Arab women, in whom the pelvis (as Kocher and others have described it) is broadly extended, show nothing of the globular fulness of the well-developed European woman. The pelvis has developed during the course of human evolution; while in some of the dark races it is ape-like in its narrowness and small capacity, in the highest European races it becomes a sexual distinction which immediately strikes the eyes and can scarcely be effaced; while the women of these races endeavour still further to accentuate it by artificial means. It is at once the proof of high evolution and the promise of capable maternity. Ancient authorities emphasised this most prominent of all secondary sexual distinctions by saying that while in both men and women the trunk represents an ovoid figure, comparable to an egg, with a large end and a small end, in men the large end is above, in women it is below. That is to say, that in men the diameter of the shoulders is greater than that of the hips, in women the diameter of the hips greater than that of the shoulders. This statement, as Mathias Duval and others have shown, is exaggerated. The correct formula would be expressed by saying that while in both men and women the trunk is an ovoid with the large end uppermost, in men the difference between the upper and lower ends is considerable, in women it is slight.[1] Thus, as Dr. Sargent shows for Americans between the ages of 17 and 20, the woman's hips, though relatively 4 inches larger, are absolutely smaller than man's; at the age of 20, girth of hip is in actual measurements $\frac{1}{2}$-inch smaller in women than in men, but if we take men and women of the same height the girth is as much as 6 inches larger in women than in men. The girth of thigh remains the only external measurement that is absolutely and almost constantly greater in women

[1] M. Duval, *Précis d'Anatomie Artistique*, p. 125.

than in men, although its size largely depends upon the relatively great size of the pelvis.

The pelvis—the bony girdle of the lower part of the body—acts under very different conditions in men from those found in quadrupeds. In animals it forms an arch which supports the posterior half of the body, while at right angles to its weight-bearing axis the arch is left free to form the gate by which offspring enter the world. In man it not only supports the weight of the whole of the trunk, but the weight falls in almost the same line as the axis of the exit from the body. The adaptation of the pelvis to the erect position becomes then a very delicate adjustment of physical forces, and as this adjustment must be carried to its highest point in women, the pelvis of women is in many respects more highly developed than that of men, which retains more animal-like characters.

The pelvis consists, above, of the hip-bones or ilia, which are in Man broadly spread out and excavated; behind, of that fused portion of the spinal column which is called the sacrum, and which terminates below in the rudimentary caudal vertebræ called the coccyx; in front, of the two pubic bones which meet to form an angle of varying degree; and underneath, of the two ischial bones which support the weight of the body in the sitting posture. All these four groups of bones which constitute the pelvis are differently arranged in man and in woman, and the differences are numerous and well-marked.[1] They may, however, for the most part be easily expressed by saying that while in man the pelvis is long,

[1] They have been studied in detail by numerous anatomists. The classic work of R. Verneau, *Le Bassin dans les Sexes et dans les Races*, Paris, 1875, may still be consulted. The French anatomist, Sappey, also gives a clear summary of the sexual differences. See also Garson, "Pelvimetry," *Journal Anat. and Phys.*, 1881. For differences in the pelvis and hips in the women of various races, see the illustrated chapter in Ploss and Max Bartels, *Das Weib*, Bd. i., "Das weibliche Becken in anthropologisches Beziehung"; also E. Marri, "Sulla forma dei Bacini in Razze diverse," *Archiv per l'Antrop.*, 1892, Fasc. 1.

narrow, and strongly built, in woman it is broad, relatively shallow, and delicately made. It is as though the comparatively primitive and ape-like pelvis of man had been pressed outward by forces acting downward from within, with the object of enlarging the door of life for the unborn child. As usually explained by obstetrical writers, the larger pelvis of women is actually due to such a force exerted by the sexual organs which in women are contained within the pelvis. A secondary and accidental result of the broadening and opening out of the pelvis in women lies in the increased size of the thigh and the greater distance between the origins of the thigh-bones, which form such conspicuous characteristics of the female form.

The distance between the iliac crests of the hip-bones in women, although to the eye it appears absolutely greater than in men, is, as we have seen, only relatively greater but absolutely smaller; the breadth of the upper opening of the pelvis is, however, both relatively and absolutely greater in women, both in the higher and lower human races. Sergi has taken advantage of the fact to devise an ilio-pelvic index, formed by multiplying the transverse diameter of the pelvis brim by 100, and dividing by the distance between the iliac crests. This gives, on the basis of Verneau's data, for European men an index of 46.5 and for women 50.8. By measuring pelves from all parts of the world, Sergi has found that the ilio-pelvic index is almost invariably greater in women than in men, differences in race appearing to produce very little change in this index (Sergi, " L'Indice Ilio-Pelvico," *La Clinica Ostetrica*, Fasc. iii., 1899).

Sexual differences in the pelvis become marked, according to Fehling, as soon as the bones begin to ossify, or in the fourth month.[1] Fehling's conclusions have been conformed by Professor Arthur Thomson of Oxford, who finds such differences discernible from the third month. In a very detailed and fully illustrated paper on this subject he gives photographs showing that the pubic angle is from

[1] " Die Form des Beckens beim Fötus und Neugeborenen," *Archiv f. Gynäk.*, Bd. x., 1876.

the fourth month onwards perceptibly larger throughout in the female, and concludes that "during fœtal
life the essentially sexual characters are as well defined
as they are in adult forms, and that any differences
that occur during growth between the adult and
fœtal forms, due, it may be, to the influence of
pressure or muscular traction, affect both sexes alike,
and that such influences are in no way accountable,
as has been maintained, for the characteristic features
of the pelvis of the female as contrasted with the
male."[1]   At birth, Romiti found sexual differences
distinct, more especially as regards greater breadth
of the subpubic arch, less height of pelvis, and less
straight ilia in the female.[2]   Jürgens, who studied
the pelves of 25 boys and 25 girls under the age of
five, found that those of the girls were markedly
larger, especially in the transverse diameter.[3]   While
sexual differences thus appear at the earliest age,
the infantile pelvis in its general aspects is long,
narrow, and straight, thus approximating to the
pelvis of the higher apes and the lower human races,
such as Kaffirs, Australians, and Andamanese; in
European children also, as Litzmann has shown,
the transverse diameter of the pelvic brim closely
approximates to the antero-posterior diameter, a
characteristic of the lower races, while in adult
Europeans the transverse diameter much exceeds
the antero-posterior, and in women more than in
men.   In nearly all respects the adult woman's
pelvis is in more marked contrast to the infant's than
is the adult man's; all the lower parts are opened out
instead of compressed, the ischial spines especially
being widely separated.   If we compare the breadth
of the pelvis to its length, as Topinard has done on

[1] Arthur Thomson, "The Sexual Differences of the Fœtal Pelvis,"
Jour. Anat. and Phys., Ap. 1899.
[2] G. Romiti, *Atti della Soc. Toscana di Sci. Nat.*, vol. viii., 1892.
[3] "Beiträge zur normalen und pathologischen Anatomie des menschlichen Beckens," *Rudolf Virchow Festschrift*, 1891.

a large scale to ascertain the "pelvic index," we find
that with vertebrate evolution from the lower animals

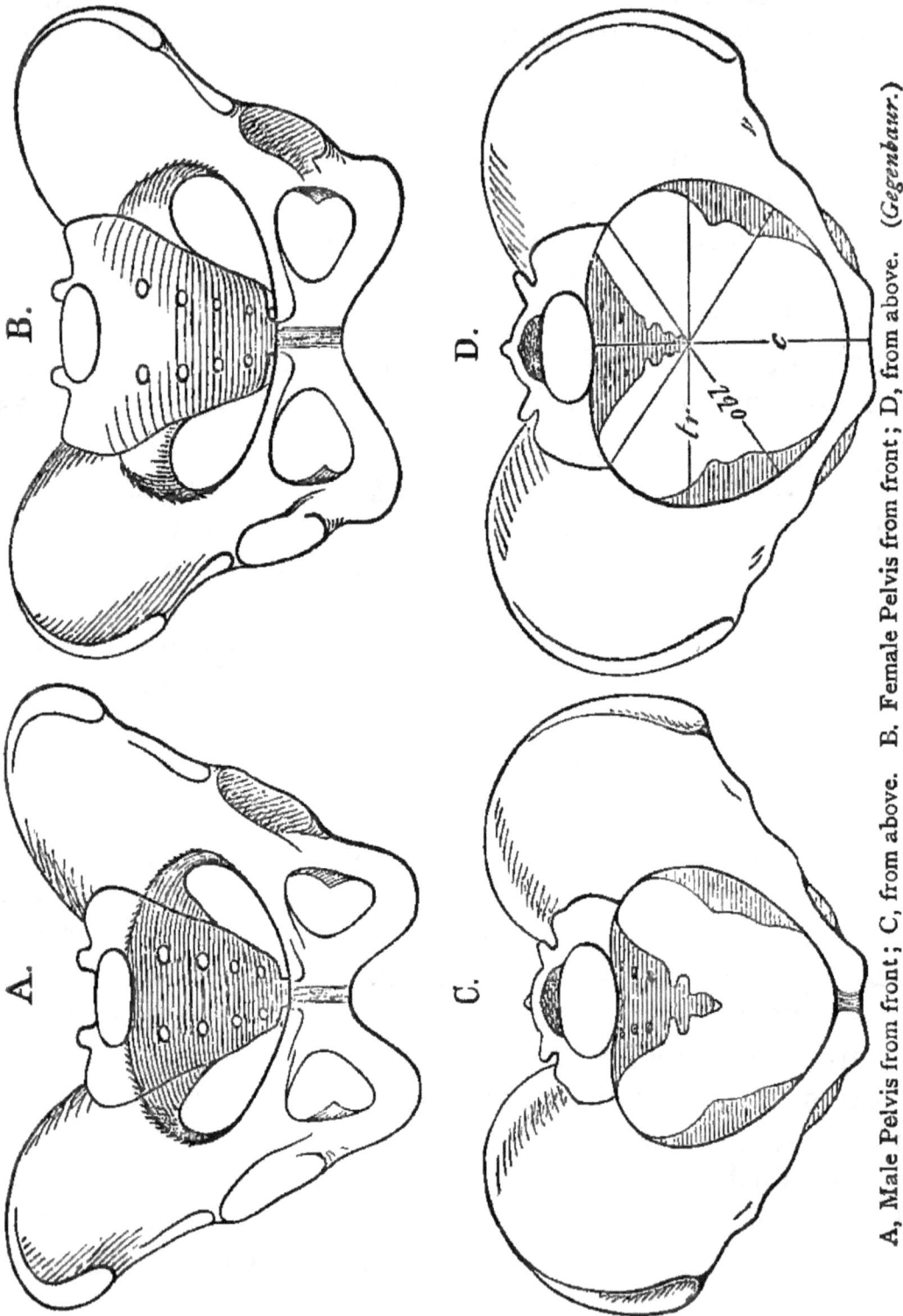

A, Male Pelvis from front; C, from above.   B. Female Pelvis from front; D, from above.   (*Gegenbaur.*)

to European man the pelvis has constantly been
becoming broader in relation to its length, and that
in women the pelvis is always broader in relation

to its length than in men. "As we rise in the human series," Topinard concludes, "the pelvis enlarges, and consequently the supremely beautiful pelvis is an

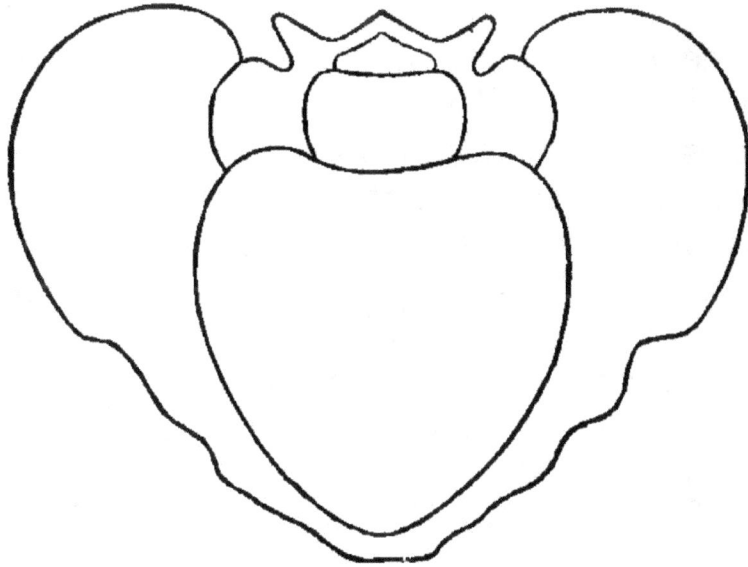

Average Andamanese Female Pelvis (adapted from Garson).

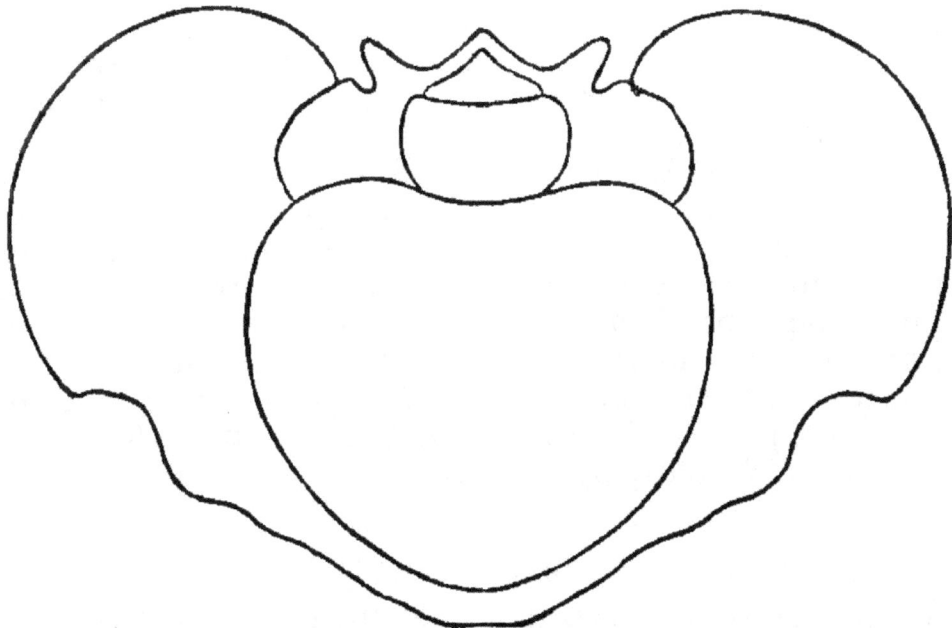

Average European Female Pelvis (adapted from Garson).

ample pelvis. The Greeks, by narrowing the pelvis in their sculpture, not only deprived woman of one of her most deserved characteristics, but made her bestial."[1]   By the breadth of her sacrum also, woman shows a higher degree of evolution than man. The sacrum in apes and in the lower human races is long, straight, and narrow, in harmony with the rest of the pelvis; the sacral index which expresses the degree of breadth of the sacrum shows a progressive rise from Hottentots to Europeans which culminates in European women.[2]

An external indication of the size of the pelvis may probably be found, as Stratz has lately pointed out, in the lozenge-shaped space on the surface of the sacrum which has been called after Michaelis. This space is formed laterally by two dimples corresponding to the superior posterior iliac spines, above by another dimple usually situated at the spinous process of the last lumbar vertebra, and below by the point at which the gluteal fissure begins. In men the lateral dimples, if found at all, are several centimetres nearer to each other.

Stratz, who has fully discussed this region, considers that these sacral dimples are secondary sexual characters scarcely inferior to the breasts in importance. This can scarcely be admitted, though, on the other hand, Brücke and Waldeyer have gone too far in denying that they are a sexual distinction at all. In all youthful and well-nourished women these dimples are large and deep, and the enclosing space well defined and inclined to the horizon. Various ancient authors refer with special admiration to these dimples, as a feature of feminine beauty, comparing them to the dimples of the face. In men they are much less marked, and, according to Stratz, only occur in from 18 to 25 per cent. cases (C. H. Stratz, *Archiv f. Anth.*, Bd. 27, 1900, p. 122; G. Fritsch, *Zt. f. Eth.*, 1898, heft 2, p. 142; Ploss, *Das Weib*, 1901, pp. 181-188; numerous illustrations are given).

We may gain a somewhat deeper insight into the problems that are grouped around the pelvis if we

[1] Topinard, *Anth. Gén.*, pp. 1049-50.
[2] The gradual evolution of the female pelvis and its departure from the male type is well shown by Dr. Garson's carefully prepared diagrams of the typical Andamanese and European pelves. (See accompanying figures.) They are constructed from the average dimensions of 13 Andamanese and 14 European female pelves.

consider it in relation to the spinal column, and more especially in relation to the various forces which influence or modify the adoption of the completely erect position. Verticality, as Delaunay pointed out,[1] is in direct ratio with evolution and nutrition, while horizontality is in inverse ratio. The apes are but imperfect bipeds with tendencies towards the quadrupedal attitude; the human infant is as imperfect a biped as the ape; savage races do not stand so erect as civilised races. Country people (even apart, according to Delaunay, from agricultural labour) tend to bend forward, and

[1] See his interesting observations on this subject, *Études de Biologie Comparée*, 1e Partie, 1878, pp. 47-52; also Dr. Frank Baker's remarkable presidential address to the Anthropological Section of the American Association for the Advancement of Science (1890) on the ascent of man to the erect position and the consequent modifications his body has undergone.

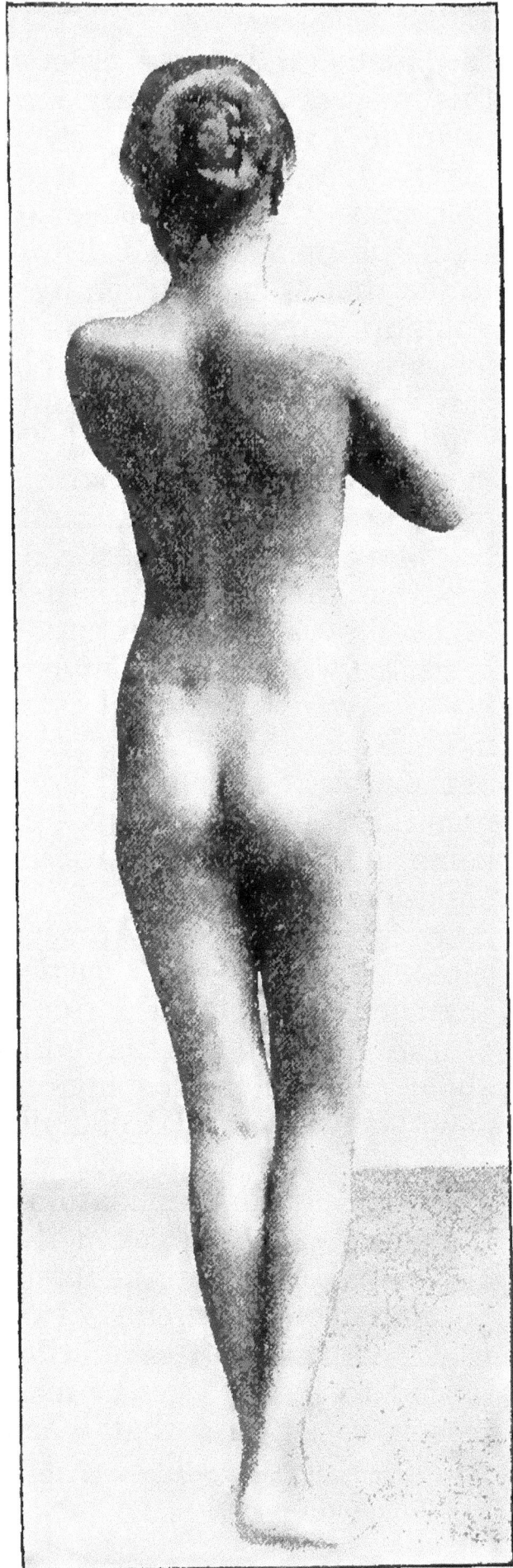

JAVANESE GIRL. (*Stratz.*)

the aristocrat is more erect than the plebeian. In this respect women appear to be nearer to the infantile condition than men. "It has been observed among the natives of Ceylon," remarks Delaunay, "that the women are more curved forwards than the men. In our European societies it is easy to see that women generally do not hold themselves quite upright and walk with the body and head bent forward." The carriage of the human female to any careful observer has (except during pregnancy) a sinuous character and a forward tendril-like movement which is full of charm, and contrasts with the more proud and rigid, almost convex, carriage of the human male. The head tends to fall forward, and that this tendency is not due to training seems to be shown by the fact that it has an anatomical basis, as was pointed out by Cleland. From childhood onwards the skull is slowly tilted more and more backwards in order to throw more and more of the weight behind. "The female skull," Cleland remarks, "is much less tilted back than the male, being in this, as in various other respects, more child-like than the male skull."[1] While the head is more tilted forward in women, the pelvis is also more tilted. This is due to partial arrest of an infantile character. The angle formed by the superior plane of the pelvis with the horizon when standing is about 70°—80° in the infant, 50°—55° in men, 55° —60° in women. (Papillault's method of measurement gives a wider angle, but a similarly large sexual difference.) This inclination—which tends to efface the mons Veneris between the thighs and to give an abdominal curve often adopted by artists—better supports the pelvic contents. In animals it appears there is also a sexual difference; thus in the horse the angle is said to be 110°, in the mare 120°. There is some reason to suppose that when the angle in women

[1] Cleland, "The Variations of the Human Skull," *Philosophical Trans. of Roy. Soc.*, 1870.

is very little inclined (from 24° to 45°) there is a tendency to uterine prolapse. The racial differences are considerable; thus in Mexican women, whose pelvis is in many respects remarkable, the average inclination is from 61° to 65°.[1]

In harmony with this the anus appears to be rather farther back and nearer to the coccyx in women than in men; in the apes (and also to some extent in the child) there is a long distance between the tip of the coccyx and the anus (Cunningham). In certain African races, even (according to Delaunay) among the Moors, the vagina is often so far directed backwards as to render necessary the quadrupedal method of coitus. The older anthropologists used to judge of the inclination of the pelvis by the direction of the urinary stream in the female. A stream directed backwards is an animal-like character rarely found, even in the lower races; a forward direction of the stream indicates that the distinctively human upright position has reached a high degree of attainment.

An anatomical explanation has sometimes been given (*i.e.*, by Wernich in the case of Japanese women) for the primitive attitude of women during urination. This attitude, it may be necessary to remark, is for both sexes the opposite of the civilised; *i.e.*, the men squat, the women stand. This was the custom even in ancient Egypt (according to Herodotus); it was also the custom in ancient Ireland (according to Giraldus Cambrensis). It is to-day, or was until lately, the custom in large part of Australia (the *mika*-operation here makes the sitting posture more convenient for men, but it would be hazardous to suggest that this operation was ever universal), in New Zealand, throughout North America—among the Apaches, in Colorado, in Nicaragua—and in Angola and some other parts of Africa. (Some of the evidence is given in Captain J. G. Bourke's *Scatalogic Rites of all Nations*, 1891, pp. 148-153.) To sit on the heels is for males the orthodox Mohammedan custom.

There is no reason to suppose that anatomical considerations come in here to any marked extent; it is partly a psychological, partly a ritual matter, partly a question of clothing. In the case of Japanese women, Professor W. Anderson wrote to me, there is no reasonable ground for supposing any anatomical peculiarities, and he pointed out that the tight skirts of the

---

[1] Sappey; also H. Meyer, "Die Beckenneigung," *Archiv f. Anat.*, etc., 1861, p. 137; Felsenreich, "Beckenneigung," *Wien. Med. Wochenschrift*, 1893; De Yta, "Le Pelvis Mexicain," *Atti dell xi. Congresso Medico* (Rome, 1894), vol. v. p. 137; Papillault, "L'Homme Moyen à Paris," *Bull. Soc. d'Anth.*, 1902.

women make it difficult to raise them. Mr. Tregear, one of the chief authorities on the Maoris, and Secretary of the Polynesian Society, writes to me that at the present day it is invariably the rule for both sexes amongst the Maoris to squat, but that in old times the women stood, and he makes the important observation that the girdle or mat of most primitive races makes it easy (bearing in mind the sexual difference in the position of the organs) for the women, difficult for the men, to urinate in the standing position without exposure.

Among most uncivilised races, it is a matter of religious ritual to avoid exposure of the sexual organs; the considerations of hygiene which the men among the Maoris and other races bring forward to explain their practice of squatting is merely an afterthought; the primary consideration is of a ritual character. The same consideration still prevailed when men (on account of the development of their garments, or for whatever reason) gave up the squatting position; and Hesiod recommends men to urinate before an object standing full before them, so that no divinity may be offended by their nakedness. (*Works and Days*, l. 727 *et seq.;* so also Pythagoras, *Laert.* VIII. i. 19.) This habit has become ingrained in civilised men unto the present day, although they have long ceased to consider how the gods view the matter.

It is curious that as men began to develop this habit women seem nearly everywhere to have adopted the custom discarded by the men. Perhaps it was fostered by the general contrariness of men and women, which everywhere makes men unwilling to adopt women's ways and women unwilling to adopt men's; for it is only within comparatively recent times that the development of women's garments has offered much obstacle to the primitive custom. In any case there are now but few countries where the habit is for both sexes the same, and these countries seem to be in a transition state. In most countries the habits of the sexes in this matter are opposed, and as a general rule also the practice of the more civilised countries is the reverse of the primitive practice. So far as I am aware, the evolution of these customs has never been discussed, but they are as instructive and as wide-reaching (also as complicated) as many more dignified problems in the origin of civilisation.

The inclination of the pelvis is related to, though it is not identical with, the saddle back or lumbo-sacral curve which in its exaggerated pathological form is called lordosis. This is only slightly marked in the ape, and does not exist in the human embryo. It is one of the superior qualities of African races, and appears to be increased by the muscular action of the back, as in rowing upright and in carrying children on the hips. It is always more pronounced in women than in men, as Duchenne first showed,[1] and is especially well marked in Spanish and Creole women, constituting the main anatomical basis to their beauty of carriage.[2]

Cunningham's lumbo-vertebral index shows the tendency to curvature; a high index indicates — though not invariably — a low curve, and a low index a high degree of curvature. In the chimpanzee the index is 117, in the Australian 108, in the male Andaman 106, in the female Andaman 105, in negroes 105, in Europeans 96, in (21) Irish males 96.2, in (22) Irish females 93.5. (An index below 100 means that the anterior measurements of the lumbar vertebræ exceed the posterior.) So that curvature increases on the whole as we ascend the scale, and tends to be greater in women. Among North

[1] *Physiologie des Mouvements*, 1867, pp. 726-734.
[2] Art. "Ensellure," *Dict. des sci. Anthrop.*

1st Dorsal

1st Lumbar

MALE SPINAL COLUMN SHOWING THE NORMAL CURVES IN THE UPRIGHT POSTURE. (*Pansch.*) In women the convexity forwards below the first lumbar vertebra is increased.

American Indians, who have a medium lumbar index, Dorsey has found that the sexual difference is marked and constant.[1] Luschka, Balandin, Charpy, Ravenel, all consider that the lumbar curve is most marked in women. Charpy points out that the degree of the curve is in proportion to the inclination of the sacrum, and this is confirmed by Papillault, who points out that the prominence of the buttocks in relation with this sacral obliquity is an index of functional utility. As sacral obliquity may be due either to an acute sacro-vertebral angle or to a pronounced lumbar curve, Papillault remarks that we have two different types which may possibly be of racial significance.

In association with this greater curvature we find, if we compare the bony spinal column of man with that of woman, that the chief difference is the relatively greater length of the lumbar region in woman. In woman also the curve seems to begin higher and to attain its summit at a higher point. This is a character which in association with the greater relative size of the abdomen fits woman for her maternal function. While in women the lumbar region constitutes 32.8 per cent. of the entire column, in men it constitutes only 31.7 per cent.;[2] and, on the other hand, the dorsal section of the column is 46.5 in men against 45.8 in women. The lumbar region of the column is thus not only longer in women than in men, but it is moulded on a different plan, being more arched and the vertebræ moulded more distinctly in adaptation to this arch.

[1] G. A. Dorsey, "The Lumbar Curve in some American Races," *Bull. Essex Inst.*, vol. 27, 1895, Salem, Mass.

[2] These are the figures given by Professor D. J. Cunningham, who has very carefully studied the relations of the spinal column in the *Cunningham Memoirs* of the Royal Irish Academy, No. 2, 1886, and in "The Lumbar Section of the Vertebral Column," *Journal of Anat. and Phys.*, Oct. 1888. G. A. Dorsey, who has studied the lumbar index in American Indians (*Bull. Essex Inst.*, Salem, Mass., vol. 27), finds it an important sexual distinction, as well as a test of racial superiority.

"All these distinctions," Cunningham believes, "may be accounted for by the different habits pursued by the two sexes. There is no part of the vertebral column which is more readily moulded by the functions that the spine has to perform, because it is that section of the column which works under the greatest degree of superincumbent pressure."

Soularue, by the method of measuring the anterior face of each vertebra separately, found the same relatively greater length of the lumbar vertebræ and ascertained that it applied also to the lower dorsal vertebræ. The difference was almost equally great in Europeans, Mongols, American Indians, and Negroes. Soularue found that the sacrum is very slightly larger and also more curved in men; in Mongol and American Indian women, however, it was relatively larger in women.[1]

Rosenberg (*Morphologisches Jahrbuch*, 1876) from his researches into the development of the spinal column has come to the conclusion that it is shortening in Man. The ancestral form, he considers, had 25 movable vertebræ anterior to the sacrum; now there are 24; in the future there will be only 23. In this connection he points out that on the transverse process of the first lumbar vertebra of the fœtus is found the cartilaginous rudiment of a rib which subsequently disappears through its fusion with the transverse process, suggesting that the ancestral type was a condition now most frequently found in the gibbon, 13 ribs and 25 movable vertebræ. This ancestral type is sometimes found in Man at the present day. Professor Ambrose Birmingham supports Rosenberg's view (*Journal Anat. and Phys.*, July 1891). Weidersheim, who also appears to support Rosenberg's view (*Der Bau des Menschen*, 1887), remarks that the spinal columns with the most reduced number of vertebræ always occur in women, so that women in this respect would be leading the evolutionary movement, a supposition in harmony with the higher morphological development of the pelvis in women. Rosenberg's view, however, is not universally accepted; thus Professor Paterson ("The Human Sacrum," *Proc. Roy. Soc.*, 1892) does not accept it, on the ground that there is more often elongation than contraction of the region above the sacrum; but his facts and arguments, as contained in the abstract published by the Royal Society, do not clearly support his objection to Rosenberg's view, and he admits that a process of fusion is going on at the caudal end of the column.

[1] Soularue, "Étude des Proportions de la Colonne Vertébrale chez l'homme et chez la femme," *Bull. et Mém. Soc. d'Anth.*, Paris, 1900.

The question has since been discussed by Professor D. J. Cunningham, who disputes Paterson's views and leans towards Rosenberg's ("The Significance of Anatomical Variations," *Brit. Med. Jour.*, 10th Sept. 1898). He believes that the lumbo-sacral region of the spine, which is in a position of very unstable equilibrium, may exhibit both retrospective and prospective variations, and points out (as against Paterson) that statistics alone do not suffice to show the direction of the movement; a prospective or prophetic variation can at first make little way against the strong counter-current of normal and atavistic tendencies, so that a long period must elapse before it wins its way to a high place on the statistical table. If we suppose, Cunningham argues, that man and the anthropoid apes have descended from a gibbon-like ancestor with at least 26 præsacral vertebræ, we find that man has 25, the gorilla and the chimpanzee 24, and the orang 23. The orang has thus travelled farthest on this line and reached its goal, for it exhibits comparatively few variations. Man and the gibbon are lagging behind, though they have made considerable progress along the same path. Cunningham adds, though not as an argument having any anatomical value, that the æsthetic taste of man emphatically condemns a long trunk with short legs.

If woman's body seems to be somewhat more reminiscent of the quadrupedal posture than man's, she has excellent reason for it. There can be little doubt that, as Dr. Baker shows, in both sexes all sorts of pathological and unwholesome conditions have been encouraged or produced by the assumption of the erect posture; it is sufficient to mention hernia, stone, disease of the vermiform appendix of the intestine, varicose veins, exposure of the great arteries to injury, torpidity of gall-bladder, greater constriction of lungs and therefore inability to sustain prolonged and rapid muscular exertion, disorders of the liver from the difficulty of raising blood through the ascending *vena cava*, and the tendency to syncope. Women share these disabilities with men, but in addition they suffer other special disadvantages. The erect position has comparatively slight effect on man's sexual organs, beyond producing a predisposition to scrotal varicosity and greater exposure to injury; it tends very seriously to affect woman's sexual organs, and enormously interferes with the maternal functions. "In the quadruped," as Dr. Baker remarks, "the act of parturition is comparatively easy, the pelvis offering no serious hindrance. The shape of the female pelvis is therefore the result of a compromise between two forms—one for support, the other for ease in delivery. When we reflect that along with the acquirement of the erect position the size of the head of the child has gradually increased, thus forming still another obstacle to delivery and to the adaptation which might otherwise have taken place, we can realise how serious the struggle has been, and no longer wonder that deaths in childbirth are much more common in the higher races, and that woman in her entire organisation shows signs of having suffered more than man in the upward struggle. In no other animal is there shown such a distinction between the pelvis of the male and that of the female —a distinction that increases as we ascend the scale. . . . The frequency of uterine displacements, almost unknown in the quadruped, has also been noted, and it is significant that one of the most effective postures for treating and restoring to place the disturbed organ is the so-called 'knee-elbow position,' decidedly quadrupedal in character."[1]

We may say, indeed, that the adoption of the erect biped position has—to use the convenient teleological method of expression—placed Nature in an awkward dilemma. On the one hand, it is necessary for the stability of the body and the due support of the organs that the pelvis should be tough, that the bony girdle should be strong and hard, and the inner channel small. On the other hand, for the higher evolution of the race it is necessary for the bony girdle to be rendered somewhat less stable by the

[1] The advantages of this posture in the treatment of the diseases of women have been summarised by Dr. Potter of Buffalo, who considers that its discovery by Marion Sims was "the turning-point in the history of gynecology." ("Posture in Obstetrics and Gynecology," *Trans. Am. Soc. of Obstet. and Gynec.*, vol. v., 1893, pp. 99-102.)

increased size of the outlet which will permit the birth of large-headed children. The most delicate adjustment is required to prevent these directly opposite necessities from conflicting with each other.[1] If we were born through the navel (as some of us supposed when we were children) the dilemma would not exist; but while such a method of parturition would be in perfect harmony with the biped position, it would have been impracticable in the quadrupedal position. On the whole, as we know, while the adjustment is not absolutely perfect and we suffer from the disadvantages of the biped position, the demands of the higher evolution of the race have caused, and will no doubt continue to cause, an increased expansion and development of the pelvis, a movement in which women are the natural leaders. But the children always tend to be somewhat too developed for the gate by which they enter the world; this cunningly contrived girdle of bone is a force on the side of mediocrity, shutting out the highly developed from the chances of life, although it is a force which tends to become weaker, for the size of the head depends on both parents, and the women with small pelves tend to produce still-born children or weak children unlikely to survive, and so it is not easy for them to transmit their small pelves. In the higher evolution of the race the increased development of the head must always be accompanied by the increased development of the pelvis.

A word may perhaps be said here on a point which has a connection with this question usually ignored. Many writers—

---

[1] The difficulty of this adjustment is shown by the cases, occasionally occurring, of congenital diastasis of the symphysis pubis. In such cases there is increased pelvic elasticity, and the pelvic ring tends to gape at the pubis. The result is (as in a case recorded by Schauta, *Centralbl. f. Gynäk.*, Aug. 1899) that labour is easy, quick, almost painless, and without bad results. But, on the other hand, additional care and artificial support are required during pregnancy.

I think especially of Strauss (*The Old Faith and the New*) and Renan (Introduction to translation of *Le Cantique des Cantiques*) —have spoken in glowing terms of a future of humanity in which sensuality, by which they mean the sexual emotions, shall have almost disappeared, to give place to pure rationality. There is no foundation whatever for any such supposition. We do not know very much of the sexual emotions (as distinguished from sexual customs) among the lower races, but while their sexual practices are often very free, there is considerable evidence to show that their sexual instincts are not very intense. (See Havelock Ellis, *Studies in the Psychology of Sex*, vol. iii., Appendix A, in which information on this point is brought together.) It would probably be found that the higher races (*i.e.*, those with the larger pelvis) have nearly always the strongest sexual impulses. As civilisation advances abnormalities become more frequent, the individuals are multiplied. in whom the sexual impulse is weak or even non-existent. But these, even if healthy or highly intelligent individuals, are not the individuals who tend to propagate the race. The persons best adapted to propagate the race are those with the large pelves, and as the pelvis is the seat of the great centres of sexual emotion the development of the pelvis and its nervous and vascular supply involves the greater heightening of the sexual emotions. At the same time the greater activity of the cerebral centres enables them to subordinate and utilise to their own ends the increasingly active sexual emotions, so that reproduction is checked and the balance to some extent restored.

CHAPTER V.

THE HEAD.

THE study of the pelvis naturally brings us to the study of the head with which it is in such intimate relation. In studying the head we may first of all consider the *skull*, unimportant in itself as being merely the comparatively inert garment of the living brain, which to some extent it moulds, and by which, to a large extent, although not in detail, it is itself moulded; at the same time we will glance at the interesting but as yet not greatly cultivated study of the face; then we will turn to the *brain*, unquestionably an organ of the first importance as being a collection of the chief nervous centres which are probably more or less concerned in every process that goes on in the organism, but unfortunately an organ which does not easily lend itself to study.

THE SKULL.

If we take up the skull of an infant we find that it is very light and very smooth, with thin, translucent walls delicately veined by the blood-vessels. The orbits appear large; the lower jaw is small and shallow, and its angles very wide; the face, taken altogether, is relatively small. The parietal bones are very large, forming the greater part of the roof and a large part of the walls of the skull, and each parietal bone presents a well-marked boss, the resultant of mixed compressive forces, which gives the impression that the skull is not yet fully expanded. The other bones are mostly in a very undeveloped condition, and their component parts are still incompletely welded together. The bony processes and corrugations, which afterwards give a foothold to powerful muscles to support or turn the head, can scarcely be traced at all. We notice, further, that the hole through which the spinal cord emerges to enter the spinal column is placed very far back, so that when supported at this point of junction between the head and the body the head tends to fall forwards.

There would be no difficulty whatever in recognising an infantile skull even if it were magnified to adult proportions. But it is another matter when we turn from age distinctions to consider the sexual characters in an adult skull. Some investigators (like Aeby), though not in very recent days, have gone so far as to declare that there are no sexual differences in the skull except size. And most competent craniologists, like Virchow, one of the most distinguished, insist that, among non-European races, it is extremely difficult to determine the sex from the skull, as the criteria furnished by one race do not hold for other races, although among some savage races (as in New Britain) the sexual differences in the skull may be "colossal." When attempting to determine by inspection alone the sex of skulls of known origin, Mantegazza, an experienced anthropologist, found that his mistakes were from three to five per cent.; Rebentisch, a younger and less experienced observer, found that his errors were nine per cent.

The skull is of incomparably less importance from this point of view than the pelvis. And although it is impossible to assert that differences between the skulls of men and of women are only those of size, it is extremely probable that, as Manouvrier argues, such sexual characters as may be found are due mainly to the differences in general physical proportion; that is to say, that they depend chiefly on the greater precocity of woman and her earlier arrest of growth. It need scarcely be added that to say that the sexual differences in the skull are largely the result of the general physical differences is not to say that they are of no significance.

Jacobæus of Copenhagen, who in 1709 wrote a book *De distinguendis Cadaveribus per Crania*, showed that there were some sexual differences in the skull. Soemmering (*De corporis humani fabrica*, 1794) considered that the head was relatively rather larger in women. His pupil Ackermann discovered a number of precise differences which have since been credited to other anatomists. Bichat (*Anatomie descriptive*, 1801) thought there was little sexual difference. Gall (*Fonctions du Cerveau*, 1822) stated that the antero-posterior diameter is longer in women, and the other diameters shorter. These statements are worth quoting as the opinions of the most distinguished authorities of their time, but they were not founded on extensive and accurate data. Barnard Davis and Thurnam (*Crania Britannica*, 1856-65) seem to have been the first to recognise the necessity of always separating the sexes in craniometrical tables. Dureau ("Des caractères sexuels du crâne humain," *Revue d'Anthropologie*, 1873, t. ii. pp. 475-487) gave an excellent summary of the history and data of the subject up to that date; and Mantegazza ("Dei caratteri sessuali del cranio umano," *Arch. per l'Antropologia*, 1872, vol. ii. pp. 11 *et seq.*) gave a brief critical summary of the matter. The most important recent studies are embodied in two inaugural dissertations : E. Rebentisch (Strassburg), "Der Weiberschädel," *Morphologische Arbeiten*, ii. 2, 1893), and Paul Bartels (Berlin), *Ueber Geschlechtsunterschiede am Schädel*, 1897. For a good general account of the history of head-measurements see Marage, " Historique des Recherches sur la Céphalométrie," *L'Année Psychologique*, 5th year, 1899, pp. 245-298. And for a discussion of methods, Manouvrier, *ib.*, pp. 558-591.

Panichi has shown by his observations on the skulls of children at Florence that sexual differences begin to be visible at the age of six, and that most of the chief sexual distinctions are fairly well marked before the age of twelve.[1] As to what the most constant sexual differences, taken comprehensively, are, it cannot be said that any two authorities are quite agreed, for each craniologist has his own preferences, and we have to bear in mind that sometimes a skull may be masculine in some of its characters, feminine in others; while a man's skull may approach a woman's in character, or (more frequently, in Mantegazza's experience) a woman's skull may resemble a man's. There is no one constant sexual character in the skull, but there are a few characters which, when taken together, unmistakably indicate its sex. I will briefly state these, following, so far as possible, the opinions of four anthropologists belonging to different countries—Broca in France, Schaaffhausen in Germany, Mantegazza in Italy, and Turner in

[1] R. Panichi, " Ricerche di craniologia sessuale," *Arch. per l'Antrop.*, 1892, Fasc. i.

Great Britain.[1]   (1.) Perhaps the most conspicous
and distinctive of all the characteristics of the male
human skull is the prominence of the glabella (or
bony projection over the nose) and of the supraciliary
ridges; that is to say, that men have overhanging
brows which are little marked in women, while they
do not exist in children; they develop at puberty and

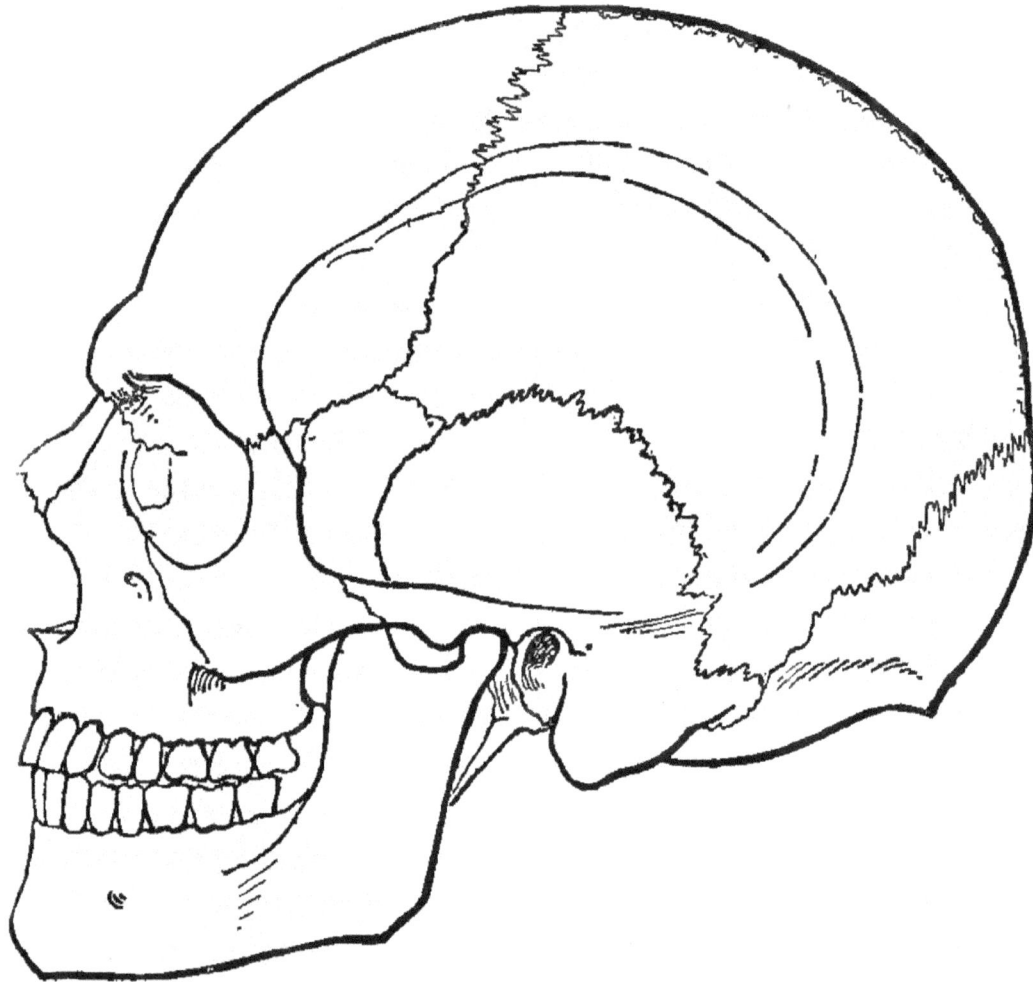

TYPICAL MALE SKULL (*Poirier*).

increase with age, and form a distinctly retrogressive
character, being exaggerated in many lower races
and to an extreme extent in the anthropoid apes.
Associated with these bony prominences in men are

---

[1] Broca, *Instructions craniologiques et craniomètriques;* Schaaffhausen, " Ueber die heutige Schädellehre," *Correspondenzblatt deutsch.
Gesell. Anthrop.,* 1889, p. 165; Mantegazza, "Dei caratt. sess. del
cranio," *Arch. per l'Antrop.,* vol. ii. p. 14; Sir W. Turner, " Report
on the Human Crania," *Challenger Reports, Zoology,* vol. x.

large frontal air-sinuses which in women are much smaller.[1] (2.) In women certain bosses which are prominent in children have usually persisted to a more marked extent than in men; these are the parietal bosses at the outer and upper part of the back of the head and the frontal bosses half-way up the forehead over the eyes; in men these present the appearance of having been largely obliterated by

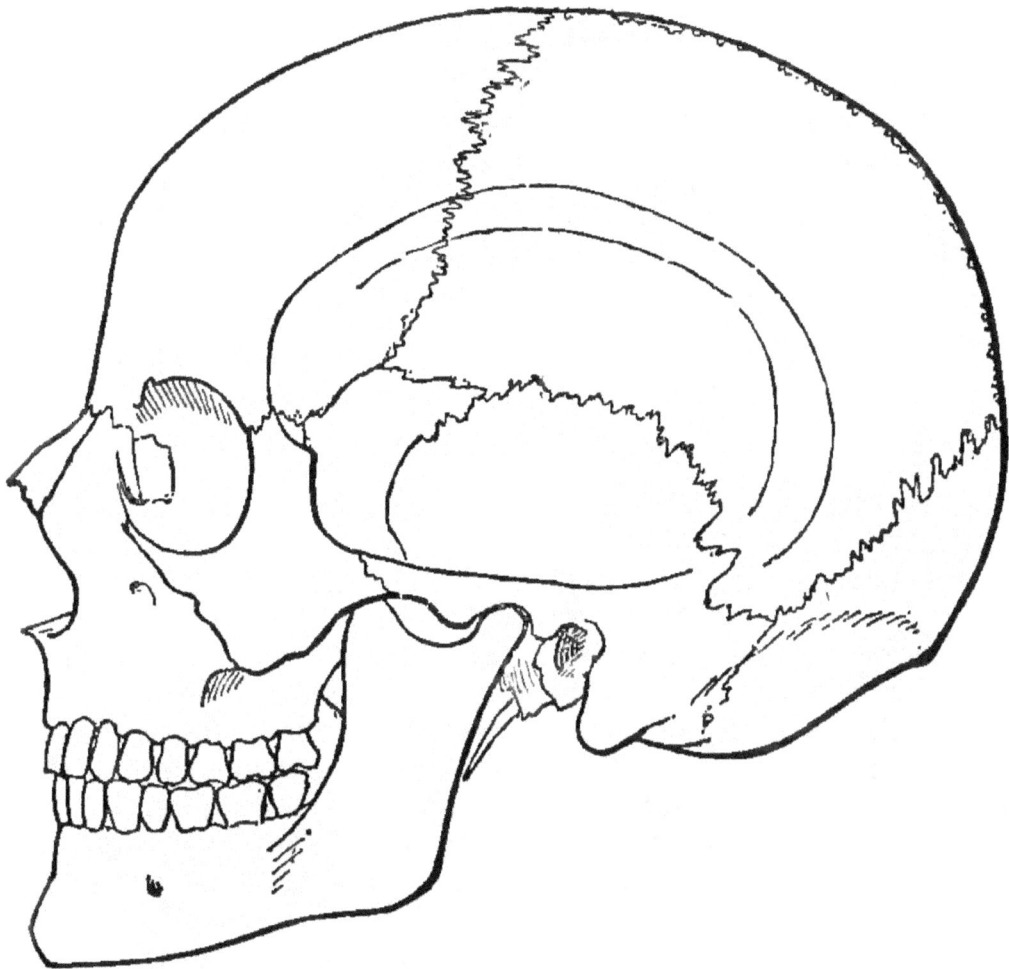

TYPICAL FEMALE SKULL (*Poirier*).

the expansion of the skull. (3.) All the muscular prominences are better marked in men, and the bones of the skull generally are thicker and stronger; thus the inion (the small occipital protuberance at the back of the head) is nearly always larger in men,

[1] The frontal sinuses have been studied by Professor S. Bianchi, of Siena, "I seni frontali e le arcate sopraccigliari," *Arch. per l'Antrop.*, 1892, Fasc. 2.

as are the mastoid processes beneath the ear, which in children are very small. The ridges on the skull for the attachment of muscles are also more marked in men. With regard to these three points it may be confidently said that there is very general agreement among anatomists. There are other sexual distinctions which seem to be fairly well marked but which are less obvious: thus in women the top of the head appears to be flatter, and at a more marked angle with the straight forehead, while in men the curve from before backwards is more smooth and even—a distinction insisted upon by Ecker and Mantegazza, and recognised by the Greek sculptors; women's skulls, also, in most races, are relatively shallower than those of men, in dependence on the greater flatness of the head; in women, again, while the base of the skull is usually smaller than in men, the arch of the skull, measured from the base of the nose to the occipital foramen, is often as large as in men.

These characters have not the same definiteness or constancy as the three characters first mentioned. The lowness of the female skull, which is accepted by Welcker, Weisbach, Ecker, Cleland, and Benedikt, seems to be due to the persistence in women of the infantile character of flatness of the roof; at birth the male and female skulls are of equal height, but the female skull in its adult shape lacks the final increments of height gained by the male. There are, however, many races among whom the skull is not lower in women than in men: such are the stone-age folk of the Homme-Mort Cavern (Broca), Auvergnats (Broca), New Caledonians (Broca), Negroes (Davis and Broca), Crania Helvetica (von Hölder), Corsicans (Broca), Ancient Romans (Davis and Thurnam), Irish (Davis), Anglo-Saxons (Davis and Thurnam). The relation of the arch of the skull to its base (the direct line between the two ends of the arch) has been worked out for various races by Cleland in his interesting paper on "The Variations of the Human Skull," in the *Philosophical Transactions of the Royal Soc.*, 1870. In infancy and childhood the base is very small compared to the arch; in women the base is almost always short, while the extent of the arch is in some instances as great as in the male. Comparing races, the Irish have the largest proportion of arch to base, the Chinese next. The short base line of women is therefore an infantile character, but on the other hand the longer base line of man is a savage character. "The most striking and altogether remarkable fact," as Cleland points out, "is that in uncivilised nations, while the length of the arch is very variable, the length of the base line is always great." Here, as is so often found, the infantile condition indicates the direction of evolution.

Cephalic Index.—A very great amount of study has been expended on the cephalic index, especially in regard to race and to sex. In regard to race, the great value of this index is unquestioned;[1] in regard to sex, although the assertions of craniologists have been equally emphatic in opposite directions, its value is by no means so clear. This index, which was devised many years ago by Retzius and perfected by Broca, shows the relation of the breadth of the skull to its length; it is ascertained by multiplying the maximum transverse diameter by 100, and dividing the result by the maximum antero-posterior diameter, certain precautions being observed in taking the measurements. A head or a skull of which the cephalic index is from 70 to 74 is (according to the international agreement of Frankfort, usually accepted in England) called dolichocephalic; from 75 to 79 it is called mesaticephalic; from 80 to 84 brachycephalic; below 70 it is hyperdolichocephalic; and above 84 it is hyperbrachycephalic. Therefore, the more an individual is relatively broad-headed the higher is his cephalic index, and long-headed persons have a low cephalic index. While some anthropologists (like Deniker in his *Races of Man*), realising that the differences are in any case slight, are content with the conclusion that there are no important sexual differences in this respect, a large number of other distinguished anthropologists—De Quatrefages, Welcker, Broca, Calori—assert that in Europe women are more dolichocephalic than men,

---

[1] Sergi (*Specie e Varietà Umane*, 1900, and *Mediterranean Race*, 1901) has shown the importance of studying the skull by a zoological method based on form, but the cephalic index, when used with discretion, still retains much value.

that is to say, that women's heads tend to be rather longer or not so broad. But, on the other hand, other eminent anthropologists — Weisbach, Mantegazza, Hamy, Topinard—find that women are more brachycephalic than men. Crochley Clapham gives the measurements of nearly 2000 insane men and about the same number of insane women at Wakefield asylum;[1] he also examined a much smaller number of normal men and women; calculating the cephalic index from the figures given by Clapham, I find that for insane males it is 80.3, for insane females 80.1, for sane males 81.2, for sane females 80.5; that is to say, that the sane are slightly more brachycephalic than the insane, and the men very slightly more brachycephalic than the women.

If we turn to consider the cephalic index among human races generally, the discrepancy continues equally great. Among the following the men are more brachycephalic than the women:—Parisians anterior to nineteenth century (Topinard), Auvergnats (Broca), Troglodytes of Lozère (Broca), Papuans of New Guinea (Mantegazza), Admiralty Islanders (Turner), Italians of Bologna (Calori), Flemish (Houzé), Annamites (Mondière), Polynesians (Clavel), Letts (Woeber), Lapps, both Norwegian and Russian (Mantegazza, Kharouzine, Deniker), Ancient Britons (Davis), Bas Bretons (Broca), Alsatians (Schwalbe, Pfitzner), English (Davis), Ancient Romans (Davis), Basques (Broca), Modern Asiatic Greeks (Neophytos), Hindus (Davis), Greenlanders (Davis). Among the following, on the other hand, the women are more brachycephalic:—Berbers of Biskra (Topinard), Neolithic men of the Marne (Broca), Californians of Santa-Barbara (Carr.), Italians of Bologna (Mantegazza), Andamanese (Flower), Negroes (Broca, Huschke, and Davis), Tahitians (Deniker and Laloy), Australians (Flower, Krause, Duckworth), Papuans

---

[1] Art. "Head, Size and Shape of," in *Dict. of Psychological Medicine.*

of Loyalty Islands (*Crania Ethnica*), Russian Mordwins (Deniker), Tyrolese (Tappeiner), Italians of Romagna (Vitali), Spaniards (Aranzadi), Portuguese (Macedo), Faroe Islanders (Arbo), Omahas (Manouvrier), New Caledonians (*Crania Ethnica*), Russians (Elkind), Ainos (Koganei, Kopernicki, Tarentzky), Veddahs (Thomson), Finns (Retzius), Sardinians (d'Hercourt), Swiss (His), Irish (Davis), French (Sappey), Danish (Davis), Germans (Krause, Daffner), Guanches (Broca), Chinese (Davis), Czechs (very slightly, Matiegka).[1] From these mixed and not always reliable data it is obvious, however, that no definite conclusion may be drawn, except that we note that while the first list contains a very large proportion of white races, the second contains a very large proportion of dark races. Among savage and dark races generally dolichocephaly prevails; among the prehistoric races of Europe dolichocephaly prevailed to a greater extent than in the Europe of to-day, and the predominance of the brachycephalic is still increasing;[2] the higher age of the dolichocephalic races is suggested (as Virchow remarks) by the existence at both ends of the long continents of dolichocephalic races whose great age we must recognise;[3] the brains of brachycephalic men are decidedly larger than those of dolichocephalic men, as Calori has shown;[4] among the criminal, insane, and degenerate generally, while marked brachycephaly is sometimes found, dolichocephaly prevails to a greater extent

[1] Topinard, *Anthrop. Gén.*, pp. 376, 377; Morselli, *Arch. per l'Antrop.*, vol. v., and various other sources.

[2] Topinard, *L'Homme dans la Nature*, 1891, p. 161.

[3] R. Virchow, *Crania Ethnica Americana*, 1892.

[4] Topinard, *Anthrop. Gén.*, p. 568. Tappeiner (*Zt. f. Eth.*, 1899, heft 5, p. 203) has found that even among a very brachycephalic people like the Tyrolese the more brachycephalic skulls tend to have the greatest cranial capacity, but as regards the extreme (ultra) brachycephalic group he found that this no longer held good. Bolk in Holland found the mesocephalic skulls the most capacious, but the brachycephals were superior to the dolichocephals; and Ammon (*Int. Ctbll. Anth.*, 1902, heft 1, p. 8) states that his results do not really contradict Bolk's.

and in a greater degree;[1] finally, some observers (Pruner Bey and Durand de Gros) found that brachycephaly tends to be associated with large pelves in women.[2]

The differences are often very small, but even in these cases they are sometimes so persistent or harmonious that hesitation is necessary in rejecting them; slight difference with harmonious arrangement was found to be the case among the Alsatians by Pfitzner, and in Spain Aranzadi found that in eight different groups belonging to eight different provinces the women were slightly, but in every case distinctly, more brachycephalic than the men.

It must be added that the various series of measurements of the head of which the results have been briefly given are of very unequal value; they have been made by a variety of individuals and sometimes on very small series of subjects. It was the opinion of Broca, the greatest of French anthropologists—an opinion founded on extensive experience—that among the dark races women are more brachycephalic than men, although he found them less so among the existing races of Western France.[3] Virchow, the greatest of German anthropologists, in a study of the skulls of the aborigines on the west coast of America, found the women much more brachycephalic than the men; dolichocephaly and hyperdolichocephaly he found chiefly, and the latter almost exclusively, among men.[4]

It is doubtful whether we can say that on the whole the course of evolution is from the dolichocephalic to the brachycephalic. As Bischoff's investigations showed, we may most properly regard the anthropoid

---

[1] See, for instance, M. Benedikt, *Kraniometrie und Kephalometrie*, Vienna, 1888, p. 23; also Clapham, Art. "Head, Size and Shape of," *Dict. Psych. Med.*

[2] Delaunay, *Bull. Soc. d'Anthropologie*, Paris, 5 Mars 1885.

[3] *Revue d'Anthropologie*, t. ii. p. 28.

[4] R Virchow, "Beiträge zur Craniologie der Insulaner von der Westküste Nordamerikas," *Zeitschrift für Eth.*, 1889, heft 5.

apes as markedly brachycephalic; moreover, they are most so in early life, and the orang, which may probably be regarded as the anthropoid with the best developed brain, is the most brachycephalic. In the human species the new-born infant tends to be somewhat dolichocephalic but quickly reaches the maximum brachycephaly.

Children nearly everywhere are more brachycephalic than adults; this occurs in dolichocephalic as well as brachycephalic races, and (as Danielli found among the Nias of Sumatra) when the mother is more dolichocephalic than the father. Thus, for example, Skoff found that for Russians the cephalic index presents its maximum in childhood and diminishes with age, so that skull-growth is more especially in the antero-posterior direction; in adult Russian skulls Popow has found little difference in cephalic index. It is worth noting that in early life, on the whole, at all events among Europeans, girls are decidedly more brachycephalic than boys. Thus Mantegazza found by measuring nearly 100 boys and over 100 girls between the ages of 4 and 14, belonging to the poorer classes at Bologna, that while the average cephalic index in the boys was only 79.10, in the girls it was as high as 83.35;[1] it may be added that the index of the girls is almost the same as that of adult Bolognese men (as ascertained by Calori), the women being rather lower. It is noteworthy that while Clapham found the average cephalic index of his insane men to a small fractional extent greater than that of the women, below the age of twenty the index of the women was markedly higher (82.9 against 78.6), and this difference was chiefly due to defective antero-posterior development in the girls. Gerald West, who has measured over 3000 children between the ages of four and twenty-one in the schools of Worcester, U.S.A., finds that

[1] Mantegazza, "Studii di Craniologia sessuale," *Arch. per l'Antrop.*, vol. v.

the maximum width of head is reached earlier in girls than in boys; that the index of girls during the period of growth is on the whole higher than that of boys; and that while the final index for girls is nearly the same as that reached at five years of age, the final index for boys is $1\frac{1}{2}$ per cent. below that attained at five years of age.[1] In line with these inquiries we may probably place the investigations of Gönner who found by the examination of 100 infants at birth that the cephalic index of the child at this period tended to be nearer to that of the mother than to that of the father; while 25 per cent. of the infants' heads fell into the same index group as the mothers', only 18 per cent. fell into the same index group as the fathers'; so that the mothers' heads were somewhat more infantile than the fathers'.[2] As regards English children, Macalister finds that the change from brachycephalism to mesaticephalism takes place shortly after the completion of the first dentition.

It is through such investigations that we may hope to learn more than we know at present concerning the significance of the cephalic index. It will be observed that the youthful brachycephaly of women is owing less to excessive breadth than to defective length of the skull. This late antero-posterior growth is due, not so much to brain development as to the expansion of the air-sinuses in the frontal bone, which in childhood scarcely exist. We have already seen that the races in which the women are

---

[1] G. West, "The Growth of the Body, Head, and Face," *Science,* 6th Jan. 1893.

[2] Gonner, "Ueber Vererburg der Form und Grosse des Schädels," *Zt. f. Geburtsh. u. Gynäk,* 1895. The special characters of the fœtal skull have been studied by Sergi (*Rivista di Scienze Biologichi,* vol. ii., 1900), who finds that the characteristic shape of the fœtal skull is pentagonal, this being due to the prominence of the centres of ossification, and that the presence of this shape in adult life, instead of the more usual ellipsoid or ovoid, indicates the persistence of a fœtal character.

more brachycephalic outnumber those in which the women are more dolichocephalic than the men. The opinion may be hazarded that if any further sexual difference is ultimately found it will be in favour, on the whole, of the somewhat greater brachycephaly of women among the darker and more primitive races, and a possibly greater tendency to dolichocephaly among the fair and civilised European races.[1]

It is not difficult to understand why this should be so when we remember that the child is brachycephalic, and that while women approximate to the child-type more closely than do men, the anatomical tendency of civilisation is also to a nearer approximation to the child-type than commonly prevails among savages.

The Face.—It will be convenient here to consider briefly the general structure of the face. Speaking of the face generally, it must be said that its evolutional tendency is to become smaller while the skull becomes larger; the apes, as is specially obvious in the gorilla, have enormous faces compared to their small skulls; the human face, comparatively, is small; and woman's face compared to her relatively large head is usually stated to be smaller than man's; so that, as Soemmering pointed out a century ago, while man is in this respect higher than the apes, woman is higher than man.

The evolution of the face from childhood to adult life has at present attracted singularly little attention, although it is full of interest. The only investigation with which I am acquainted, on a sufficiently large

---

[1] This conclusion is confirmed by the data more recently brought together from scattered sources by Karl Pearson (*Chances of Death*, vol. i. pp. 349 *et seq.*). If we divide the series brought forward by Pearson into two groups, one in which the women are more dolichocephalic, and the other in which the women are more brachycephalic, than the men, we find that the first group consists almost exclusively of civilised races, while all the very primitive races are included in the second group, which also includes various civilised peoples.

number of subjects, is that carried on at Worcester, U.S.A., by Professor West of Cambridge, Mass., on 3250 individuals between the ages of five and twenty-one.[1] There seems to be a certain amount of parallelism between face-growth and stature-growth, both in the tendency to periods of retardation of growth, in the temporary relative predominance of girls at puberty, and the more continued growth in men. The evidence points to the existence of three periods of growth, the first ending at about the seventh year, while the third begins at about the age of fifteen. Between the ages of eleven and thirteen girls approach boys in the diameter of the head, while in the diameter of the face at the age of twelve girls seem quite to reach boys. "In proportion to the length of head," West remarks, "the width of head and width of face of girls are generally greater than those of boys, and in proportion to the width of head the width of face is also greater in girls than in boys." It was found that while the face in girls ceases to grow at the age of seventeen, in boys it is still growing at eighteen, and probably continues to grow afterwards. These results seem to show that women's faces may be relatively broader than those of men, though at the same time, in accordance also with the impression gained by observation, and, indeed, with the result obtained by Kollmann's facial index, they are relatively short, as in children. These results are confirmed by Pfitzner's observations on a very large number of adult subjects in the Anatomical Institute at Strassburg; he found that the face in women is relatively broader and shorter, these characteristics leading to a greater conservation of the infantile type. Pfitzner found the sexual differences in the length-breadth index of the face very constant, regular and marked when compared with the trifling sexual differences in the

---

[1] "The Growth of the Face," *Science*, 3rd July 1891; "The Growth of the Body, Head, and Face," *Science*, 6th Jan. 1893.

length-breadth index of the head.[1] As the lower part of the face with the lower jaw is less developed in women than in men, the upper part with the orbits forms a relatively larger part of the face (as Huschke remarked) and tends to appear larger than it actually is, an appearance which is probably still further emphasised by a frequently rounder or more oval shape of the orbit in women, and perhaps a really relatively greater height of the orbit. The real difference is less than it appears. Paul Bartels found that, except among Malays and Singhalese, it is not absolutely greater in women, but, in agreement with Welcker, Weisbach, Ecker, and Rebentisch, finds that it is relatively larger. Zeiler,[2] on the other hand, finds that the capacity of the orbit is, relatively as well as absolutely, less in the females both of apes and the human species. Relatively, he concludes, it is much greater in apes than in men, and there is an increase with age which is specially marked in the case of apes.

It must be added that Topinard's fronto-zygomatic index shows the relatively greater breadth of the face as compared to the breadth at the temples; the higher this index the broader the temples or the narrower the face, so that the highest indices are found in hydrocephalic heads; the index is higher in children than in adults, and is invariably higher in women than in men.[3]

On casual inspection women's eyes seem to be generally larger and more prominent than men's. This effect is for the most part apparent only, and is due to a large extent to the over-arching of the bony ridges above the eyes in men. The races in whom this distinctively masculine character is defi-

---

[1] W. Pfitzner, "Ein Beiträg zur Kenntniss der sekundären Geschlechtsunterschiede beim Menschen," *Morphologische Arbeiten*, Bd. vii., heft 2, 1896 ; *ib.*, *Zt. f. Morph.*, Bd. iii., heft 3, 1901, pp. 524, 573.

[2] J. Zeiler, *Beiträge zur Anth. der Augenhöhle*, Inaug. Diss., 1899 ; I have not been able to see this pamphlet.

[3] Topinard, *Anthrop. Gén.*, p. 936.

cient have an infantile or feminine appearance. The eye itself, according to Priestley Smith, is at all ages very slightly larger in the horizontal diameter in men than in women, but the difference is extremely small, only about .1 mill.

The Facial Angle.—This angle, which, speaking roughly, indicates the amount of protrusion of the upper jaw, has not—in the general neglect of the face in favour of that portion of the skull in contact with the brain—led to the general recognition of any sexual distinctions. This is very largely due to the very various ways in which craniologists have determined it. As, however, defined by certain investigators, the facial index has some importance and has led to fairly clear results. Welcker (followed by a large number of craniologists) measured the facial angle by the degree of projection of the spine of the nose at its base as compared to the root of the nose. This index, in the hands of most observers, shows women to be more prognathous than men. Thus Benedikt, investigating this angle, found prognathism more marked in infants than in adults, and that while prognathism decreased with age (instead of, as among the lower animals, increasing with age) women remained slightly more prognathous than men, usually about half a degree.[1] Topinard considers that the most important of all the facial indices for indicating morphological rank is the alveolar-sub-nasal index, which in a somewhat different way also indicates the degree of protrusion of the upper jaw. The investigation of this index shows that prognathism is very much greater among lower than among higher races. Among Hottentots, for example, it is nearly 50; among English, French, and Germans, it oscillates around 20, while Mongols and Polynesians come midway. In every large Indo-European series women are more prognathous than men. Among

---

[1] Benedikt, *Kraniometrie und Kephalometrie*, 1888, p. 31.

Parisians, for example, from the twelfth to the nineteenth centuries, among Bretons, Auvergnats, Basques, Corsicans, as well as among ancient Egyptians and Javanese, women are markedly, and to a very considerable degree, more prognathous than men. But it is a curious fact that this is not so among the darker races in a lower stage of civilisation, nor does it appear to be so among the Chinese; among African negroes, Nubians and Bushmen, the women are markedly less prognathous than the men.[1] Women thus possess on the whole, at all events among European races, a tendency to alveolar prognathism. This, although a savage character, is far from being a defect; it frequently imparts, as Virchow remarks, a certain piquancy to a woman's face. Perhaps the naïve forward movement of slight prognathism in a woman suggests a face upturned to kiss; but in any case there is no doubt that while not a characteristic of high evolution it is distinctly charming.

When we investigate other forms of the facial angle, more especially those which show the projection of the upper part of the jaw in relation to the forehead, it is usually found that women are, if anything, less prognathous than men. These are, however, less characteristic and important varieties of the facial angle. It is possible to estimate the total prognathism of the face by taking the profile as a whole, with the inclusion of the lower jaw, and to measure the projection of the angle where the teeth meet. This is measured by Camper's maxillary angle (quite distinct from Camper's facial angle), which takes as its apex the junction of the teeth, while the base is at the forehead and at the point of the chin. Topinard attaches great importance to this angle, almost as much importance indeed as to the

[1] P. Topinard, "Du Prognathisme," *Revue d'Anth.*, 1872, p. 628; and 1873, pp. 71 and 251; Manouvrier, *l'Année Psych.*, 5th year, 1899, p. 582.

mass of the brain or to the biped attitude, because it enables us to arrange many zoological species in their order of morphological evolution, as well as to classify the individuals within a species. The larger the maxillary angle the higher the degree of evolution. It is found that in women, both among the higher and the lower races, the maxillary angle is always markedly smaller than in men. The angle formed, therefore, by the whole face, supports the conclusion reached by the investigation of the alveolar region of the upper jaw, that women are somewhat more prognathous than men.

While prognathism of the lower part of the upper jaw must be regarded as a reminiscence of a more primitive age, the protrusion of the lower part of the lower jaw is a distinctively human character which is most marked in the highest European races. A receding chin is a character of degeneracy and animality. In women the chin is usually less prominent. In women also, as in children, the angles of the jaw are decidedly large.

On the other hand, women show a higher degree of evolution than men, and at the same time approach the infantile type, by the relatively smaller weight of their jaws, as has been shown by Bertillon, Morselli, Orchanski, and others. The lower human races, as well as apes, have relatively larger lower jaws, and the same tendency has often been found among criminals; but while woman's skull is to man's as 85 to 100, woman's jaw is to man's as only 79 to 100.[1]

The Teeth.—It is rather surprising that very little attention has been given to the anthropological examination of the teeth among European races, although it is a promising field and one where examination is comparatively easy. A few anthropologists, Schaaff-

[1] E. Morselli, " Sul Peso del Cranio e della Mandibula in Rapporto col Sesso," *Arch. per l'Antrop.*, 1876; Rebentisch (*op. cit.*, pp. 33-39) regards this as the most important of sexual distinctions; cf. Paul Bartels (*op. cit.*, pp. 22-43).

hausen and Flower for example, have reached interesting results, but dental surgeons, so far as I have been able to elicit by inquiries of some of the heads of the profession, have added little to our knowledge of sexual differences. Gorham, who weighed several thousand teeth, says nothing whatever as to differences according to sex.[1] Among the lower as compared to the higher human races it is generally agreed that the teeth are larger and more regularly arranged, that the wisdom teeth resemble the other molars and are less cramped and not so frequently absent, while the dental arch is squarer and not so rounded as in the more civilised races.[2] There is also no doubt that among primitive races, whether of earlier or our own times, the upper jaw and palate exhibit fewer irregularities and malformations, being usually extremely well formed and developed; it would also appear that among the higher and middle classes irregularities are of more frequent occurrence than among the working classes. A powerful jaw, and perhaps also various mental qualities correlated with such a jaw, are of less primary importance under the conditions of civilised than of savage and barbarous life. The tendency of civilisation is to decrease the number and size of the teeth, and to decrease the size, and often to deform the bony cavity, of the mouth.[3]

As the lower jaw is in women markedly smaller than in men, while the teeth show no corresponding reduction, we should expect disturbances of development to occur with special frequency in women. This seems to be the case. That the jaws of women have a marked tendency to be defective in size and consequently to cramp the teeth, there is much evidence to show. Mr. C. S. Tomes, F.R.S., writes in a private letter: " Speaking from a general impression,

[1] *Med. Times*, 9th January, 1875.
[2] C. S. Tomes, *Manual of Dental Anatomy*, 1889, p. 459.
[3] See, for instance, Oakley Coles, *Deformities of the Mouth*, p. 34.

which, as you know, is nearly valueless in such a matter, I should say that contracted dental arches necessitating the extraction of teeth for space are commoner in female than in male children." An examination of the various tables appended to the fourth edition (1901) of Talbot's very interesting and instructive work, *The Irregularities of the Teeth*, seems to show that on the whole abnormalities of the jaw, more especially a tendency to the V-shaped arch, are especially frequent in women.

Magitot has found by an examination of the wisdom teeth in 241 men and 259 women that they are more precocious in women than in men in France, the maximum number appearing at 22 years, in men at 23 years,—although at 25 years there happened to be 10 women to 6 men.[1]

Galippe found the density of the teeth to be slightly greater in men than in women; but if we examine the data which have been accumulated during recent years as to the incidence of caries, there are no marked sexual differences. In some countries one sex seems more liable to caries than the other, but on the whole the incidence is equal.[2]

We owe to Professor Flower a dental index which is constructed by multiplying the dental length by 100, and dividing by the basio-nasal length (or length from the naso-frontal suture to the edge of the *foramen magnum*). He finds that the white races are microdont (possessing, that is, small teeth and a small dental index); the yellow races are mesodont; the black races megadont, with large teeth and a large dental index, while among the anthropoid apes the dental indices are still larger. Among the apes the dental index among females is always

[1] *Bull. Soc. d'Anthropologie de Paris*, 20 Fev. 1879.
[2] A summary of the observations so far made will be found in Lipschitz, "Cariesfrequenz bei Schulkindern," *Comptes Rendus XII. Int. Cong. Med.* (Moscow, 1897), vol. v. p. 6. For Report of Committee of British Dental Association, see *Brit. Med. jour.*, 21 July 1900.

greater than among males. A similar sexual difference is seen in the human species, the teeth in
women more nearly retaining their size while the
cranium with the body generally is less. The difference is, however, slight among European races.

Schaaffhausen has shown that the two upper
middle front or incisor teeth are in women and
girls not only relatively but absolutely larger than in
men and boys of the same age. Comparing 50
girls to 50 boys of the ages of 12 to 15, he found
that the average breadth of the teeth in question was
as 1.33 in girls to 1 in boys. Among 12 men
belonging to Zandvoort, in Holland, he found an
average breadth of 8.3, while 12 women gave a
breadth of 8.8. In some women the teeth in question
are conspicuously large.[1] We see therefore that while
the jaws of women may in civilised races tend to be
unduly small, there is good reason to believe that their
teeth have remained relatively and even absolutely
larger than those of men. Schaaffhausen's conclusions were criticised by Parreidt, who measured
the incisor teeth of 100 men and 100 women
at Leipzig, and found that at most decades of
life the central incisors of men were absolutely
larger than those of women, but he ultimately agreed
that they were relatively larger. Paul Bartels also
measured the teeth in over 60 skulls, and reached
the same results as Parreidt.[2] Max Bartels, it may
be added, comes to the conclusion that this sexual
distinction is world-wide, and gives many photographs in evidence. Stratz associates the large
incisors with the relatively broader face in women,
and regards them as a mark of feminine beauty.
It is probable, however, that in the lowest human
races the sexual difference is less, both men and
women possessing large middle incisors; this has

[1] Ploss and Max Bartels, *Das Weib*, 7th ed., 1901, Bd. i. p. 15.
[2] Paul Bartels, *Ueber Geschlechtsunterschiede am Schädel*, pp. 36-41;
he gives a good account of the whole controversy.

been noted to be the case among the Australians by Professor Klaatsch.[1]

In considering the lower part of the face in the two sexes we thus see that there are very notable differences, in fact constituting secondary sexual distinctions of the first order. In men the jaws develop to a much greater extent, are furnished with more powerful muscles, and become the seat of prominent hairy appendages. In women, though the incisor teeth at all events remain large, this region generally remains softer, more rounded, smaller, altogether markedly less developed, this difference extending from the external ears to the larynx. This region is in women both more infantile and more primitive, while at the same time revealing less animality and higher racial though not individual evolution. These distinctions, while of importance as secondary sexual character, may also possess a significance of quite another order, and Woods Hutchinson has ingeniously suggested that they may help to account for the varying sexual incidence of cancer. It is well known that the two organs most affected by cancer are the breast and the womb. When we leave these two feminine sexual glands out of account it is found that cancer is somewhat more prevalent in men, and the region common to both sexes in which it most markedly prevails in men is precisely the district around the mouth. Cancer of the ear, larynx, parotid, mouth, pharynx, throat, œsophagus, neck, and jaws is in nearly every case twice as frequent in men as in women, and on the whole nearly three times as frequent as in women (see *e.g.*, G. B. Longstaff, "Etiology of Cancer," *Brit. Med. Jour.*, 21 Sept. 1901). Now all these organs are closely connected with the mouth, and it is usual to put forward the idea that the greater frequency of cancer here in men is due to smoking. This explanation, common as it is, seems rather far-fetched. Woods Hutchinson points out (*Studies in Human and Comparative Pathology*, 1901, p. 268) that cancer tends to appear in those organs in which function is decaying, while the vitality of the rest of the body is well maintained. This is conspicuously the case as regards the breast and womb. But it is also the case, Woods Hutchinson observes, with regard to the highly developed masculine mouth-region. After the age of fifty senile regressive changes here begin to take place towards the infantile condition, and relatively these changes are much greater in men, because in women this region already approximates to the infantile type. The liability of this region to cancer in men would thus be a phenomenon of degeneration in a highly developed region of sexual significance, strictly comparable to the liability of the womb and breast to cancer.

---

[1] *Zt. f. Eth.*, 1901, heft 3, p. 137.

Cranial Capacity.—A considerable amount of atten-tion has been given to the question of sexual differ-ences in cranial capacity, but the results have been small. In nearly every large series of skulls, ancient or modern, savage or civilised, the cranial capacity is found to be considerably greater in men than in women. But when we consider that the body-weight is also considerably greater in men this result is not surprising, and while some anthropologists have asserted that the cranial capacity of men is relatively somewhat greater than that of women, others have been at least equally justified in deciding that the cranial capacity of women is relatively greater than that of men. At the best, cranial capacity is not an exact indication of brain size; and to measure brain size by the external size of the skull furnishes still rougher and more fallacious approximations, since the male skull is more massive than the female.[1]

A point of some interest, which was noted long ago by Retzius,[2] and has since often been raised, is the relative sexual difference in the higher and in the lower races; it is a question whether in the higher races there are not greater sexual differences than in the lower races. I have prepared the following table bearing on this point, using many of the figures obtained by Weisbach, and also working out the proportions given by Topinard, Flower's as harmon-ised by Topinard, and adding others from different

---

[1] It is worth noting that woman's skull constitutes a larger part of the total bony skeleton than man's. Thus Manouvrier's cranio-femoral index gives the relation of the weight of the thigh-bones to that of the skull, the latter equalling 100. Most women (83 per cent.) have heavier skulls than thigh-bones; in most men (81 per cent.) the thigh-bones are heavier. From this point of view the relative size of the skull diminishes in the following order : child, woman, short man, tall man, ape.

[2] Müller's *Archiv für Anat.*, 1845, p. 89; and see Rolleston's Presidential Address to Anthropological Section Brit. Association, 1875; also Le Bon, *Revue d'Anth.*, 1879, p. 56. Huschke in 1854, Vogt and Welcker a few years later, pointed out the tendency to greater sexual differentiation of the skull among civilised peoples.

sources.[1] The figures give the average cranial capacity of woman's skull if the man's be taken to equal 1000.

Negro (Davis), 984.
Bushman (Flower), 951.
Hottentot and Bushman (Broca), 951.
Hindu (Davis), 944.
Negro (Tiedemann), 932.
Eskimo (Broca), 931.
Australian (Broca), 926.
Malay (Tiedemann), 923.
Dutch (Tiedemann), 919.
Prussian (Kupffer), 918.
Irish (Davis), 912.
Andamanese (Flower), 911.
New Caledonian (Broca), 911.
Dutch (Broca), 909.
Tasmanian (Broca), 907.
Kanaka (Davis), 906.
Veddah (Davis, Flower, Virchow, Thomson), 903.
Marquisas (Davis), 902.
German (Welcker), 897.
Auvergnat (Broca), 897.
Aino (Koganei), 894.
Tyrolese (Tappeiner), 893.

Bavarian, town-dwelling (Ranke), 893.
Aino (Kopernicki), 890
Australian (Flower), 889.
Bavarian, country dwelling (Ranke), 888.
Scotch (Turner), 887.
Russian (Popow), 884.
German (Davis), 883.
Alsatian (Schwalbe), 880.
German (Weisbach), 878.
Ancient British (Davis), 877.
Javanese (Tiedemann), 874.
Australian (Turner), 871.
Chinese (Davis), 870.
German (Tiedemann), 864.
Anglo-Saxon (Davis), 862.
Parisian of 12th century (Broca), 862.
English (Davis), 860.
Parisian of 19th century (Broca), 858.
Javanese (Broca), 855.
Eskimo (Flower), 855.
German (Huschke), 838.

This table seems to brings out on the whole a gradual sexual divergence in cranial capacity under the influence of evolution and civilisation. There are naturally many discrepancies, due to some of the series included being too small, or abnormal, or to difference in methods of measurement. Thus if from the series of Veddah skulls two were to be omitted— an abnormally large masculine and an abnormally small feminine skull—it would be found that the Veddahs, a very primitive race, would come at the top of the list, where they perhaps belong. It must of course be remembered that we cannot rashly assume

[1] Weisbach, "Der deutsche Weiberschädel," *Archiv für Anth.*, Bd. iii., 1868; Topinard, *L'Homme*, etc., 1891, p. 218.

that this divergence, if real, is entirely due to civilisation. It may be largely a matter of race, as Waldeyer believes. There are, however, two great factors working for increased cranial capacity—large size of body and mental activity—which both operate in civilisation. Among the small Maravers of southern India the cranial capacity of the women is, even absolutely, rather greater than that of the men; among the large-bodied Germans the cranial capacity of the women is relatively very small. Town-dwellers have a larger cranial capacity than country-dwellers, but the muscular labour undergone by country-dwellers keeps their cranial capacity at a fairly high level; Ranke found that while the minimum of 100 large-headed male town-folk was as low as 1218, the minimum of 100 smaller-headed male country-folk was 1260.[1] The town-dweller without either manual or mental work stands very low, and in civilisation both the heaviest manual and the heaviest mental work falls to men. It is perhaps worth noting that Jacobs and Spielmann found that while West End Jewesses are distinctly inferior to West End Jews in cranial measurements, there is comparatively little difference between East End Jews and Jewesses. It must be realised, however, that there are very distinct limits to the equalisation of cranial characters by the equalisation of social conditions. Among orangs and gorillas the sexual cranial differences are enormous. The Australians are almost the lowest of human races, and live under the simplest conditions, but, as Turner remarks, examining the *Challenger* skulls, "The sexual characters were strongly marked in the Australian crania. The much smaller size and capacity of the female skull, its comparative lightness, the feebleness of its ridges and processes, more especially the glabella; its low basi-bregmatic height

[1] J. Ranke, "Stadt- und Landbevolkerung," *Beiträge zur Biologie*, 1882.

and the high orbital index, all constituted important features of difference between the female and the male skulls." The relatively greater difference in cranial capacity among civilised than among savage races generally, however, remains a fact of some interest and significance.

It has often been asserted, and more especially in the earlier days of craniology, that the frontal regions of the skull, regarded as the "nobler" regions, are more developed in men than in women. There is, however, no reason for supposing that the frontal region is higher or more characteristically human than any other cranial region; and there is just as little reason for supposing that the frontal region is more highly developed in men. Cleland, who compared the three regions of the skull—frontal, parietal, and occipital—in men and women, could find no noteworthy difference. Manouvrier, who has made the most extensive and reliable investigations on this point, found, by the examination of Broca's registers, that the frontal curve is relatively larger in women than in men in 14 series of skulls out of 17; that the parietal curve was relatively larger in women in 6 out of 17 series. He therefore came to the conclusion that women exhibit a frontal type of skull, men a parietal type.[1] That the occipital region is also relatively larger in women has been found as well by Manouvrier as by Weisbach, who in his careful investigations of the German skull came to

---

[1] Manouvrier, "Sur la grandeur du Front et des principales régions du Crâne chez l'Homme et chez la Femme," *Bull. de l'Ass. fran. pour l'avancement des Sci.*, 1882, pp. 623-639. Also Art. "Sexe," *Dict. des sci. Anthrop.* Daffner (*Das Wachsthum des Menschen*) found the frontal breadth practically the same in both sexes, although the circumference was much greater in males.

It may be noted here that a high forehead is by no means, as commonly supposed, the necessary accompaniment of high mental capacity. In women Benedikt (*Kran. u. Keph.*, p. 125) is accustomed to regard it as an indication of convulsive degeneration, and he refers to the instinctive concealment by women of a high forehead by arrangement of hair.

the conclusion that there is greater height and length in the occipital skull in women with equal breadth. Topinard's figures of the relative breadth of the different regions of the head in Parisian men and women show little or no superiority of breadth of the frontal region in women, but a very markedly greater breadth of the posterior region of the head, indicating large size of occipital lobes and cerebellum. As Topinard points out, as a rule this breadth is greatest in the superior races; "the cephalic index of Russians and Javanese is almost the same, but the former, a higher race, have greater occipito-cerebellar breadth; the Basques have, almost to a decimal, the cephalic index of the Tasmanians, but they have greater occipital breadth; Parisian men have only two units of cephalic index more than Parisian women, but the latter have eight units more of occipital breadth."[1]

Picozzo (*Arch. di Psich.*, 1895, Fasc. vi., p. 564), utilising the material collected by Macedo, has examined the cranial sutures in 1000 skulls of Portuguese origin, about equally divided between the two sexes. He found that the sutures in women were of simpler character, that fusion takes place at a later age in women, and that in women also the solidification of the sutures of the anterior part of the skull is relatively earlier than in men. The prolonged retention of the free sutures is, as Picozzo points out, an obviously infantile character. He believes, also, that the relatively earlier fusion of the sutures anteriorly in women is a sign of inferiority. This can scarcely be admitted, when we recall that there is no ground for attributing any special intellectual pre-eminence to the frontal region, and that in any

---

[1] Topinard, *L'Anth. Gén.*, p. 694. Wilks (*Lectures on Dis. Nervous System*) remarks, "We have only to look at the head of a person with his faculties well developed to see a considerable projection behind, whilst in a person of low development the neck and head are in one line." (It would perhaps be better to say "imperfect" rather than "low" development, since this small occipital development is sometimes found in men of marked intellectual ability.) Clapham has found, as a result of the measurement of 4000 heads, as regards the proportion of the anterior segment to the whole circumference, that the anterior segment increases rather than diminishes in passing from the sane to the insane, and from the insane to idiots (*Jour. Ment. Sci.*, April 1898, p. 293).

case the frontal region in women is, relatively, as fully developed as in men. It is sufficient to say that the anterior sutures close earlier in women than the posterior, because the frontal region is precociously developed in women.

On the whole, we have found no valid ground for concluding from an examination of the skull that one sex is morphologically superior to the other sex. The only well-marked and generally acceptable sexual cranial differences, so far as our present knowledge extends, are those pointed out at the outset: in men the air-sinuses and muscular projections are more marked, and in women the bosses are more prominent. In all three of these respects men approach the savage, simian, and senile type (for these, as we have seen, and as Virchow pointed out, approximate to each other), while in all these respects also women approach the infantile type.[1] It is open to a man in a Pharisaic mood to thank God that his cranial type is far removed from the infantile. It is equally open to a woman in such a mood to be thankful that her cranial type does not approach the senile.

THE BRAIN.

The history of opinion regarding cerebral sexual difference forms a painful page in scientific annals. It is full of prejudices, assumptions, fallacies, over-hasty generalisations. The unscientific have had a predilection for this subject; and men of science seem to have lost the scientific spirit when they approached the study of its seat. Many a reputation

[1] The special morphological characters of the feminine skull as intermediate between the infantile and masculine type were shown by Lissauer (*Arch. f. Anth.*, 1885), and this point was often emphasised by Virchow. Paul Bartels (*Ueber Geschlechtsunterschiede am Schädel*, 1897, p. 97) considers that the absence of animal characters in the female skull as compared to the male is one of the chief results of his investigation. The arguments of an eccentric zoologist, Albrecht, in favour of the "greater bestiality" of women in anatomical respects (*Corr.- Bl. Deutsch. Gesell. Anth.*, 1884), need not be seriously discussed.

has been lost in these soft and sinuous convolutions. It is only of recent years that a comparatively calm and disinterested study of the brain has become in any degree common; and even to-day the fairly well ascertained facts concerning sexual differences in the brain may be easily summed up.

There is no doubt whatever that in European races (for of other races our knowledge is scanty) the absolute weight of the brain in man is considerably greater than in woman. The following are a few of the averages reached by some of the chief investigators in different countries, working on a large number of brains, most of the series comprising many hundreds:—

		Grammes.	Difference.
Wagner	Men	1410	148
	Women	1262	
Huschke .	Men	1424	152
	Women	1272	
Broca	Men	1365	154
	Women	1211	
Topinard . .	Men	1360	110
	Women	1250	
Bischoff .	Men	1362	143
	Women	1219	
Boyd[1] . .	Men	1354	133
	Women	1221	
Manouvrier .	Men	1353	128
	Women	1225	

[1] These figures were obtained from Boyd's well-known investigations at the Marylebone Infirmary, London. Sir James Crichton-Browne has obtained very similar results with the brains of the insane. From an examination of nearly sixteen hundred brains he found that the average in the male was 1351 grammes, in the female 1223 grammes; the male average is a little lower than in the sane, on account of the serious nature of brain disease in men, and consequently in insanity the sexes approach each other in brain-weight more than in sanity. See Crichton-Browne "On the Weight of the Brain in the Insane," *Brain*, vols. i.-ii. ; also Clapham, Art. "Brain, Weight of, in the Insane," *Dict. Psych. Med. ;* Tigges, "Das Gewicht des Gehirns und seine Theile bei Geisteskranken," *Allgemein. Zeitschrift für Psychiatrie*, vol. 45, 1888, heft. 1 and 2.

It is clear that in Europe men possess absolutely larger brains than women. There is no doubt on this point. The difficulty has arisen at the next stage. Have men relatively larger brains than women? We have first to decide relatively to what we are going to compare the brain. Height has usually suggested itself as the most convenient term of comparison. It would be better, as Topinard suggests, to take the height of the body only, ignoring the legs, but, so far as I am aware, this is never done. It is not difficult to ascertain with fair accuracy the average height of a population, and it is evident that when we have brought the brain into relation with the stature we have made some approximation to a fair estimate. Relatively to stature, it is nearly always found that men still possess somewhat heavier brains than women. Thus, according to Boyd's average as well as Bischoff's, man's brain-weight is to woman's as 100 to 90; the average stature of men and women in England is as 100 to 93; so that, taking stature into account, men have a slight but distinct excess of brain (amounting, roughly speaking, to something over an ounce) over women. Precisely the same difference in ratio has been found in France.[1] On the strength of this ounce a distinguished brain anatomist has declared that "the difference, therefore, in the size and weight of the brain is obviously a fundamental sexual distinction," and the same assertion has often been made by others.

On consideration, however, it becomes clear that while it is very convenient, and even approximately correct, to estimate sexual differences in brain-mass relatively to sexual differences in body-height, it is not quite fair to women. Men are not only taller than women, they are larger. If human beings, while retaining their present height, were moulded

[1] A discussion on this point will be found in Topinard's *Anthropologie Générale*, p. 557.

into circular columns the same size all the way up, the male columns would be usually of greater circumference than the female columns. As we found in Chapter III., there is only one measurement—the girth of the thighs—which is almost constantly larger in women. It is clear that we should be doing an injustice by comparing the amount of brain of the female column to that of the male column, for the male column must necessarily possess an absolutely larger amount of brain-tissue per foot, merely in order to equal the percentage amount of the female column. That additional ounce is fully needed merely to place men on a fair equality with women.

The evident inaccuracy of the stature criterion has therefore led a number of eminent craniologists—Clendinning, Tiedemann, Reid, Wagner, Weisbach, etc.—to adopt the method of estimating sexual differences in brain-weight in accordance with their ratio to body-weight. This is obviously a more logical method. The almost constant result is that, proportionately to body-weight, women are found to possess brains somewhat larger than men's, or else brains of about the same size. This was ascertained many years ago by Parchappe, Tiedemann, Thurnam, and others, in England, France, and Germany.[1] More recently Bischoff, in his important and accurate work on the brain, shows similarly that while woman's brain-weight is to man's as 90 to 100, woman's body-weight is to man's as only 83 to 100; Vierordt has also illustrated the same fact, that relatively to body-weight women have larger brains.[2] It may be taken as proved that in relation to body-weight—a more logical relation than that to body-height—women's

[1] See, for instance, Tiedemann, *Phil. Trans. Royal Soc.*, 1836, vol. cxxvi., p. 306; Parchappe, *Recherches sur l'encéphale*, 1836, etc.

[2] T. L. W. von Bischoff, *Das Hirngewicht des Menschen*, Bonn, 1880; H. Vierordt, "Das Massenwachsthum der Körperorgane des Menschen," *Archiv für Anat. u. Phys.*, 1890; also tables in the same author's *Anatomische Tabellen*, 1892. Topinard (*Anthrop. Gén.*, pp. 530 *et seq.*) has also discussed this question.

brains are at least as large as men's, and are usually larger.

We have, however, not even yet reached a fair statement of the relative amount of brain-mass in men and women. To estimate brain-weight by its ratio to body-weight is satisfactory enough if we are dealing cautiously with very large averages. But it has to be remembered that we are comparing a comparatively stable element with one which is extremely unstable. The well-to-do, well-nourished, and comparatively lazy classes weigh much more than the under-fed and overworked classes. The relations between body and brain may be quite different in the individuals who die in a workhouse from what they are in the ordinary population. There are not only differences between individual and individual; there are very marked fluctuations in the same individual. A well-nourished individual dying after a slow and wasting disease has run its course, will appear to possess a relatively much larger brain than if he had died at the outset of the disease. Brain, although not the most stable tissue, is relatively stable, more stable even than bone; fat, which makes up a very large part of the general body-weight, is the most unstable tissue in the body; it is used up on the first call from the over-strained or under-fed organism; while, according to Voit's analyses, 97 per cent. of the fat has disappeared at the completion of starvation, the nervous system has only lost 3.2 per cent. of its weight.[1] When we compare brain-weight with stature we are falling into a fallacy, but we are comparing elements that are at all events fairly constant, and therefore our error is fairly constant; when we compare brain-weight with body-weight we are on sounder ground, but one of our two elements fluctuates to a much greater extent than the

[1] See, for instance, in Waller's *Physiology*, a diagram showing relative loss of different tissues under the influence of starvation.

other, and produces an error which is less constant and requires greater care to circumvent.

There is another serious and more constant error in estimating sexual differences in brain-mass by the ratio to the bulk of the body. Women, as we have already seen (p. 41), are fatter than men. There is a tendency in adult women to deposit fat about the breasts and arms, and especially in and around the abdomen, in the gluteal regions, and in the thighs, a tendency which only exists to a moderate extent in men. As we have seen, Bischoff found that the proportion of fat in the woman to that in the man was as 28.2 to 18.2, and that while the proportion of muscle to fat in an adult man is as 100 to 43, in an adult woman it is as 100 to 78. Though his results were only founded on two typical well-nourished subjects, there is no doubt as to the general tendency of women to deposit fat. It is part of what some have called the anabolic tendency of the female sex—the tendency to acquire rather than to expend—and it is further illustrated by the fact that while men attain their maximum weight at about the age of 40, women, whose growth terminates at a distinctly earlier period than that of men, do not attain their maximum weight until the age of about 50. Now fat is a comparatively non-vital tissue; it needs, compared to muscle, but very little innervation. Therefore it is not fair to women, in studying brain difference in relation to body-weight, to make no allowance for their excess of comparatively non-vital tissue.[1] Manouvrier estimates that the active organic mass of woman's body is to that of man's as at most 70 to 100. This is only an approximate estimate, but in any case the relative excess of brain-tissue in woman is very large, for the

[1] Professor Manouvrier, the well-known Parisian anthropologist, an energetic champion of the anatomical virtues of women generally, has especially drawn attention to this fact. (L. Manouvrier, *Sur l'Interpretation de la quantité dans l'Encéphale*, Paris, 1885; also Art. "Cerveau," in *Dict. de Phys.*, vol. ii.)

sexual ratio in brain-weight may be put with fair constancy, as we have seen, as 90 to 100.

The two usual and most convenient methods of estimating the sexual proportions of brain-mass—the ratio to body-height and the ratio to body-weight—are thus both erroneous, and in both cases the error leads to the assignment to women of an unfairly small mass of brain. It might be thought that there is some fallacy on the other side which would tend to restore the balance. Such a source of fallacy might be thought to lie in the massive bony skeleton of men, but this does not seem to be the case to any appreciable extent. If, for example, we take the skull, the average relation of the weight of man's to woman's is (if we accept Morselli's figures) as 100 to 86; the sexual ratio of weight of the large and well-to-do members of the Bath meeting of the British Association was 100 to 79; of the small-sized Belgian race (according to Quetelet) it is 100 to 87: so that while these two ratios of bulk differ widely (as we should expect), they oscillate around the sexual ratio of bone-mass. There is indeed one correction which must yet be made, and it is a correction which does something towards restoring relative predominance of brain tissue to men. Independently of sex, and (at all events among Mammalia) independently even of species, increase of body-size has a fairly constant and regular tendency to be accompanied by an increase of brain which is relatively less in amount. Tall men have smaller brains, relatively, than short men; tall women have, relatively, smaller brains than short women; and the shortest women have brains that are relatively much larger than those of the tallest men.[1] This law involves a correction which is not

---

[1] Bischoff, Broca, Topinard, etc., have shown that this holds good for either the stature-ratio, the bulk-ratio, or both. See, for example, Bischoff, *Das Hirngewicht*, p. 32; Topinard, *Anthrop. Gén.*, p. 533; J. Marshall, "On the Relation between the Brain and the Stature and Mass of the Body," *Journal of Anat. and Phys.*, July 1892.

large, being scarcely two per cent., and perhaps even less, for Bischoff and Tigges have shown that brain increases with height to a greater extent in women than in men. This consideration, however, serves to complicate the problem of the brain-ratio, and to reduce somewhat the estimate of the relative predominance of brain tissue in women. No satisfactory plan has yet been devised for avoiding the fallacies involved in measuring the brain by the ratios to stature and bulk. The relation of the brain to a bone (such as the femur), or to the heart or to some particular muscle, are among the methods that have been suggested. There is ample scope here in the future for the efforts of the mathematical anthropometrist. It is sufficient at present if we are generally agreed as to the nature and directions of the errors in the usual methods.

There is, therefore, no doubt that when we have eliminated the chief distributing errors, we are compelled to conclude that women possess a relatively larger mass of nervous tissue than men. This by no means necessarily implies that women have any natural advantage over men. The fact that the absolutely large brain is to a great extent the appanage of a large muscular system apparently contributes to its steadiness and tone. A relatively large brain not rooted in a good muscular foundation is not always a good gift of the gods; it is often difficult to turn on effectively to intellectual tasks; it acts uncontrollably and with too much facility; it may be liable to explosive outbursts; it is a fact of some significance that the epileptic possess relatively large brains.[1] A very considerable proportion of the good work of the world has been done by brains which were large, though, relatively to the bulk of the body, not inordinately large.

There is no doubt that some men of genius, in the

[1] See, for instance, Clapham, Art. "Brain, Weight of," *Dict. Psych. Med.*

departments both of science and of art, have possessed brains that were enormously large, both absolutely and relatively. But it is not doubtful that a brain both absolutely and relatively large is a possession of most uncertain value. Taking the six largest recorded male brains (without special research but eliminating those of dubious authenticity), we find one (guaranteed by Bischoff) as large as 2222 grs., which belonged to a totally undistinguished individual; then, slightly smaller, the brain of an imbecile, examined by Levinge at the Hants County Asylum, and said to be of normal consistence; then we have Turguenieff, the great Russian novelist, a tall but not extremely large man, with a brain of 2012 grs.; the fourth, 1925 grs., belonged to an ordinary labouring man, and was examined by Bischoff; the fifth, 1900 grs., belonged to a bricklayer; the next, 1830 grs., was the brain of Cuvier, the famous zoologist.[1] The six largest brains of women known (as recorded by Topinard) are: first, that of an insane woman, weighing 1742 grs.; she died of consumption, and her case was recorded by Skae; then comes one of 1587 grs., belonging to a sane woman, who died at the age of 63 (Sims); then another of the same weight, belonging to an insane woman, and recorded by Clapham at Wakefield Asylum; then two cases of 1580 grs., both in sane women, and recorded by Boyd; finally another, also of 1580 grs., which belonged to a medical student who is said to have possessed exceptional ability, and to have shown no signs of insanity, but who committed suicide believing that she had failed to pass her final examination. A large brain is a perilous possession,

---

[1] It may be added that since I compiled the above list, a brain larger than any of these here mentioned has been described in Holland by G. C. van Walsem (*Neurolog. Centralbll.*, 1st July 1899): it was that of an epileptoid idiot, and weighed 2850 grs. Manouvrier (*Rev. de l'École d'Anth.*, Dec. 1902) has also described a brain weighing 1935 grs.; it was that of a man esteemed for his judgment and the rectitude of his conduct, but who remained obscure. The accuracy of the weight of Turguenieff's brain has been questioned without reason.

and—so far at least as this evidence goes—it is even more likely to be a perilous possession in a woman than in a man. A large brain is often inert or disordered, and fails to receive the rich blood-supply it demands; there is much to be said in favour of a small, well-ordered, and active brain. It is possible that great thinkers generally have large brains, but among distinguished men of action a small brain seems to be quite as often found as a large one.

Some light is thrown on the significance of the relative preponderance of nervous tissue in women, by considering the course of the brain's evolution in the two sexes. At birth the boy's brain is larger than the girl's. Boyd, from an examination of about forty cases of each sex, found the average weight 331 grs. in boys, 283 grs. in girls, a difference of 48 grs., and this is accepted by Topinard (and also by Rüdinger) as about the average difference; Mies, however, who more recently recorded the result of the weighing of a large number of new-born infants, found that for 79 boys the weight is 339 grs., for 69 girls 330 grs., a difference of only 9 grs.[1] Boyd's measurements give boys a preponderance of brain in relation to body-weight; Mies's figures, founded on larger experience, give a decided preponderance to brain tissue in girls. I think that the fact that most observers have found the brains of new-born boys decidedly larger than those of girls may be very simply explained. Children with unusually large heads—that is to say, the children to whom birth is most likely to prove fatal—are more usually boys, and therefore help to raise unduly the masculine average of brain for the new-born; girls are comparatively free from this danger.

The brain grows enormously during the few months after birth, and very rapidly during the first few years of life. While at the age of three months the brain is about the fifth part of the weight of the body, in the

[1] *Wein. Klin. Wochenschrift*, 10th January 1889.

adult it forms merely about a thirty-third part. By the age of six months (according to Boyd's fairly large figures) the absolute weight of the brain has doubled in girls, and nearly doubled in boys; by the age of seven years the weight of the brain has quadrupled in girls, and before the age of fourteen it has quadrupled in boys. The precocity of the female brain in childhood is therefore extremely marked. Even Boyd's figures, which give girls a relatively small amount of brain at birth, show that between the ages of four and seven girls possess larger brains than boys in relation to height. While girls between the ages of four and seven have already gained 92 per cent. of their final brain-weight, boys at the same age have only reached 83 per cent. The girl's brain grows but little after the age of seven, and has practically ceased to grow by about the age of twenty; the man's brain does not reach its maximum size until after thirty years of age. Owing to the rapid growth of the brain in the first years of life, it is in childhood, and more especially during the ages of two to four, that both sexes possess the largest amount of brain in relation to height. The premature and fallacious maximum in the weight of the brain before the age of twenty, which is found chiefly or exclusively in the female brain by the large series of Boyd, Bischoff, and Broca in three countries, seems to show, as Topinard points out,[1] that the precocity and extent of brain-growth in women at this early age exposes them to greater chance of death than men, just as boys are more exposed at birth; for it must always be remembered that brain-statistics in early life are exclusively founded on those members of the community who have been failures in the race of life; we cannot necessarily argue from them to the successful members of the community who reach adult life. Soon after the age of twenty the average weight of the brain begins to fall; in men there is no notable fall until

[1] *Anthrop. Gén.*, p. 557.

after fifty-five; in both sexes there is a somewhat rapid decline after this age, and there is some reason to think that in old age men undergo relatively greater brain-loss than women.

The larger amount of brain in women, which we have found to exist after the elimination of fallacies caused by incorrect criteria of proportion, is correlated with the precocity and earlier arrest of growth in women which exists as well for the brain as for the general proportions of the body. Tall people have larger brains, absolutely, than small people; the tallest and largest people, on the average, have the largest brains; but their brains do not increase in the same ratio as their bodies generally; the figures of Bischoff, Broca, and others, show that as body-height and body-weight increase in both men and women, so the proportion of brain decreases. A relatively large mass of brain-tissue is a character which women share with short people generally and with children.

It is time to turn to the question of sexual differences in the relation of the various parts of the brain. In doing this we have to consider the relation of the two hemispheres of the cerebrum, or brain-mantle, to the cerebellum or smaller brain, and to the upper parts of the spinal cord called the pons and medulla oblongata; in the cerebrum we have to distinguish between the frontal lobe in front, the occipital lobe at the back, and the intermediate temporo-parietal region; and we may take these last three subdivisions of the mantle first.

It has been said by Meynert that sexual distinctions in the brain are much better marked in the relation of its parts to one another than in the organ taken as a whole. But if this is so it is not well illustrated by the curious manner in which the opinions of brain anatomists concerning sexual differences in the proportion of the cerebral lobes have of late years been turned upside down. Some years ago it was asserted with great emphasis, more especially in Germany, that even from an early period of fœtal life there are marked sexual differences in the lobes of the cerebrum, tending to show the great intellectual superiority of man over woman. Burdach considered that men are distinguished from women by the development of their frontal lobes; Huschke, in 1854, came to the conclusion that woman is a *homo parietalis*, while man is a *homo frontalis;* Rüdinger in 1877 found the frontal lobes of man in every way more extensive than those of woman, and sexual differences, according to him, are distinct during fœtal life; his pupil, Passet, as recently as 1882, confirmed these results, though in a more modified form. It is quite possible to explain these conclusions. Individual variations are very considerable; most of these results were founded on very small series of brains; the brain, moreover, is a very difficult organ to examine; and, finally, as it had always been taken for granted that the frontal regions are the seat of all lofty intellectual processes, only a result which gave frontal pre-eminence to men could be regarded as probable.

It is no longer possible to accept the opinion that the frontal lobes are defective in women. Broca examined some 360 brains with great care and uniformity of method; his results show that the whole cerebral hemisphere being taken as 1000, while the proportion of frontal lobe in man is as 427, in woman it is as 431; it is only a difference in favour of women of 4 in 1000, but it is enough to show at least a practical sexual equality; on analysing the figures according to age, it is found that while in early adult age men have some frontal advantage over women, this position is decidedly reversed in old age.[1] Among the insane, Crichton-Browne has shown that the proportion of the frontal lobe to the rest of the brain is not less in women,

[1] Topinard, *Anthrop. Gén.*, p. 580, and more especially Manouvrier, art. "Cerveau," *Dict. de Physiologie.*

but is even slightly more;[1] Clapham's figures, dealing with some 450 subjects, show practical equality in the sexes; Meynert and Tigges, dealing with a considerable number of brains belonging to the insane, have both found the frontal lobe larger in women. The most reliable and accurate measurements made with special reference to this point are probably Eberstaller's. He measured with great care no less than 270 hemispheres belonging to adults (176 male and 94 female), and he found that the upper end of the fissure of Rolando occupies relatively the same place in the two sexes, what difference there is, only 0.5, being in favour of the frontal lobe in women. The results obtained by Professor Cunningham, a very cautious and reliable observer, are in exact harmony with those of Eberstaller; so far as he found any sexual difference at all it was in favour of the frontal lobe of women. He also ascertained that the lower end of the fissure of Rolando holds relatively the same place on the cerebral surface in the two sexes, and that at no period of growth is there to be found what might safely be called a sexual difference in the fissure. It had been asserted by Passet and others that the fissure of Rolando is longer, absolutely and relatively, in men; measuring the fissure by a thread carefully inserted between its lips, so as to follow all its flexures, Cunningham found, by examining a large number of brains, that (except at birth) there was some advantage, so far as there was any advantage at all, on the part of the female fissure.[2]

While it has recently become clear that women have, so far as there is any sexual difference at all, some frontal superiority over men, it has at the same time been for the first time clearly recognised that

---

[1] *Brain*, vol. ii. pp. 62-64.
[2] Professor D. Cunningham, "Contribution to the Surface Anatomy of the Cerebral Hemispheres," *Cunningham Memoirs* of the Royal Irish Academy, No. 7, 1892.

there is no real ground for assigning any specially exalted functions to the frontal lobes. This opinion had been very widely accepted without any definite reasons at all, and even Hitzig, the pioneer of modern progress in the precise knowledge of cerebral localisation, had given it the weight of his authority by assigning to the frontal lobes the seat of logical thought. It is not difficult to account for this ancient notion; there is a deeply implanted feeling in the human mind which associates with "above," "front," "top," more dignified ideas than with "below," "back," "bottom." The frontal region exactly fits in with this implicit mental assumption; it is precisely that part of the body which is most above, to the front and to the top; it is not, therefore, surprising that the centres for the highest intellectual processes should have been placed in a position where we can scarcely believe that a quadrupedal craniologist would have placed them; nor is it surprising that it is only within very recent years that we have brought ourselves to believe that the occipital lobes are intimately concerned in so high a process as that of vision. The extreme anterior part of the brain, usually called the prefrontal lobe, gives little definite reaction to electrical stimulus (though the fact that the frontal region is inexcitable to electrical stimulus is no argument against its importance in intellectual processes);[1] and there is no decisive experimental ground for associating the frontal region with intellectual processes in any special and peculiar manner. Moreover, the frontal region is, relatively, very considerably developed in the anthropoid apes, in whom the intellectual processes are not usually regarded as highly developed. Nor is the frontal lobe relatively more

---

[1] As Sherrington and Grünbaum have pointed out, it is probable that further progress in this field will be made rather by the patient combination of clinical and microscopical research than by excitation experiments in the laboratory.

developed in the adult than in the fœtus. And it may be added that in women, in whom it is if anything more developed than in man, the relations of the frontal region (as Cunningham's results show) more nearly approach the anthropoid form than man's; although in one important respect, as Cunningham points out, men in the relations of this region approach the apes more nearly than women: the area of the frontal lobe covered by the parietal bone is relatively less in men than in women. It must be added that while at present it cannot be definitely asserted that the frontal parts of the brain are specially connected with the higher mental processes, neither can it be definitely denied.[1] A consideration which makes it very improbable is the high percentage of the frontal lobes to the brain as a whole, furnished by idiots and imbeciles; in Clapham's figures it is scarcely second to that given by even the most intellectual forms of insanity. The question remains open, though it seems most reasonable to suppose that the whole of the brain is concerned in mental operations, and certainly by no means least the sensori-motor regions of the middle of the brain cortex, of which we have the most detailed experimental knowledge.

These centres are concentrated in the parietal portions of the cerebrum, and there seems now to be no doubt that they predominate in men. This result has been obtained by Broca (though Broca's figures show only a slight preponderance of this region in men), Meynert, Rüdinger, Crichton-Browne, Tigges, etc. There is some reason to suppose that the parietal region is very largely developed in persons of exceptional intellectual power; thus Rüdinger, examining eighteen brains of distinguished

[1] The case has, however, been reported (Dide, *Rev. Neurol.*, 1901, pp. 446-462) of a woman who lived a normal life, though she eventually became insane, in whom the frontal lobes were atrophied to an extreme degree; microscopical investigation showed that this atrophy was not acquired but congenital.

men, found that in all of them the parietal lobes were largely developed in the frontal direction. In apes the parietal region is small owing to the incursion both of the frontal and occipital lobes.[1]

It is somewhat doubtful whether the occipital lobe is larger in women than in men; Broca's figures show it to be on an average relatively the same size, in earlier adult age somewhat larger, in old age somewhat smaller; Crichton-Browne found it larger in women; many authorities speak uncertainly, or are inclined to find it larger in men. Cunningham finds it larger in women. It may be added that the general tendency of the occipital lobe in the mammalian series is to decrease; it is relatively smaller in the anthropoids than in the more primitive apes, and is still smaller in Man; on the other hand, it tends to become more convoluted, so that we cannot regard it as in process of atrophy; Gambetta's brain, which was small, was a marvellous example of occipital convolution.

Sexual distinctions in the important matter of the vascular supply of the brain have as yet received little attention. Sir James Crichton-Browne and Dr. Sidney Martin have, however, made a few observations. They found that the combined diameters of the internal carotid and vertebral arteries which supply the brain, taken together, are relatively to the brain-mass rather larger in women than in men. So that women's brains receive a proportionately larger blood-supply than men's, and would not suffer as they otherwise would from the comparative poverty which, as we shall see later, characterises their blood. The same investigators have found the internal carotid slightly larger in men, the vertebral slightly larger in women.[2] These results were founded on a small

---

[1] "It would be an interesting field for speculation," Cunningham remarks, "to consider whether this parietal increase in the human brain has anything to do with the acquisition of the educated movements of the limbs—more especially of the upper limbs—and that wonderful harmony of action which exists between the brain and the hands, and which has played so important a part in the evolution of the species."—"Contribution to the Surface Anatomy," etc., p. 59.

[2] Sir J. Crichton-Browne, "Sex in Education," Brit. Med. Journal, 7th May 1892.

number of subjects, though they seem in harmony with the results already set forth; for while the internal carotid chiefly supplies the parietal regions which we have found to be large in men, the vertebral chiefly supplies, not only the doubtfully large occipital, but various other basal ganglia which are large in women.

If we turn from the consideration of the sexual differences in the divisions of the cerebrum to the larger and plainer divisions of the brain-mass into cerebrum, cerebellum, and the medulla and axial part of the brain, the points of sexual difference are somewhat clearer. The most reliable evidence points on the whole to the cerebellum being, relatively, distinctly larger in women than in men, as stated long ago by Gall and Cuvier. Broca's figures show that to a slight extent the medulla and cerebellum, but especially the latter, are relatively larger in women. Dr. Philippe Rey, who has worked up Broca's figures with much elaboration, finds that with scarcely an exception all the centres below the cerebrum are relatively larger in women.[1] Boyd's figures show that the cerebellum is to the whole cerebrum in males between the ages of 7 and 14 as 103 to 1000, and between the ages of 30 and 40 as 106 to 1000; in females at the earlier period it is as 105 to 1000, at the later period as 108 to 1000; the medulla is somewhat larger in males at the earlier age, and larger in females at the later age. Marshall, in an important paper[2] on the weight of the brain and its parts, found that the ratio of the cerebellum to the cerebrum (from Boyd's figures) is in adult males as 1 to 8.17, in adult females as 1 to 8; and he further worked out from Boyd's figures the ratio

[1] P. Rey, "Le Poids du Cervelet," *Revue d'Anth.*, 1884, p. 193.
[2] J. Marshall, "On the Relation between the Weight of the Brain and its parts, and the Stature and Mass of the Body in Man" (founded partly on facts recorded by Boyd in *Philosophical Trans.*, 1861, partly from Boyd's original MSS., and partly from fuller tables prepared by Boyd at Marshall's request), *Journal of Anat. and Phys.*, July 1892.

of the parts of the brain to the whole in decimal parts of an ounce to every inch of height :—

		MEN.			
No. of Cases.	Age.	Entire Encephalon.	Cerebrum.	Cere-bellum.	Pons and Medulla.
103	30-40	.725	.632	.077	.015
		WOMEN.			
85	30-40	.695	.611	.076	.015

This shows that while men possess relatively to height more cerebrum than women, in the distribution of the lower centres the sexes are equal. Reid, Peacock, Weisbach, Meynert, and Bischoff have agreed that there is little sexual difference in regard to the relative proportions of the cerebellum. It must be added that, in accordance with what has been already said in regard to the brain generally, this sexual cerebellar equality relatively to height really means cerebellar predominance in women. Some of the basal ganglia of the brain, according to Tigges and others, are absolutely as well as relatively larger in women. Putting together numerous facts, it seems clear that the mantle is that part of the brain which is most liable to vary. The cerebellum, the various basal ganglia, and the spinal cord seem to be more constant than the cerebrum; they do not waste to the same extent with age or with insanity.

It is worth noting that the cerebellum in women is relatively larger than is the cerebrum. But the significance of this fact is at present by no means obvious. There is less to be positively affirmed to-day about the functions of the cerebellum than there was fifty years ago. It has no connection, as was once supposed, with the sexual instinct. Its destruction does not produce either paralysis or loss of intelligence. The only definite function which, so far as is yet known, it seems to possess, is the function of, to some extent, co-ordinating muscular movement. Ferrier has suggested that visceral or organic sensory impressions are represented in the cerebellum. It may be added that the cerebellum is a characteristically adult organ; in the new-born child it may only form about one-thirteenth or less of the brain-mass; in the adult it forms about one-seventh. Its development indicates height in the zoological scale, and it is relatively largest in man.

While the sexual differences in the brain are at the most very small, it would appear that the differences in the relative amount of the spinal cord are somewhat more marked. Mies found that, both in normal subjects and in the insane, women have throughout life a larger cord, as compared to the brain, than men.[1] The results obtained by the Collective Investigation Committee of the Anatomical Society of Great Britain[2] go further than this, and indicate that as regards the length of the cord, women tend to show an even absolute superiority. In the 115 cases examined the committee found a marked tendency for the cord to descend lower in females than in males. Relatively to the length of the spinal column, the cord is longer in females, and this greater extension may be a sexual peculiarity. In females, also, there was greater variation than in males; while absolutely longer on the average in women, the longest cord measured was in a woman (47 cms., as against 46.5, the longest in a man). Relatively to the average length of the spinal column, from the foramen magnum to the base of the sac, the cord is slightly longer in females than in males; while the female spinal column to the male spinal column was as 94.8 to 100, the female cord to the male cord was as 97.1 to 100. This spinal predominance in women (which is also an infantile character, all the foetuses

---

[1] *Ctbll. f. Anth.*, heft 3, 1897, p. 273.
[2] *Jour. Anat. and Phys.*, Oct. 1894.

examined showing a long cord) may possibly be of some significance.

It can scarcely be said that the study of the brain from our present point of view leads to the revelation of any important sexual distinctions.[1]   In the future, when the facts are more precisely ascertained, and their significance more obvious, than they are now, it may be different.   At present it is necessary to insist upon the fact that the importance of the brain has been greatly exaggerated.   Its importance, unquestionably, is great, but it is an importance that is strictly related to the brain's very intimate connection with the body generally.   We have been apt to regard it as the despotic ruler of the body, whereas, so far as it is a ruler at all, it is a distinctly democratic ruler. The brain elements, for the most part, are but sensori-motor delegates brought together for the sake of executive convenience.   We must not, therefore, be surprised if we can often better study these cerebral representatives of the organism by investigating the organism itself.

While, however, the brain is at present an unprofitable region for the study of sexual difference, it is, as we have seen, an extremely instructive region for the study of sexual equality.   Men possess no relative superiority of brain-mass; the superiority in brain-mass, so far as it exists, is on women's side;[2]

[1] Gustaf Retzius, in his very careful and judicial study of the human brain, takes account of sexual differences (*Das Menschenhirn*, I., pp. 166-7, Stockholm, 1896).   He concludes that, while there are no specific or characteristic sexual differences, we may say on the whole that the brains of women show somewhat fewer deviations from the type, and a greater simplicity and regularity.   While most deviations may be found in the brains of women, the percentage of their occurrence is in general smaller.   It may be added that Waldeyer, one of the chief of German authorities, has expressed himself as in agreement in this matter with Retzius.   It is a result which accords with the results we shall find later on in various other fields.

[2] It would be interesting to know how far the same rule applies to the lower animals.   In the frog, which has been most carefully studied, Donaldson and Shoemaker ("Nervous System of Frogs," *Jour. Comp. Neurology*, 1900, p. 300) show, in opposition to Furbini, that the

this, however, implies no intellectual superiority, but is merely a characteristic of short people and children. Nor is there any well-marked sexual arrangement of the nervous elements which implies relative inferiority on one side or the other. The parietal predominance of man is possibly such a character, but, as we have seen, this predominance is so inconspicuous that it has been possible in the past to attribute it to woman. From the present standpoint of brain-anatomy and brain physiology, there is no ground for attributing any superiority to one sex over another. Broca, the greatest of French anthropologists, whose keen and luminous intelligence has brought so much light to the study of man, believed many years ago (in 1861) that women are, naturally and by cerebral organisation, slightly less intelligent than men. This opinion has been very widely quoted; it is not so well known that with riper knowledge Broca's opinion changed, and he became inclined to think that it was merely a matter of education—of muscular, it must be understood, and not merely mental, education,—and he thought that if left to their spontaneous impulses men and women would tend to resemble each other, as happens in the savage condition.[1] It must be clearly recognised that in the present state of our knowledge there is no recognisable scientific warrant for the introduction of these considerations as factors in the settlement of the questions of social and practical life.

female frog has, proportionately to her body-weight, a larger mass of brain than the male.

[1] Discussion at the Paris Anthropological Society, *Bull. Soc. d'Anth.*, 3rd July 1879.

CHAPTER VI.

THE SENSES.

TOUCH.

THERE can be little doubt that as regards tactile sensibility women are superior to men. The earlier experiments on sexual differences in this respect, made chiefly in Italy by Lombroso and others, for the most part on abnormal subjects, were inconclusive. Later experiments, frequently made with more delicate instruments, have shown that girls and women are distinctly more sensitive to tactual impressions than are boys and men. This is found to be so even in Italy. Even Lombroso, who came to the conclusion that women have a less acute tactile sensibility than men, found that it was highly developed in young girls between the ages of six and twelve. Di Mattei, examining 160 children, found the tactile sensibility of girls greater than of boys.[1] Ottolenghi, again in Italy, made an extensive examination among girls and women of all classes and ages (nearly 700 in number), and found that on the whole they are more sensitive than boys and men.[2] Den in Russia, testing sensitiveness to temperature, electric current, and locality, found little sexual difference, but such differences as occurred were in favour of the greater sensibility of women. In Germany, Stern at Munich, among a large number of individuals, found that women are decidedly superior to men in tactile sensibility of the finger, and girls to boys; compositors also showed a very high degree of sensitiveness, while the highest development of tactile sensibility was found in the blind.[3] In England also Galton, using compasses applied to the nape of the neck (thus avoiding the results of varying exercise and varying roughening of the skin), found among 1,300 individuals that women show more sensitivity than men, the relative sensitivity being, roughly, about 7 to 6. He found greater variability in the

[1] Di Mattei, "La Sensibilità nei Fanciulli in Rapporto al Sesso e all età," *Arch. di Psich.*, 1901, Fasc. iii.

[2] Ottolenghi, "La Sensibilité de la Femme," *Rev. Sci.*, 28th March 1896.

[3] A. Stern, "Zur Ethnographischen Untersuchung des Tastsinnes der Münchener Stadtbevölkerung," *Beitr. zur Anthrop. u. Urgesch. Baierns*, 1895, Bd. xi., heft. 3-4; summarised in *Ctbll. f. Anth.*, 1897.

women, and attributes this, no doubt correctly, to the fact that women, much more than men, are defective in the exercise of sustained attention; their carelessness would affect the result in the same direction as diminished sensitivity.[1] Galton's results are specially reliable because they are made on a region of the body very favourable for such a test, and one also where no extreme precision of measurement is required, the average first-perceptible interval at the nape of the neck being about as much as half an inch.

In America, Professor Jastrow[2] has brought forward a small series of observations on male and female students, which, though not conclusive, have the advantage of being perfectly comparable; the tests were selected in order to yield quickly a few typical results. The æsthesiometer used was one designed by Professor Jastrow himself: on the tip of forefinger the average for 32 men was 1.71, for 22 women, 1.52; on the back of hand the average for 30 men was 17.5, for 22 women, 15.0. The sensitiveness of the palm was tested by determining the minimum height from which the fall of a bit of cardboard (weighing .9 mgr., and cut in a rectangle of 1 by 2 mm. from a sheet of millimetre paper pasted on cardboard) could be perceived; this distance was 58.2 in 27 men, but only 21.9 in 22 women. An attempt to test the pressure sense, as exhibited in the finger resting on the beam of a modified post-office balance, showed men and women about equal, one-sixth or one-seventh of the initial weight in the scale-pan being correctly appreciated.

Dr. Arthur Macdonald found that on the volar surface of wrists girls are more sensitive to locality than boys both before and after puberty, which in

---

[1] Galton, "The Relative Sensitivity of Men and Women," *Nature*, 10th May 1894.

[2] "Studies from the Laboratory of Experimental Psychology of the University of Wisconsin," *American Journal of Psychology*, April 1892.

both sexes appeared to lead to decreased sensitivity. These results seemed to require modification in the case of adults, but the number of subjects was here very few.[1]

It may be added that Marro's observations on the sensibility of the tip of the index-finger, between the ages of ten and twenty, showed that after fourteen the boys were more sensitive, though before fourteen the girls were more sensitive. In another but very small series, in which, however, the ages were higher, he found the women superior. He recognises the influence of defective attention, and also, he believes, imperfect oxidation, as tending to decreased sensibility in women.[2]

It must be borne in mind that tactile sensibility is more variable and more educable than we are always inclined to assume. Dr. Pauline Tarnowsky's investigations into the senses of normal women, criminal women, and prostitutes in Russia showed that women who live in towns have keener senses than women who live in the country; thus while criminals as a rule have more obtuse sensory perceptions than ordinary persons, she found that town-dwelling thieves had a much keener sense of taste than honest peasant women who had never lived in a town.[3] Dr. Felkin has made some very interesting observations bearing on the same point. He tested 26 parts of the body in 150 negroes and 30 Sudanese Arabs, and found that the power of discrimination, as against 1.1 mm. on tip of tongue in Europeans, was 3 mm. in the negroes and 2.6 mm. in the Sudanese; but after two negro boys had been educated in Europe for four years, tactile sensibility became more acute and they could discriminate at

[1] A. Macdonald, *Psych. Review*, March 1896.

[2] Marro, *La Puberté*, p. 57.

[3] " Sur les Organes des sens chez les Femmes Criminelles," *Actes du Troisième Congrès International d'Anthropologie Criminelle*, Brussels, 1893, p. 226.

2 mm.[1] Again, Professor Krohn has found that the skin can be progressively educated to localise sensations of pressure more and more correctly. At first in the different individual series, the subject could generally localise but two out of seven, but after a number of sittings (130) he had no trouble in localising five out of seven. This improvement from practice is very rapid.[2] The education of the skin by means of the æsthesiometer has also been carefully studied by Dressler.[3]

SENSIBILITY TO PAIN.

Professor Jastrow made some attempts to measure sensitiveness to pain in male and female students, using a light hammer, pivoted at a point 200 mm. from its iron head, and allowing it to fall on the tip of the forefinger of each hand; both finger and hand were supported. The minimum number of degrees through which the hammer must fall in order to cause a painful sensation was found to be surprisingly constant, and, as might be expected, it was much smaller in women. The figures for the right hand were, in men, 33.9, in women, 16.6; for the left hand, men 22.7, women 14.8. It is noteworthy that as regards the left hand men and women are more nearly equal, but that there is a very considerable disproportion as regards the right hand, apparently indicating the rough usage undergone by the right hand. Macdonald found, with an algometer of his own design applied to the temples, that girls and women are at all ages more sensitive to pain than boys and men; there was in general decreased sensibility with age, and the left temple (as well as

[1] Felkin, "Differences of Sensibility between Europeans and Negroes," *British Ass. Report*, 1889.

[2] W. O. Krohn, "An Experimental Study of Simultaneous Stimulations of the Sense of Touch," *Journal of Nervous and Mental Disease*, March 1893.

[3] *Am. Jour. Psych.*, June 1894.

the left hand) was more sensitive than the right. The non-labouring classes in both sexes were more sensitive than the labouring classes.[1] Ada Carman, using Macdonald's algometer, reached similar results in a series of experiments with 1500 school children in Michigan.[2] Gilbert, again, among Iowa school children, tested the pain threshold, using an algometer which exerted pressure on the nail of the right index finger; it is claimed for this method that it not only obviates the difficulty due to varying callosity of the skin, but that there is a definite point at which pressure gives way to pain. It was found that boys are always less sensitive, and that there is a gradual decrease of sensibility throughout from the ages of six to nineteen. The average difference between the sexes continued about the same up to the age of thirteen, but after that age, while the girls remained almost stationary, retaining their youthful sensibility, the boys progressively lost sensibility.[3]

It would thus appear that we are justified on the whole, so far as exact measurements can be trusted, in concluding that women are more sensitive to pain than men. The matter is not altogether simple. As Griffing remarks, as the result of experiments with Cattell's pressure algometer and with the induction coil, while thickness of skin is an important factor, it is not the only factor concerned, some persons being more, and others less, sensitive than the appearance of the skin suggests; nor is there any necessary conformity throughout the body, so that a high pain threshold for the hand is not necessarily associated with a similarly high threshold for the forehead. Moreover, sensibility to electric stimulus is quite independent of pressure sensibility.[4]

---

[1] *Psych. Rev.*, 1896 and 1898.   [2] *Am. Jour. Psych.*, Ap. 1899.
[3] Gilbert, *University of Iowa Studies in Psychology*, 1897, p. 11.
[4] H. Griffing, "On Individual Sensibility to Pain," *Psych. Rev.*, July 1896.

It would appear that, on the whole, sensibility to pain, in its sexual variations, corresponds to the general tactile sensibility. It is, however, not a very satisfactory test to carry out, nor are its results quite easy of interpretation. On this account there is still some difference of opinion as to whether men or women are more sensitive to pain. In Italy, Ottolenghi, who found general sensibility more acute in women, found sensibility to pain more acute in men. He used Edelmann's faradimeter on the moistened back of the hand. His results show increase of sensibility to pain up to the twenty-fourth year, after which age women showed three times as many cases of obtusity as men. He admits, however, that the matter is somewhat complicated by a greater " resistance to pain " on the part of women, and at one school some of the girls, in a spirit of bravado, refused to admit pain up to the extreme limit of the faradimeter.

The question of the relative sensitiveness to pain of men and women has usually been settled by the consideration of data of a more general character. There are numerous facts and statements tending to show that women are less affected by pain and suffering than men. Professor Sergi considers that the fact that women suffer less is shown by their greater resignation, as it can scarcely be claimed that women possess greater strength of will; and he points out that men who nurse their relatives rapidly lose flesh and health, while women, even mothers, often retain their good humour and appetite.[1] Mr. Williams, a professional tattooer, stated to a representative of the *Pall Mall Gazette*, " Ladies have much more courage and bear pain much better than men, though I must tell you that tattooing, if scientifically done, is all but painless. However,

[1] Sergi, " Sensibilità Femmenile," *L'Anomalo*, Oct. 1891. Sergi states that he has examined emotional sensibility rather than organic sensibility.

men are much more fidgety than women, who keep perfectly quiet." Bouchet, an observant old French writer of the sixteenth century, remarks that women endure cold better than men, and do not need so much clothing.[1]

Some light is perhaps thrown on the matter when we turn to the very closely allied question of disvulnerability in the two sexes. Disvulnerability is the term, first used by Professor Benedikt, to signify the quick repair of wounds and comparative freedom from ill consequences after severe injuries. Among the lower animals there is a high degree of disvulnerability. Among savages it is everywhere well marked, and is associated with a measurably high degree of insensibility. The Zanzibaris, for instance, have a wonderful power of repair of wounds,[2] and Dr. Reyburn, from an analysis of the cases of over 400,000 negro patients treated by the medical department of the American Bureau of Refugees, from 1865 to 1872, found that the negro has greater reparative power after injuries and other surgical operations than the white man. Among different races there appears to be a varying degree of resistance to pain which does not seem necessarily related to the evolutionary scale of the race. Pirogoff, the distinguished surgeon, observed that Jews, Mussulmans, and Slavs bore pain well. Sir William McCormac observed that the Turks exhibit total indifference to suffering.[3] The cheerfulness of children when patients has often attracted attention.[4] Malgaigne, the French surgeon, first showed conclusively in 1842 that children from the age of 5 to 15 bear amputation better than adults, a result which has since been confirmed, and is now generally recognised; we may accept Pro-

[1] *Serées*, tom. i. p. 15.

[2] T. H. Parke, *Experiences in Equatorial Africa*, p. 435.

[3] McCormac, Art. "Gunshot Wounds," Heath's *Dictionary of Surgery*.

[4] For instance, see Dr. A. B. Judson in his presidential address to the American Orthopædic Association at Washington in 1891.

fessor Horsley's statement that "as far as operative measures go, there is no doubt whatever that the nervous system of the child is less influenced by trumatism than that of the adult." Malgaigne also showed that women bear amputation better than men, a conclusion which has also been confirmed. Legouest has united the figures of Malgaigne of Paris, Laurie of Glasgow, Fenwick for Newcastle, Glasgow, and Edinburgh. In a total of 1,244 cases of amputation in men there were 441 deaths, *i.e.*, 35.45 per cent. In a total of 284 cases of amputation in women there were 83 deaths, *i.e.*, 29.29 per cent.; that is to say, a considerable difference in favour of women.[1] According to one table, the difference in favour of women is as much as 16.2 per cent. It may be argued that the difference is due to the more serious character of the accidents to which men are liable; but the difference is marked not only in amputations due to injuries, but also in those occasioned by disease. It will probably be found that we here have a sexual difference which is closely connected with the well-recognised resistance to death shown not only at birth by female infants, but in old age by the greater longevity of women.

In a paper by Lombroso on "La Sensibilité de la Femme," read at the International Congress of Experimental Psychology (1892) in London (and published in an abridged and translated form in the *Proceedings* of the Congress, pp. 41-44), various arguments are brought forward in favour of the greater sensory obtuseness of women and their greater disvulnerability. The paper is not rich in precise details, and is somewhat open to criticism. The following passage may be quoted:—"Billroth experimented on women when attempting a certain operation (excision of the pylorus) for the first time, judging that they were less sensitive and therefore more *disvulnerable—i.e.,* better able to resist pain. Carle assured me women would let themselves be operated upon almost as though their flesh were an alien thing. Giordano told me that even the pains of childbirth caused relatively little suffering to women, in spite of their apprehensions. Dr. Martini, one of the most distinguished

---

[1] Art. "Amputations," *Dict. ency. des Sciences Médicales.*

dentists of Turin, has informed me of the amazement he has felt at seeing women endure more easily and courageously than men every kind of dental operation. Mela, too, has found that men will, under such circumstances, faint oftener than women. Proverbs of different peoples confirm the fact of women's capability of resisting pain—*e.g.*, 'a woman never dies, has seven skins, has a soul and a little soul,' etc." The same arguments are more fully stated and developed in Lombroso e Ferrero, *La Donna Delinquente*, 1893, pp. 58-66. See also Dr. H. Campbell's *Nervous Organisation*, etc., pp. 54-55, 118. Dr. Campbell points out how well women bear both loss of blood and loss of sleep, and remarks, "Nothing has surprised me more than the extraordinary resignation, almost it would seem apathy, with which many women endure physical suffering, and face impending death."

With regard to the statement attributed to Professor Billroth, I may add that I wrote to Professor Eiselsberg, who was then the celebrated Viennese surgeon's chief assistant, and he confirmed Professor Lombroso's statement: "Professor Billroth really thinks that for all operations of the abdomen women have more resistance, so that operation on them gives more chance of recovery." This opinion, from so high an authority, although unaccompanied by statistics, is entitled to attention, and it harmonises with the recorded results of amputation. The sexual difference cannot be great, since many eminent surgeons (Sir James Paget, for example) have not observed it; but it seems to be real. Since the first edition of this book appeared the question has been dealt with by Marcel Baudouin, "La Supériorité de la Femme au point de vue des Opérations Abdominales," *Le Progrès Médical*, 10th July 1807. He quotes German statistics (*Arch. f. Klin. Chir.*, 1895-96, pp. 484, 861) showing that in a large number of cases of gastro-enterostomy the mortality among men was 54 per cent., among women only 35 per cent.; while in a number of cases of pylorectomy it was 64.3 among men to 52.8 among women. Baudouin brings forward in explanation of this difference a number of possible causes, but they do not seem very convincing.

While the experimental evidence on the whole goes to show that sensibility to pain as well as general tactile sensibility is more acute in women than in men, it must be admitted that the former sensibility is of a more complex character than the latter, and in its determination we encounter elements which do not truly belong to the region of sensibility proper. According to some observers, as we have seen, it appears that even if women feel pain sooner, they have a greater resistance to pain than men, and are less affected by it. It is possible that, notwithstanding their greater nervous irritability in most respects, women are really better able than men to resist pain and discomfort. The social life of woman, her subordination to parents and husband and children, the duty of submission and concealment imposed upon her, have all tended to foster tolerance of pain. It is reasonable to suppose that women would not have so generally fallen into this *rôle* unless there were some organic basis which made it more natural and less arduous than it would be in man. We shall approach this problem from another point of view when we come to consider the affectability of women.

SMELL.

Sexual differences in keenness of smell were first accurately measured by Professors E. H. S. Bailey and E. L. Nichols. In the *Proceedings of the Kansas Academy of Sciences* for 1884 there is a paper by Mr. Bailey showing that with regard to many common odours delicacy of perception is much more marked among men than among women. I have not been able to see this paper; but in *Nature*, 25th November 1886, there is a letter from Professors Nichols and Bailey, briefly summarising their methods and results. They made use of the following substances:—(1) Oil of cloves, (2) nitrite of amyl, (3) extract of garlic, (4) bromine, (5) cyanide of potassium. A series of solutions was prepared, of which each member was half the strength of the preceding one. They were extended in successive dilutions till it was impossible to detect the substances by their odours. The bottles were then placed at random for the subject to classify by the sense of smell. In the first series of experiments there were 17 males and 17 females. The results may be expressed in the following table, which gives the amount of each substance detected:—

Average of males.	Oil of cloves. 1 part in 88,218 of water.	Nitrite of amyl. 1 in 783,870	Garlic. 1 in 57,927	Bromine. 1 in 49,254	Cyanide. 1 in 109,140
Average of females.	1 in 50,667 of water.	1 in 311,330	1 in 43,900	1 in 16,244	1 in 9,002

A second series of experiments was subsequently made on 27 males and 21 females, with the following results:—

Average of males.	Prussic acid. 1 part in 112,000 of water.	Oil of lemon. 1 in 280,000.	Oil of wintergreen. 1 in 600,000.
Average of females.	1 in 18,000 of water.	1 in 116,000.	1 in 311,000.

Three of the male observers were able to detect one part of prussic acid in about 2,000,000 parts of water—two of these persons, however, were engaged in occupations favouring the cultivation of this sense —when the most careful chemical tests failed to reveal the acid. On the other hand, some of both sexes could not detect prussic acid even in solutions of overpowering strength. "Our average shows," the investigators conclude, "that the sense of smell is much more delicate in the case of male than of female observers."

From an interesting letter (14th September 1892) from Professor Nichols (now of Cornell University), in reply to various queries which I addressed to him, I quote the following passage:—"It should be said, in considering our work, that neither Professor Bailey nor I were in any degree experts in the physiology of the senses. His interest in the matter lay in its bearings upon chemistry, mine in its relation to physics. The points of sexual difference met with were not looked for in planning our experiments. They were, almost without exception, just the opposite of our preconceived notions concerning such differences. The number of individuals tested was probably insufficient to enable one to draw very broad conclusions. We deemed the differences worthy of record, however; to be given such weight as their limited character would justify. As to the class of individuals tested: they were almost entirely students of the University of Kansas, a co-educational institution of fair grade, which at that time contained nearly equal numbers of young men and women. Ages chiefly 17 to 25 years. The only distinction which one could draw, other than sexual, was that which arises from the fact that boys, in an institution offering a considerable choice of studies, select the *sciences* rather than *letters*, gaining thereby some training of the special senses. The few cases in which we deemed it certain that *training* entered, were those of students of pharmacy who had been given much practice in the recognition of drugs, etc., by use of the unaided senses, touch, taste, smell, etc. We did not think male observers perceptibly affected by indulgence in tobacco or alcohol. The use of either was the exception, and attempts to take account of the influence of such habits by averaging smokers and non-smokers, etc., seemed to show no effect. To sum up then:—

"The class dealt with was in one way a special one (college students).

"There was no attempt to select within that class; nor to exclude smokers, etc.

"The experiments were not conducted *with a view* to sexual differences.

"The male and female observers were not the same in the various experiments, although the groups tested had many members in common."

Dr. Ottolenghi, in the Laboratory of Forensic Medicine of Turin University, made a series of observations on 30 normal men and 20 normal women (of the middle and lower classes), none of whom took tobacco or presented any disorder of the nasal passages; at the same time he experimented on 80 criminal men and women. He constructed a kind of osmometer with twelve aqueous solutions of essence of clove, ranging in strength from $\frac{8}{50000}$ to $\frac{4}{000}$; in other respects he followed the methods of Nichols and Bailey. Essence of clove was selected as being a very odorous substance, very fractionable, and well known. He found that olfactory acuteness was slightly less in women than in men.[1] Ottolenghi's conclusions have been criticised by Garbini, who remarks that they are scarcely supported by Ottolenghi's own figures. Garbini has himself studied the evolution of the sense of smell in 400 young children, and finds that olfactory sensibility is both greater and more precocious in girls than in boys.[2] This difference is, however, on the average very small, and it decreases with age, so that at the age of six boys and girls are practically equal. As Binet has remarked in criticism of Garbini's conclusions, we cannot regard them as proving that women are superior to men in olfactory acuteness; they may be merely due to the greater precocity of girls. It must be added that Di Mattei, among children between the ages of four and twelve, is in agreement with Garbini in finding that the sense of smell is superior in girls. The results reached by Toulouse and Vaschide point in the same direction.

Marro also, who has investigated this question with some care on a large number of children and young people in the North of Italy, using Zwaardemaker's olfactometer, finds that the sense of smell is generally more acute in women, and more so after puberty than before. He considers that this sense is developed in association with the sexual activities of women, and that its development at puberty is connected with a relatively decreased acuteness in the other senses.[3]

So far as it goes, the evidence furnished by experiment is not at present very clear. Cases of excessively acute keenness of smell certainly occur

[1] " L'Olfatto nei Criminali," *Archivio di Psichiatria*, 1888, vol. ix. Fasc. 5.
[2] Garbini, *Arch. per l'Antrop.*, 1896, Fasc. 3.
[3] Marro, *La Puberté*, p. 59.

not very rarely in women, perhaps much more frequently than in men, but they usually occur in young hysterical women. The possibility that women are not very sensitive to odours is often suggested to men by the perfumes of oppressive strength which women frequently use.[1] It is interesting to note that the abuse of perfumes by women is not confined to modern times. In the *Pædagogus*, that delightful manual for the use of semi-pagan Christians, I remark that St. Clement of Alexandria supplies an indication that in his day masculine nostrils seemed more sensitive than feminine. In permitting a limited use of perfumes, he says—"Let a few unguents be selected by women, such as will not be overpowering to a husband."[2] A love of strong perfumes must not, however, be held necessarily to imply a defective sensitiveness to them.

TASTE.

Men have a monopoly of the higher walks of culinary art; women are not employed in such occupations as tea-tasting, which require specially delicate discrimination; they are rarely good connoisseurs of wine; and while *gourmandes* are common, the more refined expression *gourmet* does not even possess a feminine form. On these grounds it has sometimes been asserted that the sense of taste in women, like the sense of smell, is not so highly developed as in men. This conclusion has not, however, been justified by accurate investigation.

The sexual differences in the sense of taste, like those in the sense of smell, seem to have been first accurately measured by Professors Bailey and

---

[1] I do not wish to imply that the love of strong perfumes is itself proof of deficient sensitiveness with regard to smell. It must also be remembered that the use of perfumes has often been inculcated in women as a method of covering more natural odours.

[2] Bk. ii., chap. 8, "On the Uses of Ointments and Crowns."

Nichols.[1] They made a series of strong solutions for the different classes of sapid substances: for bitter, quinine was selected (1 part in 10,000 parts of water); for sweet, cane-sugar (1 part in 10 of water); for acid, sulphuric acid (1 in 100); for alkaline, sodium bicarbonate (1 in 10); for saline, common salt (1 in 100). By successive dilutions each of these solutions became the strongest of a series of solutions, each member of which was one-half the strength of the preceding one. The bottles containing the solutions were then placed without regard to order, and the person experimented upon was requested to taste them and separate them into their proper groups. In each series the last solution was so dilute as to be unrecognisable. The persons examined numbered 128, of whom 82 were male and 46 female; the experimenters' average results are expressed in the following general table:—

	Male Observers Detected.	Female Observers Detected.
Quinine .	One part in 392,000	One part in 456,000
Sugar	,, ,, ,, 199	,, ,, ,, 204
Acid .	,, ,, ,, 2,080	,, ,, ,, 3,280
Alkali .	,, ,, ,, 98	,, ,, ,, 126
Salt .	,, ,, ,, 2,240	,, ,, ,, 1,980

From these results the experimenters concluded that the sense of taste is more delicate in women than in men. This is true in the case of all substances excepting salt. "As we had found a similar difference," the writers remark, "in an earlier and independent set of experiments, which agreed in every essential particular with the results of the present test, we do not regard it as an accidental

[1] "On the Delicacy of the Sense of Taste," by Dr. E. H. S. Bailey and Dr. E. L. Nichols. A brief abstract of the paper is given in the *Proceedings of the American Association for the Advancement of Science* for 1887. The paper is printed in full in *Science*, 1888, p. 145.

difference, or as likely to disappear in more extended investigations." They noted that wide individual differences presented themselves (as much as in the ratio of one to three), and that these variations were not explicable as results of education, men with great experience in handling drugs being surpassed by women without any such training. In a few cases the ability to detect a dilute sweet was accompanied by an inability to detect a dilute bitter. Professor Nichols' remarks on p. 135 apply equally to these experiments and to those on the sense of smell.[1]

Shortly afterwards the question was independently taken up and investigated with great care by Dr. Ottolenghi at Turin.[2] He experimented on 190 persons, i.e. 60 male congenital criminals, 20 male occasional criminals, 20 normal males of the lowest social class, 50 students and professional men, 20 criminal women, and 20 normal women; all were healthy and of robust constitution, the greater part between the ages of 20 and 50. He experimented with bitter, sweet, and salt sensations. For the first he selected sulphate of strychnine, and found that 12 per cent. of his normal persons perceived one part in 800,000; setting out from this strength he made eleven graduated solutions, the strongest being 1 part in 50,000; as a sweet substance, in place of sugar, which is not very divisible, he used saccharine, making eleven gradations between 1 in 100,000 parts (which could be tasted by 25 per cent. of the normal men and 45 per cent. of the normal women) and 1 in 10,000; the eleven common salt solutions ranged from 1 to 500 to 3 in 100. Numerous precautions

---

[1] More recently Dr. Bailey has tested the sense of taste among Indians in a similar way; he finds that the order of delicacy is about the same as in white persons, but that the ability to detect dilute solutions is less among the Indians. The sexual differences found were the same as among the whites; males had a more delicate sense for salt, while in other respects the females possessed a more delicate organ. (*Kansas University Quarterly*, 1893.)

[2] "Il Gusto nei Criminali in Rapporto coi Normali," *Archivio di Psichiatria*, vol. x., Fasc. iii.-iv., pp. 332-338.

were taken: the mouth was well rinsed with luke-
warm water; each experiment was repeated, and
control experiments with distilled water were made
to avoid the disturbing influence of expectation and
subjective sensations; the solutions were kept at the
temperature of the air. In making the test the
solution was squirted on to the tongue from a pipette,
and care was taken that the amount (half a c. cm.)
should always be the same. Ottolenghi presents his
results in a table which divides the subjects into three
groups (indicating delicate, middling, and obtuse
sensations) under each head of " bitter," " sweet," and
" salt "; the table is so arranged that it also presents the percentage of individuals in relation to each
solution. Speaking generally, the criminals, more
especially the male criminals, showed a very small
proportion of persons with delicate sense of taste; the
professional men showed keen sense of taste; in
regard to bitter, for example, there were 54 per cent.
professional men in the class showing delicate perception, as against 15 per cent. congenital criminals.
The males of low social class came midway between
professional men and criminals, but nearer to the
criminals. The criminal women may be said to rank
with the men of low social class, while the normal
women on the whole rank with the professional
men. Thus 50 per cent. normal women belong to
the refined class as regards bitter, against 54 per
cent. professional men ; while 10 per cent. belong to
the obtuse class, against 14 per cent. professional men.
The weakest bitter solution was, however, only perceived by (4) professional men. Eighty per cent. of
the normal women belonged to the refined class as
regards sweet, as against 70 per cent. professional
men; the weakest solution being perceived by 45
per cent. women to only 25 per cent. professional
men; while only 10 per cent. belonged to the obtuse
class as against 14 per cent. of the professional men.
Ninety per cent. of the normal women possessed

refined taste as regards salt, against 80 per cent. of the professional men, the difference in favour of women being marked in the case of the weakest salt solution (90 per cent. of the women to 40 per cent. of the professional men); this result is in curious contrast, it is worth while to note, to the exceptional delicacy as regards salt possessed by the men investigated by Bailey and Nichols.

Ottolenghi considers that his results show that men and women possess nearly equal acuteness as regards all three tastes, but he believes that if other conditions were equal, and male habits of smoking and drinking were taken into account, it would be found that men possess a more delicate sense of taste. It is clear, however, that an examination of Ottolenghi's carefully made and clearly reported results does not justify this conclusion. No evidence is brought forward to show that alcohol and tobacco—as used temperately by average students and professional men—produces any degeneration of the gustatory apparatus, while the observations of Bailey and Nichols bring no support to this view. Moreover, the influence of social class, as shown by Ottolenghi's males, is so evident and so marked that it is obvious we ought to know to what social class his "normal women" belonged. If they belonged to the same class as the students and professional men, then the evidence as presented by Ottolenghi simply shows that men and women are equal in this respect. It is much more probable, however, that the women chiefly belonged to a much lower social class and were more nearly comparable to the males of very low social class.[1] If so, Ottolenghi's results may be said to support those of Nichols and Bailey.

Di Mattei investigated gustatory acuteness among

[1] This seems to be indicated in Dr. Ottolenghi's remark—interesting also from another point of view—that among the normal women were some who were "given to vices and debauchery," and that these showed a percentage of obtuseness at least as great as that shown by the criminal women.

Italian school children, but his results are not decisive. He found that girls are more sensitive to sweet sensations, and boys to bitter, while the sexes are equal as regards salt solutions.[1] In Russia, Den found that both among the educated and the uneducated women have a more delicate sense of taste than men. In Paris Toulouse has also found gustatory sensation more acute in women, except as regards salt solutions, for which (like Nichols and Bailey) he found that men are apparently more sensitive.

HEARING.

Deafness (which is usually due to inflammation of the middle ear) is, in the opinion of nearly all authorities, decidedly more common in men than in women. Politzer, Troeltsch, Urbantschitsch, Wilde, Duncanson, etc., all agree on this point; Marc d'Espine found 97 deaf men to 67 deaf women; Zaufal found 698 men to 451 women.[2] Among children the sexual differences are slight.

While, however, the greater tendency of men to marked pathological disturbances of hearing seems fairly certain, I am not acquainted with any extended and reliable series of observations bearing on sexual differences in sensitiveness to sound during health. Dr. Roncoroni has examined 20 healthy men and 15 healthy women from this point of view, and finds the advantage in keenness on the side of the men; 12 of the men possessed a delicate sense of hearing as against 7 of the women.[3] Among the insane he found hearing nearly equal in men and women. Professor Jastrow about the same time published a very brief note concerning an attempt to determine from what height a shot weighing 10 mgmm. must

[1] *Arch. di Psich.*, 1901, Fasc. 3.
[2] See Gellé, *Précis des Maladies de l'Oreille*, 1885, pp. 571, 572 ; also Weil, "Untersuch. d. Ohren u. d. Gehörs v. 5905 Schulkindern," *Zeitschrift f. Ohrenh.*, vol. xi. p. 106.
[3] *Archivio di Psichiatria*, 1892, Fasc. i. pp. 108, 109.

be dropped upon a glass plate so that the sound might be heard by the subject at a distance of 25 feet. It was impossible to secure absolute and constant quiet, but the hearing of the women was decidedly more acute than that of the men, the results being 17 and 35 mm. respectively.[1]

Thus these observations, so far as they go, lead to distinctly opposite results.

In regard to range of audible sensation, Mr. Galton, using his whistle at the Anthropometric Laboratory at South Kensington, found that 18 per cent. males could hear the shrillest test-note as against only 11 per cent. females; and that 34 per cent. males heard the next shrillest test-note as against 28 per cent. of the females. This result harmonises with what we know of sight.

It is worthy of note that pianoforte tuners are usually men. I am not aware whether this is owing to the inability of women to rival men in this field.

SIGHT.

Blindness in this country (according to the census of 1891) is much more common among males than among females at all ages up to 65; the preponderance of women after this age is due simply to the greater longevity of women. It does not seem to be true, however, that minor defects of sight are more common in men. The most convenient method of estimating the sexual distribution of defective eyesight is by referring to the data collected by ophthalmic surgeons. Thus Mr. R. Brudenell Carter has analysed his notes of 10,000 cases of disease or disturbance of the eyes in his own private practice, and finds 4,621 males to 5,379 females; this is over 600 more females than there would have been had his patients been in exact ratio to the general popu-

---

[1] " Studies, etc.," *Amer. Journal Psych.*, April 1892, pp. 422, 423.

lation. In classifying his cases according to the shape of the eyeball, he finds:—

	Males.	Females.	Total.
Emmetropia or normal eye-sight .	2,123	2,318	4,441
Short-sight or myopia, including simple and compound myopic astigmatism (or irregularity of eye-ball)	1,464	1,684	3148
Long-sight or hypermetropia, including simple and compound hypermetropic astigmatism	995	1,328	2,323
Mixed astigmatism	39	49	88
Totals	4,621	5,379	10,000

Therefore among Mr. Carter's patients, belonging to the well-to-do classes, there has been, even when the sexual ratio in the general population is taken into account, a distinct preponderance of women and girls. The preponderance is not to be explained, Mr. Carter points out, by special proclivity on the part of women to any single form of eye-disease. He is "inclined to refer it to the greater sensitiveness of the female sex, to the more sedulous employment of their eyes over a variety of sedentary occupations, and to their weaker muscles, which are less able, as a rule, than those of men to maintain prolonged efforts of accommodation or of convergence."[1] Mr. Carter's cases are fairly chosen, and sufficiently large in number to be reliable. We may accept them as showing that vision is in all directions more frequently defective in women than in men.

A number of investigations have been made in schools in various countries, more especially in the United States, Germany, and Sweden, with the

[1] "An Analysis of Ten Thousand Cases of Disease or Disturbance of the Eyes, seen in Private Practice," *Lancet*, Oct. 29, 1892.

special object of determining the prevalence of eye-defect among school-children, and the more extensive and reliable of these investigations show a preponderance of the short-sighted among girls which is much more marked than among Mr. Carter's patients. Thus among 11,000 boys in Sweden, Professor Axel Key found that short-sightedness ranges from 6 per cent. at the age of 11 to 37.3 per cent. at the age of 19. But among 3000 Swedish girls he found that short-sightedness ranged from 21.4 per cent. at the age of 10 to 50 per cent, and over at the age of 20.[1]

In America Dr. West examined the sight of 793 boys and 602 girls in the public schools of Worcester, Mass., using Snellen's test-types for the younger children, the Galton eye-test for those in the higher grades. In all the nine grades, except the first, which includes the youngest children, it was found that the percentage of defective eyes was distinctly greater among the girls, the difference usually being over 10 per cent.; but among boys the defect seemed to be more serious in a larger number of cases.[2] Dr. F. Warner's observations, based on an examination of 60,000 school children, also showed that serious eye defects are more common in boys.[3]

In 1902 eight oculists were temporarily appointed to examine the eyesight of the children in London Board Schools (14,000 boys and 13,000 girls). The report of the medical officer to the London School Board, Dr. James Kerr, shows that among these children, who were between the ages of eight and twelve, the percentage with defective vision was at every age decidedly greater in the girls than in the boys. When the children were divided into two groups —precocious (younger than the average age in their standard) and retarded (older than the average)— the sexual difference was still invariably maintained,

[1] *Die Pubertätsentwickelung*, etc., pp. 30, 61.
[2] *American Journal of Psychology*, August 1892, pp. 595-599.
[3] *Brit. Med. Journal*, 25th March 1893.

though the retarded group showed more defective vision than the precocious group.[1]

When we turn to more special investigations into the relative keenness of sight of men and women, the data at hand are found to be very limited. The examination at Bath of members of the British Association, by means of Galton's test, revealed little sexual difference; the men had rather better sight with the right eye, the women rather better sight with the left. At his Health Exhibition Laboratory Mr. Galton found that men are generally slightly superior to women in keenness of vision. Jacobs and Spielmann found that the English Jewess is decidedly superior to the English Jew in keenness of sight, both in the average and in the maximum and minimum; they are in this test above both the male and female as tested at the Health Exhibition by Galton.[2]

Professor Jastrow has made some careful and interesting experiments on a small number of male and female students of Wisconsin University.[3] There were 31 men whose average age was 22 years, and 22 women whose average age was 21 years; the majority were born in Wisconsin, and three-fourths of their parents were of American birth, mostly merchants, professional men, and farmers; nearly all the students were in good health, although some of them were troubled with headaches. The printed page was first placed beyond the subject's vision, then gradually moved towards him until he could just read it. The distance at which the page could be read with maximum strain was found to be slightly greater in the men, but the difference was too slight to be of any significance; the nearest point at which the type could be read was also almost identical. The

[1] *Brit. Med. Jour.*, 14th March 1903, p. 615.
[2] "Comparative Anthropometry of English Jews," *Journal Anth. Institute*, August 1889.
[3] "Studies, etc.," *Amer. Journal Psych.*, April 1892.

smallest type was then ascertained which was visible at 25 feet; this was found to be (in dioptrics) 9.4 for the men, 6.7 for the women. Acuteness of vision was tested in several ways: it was found that a series of lines 1 mm. wide and separated by spaces of 1 mm. could be distinctly discerned at a distance of 117 inches by the men, of 97 inches by the women; a similar determination with a checkerboard pattern, both black and white squares being 4 mm. square, gave 121 inches for the men, 124 inches for the women; and it was found that irregularly arranged dots could also be counted at about the same distance by both men and women, although when the dots became rather numerous the men had a slight advantage. The strength of vision was tested by noting the smallest size of letter readable at 25 feet through one and through two thicknesses of common cheese-cloth; the result in dioptrics was, through one thickness, 24.7 for the men and 19.0 for the women; through two thicknesses 45.0 for the men, 42.0 for women.

Taking the evidence as a whole, we may conclude that in most, if not all, civilised countries women are more liable to the slight disturbances of eye-sight, due to defective accommodation, which are peculiarly associated with civilisation;[1] while men are probably more liable to serious eye-defects. If, however, we take men and women belonging to the healthiest classes of the community and test the strength and acuteness of their vision, there is found to be no marked sexual difference.

Such a result is in accordance with what we know concerning the visual acuity of savages. At present our knowledge is imperfect, but so far as it goes it

[1] Animals furnish a confirmation of the association of eye-defects with civilised conditions. Motais, in a contribution to the Paris Academy of Medicine, stated that having examined the eyes of wild beasts, captured after they had reached adult age, he found them normal; those captured earlier, and still more those born in captivity, were short-sighted.

tends to show that "in a state of nature there is no marked sexual difference in visual acuity."[1]

Colour-perception and Colour-blindness.—Newton was able to make out seven colours in the spectrum. Those who possess this power can see a dark blue band between blue and violet, and they also see a broader orange band than ordinary people; they are always very fond of colour. Green has found only three persons who saw the seven colours (and considers they are about 1 in 2000 or 3000 individuals); they were all males.[2] Professor Nichols has made some interesting experiments as to sexual differences in the sensitiveness of the eye to faint colour.[3] The pigments selected were red lead, chromate of lead, chromic oxide, and ultramarine blue. Each of these pigments was mixed in a carefully graduated way with white magnesium carbonate, so that a series of coloured powders was formed of which the pure pigment formed the first, while the succeeding number were of less and less saturated hue, and finally could not be distinguished from white. These were put into small glass phials. The four sets of bottles (labelled by means of marks)—thus containing mixtures of red and white, yellow and white, green and white, blue and white—were then mingled indiscriminately, and the observer was requested to arrange them according to hue and degree of colour-saturation. The individuals examined were 54 in number (31 males and 23 females), mostly between the ages of fifteen and thirty. Five were more or less colour-blind, but this defect was not found to injure in a marked way their ability to classify the colours. In the following table the figures indicate the amount of colouring matter present in 100,000,000 volumes

[1] W. H. R. Rivers, in *Reports of the Cambridge Anthropological Expedition to Torres Straits*, vol. ii. part i. p. 28.

[2] *Colour-Blindness*, p. 103.

[3] "On the Sensitiveness of the Eye to Colours of a Low Degree of Saturation," by E. L. Nichols, Ph.D., *American Journal of Science*, vol. xxx., 1885, pp. 37 41.

of white in the most dilute mixture which can be
distinguished from a pure white by the average
observer:—

	Red Lead.	Chromate of Lead.	Chromic Oxide.	Ultramarine.
Average for males	15.9	17.3	817.7	148.5
„ „ females	59.8	33.2	913.6	108.1

"As will be seen from the above table the average
male observer is measurably more sensitive to red,
yellow, and green, while the female shows superiority
in the blue alone." The light reflected by pigments,
as Professor Nichols points out, is not monochro-
matic, so that these results cannot be held to show
us accurately the relation of the eye to the pure
spectrum.

The individual variations were very great: 8 persons (5 males
and 3 females) could distinguish yellow in a mixture of 3
parts in 100,000,000; while 2 (both females) could only detect
it in a mixture containing 190 parts to 100,000,000. The lack
of delicacy with respect to green was a general trait, possibly,
remarks Professor Nichols, traceable to familiarity with foliage.

In arranging the phials in order in the series, women on the
average were superior to men, though the two nearest approaches
to complete accuracy were both men. In the following table
100 would indicate complete accuracy:—

	Red Lead.	Chromate of Lead.	Chromic Oxide.	Ultramarine.
Male	86.86	87.16	92.81	78.13
Female	90.81	93.24	98.28	82.92

It would be interesting to consider whether special delicacy
in discrimination of a colour is accompanied by special preference for that colour, or the reverse, but there is no evidence at
present to decide this. Professor Earl Barnes found in Cali-
fornia, among nearly 1000 children of all grades, that while the
favourite colours of boys and girls were essentially the same,
more girls select red, more boys blue. "If," he remarks, "with
increasing years children generally select more red and less blue,
as seems to be the case, this would indicate that girls are more

mature than boys on an average" (*Pedagogical Seminary*, March 1893). It may be added, however, that since (as Garbini and others have shown) red, with yellow, is the first colour to be recognised and liked in early childhood, the preference of women for red might be regarded as the retention of an infantile characteristic. There seems little doubt that (at all events in America, where most observations have been made) red is most often the favourite colour selected by women, blue by men. Thus Jastrow found at Chicago that, among 4,500 adults, of every 30 men, 10 voted for blue and 3 for red; while of every 30 women, 5 voted for red and 4 for blue. Wissler obtained somewhat similar results among students in New York, but at Wellesley College blue was preferred to red. There is a much greater range in women's preference for colour, and they prefer green (which Aars in Germany found a favourite colour among young girls) much oftener than men. (For a summary of observations on the subject, see H. Ellis, "The Psychology of Red," *Pop. Sci. Monthly*, Aug. and Sept. 1900.)

These observations, so far as they go, tend to show, as also the observations on eye-sight also seem to show, that in range of sensation women are inferior to men, but that within the limits of ordinary range common to both sexes women have perhaps slightly greater power of discrimination.

The experiments of Nichols and Bailey were made on a very small number of subjects, so that they cannot be regarded as decisive. Garbini in Italy made a very elaborate and careful study of the evolution of the colour sense in 600 children, taking note of sexual differences. He adopted two methods, one in which the child had to match the colours, and another in which he had to name them. By the first, or mute method, boys were a little superior in the third year, they were equal with girls in the fifth, and in the sixth year the girls were decidedly superior. By the second or verbal method, the girls were markedly superior in the fifth and sixth years; older children were not investigated. Girls were found more precocious than boys.[1]

[1] Garbini, "Evoluzione del Senso cromatico nella infanzia," *Arch. per l'Antrop.*, 1894, Fasc. I.

In America Gilbert tested the colour discrimination of a large number of New Haven school children between the ages of six and seventeen. His examination was confined to one colour, and the test consisted of ten shades of red closely graded; the child was given the lightest shade from one set and told to pick out all those shades that were like it from another set. The advantage was slightly in favour of the girls, but the curves for the two sexes cross and recross very frequently. The boys are ahead at six, but at seventeen, when the curves end, the girls take the lead. A general average for all ages gives a very small advantage for the girls. But they have an additional advantage in that only 18.7 per cent. of them failed to discriminate at all, while 22.3 of the boys failed in so doing.[1] The girls, probably from greater familiarity with the matching of colours, had a slight advantage in this test, which was of too limited a character to be quite conclusive.

When we turn to the sexual difference in regard to colour-blindness, a subject which has been very fully investigated, there is no doubt whatever about the results. Men are much more frequently colour-blind than women. The committee on colour-blindness of the Ophthalmological Society found that among males generally (*i.e.*, out of 14,846 individuals) the percentage of pronounced cases of colour-blindness was 3.5, the average percentage being 4.16. They found that colour-blindness was nearly always much slighter in females than in males, and even then only existed in 0.4 per cent.[2] Holmgren, from an examination of 32,000 men, found 3.17 per cent. colour-blind. Dr. Joy Jefferies of Boston, from an examination carried on chiefly in educational institutions, of over 18,000 males, found

---

[1] J. A. Gilbert, *Studies from the Yale Psych. Lab.*, vol. ii., 1894, p. 58.
[2] "Report of the Committee on Colour-Blindness of the Ophthalmological Society," *Trans. Ophthal. Soc.*, 1881.

4.1 per cent. colour-blind, and among over 14,000 females only 0.008 were colour-blind. Mr. T. H. Bickerton finds the percentage 0.16. Therefore while colour-blindness exists in about 30 or 40 per thousand males of the general population of European countries it is found in only 1 to 4 per thousand females, being thus at least ten times more frequent in men than in women. One woman to ten men is the proportion found by Favre in France.[1]

There are certain variations in the incidence of colour-blindness, among classes of the population and among races, which are of interest, and may possibly bear on the significance of colour-blindness. Among the professional classes (medical students, etc.) the Ophthalmological Society's Committee found the proportion to be 2.5 per cent.; among Eton boys 2.46 per cent.; among the boys and masters at Marlborough School (according to the Anthropological Committee of the British Association) it is 2.5 per cent. On the other hand, among the police and in schools of the same social rank the Ophthalmological Society's Committee found pronounced cases in the proportion of 3.7 per cent., and in middle-class schools 3.5. In Ireland the sons of labourers are twice as liable to colour-blindness as the boys of the wealthier classes. A comparison of urban and rural populations, so far as it shows anything, points to colour-blindness being more common in the country. Jews and Quakers are more subject to colour-blindness than the ordinary population. Among (730) females of Jewish extraction, 3.1 per cent. were affected; among females belonging to the Society of Friends, 5.5; they were, however, slight cases. It was the same among the males; among 949 of Jewish extraction 4.9 were affected; among (491) Quakers, 5.9. It must be noted that the Jews were on the whole of poorer condition of life than the average, and their defects

[1] Communication to the Académie des Sciences in 1878.

were of pronounced character; the Friends belonged to the middle class, and their defects, chiefly confined to the paler shades, were slight; the wealthy Friends were less colour-blind than the poor, though still, among males, exceeding the average.[1] Jacobs and Spielmann found no fewer than 12.7 per cent. of London Jews to be colour-blind; it must be added that while in the East End the proportion was as high as 14.8 per cent., in the West End it was only 3.4 per cent.; these observers associate this tendency to colour-blindness with the absence of great painters among the Jews and the bad taste in dress shown by Jewesses belonging to the lower social grades.[2]

It is necessary to take a somewhat wider survey in order to appreciate the significance of colour-blindness. Although among civilised races colour-blindness is more prevalent in the lower than in the higher social classes, among barbarous and savage races it is very infrequent. One of the earliest investigators of colour-blindness, Professor George Wilson, examined several foreign students in England —Chinese, Kaffir, etc.: " their appreciation of colour," he remarks, "is excellent, and certainly superior to that of the majority of our own students, who have not accidentally or designedly made colour a special object of study. The most expert of them all was the young Caffre."[3]   Later and more extended investigation has shown very clearly the freedom of lower races from colour-blindness as well as their delicacy of colour-perception. Schellong among the Papuans of the New Hebrides found that the colour-sense is highly developed; they are able without hesitation to distinguish even delicate shades of difference, although their colour vocabulary is extremely limited, and they possess only one word for

[1] " Report of the Committee on Colour-Blindness of the Ophthalmological Society."
[2] *Journal Anthrop. Institute*, Aug. 1889.
[3] *Researches on Colour-Blindness*, Edinburgh, 1855, p. 77.

green and blue.[1] Among 1200 Japanese soldiers 3.4 per cent. were colour-blind. An examination of 600 Chinese men and 600 Chinese women showed that 19 men (or 3.2 per cent.) and only 1 woman (or .17 per cent.) were colour-blind.[2] Favre among Algerian tribes found only 2.6 per cent. colour-blind. Dr. L. Webster Fox, in a lecture delivered before the Franklin Institute, Philadelphia, stated that in an examination of 250 Indian children, of whom 100 were boys, he did not find a single case of colour-blindness; on a previous occasion he had examined 250 Indian boys and only found 2, or less than 1 per cent., colour-blind; he finds the proportion among white boys of the United States to be at least 5 per cent. Blake and Franklin of Kansas University also examined Indians, and found that among 285 males there were only three cases of colour-blindness, or scarcely more than 1 per cent., while among 133 females none were found to be colour-blind.[3]

In Chili colour-blindness is decidedly rarer than in northern Europe. In a graduation thesis on colour-blindness at the University of Santiago, Senor Conrado Rios states that he has examined 1200 male persons, including 520 boys of from five to fifteen years of age, with the result that 3 per cent. of the boys and 2.1 per cent. of the men presented more or less colour-blindness. He also examined 320 females, including 143 girls of from five to fifteen years of age. One girl could not distinguish between blue and violet, and a few confounded faint shades of green with yellow. Some other girls also showed a little hesitation in picking out certain colours, but none of the adult women presented any want of appreciation of colours at all. When an examination was made some years ago by a Swedish commission of 500 naval cadets and other persons in Chili, only one or two cases of colour-blindness were found. (*Lancet*, August 1890.) Dr. Rios attributes this slighter prevalence of colour-blindness in Chili to the frequency of alcoholism in Europe; it is probable, however, that a native Indian element in the population of Chili has also to be reckoned with.

[1] " Beiträge zur Anthropologie der Papuas," *Zeitschrift für Eth.*, 1891, heft iv. p. 186.
[2] *Science*, 14th Nov. 1890.   [3] *Ibid.*, 2nd June 1893.

Colour-blindness is clearly not a result of disease, nor is it associated with diseased conditions. It is true that it is rather more common among deaf-mutes than among the average of the population, but the deaf-mutes examined have largely belonged to the low social class in which colour-blindness has been found most prevalent. Among imbeciles colour-blindness is rare. Among criminals also it has not usually been found common. Among cretins the colour sense is usually present, although speech, hearing, and smell are nearly always very defective.[1] And, on the other hand, Jews, among whom colour-blindness is specially prevalent, are a healthy class of the population (except for their tendency to nervous disease), and show a very high average of ability; and the Quakers also are a distinguished class of the community.

The precise significance of the sexual difference regarding colour-blindness cannot yet be determined. The whole question of colour-blindness and of the mechanism of colour-vision generally is still under discussion. But there can be little doubt now that the greater liability of males to colour-blindness is inherent and of world-wide extension. Training has little to do with it; and comparisons between children under ten years of age and adults (in the hands of the Ophthalmological Society's Committee) have shown few differences. On the other hand, its hereditary nature is well recognised; it is sufficient to mention one case: Dr. Pliny Earle, Professor Wilson tells us, out of 32 male and 29 female relations had 20 who were colour-blind, only two, however, being female. The undoubted fact that women are more familiar with the names of colours has been considered a source of fallacy, but modern methods of examination do not require any acquaintance with names. The greater familiarity of women

[1] Professor Horsley, Art. "Cretinism" in Hack Tuke's *Dictionary of Psychological Medicine*, 1892.

with dress has been considered to account for the difference; the colour-blindness of Quakers, who are usually considered as indifferent to dress and favouring sombre hues, might be brought forward to support this theory. But it can scarcely be used to explain the very marked sexual difference among lower races; and it may be quite as reasonably argued that the Society of Friends found a specially large number of recruits among individuals indifferent to colour and defective in perceiving it.

It is doubtless significant that such scanty evidence as I have been able to gather concerning keenness of colour-perception does not seem to agree with the very clear evidence concerning colour-blindness. It is noteworthy that in Professor Nichols' experiments —though these were not on a decisive number of persons—the colours in regard to which the men were especially more sensitive than the women were red and green, precisely the colours that are defectively seen in colour-blindness. And Mr. Green found that exceptional range of colour-perception occurred exclusively in males. It would seem that we are dealing with two different classes of phenomena. Colour-blindness is a defect comparable to albinism and to the other congenital abnormalities that are more common in males. It has nothing to do with keenness in sensory discrimination, and it is probable that, as seems to be true in regard to some other sense perceptions, there is greater range and acuteness of colour-perception in men.

COLOURED HEARING.

This is one of the names for the best known of a large group of slightly abnormal psychic phenomena. A person is the subject of coloured hearing when a particular sound immediately and involuntarily brings a particular colour to the mental eye. Usually each of the vowel sounds has a colour of its own, and words are coloured accordingly. Besides coloured hearing we may have other automatic sense-associations, such as coloured gustation, coloured olfaction, coloured tactility, coloured motility.[1]

Mr. Francis Galton many years ago investigated various of these associations. He seems to have found colour association more common in women than in men; he also found that it "appears to be rather common, though in an ill-developed degree, among children."[2] The allied phenomenon of the "number-form" ("the sudden and automatic appearance of a vivid and invariable form in the mental field of view, whenever a numeral is thought of, and in which each numeral has its own definite place") was also found by Galton to be more common in women; speaking roughly, it exists in 1 out of 30 males, and in 1 out of 15 females. Number-forms originate at an early age, and are commoner in young persons than in adults.[3] Fechner collected 73 cases of coloured hearing, 35 of men, 38 of women; they were nearly all adults and of the educated classes.[4] Krohn found that coloured hearing and

---

[1] See Art. "Secondary Sensations," by Bleuler, in Tuke's *Dict. of Psych. Med.*; Grüber's "L'Audition Colorée et les Phénomènes similaires" in *Proceedings of the International Congress of Experimental Psychology*, London, 1892; and Krohn's "Pseudo-Chromæsthesia" in *American Journal of Psychology*, October 1892. The last contains a full bibliography.

[2] *Inquiries into Human Faculty*, p. 147.

[3] *Ibid.*, p. 119, Galton remarks that the somewhat allied power of visualising—or of unconsciously storing up in the mind mental pictures which may be voluntarily recalled—"is higher in the female sex than in the male, and is somewhat, but not much higher in public schoolboys than in men. . . . There is reason to believe that it is very high in some young children, who seem to spend years of difficulty in distinguishing between the subjective and objective world. Language and book-learning certainly tend to dull it." (P. 99.) The men of science he spoke to knew nothing of it. "On the other hand . . . many men, and a yet larger number of women, and many boys and girls, declared that they habitually saw mental imagery, and that it was perfectly distinct to them, and full of colour." Cross-examination brought out the truth of these assertions. (P. 85.)

[4] Fechner, *Vorschule der Aesthetik*, Zweiter Theil, p. 316.

similar phenomena are more common in women than in men. An investigation at Wellesley College, an American women's college, of 543 persons, showed that nearly 6 per cent. possessed the faculty of coloured hearing, while about 18 per cent. showed either coloured hearing or number-forms, or both combined. This is certainly a high proportion, although I do not know of any similar investigation at a men's college with which to compare it. The results were verified and confirmed by questioning the subjects after an interval of two months.[1] Large, however, as this percentage is, it is greatly exceeded by the results of a subsequent investigation at the same college on the students who entered in the autumn of 1892; out of 203 persons not less than 32, or 15.7 per cent., were colour-hearers, while 61, or 30.2 per cent., had "forms," and 17, or 8.4 per cent., showed both psychic abnormalities.[2]

It may be asserted with little fear of contradiction that all investigators who have given attention to the point have found coloured hearing and allied phenomena more common in women than in men.

If we sum up the results as regards the various senses we find that women are unquestionably superior to men in general tactile sensibility, and probably superior in the discrimination of tastes; as regards the other senses the evidence is less conclusive, but it would not seem that in regard to any sense men are clearly and decidedly superior to women. The balance of advantage is certainly on the side of women, but it is less clear and emphatically on their side than popular notions would have led us to expect. There can be little doubt that the popular belief, although it happens to be in the main

[1] Mary Whiton Calkins, "Experimental Psychology at Wellesley College," *American Journal of Psychology*, vol. v. No. 2 (November 1892).

[2] Mary W. Calkins, "A Statistical Study of Pseudo-Chromesthesia and of Mental Forms," *American Journal of Psychology*, July 1893. This is an interesting and carefully detailed study.

correct, is really founded on the confusion of two totally distinct nervous qualities — sensibility and irritability, or, as it is perhaps better called, affectability. The first means precision and intensity of perception of stimulus; the second is the readiness of motor response to stimulus. These two nervous qualities may, and usually do, vary independently.[1] The clear distinction between sensibility and irritability in the present connection has been of late clearly stated by Sergi, and by Lombroso and Ferrero, but the keen intuition of Coleridge had long before noticed that an important sexual difference is the greater irritability of women, the deeper sensibility of men. It was also perceived some years ago by Galton, who was the first to make accurate investigations of sexual sensory differences. "At first," he remarks, "owing to my confusing the quality (sensitivity) of which I am speaking with that of nervous irritability, I fancied that women of delicate nerves who are distressed by noise, sunshine, etc., would have acute powers of discrimination. But this I found not to be the case. In morbidly sensitive persons both pain and sensation are induced by lower stimuli than in the healthy, but the number of just perceptible grades of sensation between them is not necessarily different. I found as a rule that men have more delicate powers of discrimination than women, and the business experience of life seems to confirm this."[2] When we come to consider the affectability of women this important distinction will become still clearer.

[1] The greater affectability or irritability of women may be perceived at a very early stage of primitive culture and confused with greater sensibility. An interesting example is furnished by Mr. im Thurn, who tells us that women sometimes take part in the very vigorous whipping game of the Arawacks of Guiana; on such occasions a wooden figure of a bird is substituted for the whips, and a gentle peck given in place of the more serious lash. (*Journal Anthrop. Institute*, February 1893, p. 198.)

[2] F. Galton, *Human Faculty*, p. 29.

CHAPTER VII.

MOTION.

MUSCULAR STRENGTH—WOMEN'S JOINTS SMALLER—RIC-
CARDI'S EXPERIMENTS SHOWING MAXIMUM ENERGY
MORE QUICKLY REACHED BY WOMEN—REACTION-TIME
—RATE OF MOVEMENT SLOWER IN WOMEN—BRYAN'S
EXPERIMENTS ON RATE OF MOTION—RARITY OF
WOMEN ACROBATS—WOMEN AND PHYSICAL TRAINING
—SEXUAL DIFFERENCES IN VOLUNTARY MOTOR
ABILITY—WOMEN TELEGRAPH CLERKS—HANDWRITING
—WOMEN'S SLIGHTER MUSCULAR ENERGY PROBABLY AN
ORGANIC CHARACTER—MANUAL DEXTERITY—OPINIONS
OF TEACHERS—THE GENERAL OPINION THAT WOMEN
HAVE LESS MANUAL DEXTERITY THAN MEN—DEXTERITY
OF WOMEN IN VARIOUS TRADES—SENSE-JUDGMENTS—
BUSINESS EXPERIENCE—VARIOUS EXPERIMENTS—WOMEN
PROBABLY AS WELL ABLE TO FORM ACCURATE SENSE-
JUDGMENTS AS MEN.

WHATEVER doubt there may be about sexual differences in the sensory appeal there is little doubt as to
the sexual differences in motor response, at all events
in its coarser outlines. Except among certain lower
races, and then almost exclusively in that more
passive form of muscular activity involved in carrying
burdens, women everywhere reveal a somewhat less
capacity for motor energy than men and a less degree
of delight in its display. Among civilised races the
difference is great and obvious to all. There is no
form of vigorous muscular action, with the sole

exception of dancing, for which civilised women show greater attraction and aptitude than men.

Even at that period in the evolution of puberty when girls are in most respects ahead of boys, they still remain, as Pagliani and others have shown, both in vital capacity and muscular power, very much behind boys. Roughly speaking, the force of the female hand, measured by the dynamometer, is one-third less than that of the male hand; boys can carry about one-third more than girls; and while a man can carry about double his own weight a woman can carry only about half hers (Landois and Stirling). While the average male golf player (according to Whitney) can lift the ball from 120 to 140 yards, the average female player lifts it only from 70 to 100 yards. At the Bath meeting of the British Association the mean strength of squeeze was 35-40 kilos in men, 20-25 in women. The Anthropometric Committee of the British Association found that women (chiefly shop assistants and pupils in training institutions for school-mistresses) are little more than half as strong as men.[1] Manouvrier, comparing weight of femur with dynamometric pressure, found that muscular force is to body-weight as 87.1 to 100 in men and only as 54.5 to 100 in women. Sargent found that in strength of expiratory muscles the weakest boys are stronger than the average girl, and although in strength of back, legs, chest, and arms, the girls are slightly better, still 50 per cent. girls fail to reach a point of strength surpassed by 90 per cent. boys.[2] Galton found in his laboratory that of some 1600 women of various ages the strongest could only exert a squeeze of 86 lbs., or about that of a medium man. "If we wished to select the 100 strongest individuals," he remarks, "out of two groups, one consisting of 100 males chosen at

[1] *Report Anth. Com. Brit. Ass.*, 1883.
[2] Sargent, "Physical Development of Women," *Scribner's Mag.*, 1889.

random and the other of 100 females, we should take the 100 males and draft out the 7 weakest of them, and draft in the 7 strongest females."[1]

The fundamental character of the sexual difference in motor activity appears to be indicated by the fact that not only are the muscles smaller and muscular energy less in women, but the joints are also decidedly smaller. Dwight ("Range and Significance of Variation in the Human Skeleton," *Boston Med. and Surg. Jour.*, July 1894) states that "small size of joints is characteristic of woman." Hepburn found that the same holds true among savages. G. A. Dorsey has found the same difference among skeletons from the mounds of Ohio, North-West Coast Indians, and Peruvians (*Boston Med. and Surg. Reporter*, 22nd July 1897); "the average maximum diameter of the head of the humerus in the male is 46.3 mm., in the female 37.7 mm. The average maximum diameter of the femur in the male is 47.3 mm., in the female 41 mm. The average maximum diameter of the head of the tibia through the condyles in the male is 78.5, in the female 67.4."

An interesting sexual difference in muscular force has been clearly brought out by Riccardi; experimenting with the dynamometer on over 350 men and women, he found that while, with the right hand, 36 per cent. only of the men exhibited their maximum force at the first attempt, 38 per cent. at the second attempt, and 16.8 per cent. at the third, 57.8 per cent. of the women gave a maximum result at the first attempt, 20.4 at the second, only 9.9 at the third. For the left hand the results were: for the men, 49.8 at the first attempt, 24.8 at the second, 21.9 at the third, and for the women, 49 per cent. at the first attempt, 36.2 at the second, and 9.9 at the third. This result, showing that weaker women reach their maximum quicker than men, and that the weaker left hand of men resembles women in this respect, indicates a connection between weakness and promptness of reaction, and perhaps has some bearing on the general character of motor action in women.[2]

[1] *Journal Anthrop. Institute*, 1885.
[2] P. Riccardi, *Arch. per l'Antrop.*, Fasc. 3, 1889.

Herzen made a series of experiments at Florence into the influence of age and sex in modifying reaction-time—that is to say, the time taken in reacting to a signal. He was impressed by the slowness with which children co-ordinate or associate two movements, as of the hand and foot. His figures show that girls react at first more quickly than boys, but while in the latter the reaction accelerates regularly up to adolescence, in the former it accelerates less rapidly, and stops short at a lower rapidity than that of the masculine sex.[1]

Various investigations have been made in recent years with regard to reaction-time. Thus Gilbert, in a very careful series of experiments on over 1000 children in the schools of New Haven, Connecticut, found that children grow steadily quicker in simple reaction-time as they grow older, and that boys are rather quicker than girls at all the ages investigated (6 to 17); the bright children were quicker than the dull children, though at some ages this difference was not found. When discrimination and choice were involved in addition to simple reaction, the sexual difference was diminished, and the girls were almost as quick as the boys.[2] Albert L. Lewis, who made a large number of experiments on reaction-time (for light, sound, and electric shock) in different classes of persons, found that the order of decreasing rapidity was American men, Indians (these two groups being equal), Negroes, American women; the Negroes, however, came last in response to light.[3]

Reaction is quicker (according to Buccola) among the educated than among the uneducated, but the investigation of some Italian men of genius has shown that in them reaction-time is slow,[4] and Wissler found that reaction time is a very

[1] A. Herzen, *Le Cerveau et l'activité cérébrale*, pp. 96-98.
[2] J. Allen Gilbert, *Studies from the Yale Psychological Laboratory*, vol. ii., 1894, p. 77.
[3] *Psychological Rev.*, Mar. 1897.
[4] *Archivio di Psichiatria*, 1892, pp. 394, 395.

poor measure of mental efficiency.[1] It is also very slow in the insane, and extremely slow in idiots. Some Japanese jugglers examined by Herzen reacted very slowly. The north Italians, he found, reacted more quickly than the south Italians, and a Norwegian reacted most quickly of all.

Several series of investigations have been carried on concerning sexual differences in the rate of voluntary movements. Cattell and Fullerton found that this rate, which is very constant, is decidedly slower in women than in men.[2] Jastrow found, among the students of Wisconsin University, that normal movements, when no special direction is given, are quicker in women, but that the maximum movements, particularly in the case of longer movements, are quicker in men.[3] Bryan has made an elaborate study of rate of movement on about 800 school children (the sexes being nearly equally divided) belonging to Worcester, Mass. A fairly simple instrument was devised to receive tapping movements on the button of a Morse key and to record them on a clock face; the amount of force required was insignificant, and the tapping movements could be executed by the arm, forearm, or finger, so as to give the rate for the various joints. The differences between boys and girls were not found to be considerable, but there was a slight superiority of boys over girls on the whole. It must be noted, however, that the best single record was made by a girl of twelve, who " looked the type of robust health," and when asked if she played the piano, replied, " Only by ear; but I play baseball though," adding, " I can strike two over an octave on the piano." Another interesting record was that of a girl of thirteen who had taken lessons on the violin for two years, and who showed the influence of

---

[1] " Correlation of Physical and Mental Tests," *Psych. Rev. Monographs*, vol. iii., 1901.
[2] *On the Perception of Small Differences*, Philadelphia, 1890, p. 114.
[3] *Am. Journal Psych.*, April 1892, p. 425.

special practice by the high rates of the joints involved in playing the violin and the low rates of others, such as the left shoulder, not thus exercised. The superiority of the boys over the girls increases slightly from the age of 6 to that of 9, and more decidedly from 14 to 16. They are nearest together between 10 and 12. At 13 the girls are superior to the boys for each of the eight joints tested. The period from 12 to 13 is one of retardation of rate in boys and acceleration in girls. Boys are more superior to girls as regards the right side than as regards the left, so that the two sides are more alike in girls than in boys. The acceleration of rate in girls between 12 and 13 is followed by a retardation between 13 and 14; while in boys between 13 and 14 there is an acceleration followed by a decline between 14 and 15. It is significant that the decline and antecedent accelerations are more extreme in girls, and that the recovery is slower; so that girls of 13 almost reach, and sometimes surpass, girls of 16, and girls of 13 also surpass in every joint boys of 13, and in the case of four joints are faster than boys of 14. Comparison of the increments of rate in boys from 15 to 16 with those in girls from 14 to 15 shows the former to be decidedly greater in the case of every joint, and in the case of seven of the eight joints the increment of rate in boys from 15 to 16 is greater than in girls from 14 to 16. Some additional experiments with reference to precision of movement also showed a slight superiority of boys. In summing up his general results, Bryan remarks: "It would seem something more than a reasonable surmise that the general acceleration of the rate in girls from 12 to 13, and in boys from 13 to 14, is an expression of high tension in the nerve-centres in many individuals at those ages; that the decline following is an expression of nervous fatigue consequent upon the functional charges at those periods; and that the re-acceleration is a sign of recovery from that fatigue. It is significant that the antecedent acceleration and the decline are more extreme in girls than in boys, and that the girls recover more slowly. It seems not unlikely that these facts may prove of hygienic significance."[1] It is interesting to compare these results with what we know as to the rate of growth in boys and girls about the period of puberty, and the accelerations and retardations in that growth; it is very probable that there is a real connection.

Delaunay ("Les Mouvements centripètes et centrifuges," *Revue Scientifique*, 25th December 1880) has argued with much ingenuity that motor evolution is from the centripetal to the centrifugal; that centripetal movements, of adduction and of pronation, predominate among species and individuals little advanced in evolution, and among these he includes quadrupeds, apes, the lower human races, women, children, and unintelligent persons; while centrifugal movements, of abduction and supination, predominate among the higher human races, in men and in intelligent persons. Corkscrews, etc., are worked from left to right; so are watches, though formerly from right to left; and writing, which was formerly, and still often is among children, from right to left, is now from left to right. (It appears to be a fact in harmony with Delaunay's argument that mirror-writing, from right to left, is found more frequently in girls than in boys. *Jour. Ment. Science*, July 1897, p. 361.) "Women," he remarks, "preferably execute centripetal movements. Thus they give taps or slaps with the palm of the hand, men with the back. According to my observation, men make circumferential movements like the hands of a watch, women in the opposite direction. Again, all women's garments, from chemise to mantle, button from right to left, while men's garments button from left to right. When a woman puts on a man's coat she buttons it with the left hand, with a centripetal movement." It may be added that, apart from evolutionary progress, the characteristically masculine attitude of aggression is centrifugal, the characteristically feminine attitude of defence centripetal; compare, for instance, the poses of the Apollo Belvedere and the Venus de Medici.

In strength, as well as in rapidity and precision, of movement women are inferior to men. This is not a conclusion that has ever been contested. It is in harmony with all the practical experience of life. It

---

[1] W. L. Bryan, "On the Development of Voluntary Motor Ability," *Am. Journal Psych.*, November 1892.

is perhaps also in harmony with the results of those investigators (Bibra, Pagliani, etc.) who have found that, as in the blood of women, so also in their muscles there is more water than in those of men.[1] To a very large extent it is certainly a matter of differences in exercise and environment. It is probably, also, partly a matter of organic constitution. That this latter factor can in any case account for more than a small proportion of the immense muscular difference which exists between civilised men and women is impossible, when we consider the muscular strength displayed by the women among some savage races. But it is suggested by

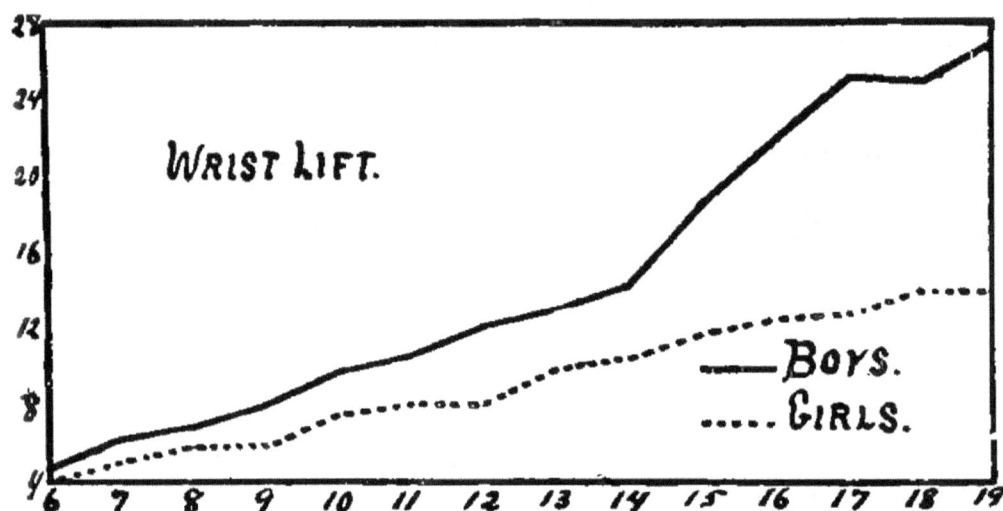

the parallelism between rate of movement and rate of growth. Gilbert, among Iowa school children, found indeed that the strength of girls, as measured by wrist-lift was fairly regular in its increase, but there was a marked sexual dividing point at the age of fourteen, boys then beginning their most rapid increase, while the rate of development of the girls was slightly but permanently retarded, so that at the age of nineteen a boy is able to lift just about twice as much as a girl (see Diagram). It is a significant fact that on the music-hall stage feats of strength are, comparatively, rarely performed by women, and the proficiency they reach is less. A

[1] *Arch. per l'Antrop.*, vol. vi. p. 173.

very competent authority remarks: " It is a question whether women should ever be trained as acrobats; it is certain that they can never attain the same proficiency as men. As a matter of fact very few women are trained for this particular kind of performance, and in some apparent exceptions—in the well-known Frantz family, for instance, where some one dressed as a woman holds a man on the shoulders and two girls at arms' length—the performer is a man in woman's clothes. Compare, too, the professional ' strong women,' such as Athleta, who is very good in her way, with the ' strong man,' such as Sandow, and you will see that no comparison or competition is possible." It must be remembered that acrobats are frequently the children of acrobats, and receive the most skilled and careful training from the earliest age, and that girls probably have as good a chance of becoming successful acrobats as men. The general tendency of men to violent muscular action, and the greater tendency of women to repose and the storing up of force, has been expressed by saying that men are katabolic, women anabolic; this generalisation, which is perhaps a little too wide, does not explain; it simply states. The motor superiority of men, and to some extent of males generally, is, it can scarcely be doubted, a deep-lying fact. It is related to what is most fundamental in men and in women, and to their whole psychic organisation. It was not an accident that at Pompeii and Herculaneum, while the men were found in a state indicating violent muscular efforts of resistance, the women were in a condition of resigned despair, or clasping their children.

If we proceed to inquire into the relative sexual differences of muscular strength in the various parts of the body, we may find precise information in a study by Kellogg of 200 men and 200 women, made with a specially devised dynamometer. He shows that the muscles of the chest are notably weak in women, agreeing with the weak inspiratory power of women; the muscles of the back are also very weak in women (whence probably the frequency with which they complain of back-ache); weakest of all are the flexors of the arm and the pronators and supinators of the forearm. It is in the legs, and especially in the thighs, that women are relatively strongest; the abductors and adductors of the thigh are the strongest muscles of the average woman. This is in accordance with the fact, already considered in a previous chapter, that thigh circumference is the only large external proportion of body in which women surpass men absolutely as well as relatively, and indicates that the larger thighs of women are not due merely to greater amount of adipose tissue.[1]

The marked weakness of the muscles of the back in women, due to defective body movements, is not only, as Kellogg notes, connected with the frequent tendency to back-ache; we must certainly associate it also with a much more serious condition. It is well known that lateral curvature of the spine (or scoliosis) is much more frequent in females than in males. Thus Bradford and Lovett, among 2,300 cases, found that there were 84.5 per cent. females to only 15.5 males, and Bernard Roth,[2] among 1000 cases, found a still higher proportion of females, 87.8 to 12.2 males. The majority of these cases occur between the ages of ten and fifteen, and there can be no doubt that defective muscular development of the back occurring at the age of maximum development—and due to the conventional restraints on exercises involving the body, and also to the use of stays which hamper the freedom of such movements—is here a factor of very great importance.

In the introductory chapter I have referred to the evidence which shows that among the lower races in many parts of

---

[1] J. H. Kellogg, "The Value of Strength Tests," a paper read to Am. Ass. Advancement Phys. Education, 1895.
[2] *Brit. Med. Jour.*, 9th Oct. 1897.

the world, the women appear to be often nearly or quite as strong as the men, if not indeed stronger. It may be proper at the present stage to point out that while such facts are undoubtedly reliable, and it would be easy to multiply them, they require some analysis before we properly understand their significance. I am in complete accord with the comments on this point of Professor Waldeyer, who remarks that the apparently greater strength of the women among, for instance, many Negro races is simply due to the division of labour by which the women act always as porters. As Waldeyer observes, a man will tire of carrying a baby before a nursemaid will ("Ueber die Somatischen Unterschiede der beiden Geschlechter," *Corresp.-Blatt. der Deutsch. Anthrop. Gesellschaft*, 1895, No. 9). It is thus that we must explain the ability of the wives of Negro soldiers (in whom the left foot had been cut off according to Abyssinian custom), after the battle of Adowa, to carry away their husbands, often finely developed men, on their backs, a distance of several miles (Fiaschi, "A Report on the Mutilated and Evirated at the Battle of Adowa," *Brit. Med. Jour.*, 29th Aug. 1896). The muscular development and strength of the women among many savage races is thus doubtless the result of special cultivation, and mostly confined to the bearing of burdens. It is not, however, without significance, since it shows the physical advantages derived from a cultivation of the muscles much greater than is common among civilised women. These advantages are, however, obtainable in Europe, as, indeed, is sufficiently indicated by the English pit-brow women of Lancashire collieries. "Their work" (I quote from a newspaper account written by a lady) "consists of stacking coal and pushing hand waggons from the shaft to a stock heap. Others stand below a large sieve which is worked by machinery, and pick stones and rubbish from the coal as it is carried on an endless iron belt from the apparatus and dropped into the railway truck beneath. Some are employed in keeping the shoot clear down which coal passes as it is shot into a canal boat. A doctor, who works in a mining village in Lancashire, considers 'the pit-brow girls much more healthy and hardy than mill girls.' Another gentleman, also a dweller among them, remarked on the fine physique of the women and the splendid children they produce." An American observer writes of the pit-brow girls of the Wigan district :—"You cannot find plumper figures, prettier forms, more shapely necks, or daintier feet, despite the ugly clogs, in all of dreamful Andalusia. . . . In the village street or at church on Sunday, you could not pick her out from her companions, unless for her fine colour, form, and a positively classic pose and grace of carriage possessed by no other working women of England." It is much to be regretted that the jealousies of male workers, aided by prejudices concerning the "unwomanly"

nature of muscular development, are in England driving women
out of healthy out-door avocations into unhealthy indoor avocations.   A distinguished American gynæcologist, Dr. G. J.
Engelmann, finds that the experiences of colleges and high
schools show improvement in the functional health of women
running parallel with greater attention to sports and physical
training.   "Physical training begun in early life," he remarks,
"the habit of exercise, will do much to remove the susceptibility to injury during the physiological fluctuations of the
functional wave, as we are taught by the acrobat, who, under
constant training from childhood on, persists in her trying
feats, requiring the greatest nerve and muscle strain, and the
highest co-ordination of all powers, unaffected by the menstrual
period" (G. J. Engelmann, "The American Girl of To-day,"
Trans. Am. Gynecol. Soc., 1900).   At the same time it is very
important to remember that the inferior strength and muscular
development of woman, as compared to man, is in relation to
her inferior size and to various fundamental and organic
characteristics.   It is highly desirable that women should pay
attention to their muscular development and their physical
training, but it is not desirable that this should be done with
the ambition of competing with men, for since men are placed
at a natural advantage, the extra strain thrown upon women
in the effort to compete with men necessarily leads to serious
sacrifices in other respects.   To women the involuntary muscular system is of special importance, more especially in its
bearing on the maternal functions, and it does not appear
that development of the voluntary muscles has any necessary
beneficial effect on the involuntary muscles.   I have noticed
that well-developed muscular and athletic women sometimes
show a very marked degree of uterine, as well as vesical,
inertia in childbirth, while on the other hand the processes of
parturition are often carried out in the most admirably efficient
manner in fragile women who show a minimum development of
the external muscles.   So far as I have made any inquiries,
this observation is in harmony with the opinion of experienced
observers.   Thus Dr. Engelmann, who, as we have seen, insists
on the importance of physical training for women, yet writes
(in a private letter): " In regard to this interesting and suggestive
question, it does seem a fact that women who exercise all their
muscles persistently meet with increased difficulties in parturition.   It would certainly seem that excessive development of
the muscular system is unfavourable to maternity.   I hear from
instructors in physical training, both in the United States and
in England, of excessively tedious and painful confinements
among their fellows—two or three cases in each instance only,
but this within the knowledge of a single individual among his
friends.   I have also several such reports from the circus

perhaps exceptions. I look upon this as a not impossible result of muscular exertion in women, the development of muscle, muscular attachments and bony frame leading to approximation to the male." It is true that peasants and labouring women are not specially liable to suffer in this way, but in such cases the muscular development is generally gradual and diffused, and probably less likely to lead to any disturbance in the nervous balance of the body.

The physical development of women should not, therefore, proceed along the same lines as that of men, and Lagrange, Mosso, and others are on sound ground when they argue that it should not be athletic in its methods. The points of greatest weakness in modern women are, as we have seen, the respiratory muscles of the chest with those of the arms, and the muscles of the back with the complementary muscles of the abdomen. Such movements as are involved in some of the slower Spanish dances are admirably adapted to correct these defects, and, as Marro insists (*La Puberté*, ch. xiii.), swimming is even more valuable. (In Stratz's *Schönheit des Weiblichen Körpers* is an interesting chapter on posture and movement in women, excellently and fully illustrated by photographs of the nude.) It may be added that, as Mosso has pointed out in a lecture on the physical education of women (translated in *Pedagogical Seminary*, March 1893), these respiratory and abdominal defects are of quite modern appearance, and by no means necessarily inherent in women. He points out that the models for the Venus of Milo and the Venus of Cnidos must certainly have been women trained in gymnastics and games. The conformation of the arm-pit of the Venus of Milo indicates a high degree of muscular development of the chest, and the muscular development is particularly noticeable in the modelling of the abdomen; "the rectal muscles of the abdomen are clearly seen; the upper part of the belly as far as the navel is divided by a line in the middle and one side, and on the other are seen two furrows marking the outer margin of the rectal muscles. I have not seen a modern statue in which this great development of the abdominal muscles was so well indicated." There is no group of muscles which it is more desirable for a woman to possess in a developed condition than those of the abdomen.

Gilbert[1] has investigated the sexual differences in voluntary motor ability with the aid of a special reaction-board with a button which the subject was required to tap as rapidly as possible for five seconds. Among over 1000 children at New Haven, between

[1] *Studies from the Yale Psychological Laboratory*, vol. ii. p. 63.

the ages of six and seventeen, it was found that rapidity increased with age to twelve years, being slightly lowered at thirteen, then increasing to a maximum at seventeen. Boys throughout showed a higher rate of tapping than girls.[1] Both sexes fall off at twelve, but while the boys go on increasing in rapidity at thirteen, the girls continue to lose up to the age of fourteen, when there is the maximum sexual difference, and again fall off at sixteen, when the boys are steadily increasing in rapidity. The tendency of the girls to fall off at these ages is undoubtedly due, as Gilbert remarks, to the influence of puberty; and sexual physical development retards nervous development in other directions. In another series of experiments the tapping was continued for forty-five seconds, in order to judge of the influence of fatigue. This influence was found to be least marked at the age of fifteen; when the data were calculated separately for boys and girls, it was found that girls tire more easily at thirteen than at twelve, while for boys this occurs between thirteen and fourteen. Boys tire more quickly than girls. At this point Gilbert makes some observations which are of considerable significance. "Boys tire more *quickly* throughout," he remarks, "in voluntary movement than girls. But the statement that boys tire more *easily* than girls could scarcely be made upon the basis of my data, for the rate of tapping by the boys was faster than that by the girls. The statement that boys tire more *easily* is unwarrantable, for, by averaging and comparing the rate of tapping for all boys and girls separately, it is found that the girls

---

[1] In another similar series of experiments at Iowa City, Gilbert found that from six to eight the girls excelled the boys, though the boys tapped faster from nine on to nineteen; the decline of the girls in rapidity at the age of fourteen was, however, less than at New Haven. It may be noted, as possibly bearing on this difference, that the physical development of the Iowa children, irrespective of sex, was superior to that of the New Haven children. (*Iowa Studies in Psychology*, vol. i., 1897, p. 27.)

on the whole tap slower than the boys, who lose but little more than the girls by fatigue, leaving the balance in favour of boys. The average boy, including all ages, taps 29.4 times in five seconds, the average girl taps 26.9 times, thus tapping 8.5 per cent. slower than boys. The average boy, including all ages, loses 18.1 per cent. by fatigue; the average girl loses 16.6 per cent. In other words, the boys

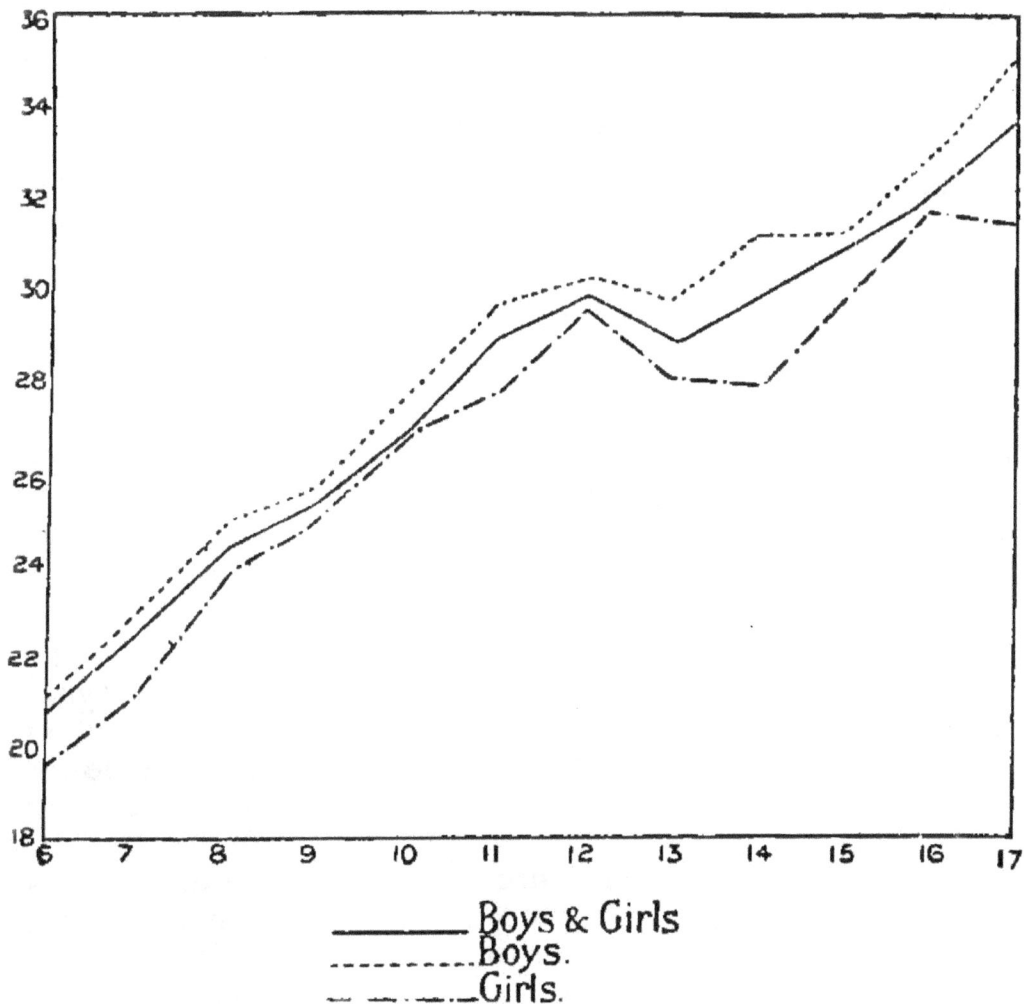

AVERAGE NUMBER OF TAPS GIVEN IN FIVE SECONDS. (*Gilbert.*)

lose 1.5 per cent. more by fatigue than girls, and yet boys tap 8.5 per cent. faster than girls. This leaves the balance greatly in favour of boys when voluntary motor ability and fatigue are considered together." This is an aspect of that more continuous character of women's activity, and more intermittent nature of men's, to which reference was made at the beginning of Chapter I. When women are working at their own natural level of energy, they tire less quickly than men do when working at their natural level of energy; but when women attempt to work at the masculine level of energy, they tire very much more rapidly than men.[1]

In practical life sexual differences in motor ability as shown in tapping may be studied in the telegraph offices. I am indebted to Mr. C. H. Garland for the following observations:—"Possibly you may know that in telegraphing use is made of a system of short and long currents, which, passing through electro magnets, move an armature working against a spring, depressing it for a longer or shorter time. This armature produces either a sound or prints a dash, or dot, on a paper ribbon. The currents are sent by a 'key,' which is essentially a brass lever pivoted in centre, one end of which bears a handle. The other end is depressed by a spiral spring. When the handle is depressed the two contacts strike together and complete the circuit, and the electro magnets at the distal end of wire move armature in corresponding manner. Sending by hand on such a key requires considerable skill and delicacy, especially when high speeds of 30 to 35 words per minute are obtained. Mr. J. Grant, speaking before the Postmaster-General on December 18th, 1893, made some interesting calculations, from which it appears that even when sending at the moderate rate of 20 words per minute, 300 signals are sent in each minute. The signals differ in length, and spaces have to be made of varying lengths between letters and words. From an experience of thirteen years, I can say that women are on an average slower senders than men. The men can for short periods send even at the rate of 45 words per minute, necessitating over 600 signals. The signals of the male clerks are cleaner cut, the distinctions between dots and dashes being more regularly and better made. The sending of women tends, as we express it, to 'drag.' The

---

[1] Many other series of experiments, chiefly carried on in America, confirm those summarised above. Thus Christopher, experimenting on Chicago school children with the ergograph, found the boys superior to the girls throughout; the girls reached their maximum at fourteen, and from then on to twenty remained stationary; the boys increased continuously up to twenty, when their energy was nearly double that of the girls. Mary Harmon, among kindergarten children, found that in flexion and extension of the arm girls are notably slower than boys. Lewis, in comparing rate of movement in flexion and extension of arms, found that American males were decidedly superior to American females, and that Indians were intermediate.

signals seem to slur into one another. The formation is more frequently faulty, although there are many excellent female clerks and many indifferent male clerks. I speak of averages. The handling of the key is another peculiar point. The normal method, and that producing the best results, is obtained when the key is grasped lightly by tips of index finger, middle finger, and thumb. This is the common method by males. The females, however, show a tendency to 'dance' on the key. That is to say, they frequently change the method of operation, alternately tapping the handle with the tips and the middle joints of index and middle finger, and grasping it. The hand is frequently lifted from the key in a sort of flourish, and has a peculiar effect when watched. The females on occasions change the position of their hand on the key two or three times during the formation of a single word. The rule seems to be to tap dots with tip of finger and dashes with middle. An experienced operator can in most cases distinguish by the marks received whether he has a male or female operator sending to him. Females also exhibit symptoms of fatigue on circuits, very quickly becoming impatient, and certainly appearing less able to talk and work at the same time. In conclusion, I might say that those stations where women are almost exclusively employed are notorious as being impatient, 'snappy,' and intolerant of any stumble." In confirmation of Mr. Garland's observation that telegraph operators can always form an opinion as to the sex of the operators with whom they are in communication, I may mention that I have been told by a female telegraph clerk that she has from time to time been addressed through the wires as "old man" by clerks who cannot be persuaded that she is a woman.

Sexual differences may be traced in handwriting, though such differences are not easy to study by methods of scientific precision. Of recent years, however, efforts have been made to study handwriting exactly, with the aid of a special curvimeter and other instruments of precision, more especially by Gross and Diehl. The latter, working in Kraepelin's laboratory at Heidelberg, finds that women write more rapidly than men. Their writing is also larger than men's, and the pressure they exert in writing is scarcely half as much as that exerted by men. But the women cannot increase their rapidity of writing to the same extent as the men, and such greater rapidity as they attain is due to diminution in the size of the writing, while in men it is produced by putting forth a greater effort.[1]

Manual Dexterity.—Carl Vogt, whose opinion is entitled to consideration, speaking of his university experience in Switzerland, where there is so large a number of women students, while bearing witness to their quickness and excellent memory for what they have learned by heart, stated that they are not skilful with their hands: "What makes laboratory work particularly difficult to women is—though one would hardly believe it—that they are often awkward and unskilful with their hands. Laboratory assistants are unanimous in complaining that they are questioned on the smallest matters, and that one woman gives more trouble than three men. One would have thought that the delicate fingers of these young women were specially adapted for microscopic work, for the manipulation of thin *laminæ* of glass, and the preparation of minute sections; but it is the contrary that really happens. One recognises the place of a female student at a glance by the fragments of glass, broken instruments, notched knives, the stains of chemicals and colouring agents, the spoiled preparations. There are exceptions without doubt, but they are exceptions."[2] This point is of some interest, and through the kindness of a friend I have obtained the opinions of several experienced and well-known teachers as to the relative awkwardness of men and women in manual operations. The letters in response cover rather more than the ground of awkwardness, but they are worth quoting. Professor M'Kendrick, of Glasgow University, writes:—"My experience has been that women are, on the average, as neat and strong and deft in manipulation as men. By 'strong' I mean that they possess sufficient and well co-

[1] A. Diehl, "Ueber die Eigenschaften der Schrift bei Gesunden," *Psychologische Arbeiten*, vol. 3, 1899, p. 37.

[2] Carl Vogt, *Revue d'Anthropologie*, 1888, quoted in Ploss, *Das Weib*, Band i. p. 34.

ordinated muscular power in their fingers, hands, and arms. Lightness and firmness of touch always imply a well-ordered muscular mechanism. In my opinion there is no average difference between the sexes as regards the capacity of performing dexterous manipulations. A certain percentage of both men and women are clumsy and inept in the movements of their fingers, and my experience does not lead me to think that the percentage is greater in women than in men. Some men possess delicate touch combined with much patience in manipulative work, and some women show the same excellences. At the same time I cannot admit that women, on the whole, are better adapted for delicate manipulative work than men. It really resolves itself into this, that many women can, in this matter, do what any man can do, and that many men can do what any woman can do. This is the result of experience in teaching women for about twenty years."

Professor Halliburton, of King's College, London, writes :—" My answer would be of much more value if I could give definite statistics, but as I have kept none, all I can do is to state my general impressions. The success of women students at examinations in science will in part answer your inquiries, but though examinational success is evidence of one kind of ability, it is not, unless taken in conjunction with other things, of superlative value in my eyes. I should rather look to the general work of the students, such as one sees in a practical class. On the whole, then, I should say that women students are on the average better than men students. This may be in part owing to the fact that women do not take up scientific work unless they are earnest about the matter and have some scientific ardour; with men one finds a large class who have no interest in their work, and who, in spite of their laziness or stupidity, or both, have been sent to college by their parents and guardians. The best women students are not, however, so good as the best men. They do not get the same grasp of the subject; they are more bookish and not so practical; they excel, however, in an infinite capacity for taking pains, such as one seldom if ever sees in a man. With both men and women one often finds that good ability, intelligence, industry, and extensive theoretical knowledge are combined with an inability to do practical work. This is not, however, the rule in either sex. Still, every now and then we come across instances of people who are not able to use their fingers, be they never so industrious or gifted in other ways; and my further impression is that one meets with this more often in women than among men."

Mr. Vaughan Jennings, who has taught Biology to mixed classes at the Birkbeck Institute for several years, writes:—" I think that in the matter of manipulation men are on the whole better than women. In a class equally divided I should expect, I think, to find more men than women showing natural skill in dissection or in using delicate apparatus. (If one had to select a number of untrained recruits to learn such work one would choose them mainly from sailors.) At the same time the men who have no capacity for such work are likely perhaps to be worse than the average woman, probably because they take less trouble. It is difficult to say where the difference lies. It is impossible to tell how much inherited habit has to do with any of the mental differences between the sexes. Some difference in the nervous system seems to be at the root of most of it. A certain lack of initiative and a hesitation about 'taking the next step' seems to cause a good deal of apparent slowness. I am sure also that greater nervous irritability is responsible for much. The ordinary words 'nervousness,' 'impatience,' etc., do not express what I mean—but there is a sort of almost unconscious and automatic exhaustion of the nervous system which often spoils delicate handiwork; and the strong man with the heavily-balanced nerves has a far greater advantage than is generally believed. However, this is only theory. My opinion is by no means a strong or decided one, but I think on the whole it goes to the masculine side."

It will be seen that the writers of two of these letters (which, I may add, were addressed to a lady) cautiously support Professor Vogt's experience, though with nothing of his characteristic *brusquerie* of expression. The opinions as to the greater awkwardness of women students in manipulation are three to one, while Professor M'Kendrick, who forms the minority, guards himself from the assertion that women are less awkward than men. That women possess in specially high degree the "well co-ordinated muscular power" which, as Professor M'Kendrick points out, is involved in skilful manipulation, there is, so far as I am aware, no precise experimental evidence to show; while, as we shall see later on, the "nervous irritability" invoked by Mr. Jennings is an important factor in the activities of women.

It is not easy, as I have elsewhere had to point out, to compare the relative skill of men and women workers, because men and women rarely perform the same work under the same conditions. The cigar and cigarette trades furnish a good field for comparison; this work requires in its more important branches very considerable manual dexterity and neatness, and a quick, accurate eye. It does not call for great muscular strength, and is therefore well fitted for women; as a matter of fact, in East London and Hackney cigar-makers are in the proportion of about 800 men to 1100 women and girls.[1] The women, however, speaking generally, are set to do a lower class of work; they receive from 15 to 40 per cent. less wages than the men, and it seems to be

---

[1] See in Booth's *Labour and Life of the People*, 1889, vol. i., the interesting Chap. vi. on "Tobacco Workers," from which the facts stated above are mainly taken.

generally agreed that their work is inferior. It should be added, however, that the physique and intelligence of the men are reckoned as above the average. A large number of women and girls are employed as cigarette-makers. This, it need scarcely be said, requires long practice and great dexterity, especially when, as is now the case, so narrow a margin of the paper is allowed to overlap. All the best work is at present done by men; the women are employed chiefly in what is called "push work," which means that the paper wrapper is first constructed and the tobacco inserted subsequently; this is much less skilled work and produces an inferior kind of cigarette. In Leeds also, according to Miss Collet, experience seems to be in favour of men's work; in the cigar trade there men are said to have a lighter touch than women, and to produce cigars, as a rule, of more equal quality.[1]

In cotton weaving (though not in cotton spinning), both in England and France, it appears that men and women are equal, and women (even as far back as 1824) have earned as much or nearly as much as men.

There is, finally, at least one occupation, chiefly involving manual dexterity, in which women are stated to be distinctly superior to men. Women stitch the serge linings to saddles as well as men and 40 per cent. more quickly. They are paid at the same rate, and earn 35s. a week as against 25s. formerly earned by men. It is an occupation for which women have been more highly trained than men.[2]

There is a general belief that women are nimble and dexterous with their fingers. If, however, we except needle-work, in which women are as a rule

---

[1] Clara E. Collet, "Woman's Work in Leeds," *Economic Journal,* September 1891.

[2] I quote the two last cases from a very able discussion by Sidney Webb, "Alleged Differences in the Wages paid to Men and to Women for Similar Work," *Economic Journal,* 1891, p. 635.

forced to possess the skill that comes of practice, there seems reason for concluding that on the whole the manual dexterity of women is somewhat inferior. This deficiency seems to be more marked in the more special and skilled departments of work. Thus, as Mr. Webb remarks, " women weavers can seldom 'tune' or set their own looms. Women heraldic engravers have, curiously enough, never been able to point their own gravers, and have, in consequence, nearly abandoned that occupation." In such cases as this we have, no doubt, to deal not so much with defective manual dexterity as with a certain lack of resourcefulness and initiative.

Sense-judgments.—Under this heading we may include various phenomena which, although closely related to pure sensory impressions, are more highly complicated by muscular, reflex, and intellectual factors. The power of forming rapid and accurate sense-judgments is of very great importance in practical life. Unfortunately, it is not easy to find or even to devise reliable investigations regarding the relative skill of men and women in forming sense-judgments; it is rare to find men and women working under absolutely the same conditions at absolutely the same work.

In the business affairs of life, where we may reasonably expect to find natural selection operating to effect a true sexual distribution, the evidence is conflicting. In salt-making, women often perform work elsewhere done by men, and are said to be more " neat-handed " in " tapping the squares "; at the same time they do less work than men, two men taking the place of three women.[1] In America an experienced peach-grower has asserted that women have quicker and defter fingers than men (as well as more natural honesty), and that they make better graders and packers than men.[2] As money-counters,

[1] S. Webb, " Alleged Differences, etc.," *Economic Journal*, 1891.
[2] *World's Work*, July 1902.

women in America are said to be much more expert than men, seldom making a mistake or passing counterfeit coin. They can tell a bad bill by feeling it only, it is asserted, and a bank cashier will make a hundred mistakes where they make one.[1] All these assertions are a little dubious.

If we turn to the more accurate and measurable determination of sexual differences in the formation of sense-judgments, it is possible to find a few, though not many, attempts to measure accuracy of motor response to sensory impressions. A few tests were applied at the Anthropometric Laboratory during the Bath meeting of the British Association. It was found that in dividing a line in half women's eyes were absolutely correct in 10 per cent. more cases than those of men—i.e., 35.6 per cent. of the men were successful, against 45.5 per cent. of the women. The division of a line into thirds was done about equally correctly by both sexes, while the men were considerably more accurate than the women in estimating a right angle—i.e., 63 per cent. men were correct, against 33.7 per cent. women. In investigating New Haven school children Gilbert found that in judgment of weight-differences both boys and girls improve with age. At six the boys are decidedly superior to the girls, from seven to thirteen they oscillate but on the whole keep pace with each other; after that there is a decided superiority of boys. At Iowa Gilbert further investigated the accuracy with which space is judged in terms of movement: the subject having first had an opportunity of measuring the distance between two points with his eyes, had then to mark it off with eyes covered. Accuracy increased with age; between the ages of six and ten girls were more accurate, but after that boys became more accurate. In the estimation of length by sight, it may be

---

[1] *Pall Mall Gazette*, 27th September 1886. The authority for this statement is not given.

remarked, Gilbert found that at nearly all ages boys are more accurate than girls.[1]

Franz and Houston in New York found that in estimating time, distance, proportion, and in quantitative measurements generally, boys are more exact than girls.[2]

Professor Jastrow, in experimenting on the male and female students of Wisconsin University, devised a series of tests of sense-judgments, though he was only able to complete a small portion of them, namely, those relating to pressure and one relating to the space-sense of the skin. The subjects were first required to pour as much shot in the palm of their right hands as they thought would weigh an ounce; the men on the average decided on 47 gm.—an exaggeration of 65 per cent.; the women on the average chose 22 gm.—an under-estimation of 21 per cent. The subjects were next asked to pour shot into a box so that both shot and box should weigh an ounce; in this test a well-recognised illusion was involved, as a stimulus appears less intense when spread over a larger area; both men and women largely exaggerated the amount necessary, but the exaggeration was somewhat greater in the case of the men. When the operation was repeated with the intention of making box and shot weigh one pound there was a slight exaggeration with the men, but the women's error was very small. The subject was then given the box which he considered to weigh one pound, and asked to put sufficient shot into another box to make it weigh double the first; in this test the women were very slightly more successful than the men. The space-test consisted in separating the points of the æsthesiometer on the back of the subject's hand until he regarded the

[1] Gilbert, *Studies from The Yale Psych. Lab.*, 1894; *ib.*, *Iowa Univ. Studies in Psych.*, 1897.

[2] Franz and Houston, " The Accuracy of Observation and of Recollection in School Children," *Psych. Rev.*, Sept. 1896. These results agree with those of Bolton.

distance between the points to be one inch; both men
and women over-estimated the separation necessary,
the men slightly more than the women.[1]   Jastrow's
observations without exception show greater accuracy
of judgment on the part of the women; here, however, it must be borne in mind that the experiments
were made through the medium of the dermal sensations of the hand, and, as has already been pointed
out, such experiments place men at a disadvantage
from the outset, and have little value in determining
sexual differences in natural faculty.   They have,
however, a certain value in relation to the practical
affairs of a world in which men and women must
be accepted as they stand, since it is thus demonstrated that the coarsening of the skin by rough
usage is a real disadvantage in forming sense-
judgments.[2]

[1] Jastrow, "Studies from University of Wisconsin," *Amer. Journal
Psych.*, April 1892.

[2] Those who wish to follow in greater detail the considerable body of
recent experimental work, bearing on the sexual differences brought out
in this and the following chapter, will find ample material in the
Psychological Review, the *American Journal of Psychology*, and the
Pedagogical Seminary.   Various other periodicals and year-books may
also be consulted, such as the *Zeitschrift für Psychologie und Physiologie der Sinnesorgone*, the *Année Psychologique*, and the *Archivio di
Psichiatria*.

CHAPTER VIII.

THE INTELLECTUAL IMPULSE.

THERE IS NO PURELY ABSTRACT THOUGHT—DIFFICULTY OF ACCURATELY INVESTIGATING INTELLECTUAL PROCESSES —JASTROW'S INVESTIGATIONS INTO THOUGHT-HABITS AND ASSOCIATIONS—MEMORY—RAPIDITY OF PERCEPTION—WOMEN READ RAPIDLY—THE READY WIT OF WOMEN—THEIR TENDENCY TO RUSE, AND ITS CAUSES —PRECOCITY—MORE MARKED IN GIRLS—CONDUCT— PUBERTY AND MENTAL ACTIVITY — INDUSTRIAL AND BUSINESS CAPACITY—EXPERIENCES OF THE POST OFFICE —ABSTRACT THOUGHT—THE GREATER INDEPENDENCE OF MEN—WOMEN AS PHILOSOPHERS AND MATHEMATICIANS—RELIGION—RELIGIOUS SECTS FOUNDED BY WOMEN—THEIR GENERAL CHARACTER—WOMEN'S CONTRIBUTIONS TO THE STRUCTURE OF THE CATHOLIC CHURCH—POLITICS.

UNDER this heading we may conveniently consider various tendencies to think and to act according to what are usually considered rational motives. As a matter of fact even our most abstract mental processes are not abstractly rational. The dryest light of the intellect is coloured in infinite ways. If we could conveniently investigate, for example, the multiplication table—an apparently abstract possession common to most persons—as it exists in individual minds from early childhood onwards, we should find it curiously tinged with emotional and pictured associations, from the simplest shadings up to the elaborate visions of the colour-hearer. It may be safely said that no two persons possess the same multiplication table.

The fact that even in so simple a shape the intellectual impulse is highly complicated makes the definite objective knowledge of psychic processes a very vast and difficult field. It is the more difficult because to get reliable results we must secure uniformity and simplicity of method working on a large body of subjects. Introspection frightens and paralyses our psychic processes; they are, as Professor Jastrow well expresses it, like children who romp and express themselves freely in the privacy of the family circle, but become bashful, silent, and conventional before strangers. At present an objective knowledge of mental processes has been sought at so few points and by so few investigators, each of them usually adopting his own methods, that our knowledge of sexual differences in the manipulation of the intellectual impulse is fragmentary and incomplete, and this character will be reflected in the present chapter. What has been said as to the comparatively little light thrown on sexual difference by the study of the brain applies, at present, in a still higher degree to the study of intellectual processes.

To arrive at any reliable knowledge of mental sexual differences it is no longer enough to formulate suggestive impressions or brilliant theories. These have a certain interest and value, it is true, but they have no part in any knowledge that can be called science. It is along the lines of precise experiment that we may reasonably hope to obtain a more definite and objective knowledge of sexual mental differences. Two series of investigation by Professor Jastrow, one of the first to inaugurate such investigations, may here be mentioned.[1] They were

[1] "A Study in Mental Statistics," *New Review*, December 1891. "A Statistical Study of Memory and Association," *Educational Review*, New York, December 1891.

carried out on male and female university students. The first investigation was into community of ideas and thought-habits, the nature of the more usual types of associations, and the time-relations of these processes. Fifty students (twenty-five of each sex) were asked to write down one hundred words as rapidly as possible, and to record the time. Words in sentences were not allowed. There were thus obtained 5000 words, and of these nearly 3000 were the same, showing how great is the community of our thoughts. This community of thought is greater in the women; while the men use 1,375 different words, their female class-mates use only 1,123. Of 1,266 unique words used, 29.8 per cent. were male, only 20.8 per cent. female. If the words are all divided into classes it is seen that among the men there was a much more frequent occurrence of words referring to the Animal Kingdom, Proper Names, Verbs, Implements and Utensils, Adjectives, Vegetable Kingdom, Abstract Terms, Meteorological and Astronomical, Occupations and Callings, Conveyances, Other Parts of Speech, Geographical and Landscape Features. Among the women there was a decidedly greater tendency than among the men to use words referring to Wearing Apparel and Fabrics, Interior Furnishings, Foods, Buildings and Building Materials, Mineral Kingdom, Stationery, Educational, Arts, Amusements, Kinship. The remaining classes of words which were used with almost equal frequency by both sexes were Parts of Body, Miscellaneous, and Mercantile Terms. The group into which the largest number of the men's words fall is Animal Kingdom (254 to 178); the group into which the largest number of the women's words fall is Wearing Apparel and Fabrics (224 to 129); " the inference from this that dress is the predominant category of the feminine (or the privy feminine) mind is valid with proper reservations; but we should remember that the dress of a woman is more conspicuous, more complex, and more various than that of a man, and that she has more to do with the making of it." In regard to Foods the difference is very great, much greater in fact than in regard to almost any other class of words; while the men only use 53 words belonging to this class, the women use 179; whether the part played by women in the preparation of food is sufficient to account for this great disproportion Professor Jastrow refrains from deciding. "In general," Professor Jastrow concludes, "the feminine traits revealed by this study are an attention to the immediate surroundings, to the finished product, to the ornamental, the individual, and the concrete; while the masculine preference is for the more remote, the constructive, the useful, the general, and the abstract." Another point worth mention is the tendency to select words that rhyme, and alliterative words; both these tendencies were decidedly more marked in men than in women. In regard to the time taken by the whole process there was practically no sexual difference.

Another series of experiments was made by Professor Jastrow in order to test the processes of memory and association. The withdrawal of a screen revealed a word upon the blackboard, whereupon each member of the class wrote upon a slip of paper the first word suggested by the word on the board, and then folded the paper so as to conceal what had been written; another word was then shown and the process repeated until each student had written ten words. (The ten words on the blackboard, it should be said, were simple monosyllables, including most of the words which the previous experiment had shown to be most generally uppermost in thought.) Exactly two days later, and without the slightest expectation on their part, the students were asked to write as many as possible of the words they had written forty-eight hours previously, and in the same order. The original ten words were then again written on the board, and the students asked to write as many as possible of the associations recorded two days before. The results of the first test may be called the " original lists," of the second the " A lists," of the third the " B lists." The first showed the most accessible associations to ten common words; the " A " lists show to what extent such can be recalled by memory alone, upon short notice, and when written with no expectation of future use; the " B " lists show to what extent the recollection is aided by the presence of the suggesting words. It was found that of the words written by the men 40 per cent. were completely forgotten, and 50 per cent. correctly recalled, while the women forgot only 29 per cent. and correctly remembered 58 per cent.; that is to say, that the women showed distinct superiority in memory. On the other hand, the " B " lists are substantially alike in both men and women; in other words, the furnishing of the original word aids the men more than the women, and this makes the proportion of totally forgotten and correctly recalled words the same for both sexes. It was also found that while men favour associations by sound and from part to whole, women prefer associations from whole to part and from object to quality. Professor Jastrow also organised some experiments on similar lines at the Milwaukee High School, and here also was shown, and in a still higher degree, the superiority of the feminine mind in the matter of memory. Here, also, the difference between the sexes was lessened when the suggesting word was supplied. The sexual difference was clearly greater in the high school; it also appears that while university boys remember better than high school boys, high school girls remember better than university girls. In many small points curious and unexpected sexual differences were found to be identical at the university and at the high school. In both, finally, there was found as usual greater community of association in girls than in boys. In a subsequent series of experiments to test the nature of associations (the results of which Professor Jastrow kindly communicated to me) each student wrote five words to each of the same ten words. A comparison of the men and the women suggested that masculine preferences are probably for associations by sound (as man-can), from whole to part (as tree-leaf), from object to activity (as pen-write), from activity to object (as write-pen), and perhaps by natural kind (as cat-dog); while feminine preferences are for associations from part to whole (as hand-arm), object to quality (as tree-green), quality to object (as blue-sky), and miscellaneous (including all that are ambiguous or not easily classi-fied). This more special study of sexual differences in the association-element in thought does not entirely confirm the results suggested by the previous study; and it need scarcely be remarked that a few series of investigations can only lead to provisional results. Such investigations place our knowledge of psychology upon a sure and positive foundation, but they need to be extended to a very large number of individuals before any wide-reaching generalisations can be attained.

Various series of experiments have been made during recent years on memory in school children. The general tendency is to show a slightly greater superiority in the girls, although this superiority is not found in every kind of memory. Thus in an elaborate series of experiments made by Max Lobsien on over 450 children at Kiel,[1] it was found that the total increase in memory power during school years was greater in the girls than in the boys; in girls there was a general development in all kinds of memory about the age of twelve, but this uniformity

[1] Max Lobsien, "Experimentelle Untersuchungen über die Gedächt-nissentwickelung bei Schulkindern," *Zt. f. Psych. u. Phys. d. Sinnes-organe*, Bd. 27, heft. 1 and 2, 1902.

was not marked in boys; the memory of girls for sounds rose chiefly about the thirteenth year, and for visual representations about the fourteenth year. When a comparison is made between boys and girls of the age of ten to eleven, there is, on the whole, a very slight superiority of girls; between twelve and thirteen—when the precocity of girls comes into play—there is a decided superiority of girls, shown in six kinds of test out of eight; at the final stage, between the ages of thirteen and fourteen and a half the superiority of girls has very slightly fallen, but is still shown in six tests. The memory for words and also for visual representations was decidedly better developed in the girls. In tests involving reproduction in exact succession boys were slightly superior as regards figures and sounds, but in the sphere of real objects the girls were decidedly superior.

In an article by Professor Stanley Hall on "The Contents of Children's Minds on entering School" (*Pedagogical Seminary*, June 1891; also *Berlin Städtisches Jahrbuch*, 1870, pp. 59-77), a detailed summary is given of an investigation carried on at Berlin into the ideas and knowledge of several thousand children on entering school. Although the carrying out of this investigation was left to the teachers, certain fairly reliable results seem to emerge. The familiarity of the children with 75 different objects and ideas was tested, and it was found that "the easily and widely diffused concepts are commonest among girls, the harder and more special or exceptional ones are commonest among boys. The girls clearly excelled only in the following concepts:—Name and calling of the father, thunder-shower, rainbow, hail, potato-field, moon, square, circle, Alexander Square, Frederick's Wood, morning-red, oak, dew, and Botanical Garden. The girls excel in space concepts, and boys in numbers. Girls excel in fairy tales [girls 60.5 per cent. to boys 39.5], and boys in religious concepts [boys 60.3 to girls 39.7]. As the opportunities to learn both would not probably differ much, there seems here a difference of disposition. Rothkäppchen was better known than God, and Schneewittchen than Christ. More boys could repeat sentences said to them, or sing musical phrases sung to them, or sing a song, than girls." Professor Hall proceeds to give an account of a more careful study on similar lines of several hundred children at

Boston. The results, although not carried out on a sufficient number of children, confirm on the whole those reached at Berlin. "In 34 representative questions out of 49 the boys surpass the girls, as the German boys did in 75 per cent. of the Berlin questions. The girls excel in knowledge of the parts of the body, home and family life, thunder, rainbows, in knowledge of square, circle, and triangle, but not in that of cube, sphere, and pyramid, which is harder and later. Their stories are more imaginative, while their knowledge of things outward and remote, their power to sing and articulate correctly from dictation, their acquaintance with numbers and animals, is distinctly less than that of the boys. The Berlin reports infer that the more common, near, or easy a notion is the more likely are the girls to excel the boys, and *vice versâ.* . . . Boys do seem more likely than girls to be ignorant of common things right about them." These interesting data bear on the respective capacity of men and women for abstract thought and for practical life, which it will be necessary to touch on later.

One other series of observations may be mentioned. Professor C. S. Minot sent out cards with the following request :— " Please draw ten diagrams on this card, without receiving any suggestions from any other person, and add your name and address." Five hundred sets were received from persons of both sexes. Circles were most common, then squares, then triangles, then four-sided figures, and so on. It was found that repetitions much preponderated among the women, though this is not true of all classes of diagrams; the men exhibit on the whole much more variety than the women. (C. S. Minot, "Second Report on Experimental Psychology : Upon the Diagram Tests," *Proceedings Am. Soc. for Psych. Research,* vol. i., No. 4, 1889.)

Rapidity of Perception.—This is an interesting example of a characteristic which has been nearly always attributed to women, but which cannot be said to have yet been demonstrated in a very satisfactory manner. It cannot, however, be entirely passed over. We must for the most part speak of it as complicated with various motor and intellectual processes such as have been in part discussed in the previous chapter.

Reaction-time merely indicates the more or less rapid manner in which a person can respond muscularly to a signal. It is perhaps in more complicated processes, involving a larger element of intelligence, that we may expect to find more marked sexual differences. Romanes once tested rapidity in reading; the same paragraph was presented to various well-educated persons, and they were asked to read it as rapidly as they could, ten seconds being allowed for twenty lines. As soon as the time was up the paragraph was removed, and the reader immediately wrote down all that he or she could remember of it. It was found that women were usually more successful than men in this test. Not only were they able to read more quickly than the men, but they were able to give a better account of the paragraph as a whole. One lady, for instance, could read exactly four times as fast as her husband, and even then give a better account than he of that small portion of the paragraph he had alone been able to read. But it was found that this rapidity was no proof of intellectual power, and some of the slowest readers were highly distinguished men.[1] In youth we read rapidly, but it is within the experience of many of us that on reaching adult age we come to read more and more slowly. It is as though in early age every statement were admitted immediately and without inspection to fill the vacant chamber of the mind, while in adult age every statement undergoes an instinctive process of cross-examination; every new fact seems to stir up the accumulated stores of facts among which it intrudes, and so impedes rapidity of mental action. It is the same with the impulse to action; in the simply organised mind this is direct and immediate; "I do just what I think of," said to Dr. Mendel an imbecile who had committed an offence against morality; "afterwards I consider it." In the more highly organised brain the consideration comes before

---

[1] G. J. Romanes, "Mental Differences between Men and Women," *Nineteenth Century*, May 1887. There is a discussion on "Perception in Man and Woman," but without any contribution of new facts, in Dr. H. Campbell's *Differences in the Nervous Organisation of Man and Woman*, Part II., chap. xii.

the action and retards it. We may say that the impulse and the action form the two ends of a circuit which at the centre of its course is intellectual. The longer and more infolded the intellectual portion of the circuit the longer it will be before the impulse is transmitted into action.

The masculine method of thought is massive and deliberate, while the feminine method is quick to perceive and nimble to act. The latter method is apt to fall into error, but is agile in retrieving an error, and under many circumstances this agility is the prime requirement. Whenever a man and a woman are found under compromising circumstances it is nearly always the woman who with ready wit audaciously retrieves the situation. Every one is acquainted with instances from life or from history of women whose quick and cunning ruses have saved lover or husband or child. It is unnecessary to insist on this quality, which in its finest forms is called tactfulness.

The method of attaining results by ruses (common among all the weaker lower animals) is so habitual among women that, as Lombroso and Ferrero remark, in women deception is "almost physiological." As Diderot somewhere says, the one thing that women have been thoroughly well taught is to wear decently the fig-leaf they have inherited from their grandmother Eve. The same fact is more coarsely and ungraciously stated in the proverbs of many nations, and in some countries it has led to the legal testimony of women being placed on a lower footing than that of men. But to regard the caution and indirectness of women as due to innate wickedness, it need scarcely be said, would be utterly irrational. It is inevitable, and results from the constitution of women, acting in the conditions under which they are generally placed. There is at present no country in the world, certainly no civilised country, in which a woman may safely state openly her wishes and desires, and proceed openly to seek their satisfaction.

Lombroso and Ferrero have admirably analysed this habit of mind, the persistency of which in women no one will doubt, and which is found to some extent even in the most highly intellectualised women. They trace it to seven causes, which all act chiefly or exclusively on women : (1) *Weakness;* for cunning and deception are the necessary resort of the weak and oppressed; only the strong can afford to be frank. (2) *Menstruation;* this function is treated with a certain amount of disgust, therefore women try to conceal it; so that every month they are exercised in dissimulation for three or four days, during which they either endeavour to conceal their condition altogether, or else simulate some trivial malady. (3) *Modesty;* thus in a woman any demonstration of love which has not been invited by a man is regarded as immodest, whence a training in deception which in the excitable nervous systems of women is peculiarly severe; again, in women the exercise of the natural functions of urination and defæcation is regarded as immodest, so that any natural call of this kind must either be repressed, or some ingenious ruse must be invented in order to gain an opportunity for its satisfaction; the facts concerning sexual relationships, again, are also regarded as immodest, and are so far as possible concealed from women and girls; when women find them out, as they inevitably do sooner or later, they have become habituated to the idea that to be modest means telling lies about such things, and so they continue the tradition. (4) *Sexual Selection;* a woman instinctively hides her defects, her disorders, if necessary her age—anything which may injure her in the eyes of men, including even her best qualities, if she thinks that these may call out ridicule or dislike. A woman usually finds it easy to mould herself on the ideal of the man she is with at the moment, provided she admires him. He would usually be repelled if she were independently to assert her own individuality. The artifices of the toilet have the same source, although, as has often been pointed out, they no longer refer to men alone, but are also intended to impress other women, or to obtain a triumph over them. (5) *The desire to be interesting*, leading to simulated weaknesses, etc., and a supposed need for protection; this seems to be merely an extension of the previous heading. (6) *Suggestibility;* the greater suggestibility of women (elsewhere pointed out, Chap. XI.) necessarily involves an overlapping of the real and the simulated—which is really unconscious and involuntary. (7) *The duties of Maternity;* a large part of the education of the infantile mind at the hands of mothers consists of a series of more or less skilful lies, told with the object of hiding from children the facts of life which are not considered proper or right for them to know; frequently also various false ideas are taught in order to frighten or otherwise influence children; so that in training their children women are also training themselves in dissimulation. (*La Donna Delinquente*, 1893, pp. 133-139.) I think it might be added that another cause of dissimulation lies in their compassion, a feminine quality on which Lombroso and Ferrero elsewhere rightly insist; an exaggerated desire to avoid hurting or shocking others is one of the most frequent causes of minor dissimulations, and works more powerfully in women than in men. I would also add that this tendency to caution and ruse is by no means confined to the human female; it appears to be a fact of considerable zoological extension, and is rooted in the necessity the female is under of guarding her offspring from danger. (See, *e.g.*, "Les Ruses Maternelles chez les Animaux," *Rev. Sci.*, 1901, pp. 80-84.) Female monkeys are more cautious and cunning than the males, and it is said that trappers on the average can only catch one nursing mother and three or four females of any kind for two score specimens of the less wary sex.

Buckle has dignified the ready wit of woman by terming it a tendency to start from ideas rather than from the patient collection of facts: men's minds, he asserted, are naturally inductive, women's deductive.[1] It would perhaps be more correct to say that women start more readily, perhaps without any conscious intellectual process, from the immediate fact before them. It is unquestionably a valuable possession, and, as Buckle remarks, women's fine and nimble minds are no doubt often irretrievably injured by "that preposterous system called their education." He refers to the notable superiority of women in quickness of intelligence among the lower classes, and to the fact that a stranger in a foreign land will always find that his difficulties are more readily understood by women. I think there can be little doubt as to the more ready intelligence of women among the uncultivated classes, whatever the cause may be. In the solitude of the Australian bush, for

[1] "The Influence of Women on the Progress of Knowledge," Buckle's *Miscellaneous Works*, vol. i.

instance, one finds repeatedly that while the settler is embarrassed and silent, or scarcely able to utter more than monosyllables, his wife is comparatively fluent and in possession of a fairly rich and precise vocabulary. It may be thought that this is merely the result of greater practice in the course of domestic avocations, but Fehling states that the little girl's command of speech is superior to the little boy's at a very early age, and it is a curious but undoubted fact that women are seldom liable to stammer.[1] Marro found that among school-children the only active class of faults that prevails more among girls than boys is sins of the tongue; otherwise, the faults of girls were mainly passive. It may be said that this facility of apprehension has been generally recognised in women. An eminent physician, Currie, mentions (according to Buckle) that when a labourer and his wife came to consult him it was always from the woman that he gained the clearest and most precise information, the intellect of the man moving too slowly for his purpose. This is by no means an uncommon medical experience. It appears also that Parisian lawyers have discovered that women can explain things best, and they say to their working-class clients, " Send me your wife."[2]

Precocity.—Rousseau long ago said in *Émile* that girls are more precocious in intelligence than boys. This is in harmony with what we know of the physical development of the sexes. Thus Delaunay remarked that among children under the age of twelve, teachers in mixed schools find that girls are

[1] Men are three times more liable to this defect, according to Ssikorski, *Ueber das Stottern*, 1891. Hartwell, director of physical training in the Boston Public Schools, who has studied the phenomenon of stuttering in a very interesting manner, found that among Boston school children the exact proportion of stutterers was 1.12 per cent. of all boys and .42 per cent. of all girls. Chervin states that the proportion of female to male stutterers is only 1 to 10. This is associated with the generally greater variational tendency of men. The proverbs of many nations bear witness to women's facility of speech ; see, for example, Lombroso and Ferrero, p. 175.

[2] Delaunay, *Revue Scientifique*, 1881, p. 309.

cleverer than boys.[1] Bellei, again, in Italy found
that school-girls of an average age of nearly twelve
years were more developed mentally than boys of
the same class, and nearly the same age.[2] Shaw,
also, in investigating memory in school children,
found that the chief difference was the greater precocity of the development of memory power in
girls.[3] Among 1000 Washington school children,
Macdonald's elaborate data show that on the whole
the girls are at the usual school age ahead of the
boys.[4] In average ability the girls were superior in
nine studies, inferior in four, and equal in one. The
precocity of girls seems to extend beyond the school
age; in America Scott Thomas has found that young
women graduate at an earlier age than young men
in the same college.[5]

It is an interesting fact, and perhaps of some significance,
that among primitive races in all parts of the world the children at an early age are very precocious in intelligence. It is
so among the Eskimo as well as among the Australians.
Among the African Fantis, Lord Wolseley remarks, " The boy is
far brighter, quicker, and cleverer than the man. You can apparently teach the boy anything until he reaches puberty, then he
becomes gradually duller and more stupid, more lazy, and more
useless every day." Kaffir lads, also, Galton was told, are often
ahead of white boys in the early stages of education, but the
limits of their development are soon reached. Among the lower
yellow races the same phenomenon is witnessed. Thus Leclère,
in his study of the Cambodgians, found that the children are
very intelligent when young, but that at the age of fifteen they

---

1 *Revue Scientifique*, 1881, p. 308.
2 *Rev. Sper. di Fren.*, vol. xxix., p. 446.
3 *Pedagogical Seminary*, Oct. 1896. Earl Barnes writes: "With a
study now in progress on 2900 children from Monterey County, Cali-
fornia, following Binet's tests in perception, we are certainly able to
demonstrate that the girls in that county from eleven to thirteen years
old have a considerably more detailed and extended knowledge of
common objects about them than is possessed by boys of the same
age, or else they have superior power of expression."—*Pedagogical
Seminary*, March 1893.
4 *Education Report*, 1897-98, pp. 1043, 1046.
5 *Pop. Sci. Monthly*, June 1903.

become stationary and less active; a certain obscurity—*un peu de nuit*—comes on their minds, and at the same time their features become less regular and beautiful than they were before. (Leclère, "Mœurs et Coutumes des Cambodgiens," *Revue Scientifique*, 21 Juin 1893.) It seems that the lower the race the more marked is this precocity and its arrest at puberty. It is a fact that must be taken in connection with the peculiarly human characters of the youthful anthropoid apes and the more degraded morphological characters of the adults.

Among the civilised European races precocity of intelligence, speaking generally, is not a fact of good augury for intelligence in after-life. This statement is scarcely qualified by the fact that among persons of abnormal intellect or genius, extraordinary precocity is sometimes found. The average results of precocity on after-development cannot at present be definitely stated as regards intelligence, but appear more clearly in other fields which are more easily open to exact observation. Thus Galton, considering the results of certain tables of the height of the male population which he had prepared, and which appear in the Report of the Anthropometric Committee of the British Association (1881), remarks: "Precocity is, on the whole, of no advantage in later life, and it may be a disadvantage. It is certain that the precocious portion do not maintain their lead to the full extent; it is possible that they may actually fall back, and that many of those who occupied a low place in the statistical series between the ages of 14 and 16 occupy a high place after those years."

It is probable that results of interest in reference to sexual differences in intelligence and its development would be obtained by the careful use of school-records. Something has already been done in this direction by Roussel, by Riccardi, and others; and such questions are now being seriously taken up in America. Roussel, for instance, has compared the punishments received by boys and girls at different Belgian schools. He found that out of 100 boys, 9 or 10 are punished for pilfering; out of 100 girls not one; out of 100 boys, 54 are punished for quarrelling and striking; out of 100 girls only 17. On the other hand, he found that girls are more idle than boys in the proportion of 21 girls to 2 boys. On the whole, during 1860-79, 31 per cent. of the boys were punished, 26 per cent.

of the girls.[1] Riccardi finds from an examination of several hundred school children of Modena and Bologna that girls have a greater fondness for study than boys (61 per cent. against 43 per cent.); that girls have also a greater fondness for manual work (27 per cent. against 22 per cent.); while the number of boys without any preference is much greater than of girls (35 per cent. against 12 per cent.). Riccardi considers that women have greater educability, sociability, domesticity, diligence, and a more profound psychic atavism than men.[2] It is not until after the age of sixteen that the intellectual superiority of boys asserts itself. It will be seen that Riccardi's results do not seem quite to accord with Roussel's as to the frequency of idleness among girls. It may be added that in lunatic asylums there is usually said to be more difficulty in persuading the women to work than the men. The best field for studying objectively the development of sexual differences in character and mental development is in mixed schools.

It would appear from various series of observations that in both sexes the onset of puberty has a very considerable effect in modifying, heightening, or depressing mental activities. It may not be out of place to refer here to its very marked influence on conduct. This is clearly seen in the investigations made by Marro in North Italy.[3] The value of Marro's observations is due to the fact that in both boys and girls he distinguishes between those who did and did not show the signs of puberty. Considering age alone, he found that there is a descent from the age of eleven, when conduct is good, to fourteen, when it is at its worst; after that age there is a steady and unbroken rise up to the age of eighteen. It was found that at the ages of thirteen and fourteen the conduct of those boys who had reached puberty was

[1] T. Roussel, *Enquête sur les Orphelinats*, etc., 1881.
[2] Riccardi, *Antropologia e Pedagogia*, Part I., 1891, pp. 121, 161.
[3] Marro, *La Puberté*, pp. 67 *et seq.*

worse than that of those who had not; in the two following years, however, the reverse was the case, so that it would appear that delayed puberty is associated with tendencies to bad or abnormal conduct. In the well-nourished classes it was found that the period of bad conduct was reached sooner than in the lower classes. Among girls, also, it was found that good conduct was much more constant before the first appearance of menstruation, after which conduct was very variable, being at its worst at the ages of fourteen and fifteen, when it began to improve steadily. The maximum of bad conduct in women, Marro remarks, would appear to be associated with the maximum of physical development and the appearance of menstruation, and so to be dependent partly on increased nutritive assimilation and partly on sexual nervous disturbance. Irregularity of conduct at this epoch is, however, less marked in girls than in boys.

Industrial and Business Capacities.—The gradual opening up of various occupations has caused many practical experiments to be made concerning sexual differences in business capacity, though it can scarcely be said that the results have been very accurately observed and recorded.[1] It must be added also that it is by no means easy to find men and women doing the same work under the same conditions; a process of sexual differentiation seems always to come immediately into operation by which the women are enabled to do lighter work under easier conditions; this is so even in the Post-office, where a very large number of women are employed.

[1] The opportunities for such observation are rapidly increasing; thus, for instance, in Massachusetts the proportion of women employed in "gainful occupations," which in 1875 was 21.3 per cent. of the whole, had increased to 30 per cent. in 1885; or, stated in another way, while the female population had increased 17.7 per cent., employed women had increased 64.6 per cent. See also "Contribution au Mouvement Féministe," *Journal des Economistes*, Mars 1883.

Delaunay consulted a number of merchants concerning sexual differences in industrial occupations, and they generally agreed that "women are more industrious but less intelligent than men;" thus in printing establishments, for instance, women were found to work mechanically, with minute attention to detail, but without fully understanding what they were doing, so that they composed very well from printed copy, but not so well from manuscript as men.[1]   Mr. Sidney Webb remarks that the Prudential Life Assurance Company employs considerably over 200 ladies in routine clerical work (copying letters, filling up forms, etc.). "This work they perform, I am assured, rather better and more rapidly than men. But they are absent from sickness (usually only slight indisposition) more than twice as much as the men."   Moreover, it has been found impossible to entrust them with more than routine work, which is a drawback to their advantageousness to the employer.[2]   In routine work, however—that is to say, continuous work at a low pressure—it is probable that they are superior to men, possessing thus greater application and patience; this seems a characteristic of the work of both civilised and uncivilised women.[3]

It seemed to me a matter of some interest to ascertain the experiences of the Post-office, so large an employer of both men and women, as to sexual differences in capacity. It is not altogether easy to obtain such information, and it does not seem possible at present to obtain it in a definite and precise form. I have, however, received from an authoritative source a number of opinions which represent the experience of various large post-offices in different parts of the kingdom, and which are regarded as being typical and reliable results. Thus, one of the chief post-

---

[1] *Revue Scientifique*, 1881, p. 307.

[2] S. Webb, "Alleged Differences in the Wages paid to Men and to Women for Similar Work," *Economic Journal*, 1891, p. 635.

[3] Lombroso and Ferrero (pp. 177-178) bring forward evidence on this point.

masters is of opinion that as counter and instrumental clerks, doing concurrently money order and savings bank duties, taking in telegrams, and signalling and receiving telegrams, and in attending to rough and illiterate persons, women clerks are preferable to men. They keep their stocks in neater order, and are more careful with money; they speak better, as a rule, and are more patient. In another (west country) district where the telegraph work is entirely performed by women, it is stated to be admirably done. At a very large provincial office it is found that women compare favourably with telegraphists of the other sex, doing their work, as a rule, with equal intelligence and accuracy. But it is found that their handwriting is not usually so good, and that they rarely exhibit the same desire as men to obtain a technical knowledge of telegraphy. On the postal side they are also regarded as a distinct success at the city in question. Complaints from the public of inattention and incivility are less frequent in the case of offices where women are employed; and women keep their stamp stocks in better order, are less troublesome in matters of discipline, and are regarded as less liable to go wrong in money matters than men. As a rule they do their work with intelligence and accuracy, and under ordinary conditions they probably do it almost as quickly; but at times of pressure they are not able to maintain a competition with men at the heavier kinds of work, especially at Wheatstone circuits, etc., owing to a lack of staying power. Another report also expresses doubt as to the strength and staying power of women for the continuous work of a heavy head office counter, and male assistance has been required. As a general rule, in the opinion of another postmaster, female telegraphists perform counter duties satisfactorily, but in cases of emergency they are not equal to male officers, and the proportion of errors is generally greater among females than males. The latter also are found better able to maintain order and discipline among the messengers. As regards instrument room duties, women work moderately busy circuits just as well as men, but it is considered generally necessary to staff the busiest circuits with male telegraphists; this applies more particularly to news wires, the work being too heavy for women, who do not seem to possess the wrist-power requisite for rapid writing, and at the same time for making the required number of copies. Moreover, for this class of work male telegraphists are better qualified because, as a rule, they are much better informed on all topics of general public interest, which is an element of importance in dealing with news traffic. According to another opinion, finally, as supervising officers women cannot so well stand the continuous walking about the instrument room which is regarded as very necessary, and it is also found that they evince no desire to acquire technical knowledge.

The general sense of these and other authoritative opinions is fairly harmonious as to the relative capacity of men and women for post-office duties. There appears to be general agreement that women are more docile and amenable to discipline; that they can do light work equally well; that they are steadier in some respects; but that, on the other hand, they are oftener absent on account of slight indisposition, they break down sooner under strain (although consideration is shown them in the matter of hours, etc.), and exhibit less intelligence outside the ordinary routine, not showing the same ability or willingness (possibly because they look forward to marriage) to acquire technical knowledge. In London it is the general experience that women are lacking in courtesy to the public; many complaints are received concerning the discourtesy of the female clerks, and some post-officers have an objection to the employment of women on this account. In some of the large provincial offices, however, it is found that women are more courteous than men. These results seem to coincide fairly with those obtained from other sources.

The employment of women in the Post-office is much cheaper (by about 25 per cent.) than that of men, but from the official point of view it is attended by various disadvantages : (1) They are much more frequently absent on account of sickness, the average for London (1900) being 11.4 days to 8.1 days for men. (2) They are not required to work at night, and it is at night that a large part of the work is done. (3) They cannot do much overtime work, and at Christmas, etc., there is great additional pressure. (4) In offices where women are employed (as at Hatton Garden) it is necessary to have the presence of a man during part of the day to afford protection in case of an attempt at robbery. When women are substituted for men an office worked by three or four men will require four or five women, chiefly, it seems, because it is not considered safe to leave a woman alone at any time. (5) The provision of separate lavatories, etc., for women is expensive and often, for want of space, impracticable. The last reason, more perhaps than any other, has militated against the immediate employment of women in provincial offices generally.

It is to be regretted that the Post-office authorities by no means offer facilities for the registration, or at all events for the publication, of facts regarding sexual differences in capacity. Now that the employment of women is becoming so widespread this question becomes one of considerable general interest and importance. Instead of discouraging such inquiries (which need not involve the publication of any facts it is for any reason desirable to withhold) a post-office official, whose sole duty it would be to obtain returns regarding such sexual differences, and to put them into statistical shape, would be performing a useful public duty. His reports would give, in a reliable and well-supported form, valuable indications as to the advantageousness of employing men or women in a variety of occupations.

Mr. Sidney Webb, who has studied some of the points touched on in this section, although from an economic rather than a psychological standpoint, reaches the following conclusions :—
" The attraction to the employer of women's labour is often less

in its actual cheapness than in its 'docility' and want of combination. 'Women strike less,' says one. A similar fact is
recorded as to the employment of the negro in manufacturing
industries in the 'New South' (United States). . . . I find it
difficult to draw any general conclusion from the foregoing
facts. But they suggest to me that the frequent inferiority of
women's earnings in manual work is due, in the main, to a
general but not invariable inferiority of productive power,
usually in quantity, sometimes in quality, and nearly always in
nett advantageousness to the employer. . . . The problem of
the inequality of wages is one of great plurality of causes and
intermixture of effects, and one might not improbably find that,
as is often the case, there is no special women's question
in the matter." (Sidney Webb, "Alleged Differences in the
Wages," etc., *Economic Journal*, 1891.)

It is interesting to find that the experience of the Post-office
in England is confirmed by the experience of other European
countries. This question has been studied by Mr. C. H.
Garland, Secretary of the Postal Telegraph Clerks' Association,
in a paper on "Women as Telegraphists," in the *Economic
Journal* (June 1901). He finds that in 35 of the 47 Administrations of the Postal Union women are employed or have been
employed as telegraphists. Belgium no longer receives women
into the telegraph service, and female telegraphists are a mori-
bund class in Germany. The Austrian Administration finds that
women are not inferior to men in all occupations more or less
mechanical, but that they are not satisfactory in the higher
grades, not having sufficient energy to obtain authority over
other persons, so that it is always necessary to entrust the
surveillance of women to men. In France, as in England, it is
found that in replacing a male by a female staff the number must
be considerably increased, and sick-leave is much greater in the
case of women. Retirement is not compulsory on marriage, but
it is found that marriage decreases their interest and energy in
their work; and although it is considered that the employment
of women is on the whole satisfactory when the work is regular
and equal, their technical knowledge is found to be defective,
they are less rapid than men, and more liable to become confused. Germany is undecided in its opinion, and in the meanwhile no more are being admitted into the service. Belgium
has come to the conclusion that, although women are apt and
intelligent in telegraph work, their employment is not compatible
with the highest efficiency, as they could not work at high pressure or meet sudden emergencies, and were more frequently ill.
In Holland they are found quicker to tire than men, and the
sexual ratio of sick absence is as 1 to 2 or even 3. Sweden
and Denmark in the north and Roumania in the south alike
speak of the lack of endurance. In Italy, women are appointed

to high-grade posts in the service after passing examination in a variety of subjects, but they are found to lack authority over their staff, to be wanting in judgment and decision, and unable to apply effectively the technical knowledge they possess. The characteristics thus revealed resemble those found in England, but it must be added that on the whole English women telegraphists seem to compare favourably with their Continental sisters. Possibly on account of the greater freedom of English life they seem to show more business capacity, nor are there any complaints in the English service of the inability of women to exercise supervision over their own sex, though the discipline in the female sections is less severe and mechanical, and the higher duties of organisation and management are always in the hands of a male superintendent. Mr. Garland mentions that one of the divisions of the Central Telegraph Office in which practically all classes of ordinary telegraphic work are performed, and in which the wires are of considerable import-ance, is staffed and supervised entirely by women under the further surveillance of a man. "It is admitted that the staff is a picked one, but the results obtained are stated to compare even to the disadvantage of the average male division."

Abstract Thought.—It is easier to compare the higher and more exceptional intellectual qualities of men and women than their average mental qualities, although in both cases we have the same difficulty —which cannot at present be definitely resolved— in determining precisely the boundary between organic constitution and education.

It is doubtless in accordance with what Buckle termed the special deductive bent of their mind that in science it has always been in the mathematical field that women have attained the highest amount of success.[1] This has been the case for some centuries past, and even to-day, when the biological sciences are so widely cultivated and are everywhere open to women, it would still appear that it is in the more mathematical regions of physics that they attain most success.

[1] Possibly there is some connection between this fact and the fact, which we may regard as unquestionable, that mathematicians tend to show more admiration for the intelligence of women than do men belonging to any other branch of science.

There is no such thing, however—one cannot too often repeat it—as pure rationality. The thought that we call abstract has its foundation in the organic and emotional character of the individual. Abstract thought in women seems usually, on the whole, to be marked by a certain docility and receptiveness. Even in trivial matters the average woman more easily accepts statements and opinions than a man, and in more serious matters she is prepared to die for a statement or an opinion, provided it is uttered with such authority and unction that her emotional nature is sufficiently thrilled. This is allied with woman's suggestibility, and it seems to have to some extent an organic basis, so that while the culture of the more abstract powers of thought may make it impossible to obey this instinct, there is still a struggle; or else the more purely rational method is attained—and often distorted in the attaining—by the complete suppression of the other elements. Professor Stanley Hall, in the course of a series of very careful and suggestive observations on children, remarks that "the normal child feels the heroism of the unaccountable instinct of self-sacrifice far earlier and more keenly than it can appreciate the sublimity of truth."[1] In this respect women remain children, and that they do seems to result from the organic facts of women's life.[2] I think we may agree that, as Burdach said long ago, "Women take truth as they find it, while men want to create truth." The latter method leads further, if only further into error. It is not simply that women are more ready than men to accept what is already accepted and what is

---

[1] "Children's Lies," *Am. Journal of Psychology*, January 1890.

[2] There are far more women than men who can say with Mrs. Besant : "Looking back to-day over my life I see that its key-note—through all the blunders and the blind mistakes and clumsy follies—has been this longing for sacrifice to something felt as greater than the self."—*Autobiography*, xiv. While the instinct of self-sacrifice is common among women it cannot be said that the appreciation of "the sublimity of truth" is a masculine characteristic in anything like a corresponding degree.

most in accordance with appearances[1]—and that it is inconceivable, for instance, that a woman should have devised the Copernican system—but they are less able than men to stand alone. It is difficult to recall examples of women who have patiently and slowly fought their way at once to perfection and to fame in the face of complete indifference, like, for instance, Balzac,—apart from the fact that a woman of talent is usually in more command of her means and able to reach a certain degree of success at an early period. It is still more difficult to recall a woman who for any abstract and intellectual end has fought her way to success through obloquy and contempt, or without reaching success, like a Roger Bacon or a Galileo, a Wagner or an Ibsen. Not only does the woman crave more for sympathy, but she has not the same sturdy independence. The hero of Ibsen's *Enemy of the People*, who had realised that the strongest man in the world is the man who stands most alone, could scarcely have been a woman. When a man is attacked by general paralysis he usually displays an extravagant degree of egoism and self-reliance; when a woman is the victim of the same disease it is not self-reliant egoism but extreme vanity which she displays. The disease liberates the tendencies that are latent in each—the man's to independence, the woman's to dependence, on the opinion of others. It must be added to this that

---

[1] The influence of education must here be taken into account; women are trained to accept conventional standards. Thus a careful investigation (inaugurated by Professor Stanley Hall) of many hundred American children as to their ideas of right and wrong showed that the answers of the girls differ from the boys in two marked ways; they more often name specific acts and nearly twice as often conventional ones, the former difference being most common in naming right, the latter in naming wrong things. Boys say it is wrong to steal, fight, kick, break windows, get drunk, stick pins into others, or to "sass," "cuss," shoot them, while girls are more apt to say it is wrong not to comb the hair, to get butter on the dress, climb trees, unfold the hands, cry, catch flies, etc.—*Pedagogical Seminary*, vol. i., 1891. p. 165.

what appears to be women's tendency to be vividly impressed by immediate facts, and to neglect those that are remote, is fatal to the philosophic thought which must see all things *sub specie æternitatis*. It is probably to such causes as these that we must attribute the fact that in the first rank of those who have devoted themselves to metaphysics there is not one woman, while in the second and third ranks, from Hypatia to Constance Naden, it is very hard to find women who occupy an honourable place.

It can scarcely be said that we have much warrant beyond her fame for assigning a high place to Hypatia. That she was of a curiously analytical and unemotional—to the ordinary masculine person it may even seem cynical—habit of mind is indicated by the untranslatable anecdote recorded by Suidas (though we cannot accept this as unquestionably authoritative): "Cum de auditoribus quidam eam deperiret, pannos mensibus fœdatos illi ostendisse dicitur et dixisse: 'Hoc quidem adamas, o adolescens'; et sic animum ejus sanasse." It is a curious fact, referred to by Lombroso and Ferrero (p. 171), that among the Greeks thirty-four women distinguished themselves in the Pythagorean school of philosophy, and scarcely three or four in any other school, only one among the Cynics. This is due, according to these writers, to the Pythagorean school being "a sort of company of Jesus, appealing to the emotions rather than the intelligence, a monastic association with rites possessing special moral aims and inculcating family virtues." That Constance Naden possessed in a high degree the purely metaphysical impulse there can be no doubt, although, whether in consequence of her early death or otherwise, she achieved no monument of philosophic thought. It is worth while to quote Herbert Spencer's estimate of her intellect and remarks on intellect in women generally (contained in a letter published in the newspapers a few years ago):—"Very generally receptivity and originality are not associated, but in her mind they appear to have been equally great. I can think of no woman, save George Eliot, in whom there has been this union of high philosophical capacity with extensive acquisition. Unquestionably her subtle intelligence would have done much in furtherance of rational thought, and her death has entailed a serious loss. While I say this, however, I cannot let pass the occasion for remarking that in her case, as in other cases, the mental powers so highly developed in a woman are in some measure abnormal, and involve a physiological cost which her feminine organisation will not bear without injury more or less profound."

Paul Lafitte (*Le Paradoxe de l'Égalité*, 1887, pp. 117 *et seq.*) has some observations on the differences in the higher mental qualities of men and women which are worth quoting, as they are much fairer and more judicious than such observations usually are. He remarks that in women the receptive faculties are most developed, and continues:—"When children of both sexes are educated together, it is the girls who are at the top during the first years; it is at that time above all a question of receiving impressions and keeping them, and we see every day that women by the vivacity of their impressions and their memory are superior to the men who surround them. To this facility in seizing and retaining facts must be added the taste for symmetry which seems innate in them; you will understand the aptitude which they always show for the study of geometry. In the same way at the examinations at the School of Medicine we may see young women shine in physiology or pathology; they have seized the series of facts with a clearness which strikes the examiners; but for the most part they are inferior in the clinical tests which bring other mental faculties into play. Generally speaking, a woman seems more touched by the fact than by the law, by the particular idea than by the general idea. If it is a question of pronouncing an opinion on a known individual, that of the man will perhaps be more exact in general outline; but if we pass to shades of character, the woman immediately has the advantage: a familiar gesture, a word employed more often than another, a wrinkle forming at certain moments, a look, a smile, all are noted by her, catalogued, and appreciated at their just value. The same differences are found in literary works: a woman's book, whether by Madame de Staël or George Eliot, is worth more in detail than as a whole. No one questions that women are superior to us in the epistolary style. Whence comes this superiority? We compose a letter as we would draw up a report, and write coldly: a woman, on the contrary, writes under the impression of the facts; she retraces them, leaving to each its own physiognomy, and naturally, without research or rhetoric, she finds life and movement at the tip of her pen. The habit of mind differs as the faculties differ; we are more interested in the relations of things than in the things themselves. La Bruyère, on more than one side, is a feminine genius; Descartes is the type of the masculine genius; it would have been possible for a woman to write the *Caractères*, but I doubt if any woman could ever remake the *Discours de la Methode*. In a word, there are equivalent faculties, but they are not the same: the woman's mind is more concrete, the man's more abstract."

It may be added that a certain number of women have attained eminence in mathematics, although none are associated with any great achievement. Thus Maria Lewen published a book of astronomical tables in the seventeenth century; the Marquise du Châtelet translated Newton's *Principia;* Sophie Germain was a highly gifted mathematician; Madame Lepaute contributed to her husband's work, and assisted Lalande; Maria Agnesi wrote a book on the Differential and Integral Calculus which has been highly praised by mathematicians; Laura Bassi was appointed to a professorial chair at Bologna; Miss Herschel was distinguished as an assistant to her brother; Mrs. Somerville obtained a wide reputation by her mathematical and general scientific abilities; and Sophie Kowalevsky possessed great mathematical powers, which obtained for her a professorial chair in Sweden. I take many of these facts from J. Boyer, "Les Femmes dans la Science" (with portraits), *Revue des Revues,* 15th September 1898; Mrs. G. C. Frankland, "Women and Science," *Nature,* 19th July 1894; and cf. D. Beale, *Reports issued by the Schools' Inquiry Commission on the Education of Girls* [no date], p. xiii. In this collection of Reports by highly competent inquirers will be found a number of interesting opinions on the mental capacities of women, as well as on the nature and results of their educational training.

Even within the philosophical field it appears that women have certain rather restricted tastes. Ladies' philosophers, according to the experience of a well-known West End bookseller, are Schopenhauer, Plato, Marcus Aurelius, Epictetus, and Renan.[1] That is to say, that women are attracted to the most concrete of all abstract thinkers, to the most poetic, to the most intimately personal, and above all to the most religious, for every one of these thinkers was saturated through and through with religious emotion.

Religion.—This leads us to inquire what part women have had in the creation of religions. No one will question women's aptitude for religion, whatever the organic basis of that aptitude may be: what part have women had within historical times in the making of religions?

In order to answer this question I have searched *A Dictionary of all Religions* published in the early part of the last century. It constitutes a fascinating but painful page in the history of humanity.

[1] *Westminster Gazette,* 13th May 1893.

Some record is here given of about 600 religious sects, and I find that of these only seven were founded by women. That is to say, that of all the great religious movements of the world nearly 99 in every 100 have received their primary impulse from men, however willing women may have been to follow. The seven sects in question are the Bourignonists, the Buchanists, the Philadelphians, the Southcottians, the Victims, the Universal Friends, and the Wilhelminians. (Some others could be added from more recent times, but it is not probable that the percentage would be greatly changed.) It is of some interest to determine the character of these sects, which are all of a more or less Christian tendency, and mostly arose within the last few centuries. Madame Bourignon was a native of Flanders, and so deformed that at birth there was some question of stifling her as a monster. She combined great intellectual power with a broad and tolerant mysticism—a combination by no means uncommon—inculcating reliance on inward impulses, the rejection of outward forms of worship, and acquiescence in the divine will. She was equally opposed to Catholicism and Protestantism, and her personality was greater than any movement she initiated. Mrs. Buchan, of Glasgow, belonged to a different type. She believed she was the woman spoken of in the Apocalypse (Rev. xii.), and that she could conduct her followers to heaven without dying, but she soon died and her sect with her. She was probably insane. The Philadelphians were a sect of mystics and universalists founded by Jane Leadley in the latter part of the seventeenth century. Her views in many respects resembled Madame Bourignon's, and the Philadelphian Society was a body of considerable importance, including many men of learning. Joanna Southcott and her delusions produced so great an impression at about the beginning of the last century that she is still well remembered. She was scarcely sane. The

Society of Victims was a curious body of ascetics founded by Madame Brehan in the eighteenth century; it was of somewhat crazy character, and appears to have had no elements of vitality. The Universal Friends were established by Jemima Wilkinson in America in the last century. She had a trance in early life, became inspired and able to work miracles, seceded from the Quakers, and founded a town called Jerusalem. She was an eloquent preacher, and is said to have been an ambitious and selfish woman who died very wealthy from the donations of her followers. The Wilhelminians were the disciples of Wilhelmina, a Bohemian woman of the thirteenth century. She believed that the Holy Ghost was incarnated in her anew, and she had the somewhat beautiful thought that while the blood of Jesus only saved devout Christians, through her there was salvation for Jews, Saracens, and unworthy Christians. On the whole, it can scarcely be said that this group of sects shows badly; they were mostly tolerant, with a strong tendency to mysticism and disregard of ritual and method, and with a very pronounced element of human charity. Still the curious fact emerges that while women usually form the larger body of followers in a religious movement, as well as the most reckless and devoted, they have initiated but few religious sects, and these have had little or no stability. Women have usually been content to accept whatever religion came to hand, and in their fervour they have lost the capacity for cold, clear-sighted organisation and attention to details. They can supply much of the living spiritual substance, if a man will supply the mould for it to flow into. The study of the Salvation Army, the most remarkable religious movement of recent times, is instructive from this point of view.

Women have played a very large part in Christianity from the first, though in early times it was an undistinguished part. As a rule women take but a small part in revolutions (although a large part in revolts which are of more hasty and temporary character), but an analysis of the mortuary epigraphs from the Catacombs of Rome, contained in De Rossi's works, *La Roma Sotterranea*, showed that 40 per cent. of them were of women. (Lombroso and Laschi, *Le Crime Politique*, 1892, tome ii. p. 10.) They doubtless played an equally large part in religion before Christianity arose. Among the *donaria*, or votive offerings of grateful Romans to the gods of healing, are found heads of every size and age; "some few," says Dr. Sambon, "are of bearded men, a large number of youths and children, but the great majority is of women of every age" (Luigi Sambon, "Donaria of Medical Interest," *Brit. Med. Jour.*, 20th July 1895).

If we ask what definite and permanent contributions to the structure of the Catholic Church have been made by its vast army of women followers, we may find a brief but authoritative answer by Cardinal Manning in his Preface to the translation of St. Catherine of Genoa's very beautiful little devotional work, the *Treatise on Purgatory:*—"Two of the greatest festivals of the Catholic Church had their origin in the illumination of humble and unlearned women. The Feast of Corpus Christi was the offspring of the devotion of the Blessed Juliana of Retinne; the Feast of the Sacred Heart of that of the Blessed Margaret Mary: to St. Catherine of Sienna our Lord vouchsafed the honour of calling back again the Sovereign Pontiff from the splendid banishment of Avignon to the throne of the Apostolic See; to St. Teresa the special gift of illumination, to teach the ways of union with Himself in prayer; to Blessed Angela of Foligno the eighteen degrees of compunction, and His own five poverties; and to St. Catherine of Genoa an insight and perception of the state of Purgatory, which seem like the utterances of one immersed in its expiation of love."

Politics.—It is somewhat remarkable that women have shown far less intellectual ability in the creation of religions than in the very different sphere of politics. More than sixty years ago Burdach remarked that women are probably more fitted for politics than men, and he instanced the large number of able queens.[1] J. S. Mill many years afterwards also made some remarks to the same effect in his *Subjection of Women.* Among all races and in all parts of the world women have ruled brilliantly and with perfect control over even the most fierce and

[1] *Physiologie*, tome i. p. 338.

turbulent hordes. Among many primitive races also all the diplomatic relations with foreign tribes are in the hands of women, and they have sometimes decided on peace or war. The game of politics seems to develop very feminine qualities in those who play at it, and it may be paying no excessive compliment to women to admit the justice of old Burdach's remarks. Whenever their education has been sufficiently sound and broad to enable them to free themselves from fads and sentimentalities, women probably possess in at least as high a degree as men the power of dealing with the practical questions of politics.

It cannot be said that in this chapter we have reached many definite results. A few careful experiments which need confirmation and extension, a certain number of observations on irregular masses of data, accumulated in the practical experiences of life, which have their value although they are open to varied misinterpretation—this is about all that experimental psychology has yet to show us in regard to the intellectual differences of men and women. Beyond that is mere speculation, founded, to what extent we cannot yet tell, on temporary social and educational differences.

CHAPTER IX.

METABOLISM.

THE BLOOD—RED CORPUSCLES MORE NUMEROUS IN MEN—
AMOUNT OF HÆMOGLOBIN GREATER IN MEN—SPECIFIC
GRAVITY HIGHER IN MEN—THE SEXUAL DIFFER-
ENCES IN THE BLOOD COINCIDE WITH THE
APPEARANCE OF PUBERTY—RISE IN THE SPECIFIC
GRAVITY OF THE BLOOD OF WOMAN IN OLD AGE—THE
PULSE-RATE—ALWAYS HIGHER IN SMALL THAN IN LARGE
ANIMALS—SEXUAL DIFFERENCES IN THE HUMAN AND
OTHER SPECIES—NOT NOTABLY GREATER THAN DIFFER-
ENCES IN SIZE WOULD LEAD US TO EXPECT.
RESPIRATION—VITAL CAPACITY MUCH GREATER IN MEN—
MEN PRODUCE MORE CARBONIC ACID—COSTAL RESPIRA-
TION OF WOMEN AND ABDOMINAL RESPIRATION OF MEN
—RECENT INVESTIGATIONS SHOWING THAT THIS SEXUAL
DIFFERENCE IS PURELY ARTIFICIAL—IT DOES NOT EXIST
AMONG SAVAGE WOMEN, NOR AMONG THOSE WHO DO
NOT WEAR CORSETS—THE ORIGIN OF CORSETS—THEIR
INFLUENCE ON THE ACTIVITY OF WOMEN—DEVELOP-
MENT OF CHEST—ITS RELATION TO CONSUMPTION—
TEMPERATURE—NO SEXUAL DIFFERENCE YET CLEARLY
SHOWN.
EXCRETION—URINE PROBABLY RELATIVELY GREATER IN
AMOUNT IN WOMEN, AND UREA RELATIVELY LESS—
SPECIAL INFLUENCES AFFECTING WOMEN.
SUSCEPTIBILITY TO POISONS—SEXUAL DIFFERENCES IN THE
SELECTIVE ACTION OF POISONS ON DIFFERENT ORGANS
—ARSENIC—OPIUM—MERCURY—SPECIAL SEXUAL SUS-
CEPTIBILITIES TO POISONS — CHLOROFORM — LEAD —
ALCOHOL THE BEST EXAMPLE OF SEXUAL SELECTIVE

ACTION ON NERVOUS SYSTEM—TENDS TO ATTACK THE
BRAIN IN MEN, THE SPINAL CORD IN WOMEN.
HAIR AND PIGMENTATION—SEXUAL DIFFERENCES IN DIS-
TRIBUTION, ETC., OF HAIR—THE EYES AND PROBABLY
HAIR ARE DARKER IN WOMEN—POSSIBLE ADVANTAGES
OF PIGMENTATION.

THE BLOOD.

BY "metabolism" we mean the intimate vital process
—so far as chemistry and physics can reveal it—which
is for ever changing and renewing the tissues of the
body. When we reach the blood we come close to
the central metabolic process of life, for it is the
blood which is the direct source of the material for
this process. Except such elementary creatures as
the Protozoa, all animals possess blood, though
with great individual varieties with regard to constituents, character, and colour. Roughly speaking, the blood of vertebrates consists of three
elements, the plasma or fluid portion, the white corpuscles, and the red corpuscles. Of these, the plasma
is the most primitive, and the red corpuscles the latest
to appear in the course of evolution. In the human
species during childhood we naturally find that there
are fewer red corpuscles than in adult age, and also
that the hæmoglobin (the oxygen-carrying element in
the red corpuscles) is less in amount, while the white
corpuscles are more abundant than in later life
(Hayem).

Denis, and afterwards Lecanu, were the first to
draw attention to the fact that there are any sexual
differences in the blood; and the results of these investigators, confirmed at a somewhat later period by
Becquerel and Rodier, showed that the blood of men
contains less water and more red corpuscles, and is
consequently of a higher specific gravity, than that
of women; these statements have since often been
demonstrated.

There appears to be no evidence showing conclusively that the white corpuscles are more or less numerous in women than in men,[1] but all physiological chemists are agreed that there are more red corpuscles in the male than in the female, not only in man, but also in many lower animals.

Cadet found in men on an average 5,200,000 red corpuscles to 4,900,000 in women, and Korniloff, using a different method—Vierordt's spectroscope—found a similar slight difference. (See Hayem's great work, *Du Sang*, Paris, 1889, pp. 184 *et seq.*) Welcker gives the number of red blood corpuscles per c. mm. as 5,000,000 in men, 4,500,000 in women; or, otherwise expressed, as 100 to 90. Laache, in an analysis of sixty cases, has found the mean to be 4,970,000 per c. mm. for men, and 4,430,000 per c. mm. for women. Macphail finds 5,075,000 for healthy men, and 4,676,000 for healthy women. (Macphail, Art. on "Blood of the Insane" in *Dict. Psych. Med.*) Ehrmann and Siegel found 5,560,000 in men to 5,000,000 in women; Otto, 4,990,000 in men to 4,580,000 in women. During menstruation, as Gowers, Stockman, and others have found, there is a reduction to the extent of from 10 to 20 per cent.

It is, however, by the amount of hæmoglobin that we more accurately measure the functional power of the blood. Leichtenstern states that women from the ages of eleven to fifty average 8 per cent. less hæmoglobin than men.[2] According to M'Kendrick, there is 14.5 per cent. hæmoglobin in man's blood, 13.3 per cent. in woman's; according to Preyer, it is 22 to 15 per cent. in man, 11 to 13 per cent. in woman; during pregnancy the amount of hæmoglobin is only about 9 to 12 per cent. Bunge has suggested that a storage of the iron in hæmoglobin takes place in the maternal organs even before the first conception, in readiness for the supply of the fœtus through the placental circulation, and he has supported this

[1] Robin asserted that they are more numerous in women; Hayem has denied it. Dilution of the blood tends, however, in general to increase of the white cells, as has been shown by, for instance, Beard and Wilcox, "Studies in the Metabolism of the Body Fluids," *Brit. Med. Jour.*, 13th November 1897.

[2] *Untersuchungen über den Hämoglobingehalt des Blutes*, Leipzig, 1878.

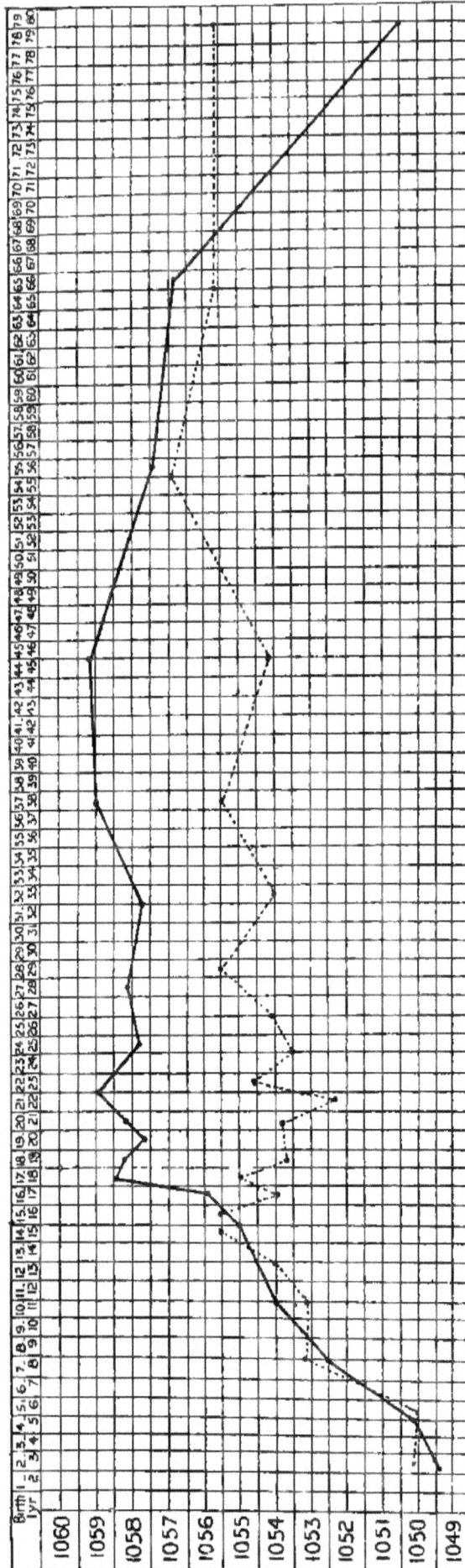

CURVE OF THE SPECIFIC GRAVITY OF THE BLOOD THROUGHOUT LIFE. ——— MALES; ·········· FEMALES. (*Lloyd Jones.*)

position by showing that young animals contain a much greater amount of iron than adult animals. In harmony with these observations are the results of Friedjung, who found that human milk contains a small but steady amount of iron, not diminishing in the course of nursing; there is less iron in the milk of mothers of mature age, and its diminution is liable to produce derangement of nourishment in the infant. We may say, as Lloyd Jones expresses it, that this is part of a general storing up of tissue food, partly as fat, partly as proteids, and a general reduction of katabolic energy.

A convenient and widely-used method for estimating the quality of the blood is by obtaining its specific gravity. It is well recognised that the specific gravity of the blood is higher in men than in women, and that it falls in pregnancy (though very slightly), after exercise, and after taking food (especially if much water is drunk). In this country the specific gravity of the blood has been very carefully investigated with interesting results by Dr. Lloyd Jones.[1] He has taken the specific gravity of the blood (by Roy's method) of over fifteen hundred persons, in ordinary health, of both sexes and all ages, from birth to over ninety. The specific gravity, Lloyd Jones has found, is at its height at birth, and although generally lower in women than in men, it is about the same in both sexes before the fifteenth year, and is higher in old women than in old men.

In males the specific gravity is about 1066 at birth, and falls during the subsequent two years, being about 1050 in the third year; thence it rises till about seventeen years of age, when it is about 1058. It remains at this height during middle life, and falls slightly in old age.

In females the specific gravity, starting at about 1066 at birth, falls in infancy, as in males, to about 1049 in the third year. Thence it rises till the fourteenth year, when it is 1055.5. Between seventeen and forty-five years of age it is lower than at the age of fourteen, and is about three degrees lower than in men.

Lloyd Jones also points out that the specific gravity of the blood varies with individual constitution; it is lower in persons with light than with dark hair, eyes, and complexion. He suggests that this difference is perhaps due to the incomplete fusion of British races, and that the more watery blood may belong to the Saxon and Scandinavian elements. "By the appearance of an individual, noting the age and sex and the

---

[1] E. Lloyd Jones, "On the Variations in the Specific Gravity of the Blood in Health," *Journal of Physiology*, 1887; "Further Observations on the Specific Gravity of the Blood," September 1891. The latter paper is a lengthy and important monograph. Also the same author's "Preliminary Report on the Causes of Chlorosis," *Brit. Med. Journal*, 23rd Sept. 1893.

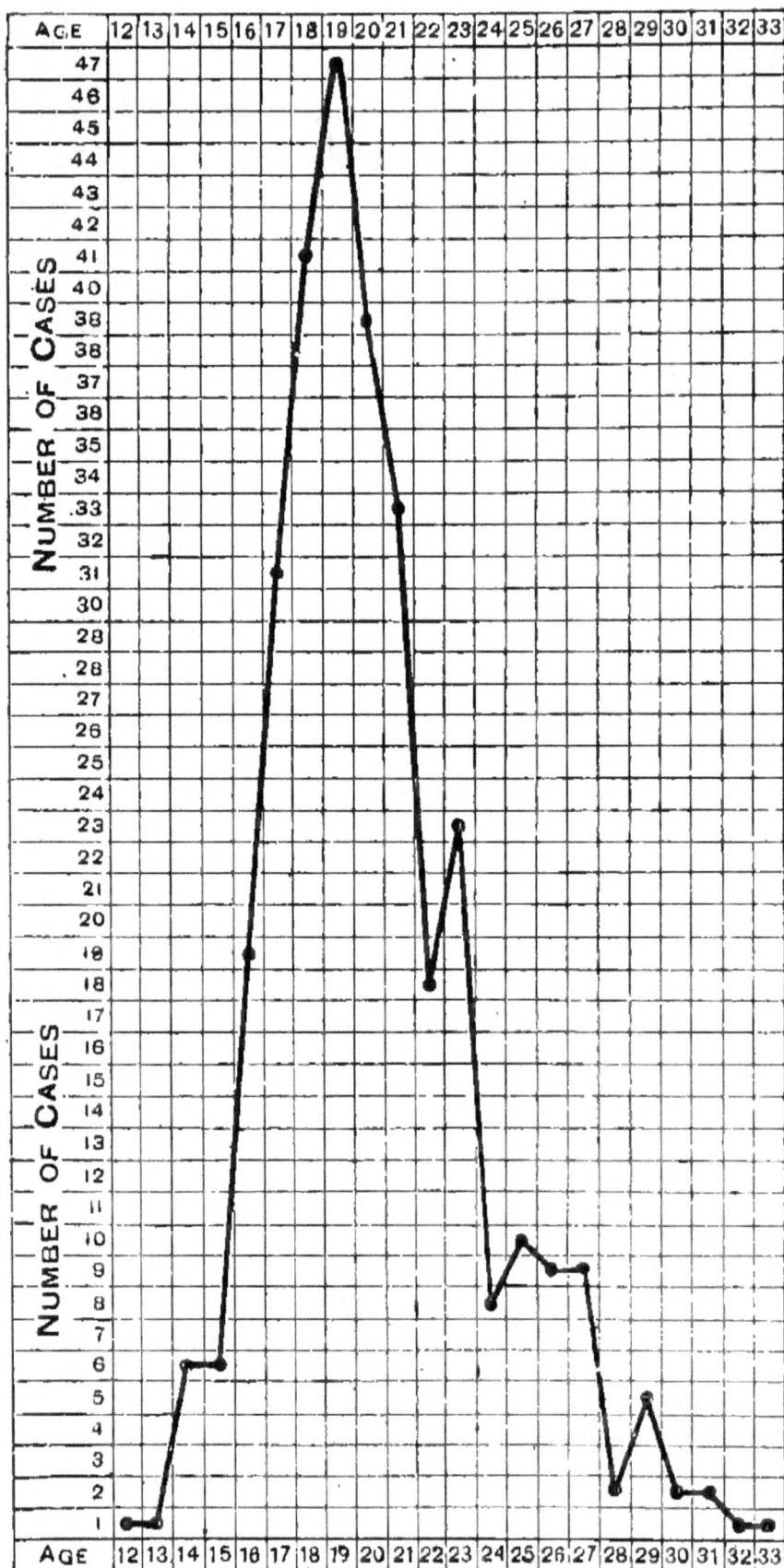

AGE FREQUENCY IN 314 CASES OF CHLOROSIS.
(*Byrom Bramwell.*)

colour of the iris, hair, and complexion, one can form a fairly accurate estimate of what the specific gravity of his or her blood ought to be."

Lloyd Jones has recently made the interesting discovery that, notwithstanding the general low specific gravity of the blood in women, the plasma in women has a somewhat higher sp. gr. than in men, rising at puberty, while in men it remains stationary.

It will thus be seen that it is at puberty the sexual difference becomes marked. The appearance of menstruation coincides with low specific gravity, and the periodical recurrence of menstruation appears to produce a slight fall in the specific gravity. A very noteworthy sexual difference is the great range in the specific gravity of the blood, consonantly with health, in girls from the ages of fifteen to twenty-two; and the lower limit during this period falls to a very low point. It is the age of anæmia, and Dr. Lloyd Jones makes the very reasonable suggestion that chlorosis, which is essentially a disease of young women, is but an exaggeration of a condition which is physiological at this age. (See chart on opposite page.)

In old women the specific gravity rises, and Dr. Lloyd Jones suggests that this rise may be a factor in the greater longevity of women. It is certain that good physique is associated with high specific gravity of the blood, and poor physique with a low specific gravity; the blood of Cambridge undergraduates is of very high specific gravity; the blood of workhouse boys of very low specific gravity.

This difference in the quality of the blood of men and women is fundamental, and its importance cannot be exaggerated; although it is possible that its significance may be to some extent neutralised by other factors.

Pulse-rate.—The rapidity of the heart's action varies very greatly among animals, the heart beating more slowly in proportion to the animal's greater size, but the rule not being perfectly correct if we compare, for example, birds with mammals. The pulse-rate usually preserves with the respiration-rate a relation of about 4 to 1. In birds the pulse-rate is very rapid; in the mammalian series we find, for instance, that the pulse-rate of the mouse is 120, that of the dog 75, of the horse 42, of the elephant 28. In the same species there are differences which are clearly associated with the bulk of the organism. Large vigorous races of dogs have a slower pulse than smaller races. Dr. Seymour Taylor remarks that he has taken the pulse-rate of gigantic muscular men employed in quarrying and other laborious occupations, men of the Cumberland fells, accustomed to violent struggles in the wrestling arena but of naturally ponderous, deliberate nature, and has been surprised to find that their hearts, when at rest and in perfect health, have gone through but 60 cycles in the course of a minute, in one case only 40.[1] There are variations among human races which seem to be accounted for by considerations of size, and not, as Delaunay[2] tried to show, by a connection between inferiority and a quick pulse: thus if we take 72, which is Béclard's standard for the Frenchman, the pulse-rate of the small-bodied Javanese is said to be as high as 84, that of the Chinese and Nicobar Islanders 77, while Jousset states that among Asiatics and Africans generally the pulse-rate varies between 77 and 86. Among Bashkirs, however, whose average height was not more than mm. 1661, Weissenberg found that the average pulse-rate was 63.

Among nearly all animals the heart of the male beats more slowly than that of the female. In some animals, if we are to accept observations that are probably not very reliable, the differences are considerable: the lion's pulse-rate is 40 (Dubois), the lioness's 68 (Colin); the bull's 46, the heifer's 56

---

[1] "Remarks on the Slow Heart," *Lancet*, June 6th, 1891.

[2] See his interesting discussion of the various influences which modify the pulse, *Études de Biologie Comparée*, 2me Partie, "Physiologie."

(Girard); the ram's 68, the sheep's 80.[1] In the human female there is a slighter but still well-marked difference. According to Frankenhausen, the pulse-rate of the male before birth is 124 to 147, of the female 135 to 154. Depaul, from an examination of 41 male and 29 female fœtuses during pregnancy, found that the average pulse-rate in the former is 139, in the latter 142. At birth and for some time later the two sexes remain very near together; in old age the pulse-rate of women seems to have a greater tendency to increase than that of men. Guy's table of the pulse-rate, according to sex and age, is as follows:—[2]

Age.	Male.	Female.
2- 7 years	97	98
8-14 ,,	84	94
14-21 .,	76	82
21-28 ,,	73	80
28-35 ,,	70	78
35-42 ,,	68	78
42-49 ,,	70	77
49-56 ,,	67	76
56-63 .,	68	77
63-70 ,,	70	78
70-77 ,,	67	81
77-84 ,,	71	82

The observations of Gilbert on school children in Iowa tend to show that the pulse is not at all ages slower in boys than in girls. He found that at six the boys' pulse is slower; from then to eleven, however, faster than that of the girls; between thirteen and fourteen faster; and again slower from sixteen onwards. There appeared to be an acceleration in both sexes at puberty, more marked in boys.[3] On

[1] Delaunay, Études, etc., p. 47.
[2] Todd's Cyclopædia of Anatomy and Physiology, p. 181, and Guy's Hospital Reports, vols. iii. and iv. See also Raseri, Arch. per l'Antrop., 1880, pp. 46 et seq.
[3] Studies in Psychology Univ. of Iowa, vol. i., 1897, p. 32.

the whole, we may say with M'Kendrick, that, at all events in Northern Europe, 72 is the usual pulse-rate in men, 80 in women; other observers give the average difference as somewhat greater; thus, according to Hardy and Béhier, women show 10 to 14 more pulsations a minute than men. Quetelet's figures (absolutely rather lower than Guy's), giving a rather greater sexual difference for early manhood and womanhood, a rather less difference for adult age, produce the same average difference as Guy's. Accepting, therefore, Guy's careful figures, we see that the average pulse-rate of civilised women is the same as that of boys about the age of puberty. It cannot be said that this difference is very notably greater than the general physical proportions of the sexes would lead us to expect.

RESPIRATION.

It is well recognised that the " vital capacity," as the breathing power indicated by the spirometer is commonly called, is decidedly less in women than in men. Even during that stage of the evolution of puberty when the girl is heavier and taller than the boy, she is still, as Pagliani and others have shown, very markedly inferior in vital capacity as well as in muscular force. Gilbert found, by the examination of several thousand school children, at New Haven and at Iowa,[1] between the ages of six and nineteen, that the boys were throughout superior in lung capacity; the difference was slight until the age of twelve, but while the girls had almost reached their maximum lung-capacity at that age, it was not until after the age of thirteen that the period of most rapid increase even began in boys. Among the Iowa children, who were better developed than those at New Haven, it is noteworthy that not only was the lung-capacity

[1] J. A. Gilbert, *Studies from the Yale Psychological Laboratory*, 1894, p. 75; *ib., Iowa University Studies*, 1897, p. 23.

greater in both sexes, but that the initial difference between the sexes was less. In adult age, when there is the same height and circumference of chest,

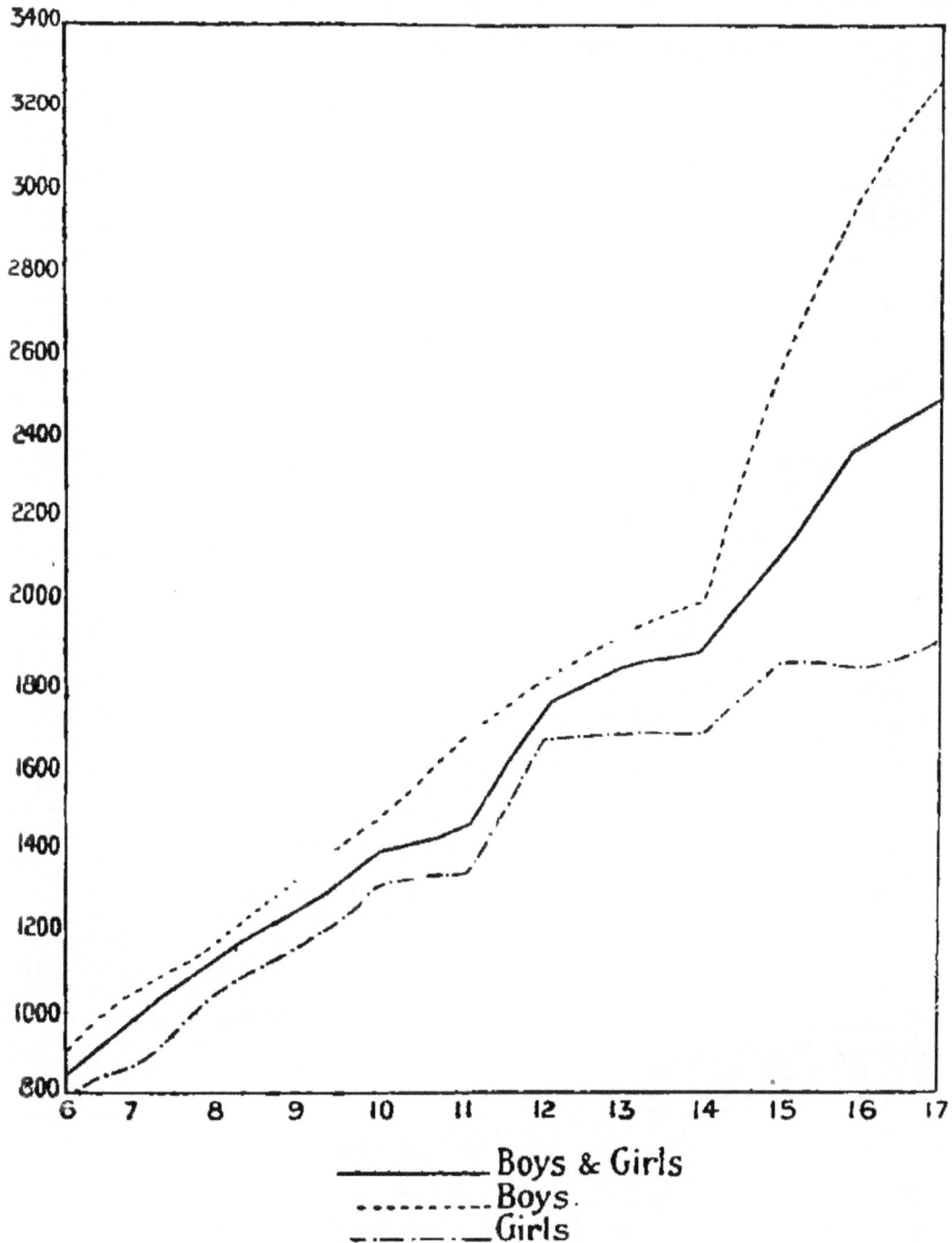

LUNG CAPACITY OF NEW HAVEN CHILDREN. (*Gilbert.*)

the ratio is 10 to 7 (Halliburton). The vital capacity of a man 1½ metres in height is usually 2350 c. cm.; in a woman of the same height, 2000 c. cm. (M'Kendrick). The vital capacity is 3 litres in women to 3½ in men, at equal height the volume expired being 700 c. cm. less in women. According to Arnold, for an increase in height of 25 centimetres, there is in men an increase in vital capacity of 150 c. cm., in women of only 130 c. cm. (Delaunay). The investigations of the British Association have shown that in England in males the mid breathing capacity is 217 c. ins., in females about 132 c. ins., the maximum difference being at the ages of 20-40, after which there is a regular decrease in the breathing capacity of men, but less falling off in that of women.

The number of respirations at birth is 44 per minute, and gradually decreases to 18 in the adult, being very slightly higher in women than in men (Quetelet). Size has much to do with the number of respirations in every zoological group; thus the rhinoceros has 6 respirations a minute, the rat 210. This matter has been studied in recent years by Richet,[1] who argues that it is one of the greatest laws of comparative physiology that "all the functions in their activity and in their intensity are determined by the size of the animal." According to Sibson, the ratio of inspiration to expiration in male adults is 6 to 7; in women, children, and old persons, 6 to 8 or 9; other observers give rather different results.

Men produce more carbonic acid than women. According to Andral and Gavarret, the amount of carbon burnt per hour is, from eight to fifteen years of age, in the boy 7 gr. 8, in the girl 6 gr. 4; from sixteen to thirty, in the man 11 gr. 2, in the woman 6 gr. 4; that is to say, the amount consumed in man rises at puberty to nearly double that consumed in woman. There is an increase in women during pregnancy, and also after the cessation of the menses. Energetic people excrete more than less active people of the same weight, and, relatively, a child gives off twice as much as an adult.

[1] *La Chaleur Animale.*

One result of this marked sexual difference is that women have a less keen need of air. This was noted by Burdach, who remarked that it began at birth. It appears that when both men and women are exposed to charcoal fumes, women, having less need of oxygen, possess a greater chance of surviving. In the process of salt-making, according to Mr. S. Webb, it is found that women can work better than men in the heat of stoves. The same result has been alleged to follow when the privation of oxygen is due to extreme altitude, so that women can live at heights where men would soon fall ill (Delaunay). It is possibly in part owing to this cause that women criminals have survived hanging much more frequently than men, from the time of Tiretta de Balsham, who was pardoned by Henry III. in 1264 because she had survived hanging, onwards; sometimes they have revived from the jolting of the cart on being conveyed from the gallows, and at other times by the skill of surgeons to whom the body had been given for anatomical purposes; Sir William Petty acquired popular fame by thus restoring to life a woman who soon afterwards married and lived for fifteen years.

During normal respiration in civilised races, when the individual is awake, man's respiration is *diaphragmatic* or *abdominal*, woman's is *costal*, the chest chiefly moving. The cause of this apparent sexual difference was at one time much disputed. Boerhaave noticed the difference of type in male and female infants; this has not, however, been confirmed by later investigators. It is now, as Dr. Ballantyne remarks,[1] " usually admitted that respiration is chiefly abdominal in type during the first three years of life." The diaphragm is thus the most important respiratory muscle in the infant as well as in the adult male, or to an even greater extent. The characteristic costal

---

[1] *Introduction to Diseases of Infancy*, p. 170. It is not, however, universally admitted. Depaul, Sergi, and others take for granted that children's respiration is costal.

breathing of women begins, according to Sibson, about the tenth year of life. Sibson, as well as Walshe and other investigators, attributed its appearance to the use of corsets and similar external impediments. Jonathan Hutchinson studied the matter carefully,[1] and came to the conclusion that the difference of breathing was not due to the restraints of clothing, for he found costal breathing in young girls who had never worn tight-fitting clothes. He argued that it was a natural adaptation to the child-bearing function in women. Hutchinson's investigations were for many years accepted as final; it became at least necessary, as Rosenthal pointed out, to admit that the costal breathing of women had become fixed by heredity into a secondary sexual character.

During the last few years, however, some fresh series of investigations, on a wider basis and with more accurate methods, have changed the accepted aspect of the matter. At the Birmingham meeting of the British Medical Association in 1890, Dr. Wilberforce Smith read a paper concerning some investigations he had made "On the Alleged Difference between Male and Female Respiratory Movements."[2] Using Burdon Sanderson's stethograph in a modified form, Dr. Smith took tracings of about fifty persons at the anterior middle line, over (1) sternum, (2) liver below ensiform cartilage, (3) just above navel, (4) just below navel, (5) midway between navel and pubes. The dress was entirely loosened; and it was rightly regarded as of considerable importance to keep the subject of the experiment ignorant of its object. It was found that at the sternal level of the chest in both sexes there was free respiratory movement, and also that over the liver there was free and regular movement in both sexes; just above

---

[1] Todd and Bowman, *Cyclopædia of Anat. and Phys.*, Art. "Thorax."

[2] Published in the *Brit. Med. Journal*, 11th Oct. 1890.

the navel the results were variable, and between the navel and pubes in many cases there was no respiratory movement. The most characteristic differences occurred just below the navel: among the men a principal group showed free movement, while a smaller group, having soft abdominal walls, only showed slight movement; among the women, habitually dressed and corseted in the usual manner, a large group showed excessive diminution or entire abolition of movement, while a smaller group of young and muscular women, wearing corsets, retained free movement; among women habitually wearing no corsets, a large group showed free movement in no degree less marked than among males, and in at least one case actually freer than among most males, and a smaller group of non-corseted women, having soft abdominal walls, showed only slight movement. Dr. Smith also independently examined nine ayahs; they all wore Oriental dress and had all borne more than one child. Without exception they exhibited respiratory movement below the navel not less free than in average English men.

As a result of his investigations, Dr. Wilberforce Smith concluded "that the tracings exhibited tended to invalidate the routine physiological teaching that there is a natural difference in the respiratory movements of the sexes, and they tended to confirm the belief of Sibson that the alleged difference is chiefly or wholly due to the effects of woman's conventional dress." Professor Cunningham, after the paper was read, remarked that these physiological experiments confirmed his own views, founded on anatomical grounds, that there ought to be no essential difference in respiratory movements in man and woman. Charpy, I may add, had also previously come to the conclusion, from extensive anatomical investigations, that up to the age of 15 boys and girls have identical chests, and that the thoracic type of breathing is only found in women of at least 25 years of age who bear on their viscera, especially the liver, signs of deformation produced by tight clothing.[1]

Dr. Smith made the following supplementary remarks in a private letter (5th Oct. 1892):—"I might have added in 1890 that the cases of which I had obtained graphic record were preceded by daily observation for many years without such record. They have been followed by similar daily observation ever since, and are, I have no doubt, founded on unalterable truth.

"The only fact of interest I have to add is, that so far from pregnancy affording a reason for a different mode of respiration, it is associated with marked abdominal respiratory movements. I take it that the comparatively firm mass of the gravid uterus, like the liver, readily conveys movements of the diaphragm to the surface.

"The same difficulty occasionally occurs in men where the action of the diaphragm is impeded by an enlarged stomach, the result of a recent meal, or undue corpulence."

I may here add that Mr. Lennox Browne, from another point of view, had reached the same conclusion that there are no sexual differences in respiration. He wrote in a private letter: "It is only where the corset confines the lower ribs or in cases of pregnancy or abdominal tumours that diaphragmatic breathing is impaired, and that costal breathing is resorted to."

Simultaneously with the publication of Dr. Smith's investigations, additional evidence on the same point from America was published in a paper by Professor H. Sewall (Michigan University) and Myra Pollard.[1] Some original observations were here given by Dr. Mays, of Philadelphia, made by means of the graphical method on the respiratory movements of female descendants of an uncivilised race. He writes:—" In all I examined the movements of 82 chests, and in each case took an abdominal and a costal tracing. The girls were partly pure and partly mixed with white blood, and their ages ranged from between ten and twenty years. Thus there were 33 full-blooded Indians, 5 one-fourth, 35 one-half, and 2 were three-

[1] A. Charpy, "L'Angle Xiphoïdien," *Revue d'Anthropologie,* 1884.
[2] "On the Relations of Diaphragmatic and Costal Respiration, with particular reference to Phonation," *Journal of Physiology,* 1890, No. 3.

fourths white; 75 showed a decided abdominal type of breathing, 3 a costal type, and in 3 both were about even. Those who showed the costal type, or divergence from the abdominal type, came from the more civilised tribes, like the Mohawks and Chippewas, and were either one-half or three-fourths white; while in no single instance did a full-blooded Indian girl possess this type of breathing." Dr. J. H. Kellogg of Michigan supplied the authors of this paper with unpublished observations (made with a Marey's stethograph and rotating cylinder) to the same effect. He wrote:—" I observed the breathing of 20 Chinese women and the same number of Indian women, and I found the abdominal type very marked in every case. The tracings given by the Chinese women were not like those of robust men, but were identical with those from men of sedentary habits. . . . Of the Indian women 14 were of the Yuma tribe, the most primitive Indians in the United States. . . . The majority of them still wear their bark dresses; the only garment in addition to this is a long strip of red cloth thrown over the shoulders and folded about the body. . . . The waist is not restrained in the slightest degree. In these women the abdominal movements were 4 to 6 times as great as the costal movements. I examined several of the Cherokee and Chickesaw women in the Indian Territory. These women had all worn civilised dress, and some of them had worn corsets. Those who had worn corsets and tight dresses gave tracings like civilised women; those who had worn only loose dress gave normal tracings. I also found a few civilised women who had never worn corsets or tight bands, and obtained from them tracings like those from the Chinese and Yuma women."

Dr. Kellogg has somewhat more recently made, and caused to be made, various series of observations on women in different parts of the world which confirm and extend these conclusions. (" The Value of Exercise," *Trans. Am. Ass. Obstetricains*, vol.

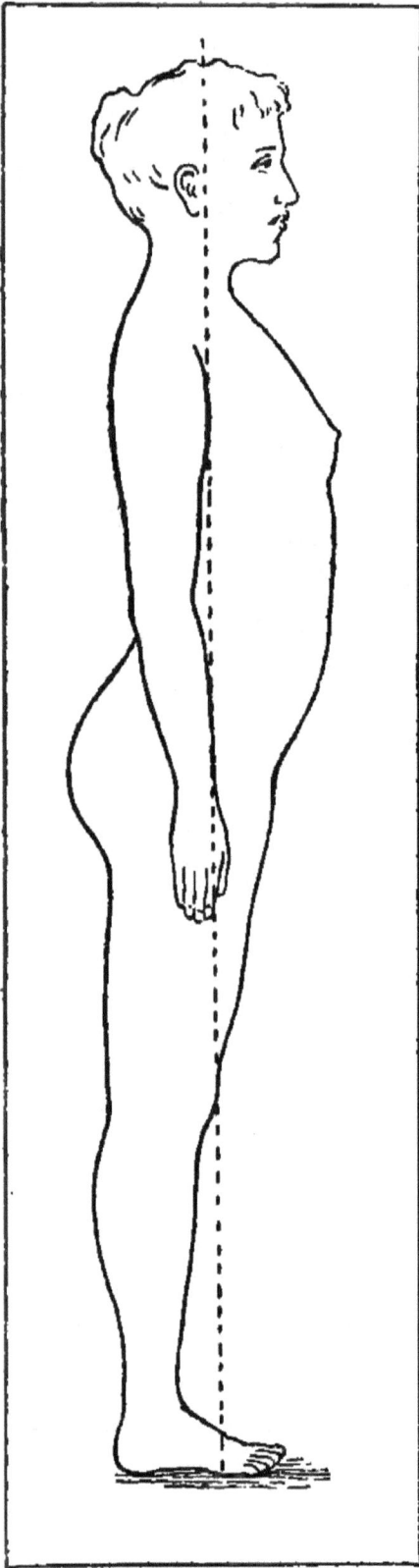

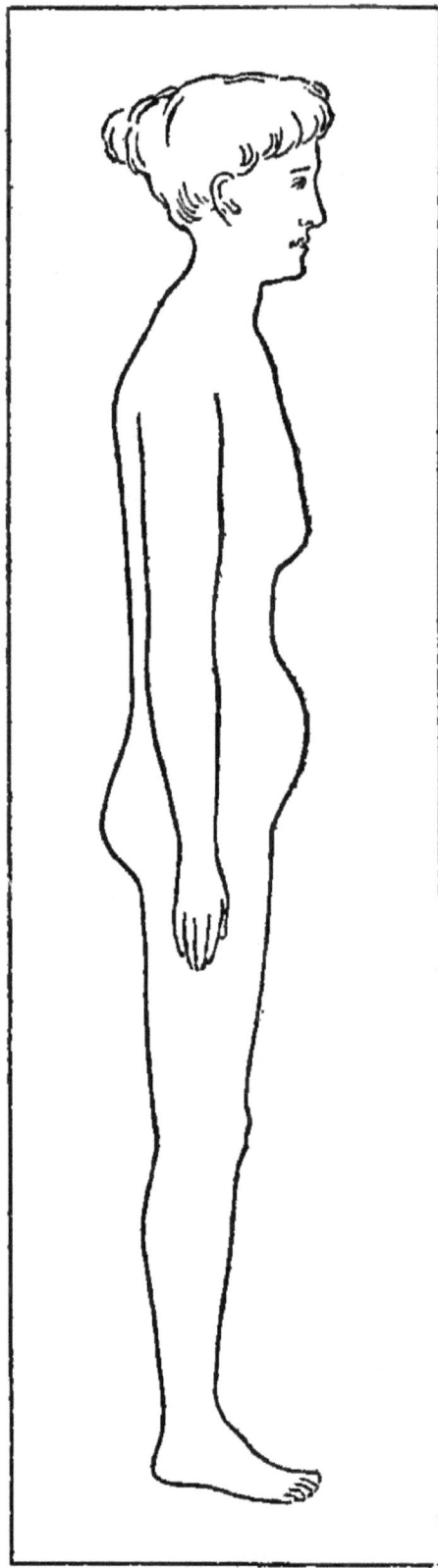

GERMAN PEASANT WOMAN.   AMERICAN WOMAN.

(After Kellogg.)

iii., 1891, and an interesting pamphlet on *The Influence of Dress*, both fully illustrated.) The two accompanying figures are reproduced by Dr. Kellogg's permission. One represents a German peasant woman, aged 29, who had never been trained in gymnastics, but who had been accustomed to carry heavy weights on her head up to the age of 20; she shows the natural healthful female form. The other figure is that of an ordinary American woman of the same age, who wore the ordinary civilised dress and took little exercise. When in England Dr. Kellogg went to the "black country" to study the women nail-makers and brick-makers, and found among them some of the best developed women he had ever seen. He ascertained also that they are extremely healthy.

It may be mentioned that Hultkrantz, of Upsala, endeavouring to avoid the possible fallacies of external measurement in estimating the influence of the diaphragm in respiration, introduced an elastic ball into the stomach and then inflated it. His experiments were performed on too small a number of persons to lead to any general conclusions, but he was able to demonstrate the lesser diaphragmatic movement in women, and also to show that pressure by a band in men produced lessened diaphragmatic movement. ("Ueber die respiratorischen Bewegungen des menschlichen Zwerchfells," *Skandinavisches Archiv für Physiologie*, 1890, heft i.)

The evidence clearly points to the conclusion that the sexual differences in respiration found among civilised races are not natural secondary sexual characters, but are merely the result of the artificial constrictions of the dress usually worn by women.

It would be interesting to trace the origin and development of the modern waist in women. The Greeks of the finest period knew nothing of it, but during the period of decadence women began to compress the body with the apparent object of emphasising the sexual attraction of a conspicuously large pelvis. Hippocrates vigorously denounced the women of Cos for constricting the waist with a girdle. Among the Romans, who adopted this practice from the depraved Greeks, Martial often alludes to the small waists of the women of his time, and Galen speaks much in the same way as a modern physician regarding the evils of tight-lacing. Since then matters have changed but very slightly. The apparent development of the pelvis has been further artificially exaggerated by that contrivance which in Elizabethan times was called a "bum-roll," and more recently a "bustle." The tightening of the waist does not merely emphasise the pelvic sexual characters; it also emphasises the not less important thoracic sexual characters; as Dr. Louis Robinson expresses it (in a private letter):—" I think it very likely one of the reasons (and there must be strong ones) for the persistent habit of tightening up the belly-girth among Christian damsels is that such constriction renders the breathing thoracic, and so advertises the alluring bosom by keeping it in constant and manifest movement. The heaving of a sub-clavicular sigh is likely to cause more sensation than the heaving of an epigastric or umbilical sigh." This double effect of waist-constriction upon hips and chest is fully sufficient to account for its origin, and it has been kept up partly by custom and partly from that "sense of support" always felt by those who have for years been subjected to the practice.

All the evidence that has since appeared confirms the conclusion that there are no true and natural sexual distinctions in respiration. Thus, among the Japanese Baelz has found that only those women who bind themselves round by the broad woman's girdle (*obi*) show thoracic respiration, while the peasant women who do not thus constrict themselves breathe abdominally like the men.[1] Fitz, in an important paper,[2] has also studied the whole question thoroughly, and found no sexual differences. The idea that waist-belts and corsets may perform a useful purpose in assisting the flow of blood to the brain and muscles (as suggested by Roy and Adami) appears to be without foundation; and, in any case, such methods are unnecessary, since perfect compensation is attained under normal conditions.[3] On the other hand, there is reason to believe that the influence of women's clothing in causing costal respiration and so diminishing the action of the diaphragm has an injurious influence, not only on the thoracic but also on the abdominal viscera. Thus it is everywhere found that women suffer much more from gall-stones than do men. In a careful and thorough study of this question Dr. Clelia

[1] *Zt. f. Eth.*, 1901, heft iii. p. 211.
[2] *Jour. Exper. Med.*, vol. i. p. 677.
[3] Leonard Hill, *Cerebral Circulation*, 1896, p. 112.

Mosher[1] found that in America the liability of women to gall-stones is 9.4 per cent., and of men only 5.6 per cent., while in Germany the frequency of gall-stones among women is twice as great, and in the negro race less. In the first line of causes for this sexual difference she mentions the costal respiration of women induced by clothing, the absence of diaphragmatic action producing stasis of the bile, and she refers to the experiments of Heidenhain and his pupils, showing experimentally that the action of the diaphragm is an important factor in emptying the gall-bladder.

Meinert has shown reason for believing that too tight-fitting clothes, even in those who have never worn corsets, may be a factor in the causation of anæmia, through the abdominal constriction leading to gastroptosis, or falling of the stomach, and consequent sympathetic nervous disturbances.[2] Of 31 young girls received into the training-school for servants at Dresden, 12 of whom had never worn corsets though their clothing was too tight, 28 were found with gastroptosis; of the 28, 17 had chlorosis, and 3 anæmia of non-chlorotic character. Meinert refers to the fact, to which attention was drawn by Hirsch, that chlorosis was unknown in antiquity and in the Middle Ages; in Saxony it is said to have appeared among the peasant girls since they adopted modern fashions; in Persia, where no constriction of the thorax takes place, it is said by European physicians to be unknown; and in Japan only to appear among those who have adopted European dress. While, however, constriction of the lower thorax may well be, as Meinert argues, an exciting cause in the production of chlorosis, there is probably, as we have already seen, a special predisposition to anæmia in women.

[1] *John Hopkins Hosp. Bull*, Aug. 1901.
[2] *Verhandl. d. zehnten Versammlung d. gesell. f. Kinderheilk*, 1893.

That costal respiration will become less common, and this artificial sexual difference be gradually abolished, we may reasonably expect, now that the advantages of allowing free play to the diaphragm are being slowly recognised. It is probable, as Professor Sewall and Miss Pollard (in the paper in the *Journal of Physiology* already referred to) point out, that diaphragmatic contraction by pressing upon the abdominal viscera has an important function in squeezing blood to the heart and so assisting circulation; it also promotes, as these authors show, the mechanical mixture of air in the lungs, thus causing in the most perfect manner possible the mixture of fresh with foul air, which is the great function of respiratory movement. It is noteworthy that women who expend an unusual amount of energy in work in a large number of cases find it better to discard or minimise the use of corsets. So far as accurate observation has gone, it is also clear that the corset-wearing woman is inferior in muscular power and physical endurance to the non-corset-wearing woman. This is, for instance, well shown in some observations on the pupils at the North London Collegiate School for Girls, the results of which were published in the *Women's Gazette*, January 1890, by Mrs. Bryant. The trial included a high leap, a long leap, a tug-of-war, and a running competition. The struggle was between " loose stays and none," and there were sixteen girls on each side. In a brief muscular effort, such as leaping, the corset-wearers came out as well as the non-corset-wearers, but in efforts requiring more sustained endurance, as in running and the tug-of-war, the non-corset-wearers had much the best of it. The results, as measured by the pulse-rates and breathing capacity, after " endurance running," were decidedly unfavourable to the corset-wearers.

Dr. Sargent, of Harvard University, has also recorded some interesting experiments on women students ("The Physical Development of Women," *Scribner's Magazine*, 1889):—" In order to ascertain the influence of tight clothing upon the action of the heart during exercise a dozen young women consented this summer to run 540 yards in their loose gymnasium garments and then to run the same distance with corsets on. The running time was two minutes and thirty seconds for each person at each trial, and in order that there should be no cardiac excitement or depression following the first test, the second trial was made the following day. Before beginning the running the average heart-impulse was 84 beats to the minute ; after running the above-named distance the heart-impulse was 152 beats to the minute ; the average natural waist-girth being 25 inches. The next day corsets were worn during the exercise, and the average girth of waist was reduced to 24 inches. The same distance was run in the same time by all, and immediately afterward the average heart-impulse was found to be 168 beats per minute. When I state that I should feel myself justified in advising an athlete not to enter a running or rowing race whose heart-impulse was 160 beats per minute after a little exercise, even though there were not the slightest evidence of disease, one can form some idea of the wear and tear on this important organ, and the physical loss entailed upon the system in women who force it to labour for half their lives under such a disadvantage as the tight corset involves. In order to ascertain the effect of tight clothing upon respiration the spirometer was tried. The average natural girth of the chest over the ninth rib was 28 inches, and with corsets 26 inches. The average lung capacity when corsets were worn was 134 cubic inches; when the corsets were removed the test showed an average lung capacity of 167 inches—a gain of 33 cubic inches."

It may be added that the evidence before us does not necessarily prove the desirability of the disuse of corsets by adult civilised European women. Some of the most serious cases of the results of waist constriction found by Meinert were in young Bavarian women who had never worn stays at all. If a number of heavy lower garments are worn, suspension from the waist is still the most convenient method for their support, and this involves a tight waist-band. Some of the modern kinds of corsets which enable the garments to rest on the hips without undue compression of the chest and abdomen are, when sensibly used, probably better even than none at all. In this matter the position taken up by Stratz (*Schönheit des Weiblichen Körpers*, chaps. viii. and xvi.) is entirely reasonable, alike from the point of view of health and of beauty. In young girls he entirely prohibits stays and the use of garments necessitating them; when full bodily development has been attained, and certainly not earlier than the age of fifteen (or much later if full development of hips is delayed), he recommends the use of certain kinds of corsets adapted to the natural form of the body.

We have seen that the chest region tends to remain unduly undeveloped in women as compared to men. The vital capacity of women is inferior to that of men out of all proportion to the smaller size of women; their lungs also, as we shall see reason to believe, are unduly small; while in strength of arm and of chest muscles, as we have found in a previous chapter (p. 170), they are very much weaker as compared to men than they are in strength of leg muscles, feebleness of arms and chest being indeed,

16

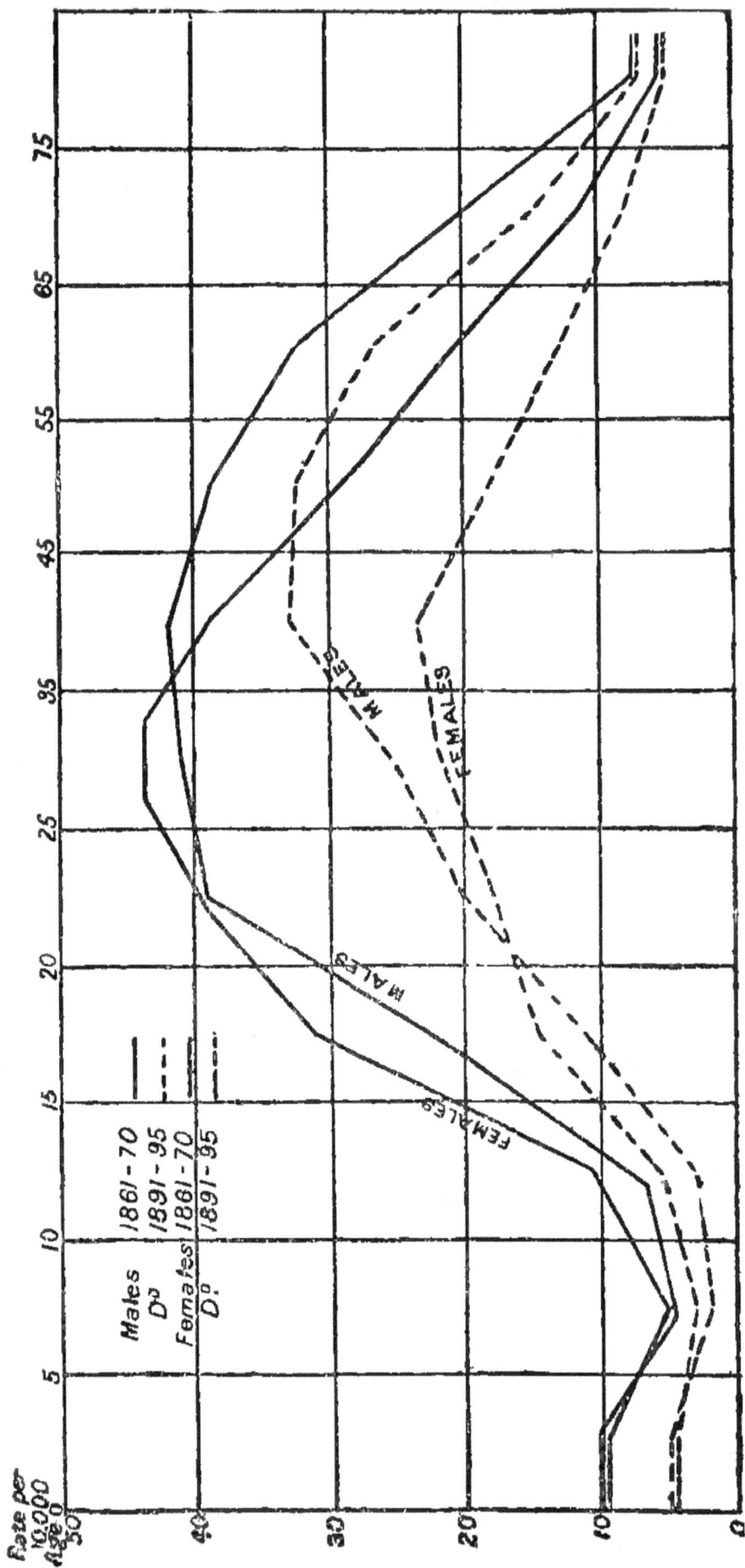

PHTHISIS DEATH-RATE IN ENGLAND AND WALES PER 10,000 LIVING, SHOWING DECLINE FOR BOTH SEXES IN RECENT YEARS, WHILE GREATER MORTALITY OF GIRLS BELOW AGE OF 20 IS MAINTAINED. (*Beevor.*)

relatively to men, women's weakest point. It is probable that this unduly feeble condition of the chest is of much significance in connection with the special tendency of young girls to become consumptive. Constantly from 1860 onwards in England and Wales the mortality of girls from phthisis, up to the age of twenty, has exceeded that of boys, in sexual ratio to the population, by as much as thirty per cent. Sir Hugh Beevor, who has specially studied the sex incidence of phthisis,[1] traces this special liability of girls to consumption to the early arrest of chest growth.[2] In later adult life the mortality of men is much greater than of women, but here we have to remember not only that the women with the least resistant lungs have already been weeded out by death, but that the influence of unwholesome occupations, and also, it is probable, the greater need of good nutrition in men, exert a very important influence. Beevor's results receive valuable confirmation in Woods Hutchinson's study of phthisis and of the consumptive chest.[3] He has found that the consumptive chest really tends to exhibit a measurable degree of inferior development. It would thus appear that the special liability of girls to become the victims of this disease is in some measure due to their inferior chest development, and therefore in part avoidable, if girls were to live a vigorous life in the open air, and with less restraint on their natural activities than is now customary.

It is usual for foolish parents and others to repress the impulse to climb trees, which is very often felt

[1] *Lancet*, 15th April 1899.

[2] In a subsequent paper ("Sex Constitution and its Relation to Pulmonary Tuberculosis," *Medical Magazine*, June 1900), Sir Hugh Beevor is inclined to regard the arrest of lung-growth and the associated greater tendency to consumption as due to ultimate differences in sex constitution. This is a conclusion which I do not think we are yet entitled to accept.

[3] *Studies in Human and Comparative Pathology*, chap. v.

by girls in the country. This is, however, as Hutchinson points out, precisely the kind of exercise they need to develop their chests. "It would almost seem," remarks Hutchinson, "as if a reversion to the arboreal habits of our ancestors was the chief requisite for proper chest development in the individual as well as in the race. The well-marked child-instinct for tree-climbing ought to be regarded with respect in both girls and boys, even at the risk of torn clothing or an occasional broken limb." At present the sexual difference in mortality from consumption is even more marked in rural than urban districts; although the country boy enjoys great advantages over the town boy, his sister's life is much more likely to be regulated by the same maxims as that of the town girl. The natural instinct of girls to climb trees as well as the persistency with which it is repressed are alike evidenced by the frequency with which Stanley Hill found that girls state that climbing trees is one of the things which it is "wrong" to do.

Temperature.—The evidence concerning sexual differences in temperature is small and inconsistent. We know that increased metabolic activity, as well as a greater afflux of blood, produces higher temperature. In children and adolescents it is well recognised that the temperature is higher than in adults, and more liable to variations which are of less significance than in grown-up persons. Davy, Roger, Mignot, and Delaunay found the temperature of men higher than that of women by about .5° C.; Ogle and Wunderlich found the temperature of women higher by about the same amount. Stockton Hough found that males have, as a rule, from the beginning to the end of life, a higher temperature than women and greater individual variations.[1] We are probably justified in agreeing with those physiologists

---

[1] Paper in *Philadelphia Medical Times*, 8th Nov. 1873, summarised in *Popular Science Monthly*, 1874, p. 97.

who assert that no sexual difference has yet been established.

Waller states that the variations of temperature in women from time to time are greater than in men and of less significance. Squire found a slight rise of temperature before menstruation and a fall after it. Dr. Mary Jacobi from an examination of six cases found that "the temperature rises from one to eight-tenths of a degree during the week preceding menstruation. It falls gradually during the flow, but in the majority of cases does not even then reach the normal average." (M. P. Jacobi, *The Question of Rest for Women during Menstruation*, New York, 1877.)

Martius took the temperature of 85 domestic ducks—in the north and south of France—under various conditions, and found the temperature of the females higher (averaging 42.2 against 41.9 for the males) and also more variable. (Gavarret, Art. "Chaleur Animale," in *Dict. ency. des Sciences Médicales;* and in the same writer's *Phenomènes Physiques de la Vie*, 1869, pp. 80-89, the temperature of a large number of animals is given.)

Excretion.—The sexual differences in the metabolic processes which we have already found are also indicated by an examination of the excreta; the best known and most important results concern the urine. Not only does the amount of liquid and of nitrogenous food very largely influence the urine and its composition, but the kidneys are especially susceptible to a variety of influences; the nature of the food, of the salts it contains, emotional excitement, mental exertion, nervous tone,[1] frequency of urination, the temperature of the air, are among the factors to be taken into account, and there is a compensatory relationship with the excreta by the skin. During

[1] "Beneke (*Archiv des Vereins für wiss. Heilk.*, Bd. i.)"—remarks Parkes, *Composition of the Urine*, p. 100—"from observations on himself has noticed that when the nervous system is, so to speak, in good tone, *i.e.*, when there is a feeling of vigorous health, and when all the functions are rightly performed, the amount of urine increases. On the other hand, when there is languor and depression, the urine is less in amount. The difficulty here, of course, is to define the term, 'tone of the nervous system'; that something real is meant is certain; and the immediate influence on the amount of the urine is, I think, put beyond doubt by Beneke's elaborate inquiry."

the night we should expect these influences to cause less disturbance than during the day; and Beigel's observations seem to confirm this; he found that the amount of urine excreted during the night is almost equal in men and women, but that during the day there is a marked excess in men. Beaunis has found that, notwithstanding the disturbing elements, and independently of the water drunk, a regular diurnal rhythm may be traced in the excretion of urine.[1]

A slight sexual difference appears soon after birth, both the solid and liquid constituents of the urine of the female infant being less. At from 3 to 7 years of age the amount of urine excreted by boys during 24 hours, according to Beaunis, is 750 c. cm., by girls 700 c. cm. This is 1½ times more than in the adult in proportion to body-weight. The amount of urea excreted by the child is even greater relatively than that of water, and the importance of this function of elimination in children is indicated by the large size of their kidneys. At the age of eighteen the urine reaches the adult standard.[2] The amount is, absolutely, usually rather smaller in women, but relatively it is usually greater.

The amount is, roughly speaking, in a man about 1000 to 1500 c. cm. (or about 50 ozs.), and in a woman about 900 to 1200 c. cm., during the 24 hours (Landois and Stirling); according to Yvon and Berlioz, in man 1360 c. cm., in woman 1100 c. cm. (*Revue Méd.*, viii. p. 713); according to Beaunis, the amount is practically identical in both sexes, and therefore relatively greater in woman, in man the average being 1875 c. cm., in woman 1812; while M'Kendrick places it at 1500-2000 c. cm. for a man, and 400-500 c. cm. less in a woman. Becquerel and Rodier, on the other hand, as the result of a large number of experiments, came to the conclusion that the quantity of urine discharged by women during 24 hours is, even absolutely, slightly greater than in men, the average being as 1227 in men to 1337 in women (Becquerel and Rodier, *Traité de Chimie pathologique*, 1854). Mosler found (comparing men

---

[1] *Recherches Expérimentales*, Paris, 1884, p. 14.
[2] Parkes, *Composition of Urine.*

from the age of 18 to 21 with women of from 17 to 26) that while the absolute amount of urine was greater in men, in proportion to body-weight it was greater in women (*Archiv des Vereins für gemeinschaft. Arbeiten zur Förderung der wissen. Heilkunde,* iii., 1858, pp. 431, 441). English physiologists usually find the sexual difference rather considerable. French physiologists more frequently find the amount nearly equal, and thus relatively greater in women; this is probably due to differences in national habit and custom.

While the amount of water excreted by the kidneys in women is probably above what the difference in body-weight would lead us to expect, there seems little doubt that the amount of urinary solids excreted by women is both absolutely and relatively rather below that excreted by men. The urine of women is usually of lighter colour than men's, and its specific gravity is lower. All physiologists are agreed on this point,[1] and the fact is a more important index of metabolism than the relative amounts of water excreted. Children in whom metabolism is very active excrete relatively considerably more urea and salts than adults; among adults the amount in women is relatively less than in men; in old age, when the metabolic processes of life are low, there is in both sexes a great diminution in the excretion of both solid and liquid constituents. The urine of women, like the blood of women, is more watery than that of men.

In women the influence of the menstrual cycle, which so largely affects the organism, has its effects here also. That the urine is frequently increased in amount at this period is a matter of common observation, and according to the usual rule this increase should involve an increase in the solids. This does not, however, appear to be always the case. Delaunay stated that menstruation diminished the urea 20 per cent., but without mentioning the extent of the data on which this opinion was founded.

[1] See, for instance, E. A. Parkes, *Composition of the Urine*, 1860, pp. 39-41.

Beigel found lessening of urea during, and increase after, menstruation. Dr. Mary Jacobi made fourteen series of observations on six women, and found that in nine the urea was diminished during the flow, in five increased. But in the majority the urea during the menstrual period was more abundant than during the following week, when the lowest point was reached, and before the flow there was usually an increase of urea. Marro found by a series of observations on eight girls and young women between the ages of eleven and twenty-six, that there was a gradual increase of urea in proportion to body-weight in the years preceding puberty, but that the establishment of menstruation produced not merely arrest but even diminution in the elimination of urea. He found that the amount of urea was nearly always diminished during menstruation, slowly rising afterwards, and apparently reaching a maximum at the period most removed from menstruation.[1] A larger series of observations is, however, necessary to obtain definite results. Our knowledge of the influence of pregnancy and lactation on metabolic activity, as measured by the urine, is very slight. Dr. Hagemann, at a meeting of the Berlin Physiological Society (6th June 1890), gave an account of some experiments on two dogs with reference to this point. They were supplied with a constant nitrogenous diet, and it was found that during the first half of the period of pregnancy more nitrogen was excreted than was taken with the food, so that the nitrogen requisite for the growth of the fœtus must have been derived from the tissue-proteids of the mother; after this period the nitrogenous excretion sank to a condition of equilibrium in the middle of pregnancy, and then fell further, until the birth of

[1] Marro, *La Puberté*, p. 44. He believes (p. 241) that this diminution of urea at puberty, in association with the diminished output of carbonic acid, constitutes a state of lowered metabolism which is one of the physiological bases of hysteria.

the offspring; while immediately after parturition there was a very marked increase in the excretion of nitrogen, followed by a sudden fall, which led to the output being, during four weeks of the period of lactation, less than the intake. It is probable that in women the metabolic cycle during pregnancy and lactation is somewhat similar; thus Laulanié and Chambrelent have noticed a marked diminution in the toxicity of the urine of pregnant women, especially towards the end of this period (when in the dogs the excretion of urea was also lowest); in two experiments out of ten the urine of pregnant women was entirely free from the toxic substances present in normal urine, so that these appear to be retained towards the period of childbirth.

SUSCEPTIBILITY TO POISONS.

There are various ways in which the varying effects of poisons on men and women might throw an interesting light on differences in metabolism and in nervous organisation. We know something of the special susceptibilities of children with regard to poisons, when given in small doses as drugs to produce beneficial effects, and also as to their effects on various animals, but not much is known as to sexual differences. These differences are usually of so slight a character that considerable precision of observation and a large body of cases are necessary to reach definite results. The poison which has most persistently been observed to exhibit sexual differences in its effects is alcohol; it is evident that this is simply because the effects of no other poison have been so widely studied. If medical men took the trouble to note systematically the effects of the drugs they administered we should be in possession of a considerable body of evidence; but they have rarely, if ever, done so on an extended scale.

From our present point of view, there are various

questions which observation of the effect of drugs would help to elucidate. For example: (1) Do any drugs tend to produce greater effect on an organ in one sex than in the other? (2) Are there in one or the other sex examples of such marked susceptibility to a poison that the therapeutical doses must be decidedly smaller than considerations of size, etc., would lead us to anticipate? (3) Especially, are the higher nervous centres more apt to be affected in one sex than in the other?

(1.) Observations on a large scale, or carefully recorded in their details, tending to prove or disprove any selective action of poisons on different organs in the two sexes are, so far as I am aware, very few. I have met with a paper, by Dr. F. Augustus Cox, containing a summary of the notes of over 1700 cases treated with arsenic which had been under his observation. In this paper[1] some sexual differences in symptoms are noted, although it was not found that the influence of sex was marked in the evolution of unpleasant symptoms. Gastric symptoms were commoner in women, intestinal in men; conjunctival symptoms were met with rather oftener in the male sex; nervous symptoms were of more frequent occurrence in women. It may be added that, in Mr. Jonathan Hutchinson's experience, children and the young bear arsenic well, while the old are susceptible to it, and it is specially apt to call out the signs of nerve degeneration whenever this is present.[2]

Trousseau and Pidoux record some interesting observations on the varying action of opium on men and women. They found that in women it acts more on the skin, in men on the kidneys; they only observed hypersecretion of urine twice in women. They found also from observation on 22

[1] "The Administration of Arsenic," *Provincial Medical Journal,* Feb. 1891.
[2] "Arsenic as a Drug," *Brit. Med. Journal,* 6th June 1891.

men and 20 women that vomiting with opium, when administered by the skin, was three times more frequent in women than in men. When given internally it produced vomiting 4 out of 10 times in men, 6 out of 10 times in women. The women who vomited were mostly nervous or neuralgic. Lauder Brunton also states that women, under the influence of opium, are more liable to nausea and also to headache.

Trousseau and Pidoux also found that the administration of mercury more easily produces salivation in women than either in men or in children, who easily bear large doses.[1] This, also, is confirmed by Lauder Brunton.

(2.) Men are said to bear the action of antimony much better than women; children bear it badly (De Savignac). Zuccarelli found in 37 cases in which he treated epilepsy by injection of atropine that the benefit was much less in the case of women than of men; children also are very tolerant of belladonna, as is well established. Sulphonal, which is apt to produce nervous symptoms, should be given to women in much smaller doses than to men; Monod found that to produce the hypnotic effect women only required half the dose required by a man.[2] On the other hand, in treating the insane with somnal, Umpfenbach found that women are much less susceptible to its influence than men. Germain Sée has found that women are especially sensitive to antipyrin.[3] Women are also said to be very readily affected by bromide (which affects the cerebral and especially the spinal system), while children (according to Voisin) bear it well, but (according to Radcliffe Crocker) bromide eruptions are most common in children.

It is remarkable that, as first noted by English

[1] R. W. Parker has suggested that this is merely due to the large amount of milk taken by children, which may deprive the mercury of its irritant effects.
[2] *Arch. für exp. Path. und Pharm.*, i. 31.
[3] Paris Académie de Médecine, 14th February 1888.

authors, the overwhelming majority of deaths from chloroform are in males. The materials furnished by Sansom show that, according to various authorities, the proportion is at the highest estimate two men to one woman, and according to one estimate four men to one woman, although, as Sansom remarked, chloroform is so extensively used in childbirth. The Report of the Anæsthetics Committee of the British Medical Association (1901) founded on nearly 26,000 cases, showed that the percentage of complications under all anæsthetics together was in the ratio of about 1.5 males to 1 female, while the percentage of danger cases was still higher in males, being in the ratio of about 1.7 to 1. Under chloroform the danger-rate was found to be greater for males in the ratio of over 2 to 1. Under ether, indeed, the danger-rate was somewhat greater for females than for males (.6 to 1), but minor complications were notably more frequent with males even under ether. Children, as the very large experience of the Moorfields Hospital shows, bear chloroform extremely well. The robust and healthy, according to Sansom, seem more exposed to the dangerous effects of chloroform than the delicate and weakly, and the largest relative number of fatal cases has occurred in very trifling surgical cases when the general health of the patient has been tolerably good.

Some allusion may here be made to the group of lead salts (which, according to Goetzke and others, primarily affect the central nervous system), as there is reason to believe that women are more susceptible to their action than men. Sir J. Alderson in his Lumleian Lectures in 1852 concluded that men are more frequently affected, but Tanquerel found that women are more susceptible to lead-poisoning, and Professor T. Oliver of Newcastle, one of the chief centres of the lead industries, is decidedly of this opinion. In his Goulstonian Lectures on *Lead-Poisoning* (1891, pp. 21-25) he remarks:—"There is, in my opinion, no doubt in regard to the very much greater susceptibility of the female to be contaminated with lead compared to the male; and this is not due simply to the fact of exposure in a lead factory to what may be regarded as the greater dangers, but depends upon sexual idiosyncrasy. This is an opinion so totally at variance with that given by several authors that I require to explain myself. My experience drawn from hundreds of cases is that, both as regards the acute and chronic forms of lead-poisoning, women are much more quickly brought under its influence than men. The ratio of men to women employed in lead factories is in favour of the women, and at first sight it might appear as if the liability was explained by the greater number of women exposed. Taking a period of five years, I find that 135 cases of lead-poisoning were admitted as in-patients at the Royal Infirmary, in Newcastle. Of these, ninety-one were women and forty-four were men. To me there is no comparison of the greater susceptibility of the female; and that it is not altogether a question of trade is shown by the fact that in the recent epidemic of lead-poisoning in Yorkshire, where out of 1000 cases due to the drinking of water contaminated by the metal, the special correspondent of the *British Medical Journal*, 1890, vol. i. p. 974, found the proportion of females to males to be as four to one. Against this may be urged the fact that women probably drink more water than men; but allowing for this, the proportion would still be in favour of the female; Brown found 153 males as against 251 females. Not only is the female more susceptible, but she is so at an earlier age than the male, and is more likely to suffer severely, and from such nervous accidents as epilepsy. The interesting point in regard to exposure to lead is that whilst young women suffer readily from saturnine poisoning, recovering quickly from colic only to be more readily and severely affected on again exposing themselves, men may go on working for years, ten to twenty, having only one or two attacks of colic, and then, after a very lengthened period of service, may still fall victims, either to lead paralysis, or die from the effects of a kidney leison due to the poison. . . . One of the first noticeable effects of the pernicious influence of lead is the production of anæmia or cachexia. Nearly all young women, those particularly between the ages of eighteen to twenty-four, when thus exposed suffer from deranged menstrual function; hæmatosis and ovarian activity are interfered with, and the result is either amenorrhœa or menorrhagia. Once the functional activity of the ovaries and blood-making is interfered with, then is that woman already in a critical condition, and at any moment she may become the subject of any of those explosive outbursts of plumbism known by the name of lead encephalopathy. To sexual peculiarity I therefore attribute much of the danger from exposure to lead. Lead as a poison strikes early at the functions of blood-making and reproduction, producing sterility, liability to abortion, and amenorrhœa or menorrhagia. Woman, from her constitutional idiosyncrasy, is therefore more liable to be impressed by lead." Mr. W. Bevan Lewis (*Text-Book of Mental Diseases*, 1889, p. 350) indirectly confirms Dr. Oliver by the vivid picture which he presents of the various nervous symptoms which are found among the young girls ("white-lead ghosts" they are called in the neighbourhood) who work in lead manufactories. These include arrest of sexual development with perverted instincts and unnatural desires, hysteria, chorea, epileptiform seizures, cataleptic states, and actual insanity. If we are justified in concluding that women suffer earlier and more severely from lead-poisoning, we may perhaps connect this with the less metabolic activity of women. In lead-poisoning there is marked metabolic deficiency. If this is so, we should expect to find that women are more susceptible than men to all these slow poisons of which lead is the subtle and terrible type. But the evidence before us is not convincingly presented.

(3.) Women, as well as children, it is generally admitted, are very sensitive to the influence of opium. "There can be little doubt," Fonssagrives states, "as to the extreme impressionability of women to opium, and most of the cases of toxic saturation following the use of opium are in women.[1] Lauder Brunton makes a similar statement.

Opium acts chiefly on the nervous system, but more especially on the brain. Children possess a greater proportion of nervous tissue and brain than adults, greater cell activity, and a greater power of absorption.[2] Therefore it is not surprising that children are susceptible to opium. The same is true of mammals generally. If poison is given to an adult rabbit and to a young rabbit, the poison in each case

---

[1] Art. "Opium" in *Dict. ency. des Sciences médicales.*

[2] The greater rapidity of absorption in children has been well shown by Yatsuty, who selected healthy male subjects from eight years old to eighty, and experimented with iodide of potassium and salicylate of soda. The dose was made to depend on the body-weight, and the urine was examined every three minutes. The general result was that the younger the subject the more rapid the absorption. Thus while the salicylate was absorbed in boys and young men in about fifteen minutes, in middle-aged men it required about twenty minutes, and in old men about twenty-five minutes. (*Lancet,* 10th January 1891.)

being proportionate to the animal's body-weight, the adult will be uninjured, the young one will succumb.[1] Among female animals generally, Cornevin states, there is greater susceptibility to poison, more especially nerve-poison, than among male animals; and in woman than in man. In cold-blooded animals like the frog, in which the cerebrum occupies a more subordinate position in relation to the spinal cord, opium causes tetanic convulsions, as it sometimes does also in children.

The best example of sexual selective action in the effect of a poison on the nervous system is, as already remarked, the case of alcohol. Alcoholism generally is much more common in men than in women; according to Hermann's figures, the proportion is 2800 men to 400 women; that is to say, women furnish one-seventh of the cases. Notwithstanding this considerable proportion of women, the cases in which the brain is chiefly affected, and which result in the symptoms of *delirium tremens*, occur almost exclusively in men. Rayer (according to Lancereaux) found among 170 cases of *delirium tremens* only 7 women; in Italy Verga found that 9 per cent. of the cases were in women; at Copenhagen, Bang found only one woman in 456 cases; Hœgh-Guldberg, one woman in 173 cases; at the Charité in Berlin the proportion of cases in women is between 3 and 4 per cent.; in England Clifford Allbutt in 1882 had never seen *delirium tremens* in a woman. On the other hand, it is a familiar fact in England and France, and no doubt elsewhere also, that chronic alcoholism tending to affect the spinal cord and nerves, and to result in muscular paralysis, is found chiefly in women. Lancereaux, who has given special attention to this matter, finds that the ratio is twelve women to only three men. Broadbent and Clifford Allbutt have made similar statements as regards England, and the fact may easily be confirmed in

[1] Ch. Cornevin, *Des Plantes Vénéneuses*, Paris, 1887, pp. 27-29.

any large hospital.   It is worth mention in the same connection that Ball found that sexual excitement, as a complication of dipsomania, is more frequent in women than in men.[1]

This well-marked differential action of alcohol on the nervous centres in men and women is of some interest, and must be taken in connection with other facts referred to elsewhere.

There is comparatively little opportunity of studying chronic alcoholism in children. Professor Demme of Berne has, however, found it somewhat common among the poor in certain districts, and has written a pamphlet on the influence of alcohol on children. I have not seen this, but it appears that he finds that the main symptom of alcoholic poisoning in children is abnormal excitement, ending, in extreme cases, in convulsions, and followed by mental and bodily debility of the nature of paralysis (*Lancet*, 19th Sept. 1891, p. 691). There is here considerable resemblance to the symptoms of chronic alcoholic poisoning in women. It is also of some interest to observe that *delirium tremens* is an extremely rare result of alcoholism among lower races. Thus in American negroes (as Dr. Reyburn has shown from an analysis of over 400,000 negro patients treated by the Medical Department of the American Bureau of Refugees) *delirium tremens* is of very rare occurrence, alcoholism being much more apt to lead to epileptiform convulsions or mania.

HAIR AND PIGMENTATION.

It is probable that the growth of the hair, its colouring, and that of the body generally, have an intimate connection with the metabolic activity of the organism. Among animals of all kinds hair, and more especially pigmentation, play a part of the first importance as secondary sexual characters. Among animals generally, in a very obvious manner, brilliant pigmentation and abundant hair predominate among the males. But in man pigmentation has become very rudimentary and comparatively stable, while sexual hair distribution has become fairly equalised. It is true that men have a growth of hair on the face,

[1] *L'Encéphale*, 1882, No. 3, p. 446.

but, on the other hand, women have a more vigorous growth of hair on their heads; even among races like the Singhalese, who preserve their hair long, that of the women is longer than that of the men, and, according to Pfaff and Waldeyer, the individual hairs are in Germany thicker in women than in men. Even among children (as Waldeyer points out) boys' hair, if left uncut, does not grow to the length of girls'.[1] Women do not tend to become bald either in Europe or among lower races like the Nicobarese, and do not suffer so often as men from *alopecia areata*. Again, while men in Europe on the average have a more extended growth of hair on the body generally, the more concentrated hair regions of women tend to be more vigorously developed; thus on the pubes it is frequently greater in amount in women than in men, and the individual hairs in this region are also (as both Pfaff and Waldeyer have found) of greater size than those of men. The sexual differences are therefore on the whole compensatory.[2] It must be added, however, that a real sexual distinction, and one of some interest, lies in the greater persistence in women of the fœtal *lanugo* or down. On their faces, necks, and bodies generally women retain this infantile characteristic of down to a much greater extent than men, and in some cases its presence is very marked.

The presence of hair on the face in men is one of the most pronounced of all the secondary sexual characters. There is perhaps some interest in remarking that, probably as a result of this, the special prevalence of acne (or of pimples not amounting to acne) in young male adults has also been regarded as a secondary sexual character, since it is comparatively rare in

---

[1] The average length of the hair in women is usually stated to be between 60 and 75 cm., but a considerably greater length is frequently attained; thus in Munich Stratz found a lady, 164 cm. (about 5 ft. 4 in.) in height, whose hair was 155 cm. (5 ft. 1 in.) in length, and he has also met four other women with notably beautiful hair which varied between 120 and 153 cms. in length.

[2] A fairly full discussion of the characteristics of the hair and its distribution will be found in Ploss and Bartels, *Das Weib*, 7th ed., pp. 28, 246-256.

women. As Woods Hutchinson points out (*Studies in Human and Comparative Pathology*, p. 180), acne is a disease of the so-called sebaceous glands, which are immature or aborted hair follicles, and it is therefore impossible not to connect the occurrence of acne, which usually appears at adolescence, with the normal impulse to the growth of hair on the face at this time.

There is, however, one question which, as we shall see, has a certain definite significance, and to which it seems possible to give a guarded answer: Are women darker than men?

There is no doubt that children have fairer hair and fairer skins than adults in very various parts of the world, such as South America, Japan, New Guinea.[1] Among many different races, also, travellers have recorded that the women are fairer than the men; Bälz says that the Japanese women have a somewhat lighter-coloured skin than the men; D'Albertis found that Papuan women in New Guinea are always lighter-coloured than the men; the Ainu women are also said to be fairer than the men, while among the Veddahs (as Deschamps noted) the women are not fairer than the men, though the children are fair. Among the Fuegians Hyades and Deniker remark that the skin colour is lighter in women than in men, but before puberty darker in the girls. Among many African peoples the women are less black, though both sexes alike are exposed to the sun, and Mantegazza made the same observation regarding the Todas in India. But among a large number of Jews and Jewesses in America Fishberg found the women much darker, 74 per cent. of Jewesses having dark skin, and only 23 per cent. Jews.[2] The determination of sexual difference in skin-colour is not very satisfactory, nor can we always be sure that both sexes receive the same amount of exposure to the sun.

It is of more interest to investigate the colour of

[1] See, for instance, Fritsch, "Bermerkungen zur anthropologischen Haaruntersuchung," *Zeitschrift für Ethnologie*, 1888, heft iii. p. 190.
[2] *Am. Anthropologist*, 1903, p. 92.

the hair and eyes. Alphonse de Candolle stated some years ago as a general proposition that the women in a population have a larger proportion of brown eyes than the men, but without bringing forward any definite evidence on the point.[1] In recent years, however, various investigators have occupied themselves with this matter. The question has been fully studied in England, and especially by Dr. Beddoe, who is unquestionably the chief authority on the matter. So far as the evidence goes, it appears that among children (in industrial and workhouse schools), girls with light eyes and light hair (and also girls with light eyes and red hair) are much commoner than boys; this applies to nearly all ages between six and fifteen. Boys having dark eyes and dark hair are on the whole commoner than girls.[2] The darkening of the hair has been found by Dr. Beddoe to take place in men most markedly between the ages of twenty to twenty-three; but in women it takes place somewhat earlier.[3] This accords with what we already know as to the greater precocity of women. It is possible that the pigmentary process being earlier established in women, becomes in them more intense. I am indebted to Dr. Beddoe for a series of figures showing the sexual differences in various parts of Great Britain; in his *Races of Britain* they are given without regard to sex. Dr. Beddoe recognises the fallacies that may arise from differences in the mode of dressing the hair and from cosmetics, and also by a possible difference in the mean ages of the men and women. Moreover, more young women than young men are met in the streets in most English towns, and Dr. Beddoe thinks that the women may come out with too low a proportion of dark hair on this account, though it seems to me that this fallacy may be counterbalanced by

[1] *Rev. d'Anth.*, 1887, p. 265.
[2] *Report of Anthropometric Committee of British Association*, 1883.
[3] *Report of Anthropometric Committee of Brit. Ass.*, 1880.

the later darkening of hair in the men, which would lead young men to be counted as somewhat fairer than if they had reached that pigmentary maturity which has been reached by young women of the same age. From an examination of Dr. Beddoe's table it appears that women have darker hair than men in Comrie (Perthshire), Thirsk, Boston, Leicester, Worcester, Norwich, and Southampton, while men have darker hair in Forteviot (Perthshire), Stoke-on-Trent, Shrewsbury, Hereford, and North Wales. It can scarcely be said that this particular list strongly supports Dr. Beddoe's opinion as to the prevalence of dark pigment among women. The evidence furnished by the eyes is clearer. Dark eyes were almost constantly more numerous in women than in men, this being found at Forteviot, Comrie, Thirsk, Boston, Leicester, Shrewsbury, Hereford, Worcester, London, Southampton, and North Wales; only Ipswich showed men to possess darker eyes, while Stoke-on-Trent and Norwich showed the sexes to be equal. Dr. Beddoe regards these results as fairly representing the facts as they would emerge from a more extensive investigation of his materials, and it certainly fully illustrates his general conclusion: "I have usually found a decidedly larger proportion of dark eyes among the women, but not so often of dark hair." I gather that he regards brown hair and brown eyes as chiefly common among women, black hair and grey eyes as more prevalent among men. An independent investigation of the members of the British Association during the Bath meeting, at a laboratory established for the occasion, entirely confirmed Dr. Beddoe's results as regards eye-colour; while the eyes of medium colour were about equal in the sexes, 44.6 per cent. of the men possessed light eyes, against only 34.2 per cent. of the women, while 20.7 per cent. of the women possessed dark eyes, against only 12.3 per cent. of the men. At the Newcastle meeting it was found that a larger percentage of the men had light hair and light eyes, a slightly larger percentage of the men showed light eyes and dark hair, and a considerably larger percentage of the women possessed dark eyes and dark hair; this result in a part of the country of very different ethnological character from Bath (and 50 per cent. of those examined at Newcastle were natives of Newcastle) also confirms Dr. Beddoe's results. Still more recently, Professor Haddon and Dr. Browne have investigated the hair and eyes of over 400 inhabitants of the Aran Islands, on the west coast of Ireland. They adopted Beddoe's methods, and independently confirm his results as to sexual differences. Both dark eyes and dark hair were found more prevalent among females than among males, the results being more symmetrical as regards the eyes than as regards the hair.[1]

In a private letter Dr. Beddoe makes some interesting remarks on sexual differences in pigmentation, and raises the question as to their causes: "It is especially on the Welsh border [*i.e.*, for example, Hereford and Shrewsbury] that the men come out with darker hair. That may have been due to the presence of more Welsh-bred men than women. I think the excess of dark women is most marked in the most purely Anglian (or, say, Teutonic) districts, such as Boston. Do the women still repeat the colours of their ancestresses, the British women who espoused the Saxon invaders? Possibly; no doubt there was intermarriage of that sort, though as the Saxons brought their cows over, I don't doubt that they brought a good many women too. Do the women deposit more pigment in their irides and hair because they have no beards wherein to expend it?" The latter supposition may seem to find support in the fact that the darkening in women occurs at about the time at which the beard begins to grow in men; but we must remember that in amount of hair there does not seem any marked sexual inequality on the whole.

The most elaborate recent investigation in Great Britain is that of Gray and Tocher in East

---

[1] See the carefully detailed statistics, A. C. Haddon and C. R. Browne, "Ethnography of the Aran Islands," *Proceedings Royal Irish Academy*, 1893, pp. 782-786. In a later investigation in Galway (*ib.*, 1899, p. 228) Browne found the index of nigrescence higher in girls than in boys, and much higher in women than in men.

Aberdeenshire. These observers noted the eye and hair colour of over 14,000 children, and found that in percentage of dark hair the sexes were about equal, while as regards eye-colour the girls show a small (3 per cent.) excess of dark eyes. Among several thousand adults, however, the greater darkness of the women was clearly marked; the women had 11 per cent. more dark hair than the men, and $16\frac{1}{2}$ per cent. more dark eyes.[1]

In Germany this question has been most fully studied by the late Professor Pfitzner. At the Anatomical Institute at Strassburg, Pfitzner found that fair men are always in excess of fair women. Taking over 500 subjects, his percentages were as follow:—[2]

Age.	MALE.		FEMALE.	
	Fair.	Dark.	Fair.	Dark.
1-10	86.0	13.9	63.4	36 6
11-20	48.5	51.5	36.4	64.6
Above 20	30.9	69.1	22.6	77.4

These figures show a very marked and constant sexual difference at all ages. Pfitzner endeavoured to find an explanation in the possibility of the sexes reaching the Institute in different racial mixtures. This is not impossible, but, as was pointed out in the first edition of the present book, this sexual difference is international, and has been observed among the living as well as among the dead. The same differences exist in Denmark. In that country Professor Waldemar Schmidt (as Dr. Beddoe kindly informs me) found more fair-haired and fewer dark-

[1] J. Gray and J. F. Tocher, "Physical Characteristics of Adults and School Children in East Aberdeenshire," *Jour. Anth. Inst.*, January-June, 1900. Karl Pearson and Alice Lee confirm the conclusion that the eyes of women are darker than those of men, *Proc. Roy. Soc.*, vol. lxvi., 1900, p. 324. Cf. K. Pearson, *Phil. Trans.*, 1901, vol. 195 A, p. 108.

[2] Schwalbe's *Morphologische Arbeiten*, Bd. ii., 1892.

haired among the men than among the women, red hair being about equal, or rather less in the men. The eyes also in men are far more often light; there are fewer of medium colour, and immensely fewer are dark. The great majority of the men have light eyes and medium hair, while among the women fair, medium, and dark hair are about equally common, and about one-half have medium hair, and one-third dark hair.

In consequence of this criticism Pfitzner took up the matter again and investigated it in a very exhaustive manner, eliminating so far as possible all fallacies, on the wider basis of over 2000 subjects of all ages. The result proved that among the native population of Lower Alsace females really are at all ages distinctly darker than males, both as regards eye-colour and hair-colour. Dark eyes were found to be 6 to 7 per cent. more numerous in the females; or, according to his final results, there are 7 per cent. more fair-haired individuals among males than among females, and 3 per cent. more brown-eyed individuals among females. This greater pigmentation of the female sex Pfitzner regarded as a specific sexual character.[1]

Elkind examined men and women working in the factories of Warsaw, all being Poles belonging to the city, and found three types—a fair, a dark, and a mixed; only 17 per cent. of the men belonged to the dark type, but 25 per cent. of the women; this greater prevalence of the dark type among the women was at the expense of the mixed, the fair being equal. All authorities agree that Jewesses are darker-eyed than Jews, and most find them also darker-haired, but not Elkind and Fishberg.[2] Among

[1] W. Pfitzner, "Ein Beitrag zur Kenntriss der sekundären Geschlechtsunterschiede beim Menschen," *Morphologische Arbeiten*, Bd. vii., heft 2, 1897; *ib.*, *Zt. f. Morph.*, Bd. iii., heft 3, 1901. Among school children in Upper Bavaria, Daffner (*Wachstum des Menschen*, p. 126) found the girls somewhat fair, but he only examined 300.

[2] *Am. Anthropologist*, 1903, p. 95.

a large number of Bulgarian school children, both in Bulgaria and in Turkey, between the ages of six and twenty, Wateff has found that the dark type prevails among the girls to a slightly greater extent than among the boys, the blond type being equal in both, so that, as in Poland, there was a deficiency of the mixed type among the girls. Considering eyes and hair separately the girls had more dark eyes, but the boys more light hair.[1]

We thus see that, though among children this distinction is less marked, or non-existent, women have darker hair than men, and decidedly darker eyes. We seem to be justified in concluding that this holds generally good for the fairer races of Northern Europe.[2]

Among the extra-European and darker races, observations have been made on a smaller scale, and do not always point in the same direction. Chantre found the women darker among the Armenians to a very decided extent; there were 51 per cent. dark-haired men to 71 per cent. dark-haired women, and 51 per cent. dark-eyed men to 77 per cent. dark-eyed women (darkness of the eyes being thus, as usually in Europe, even more marked in women than darkness of the hair); as regards the light-haired, there were 12 per cent. men against 3 per cent. women, and as regards light-eyed 12 per cent. men and no women. Among Tartars he found 63 per cent. dark-haired men to 78 per cent. dark-haired women, and 56 per cent. dark-eyed men to 72 per cent. dark-eyed women. Among the Kurds the sexes were equal as regards dark hair, but as regards dark eyes there were 66 per cent. men to 80 per cent. women. (E. Chantre, "Mission Scientifique en Arménie Russe," *Nouv. Arch. des Miss. Sci.*, vol. iii., 1892.) Among the Lapps Mantegazza and Sommier found that about 50 per cent. of the women, and only about 30 per cent. of the men, had brown eyes, but there was no similar preponderance of dark hair among the women. Among the Japanese (according to Collignon) sexual differences in the colour of the hair and eyes are slight, the women being a little less dark. Among the Fuegians, according to Hyades and Deniker, there is a larger proportion of dark eyes among the men, but the hair is exclusively dark among the women, and only predominantly dark among the men.

---

[1] S. Wateff, *Corresp.-Blatt. deutsch. Gesell. Anth.*, March 1902.
[2] Cf. Ripley, *The Races of Europe*, pp. 322, 357, etc.

CHAPTER X.

THE VISCERA.

THERE can be no doubt that the consideration of the
internal organs of the body, their varieties according
to age, sex and race, and the changes they undergo
under varying conditions, constitutes a study of great
importance. But it has scarcely yet been undertaken
in any serious or comprehensive manner. It is not
yet generally recognised that just as anthropology
is founded on anatomy, so psychology is founded on
physiology. When we say that the suprarenal
capsule is a ganglionic body moulded on to the top
of the kidney, we assert an anatomical fact; when we
go on to say that the suprarenal capsule is larger in
women than in men and very large in Negroes, we
assert an anthropological fact. In the same way,
when we accurately estimate or graphically represent
the ordinary action of the heart or the pulse, we are
well within the region of physiology. But when we
begin to make the same observations on the heart

and pulse under varying conditions of the individual organism, we are not far from the region of psychology. Thus the elaborate physiological studies of Mosso on the vascular system have a very intimate connection with psychology. No one now can be a competent psychologist who is not something of a physiologist, just as no one can be a competent physiologist who is not something of a chemist and a physicist. The physiology of the senses leads us to the psychology of intellect, and the physiology of the viscera leads us to the psychology of emotion. If we possessed, for instance, a thorough physiological knowledge of the thyroid gland, we should probably know more of the nature of emotion than all mere introspection, or mere general picturesque description, has ever taught us.

The Thyroid Gland.—This interesting gland of the neck is intimately connected with the metabolism of the blood and the functioning of the nervous system. It is associated to a remarkable extent with the sexual system.[1]

It is generally agreed that as a rule the gland is absolutely larger in women than in men, and that relatively it is very large in childhood. While in the new-born child its proportion to the weight of the body is as 1 to 400, or even to 420, in the adult it is only 1 to 1800 (Huschke and Krause). In old age the thyroid is very considerably diminished in size, and, as Kocher and others have shown, while total extirpation of the thyroid in old age is not likely to be followed by serious results, before the age of puberty it will almost certainly be followed by serious injury to health.

[1] See Sir Victor Horsley, "The Function of the Thyroid Gland," in the Virchow *Festschrift* and in the *Brit. Med. Journal*, 30th Jan. and 6th Feb. 1892; Rosario Traina, "Ricerche sperimentali sul sistema nervoso degli animali tireoprivi," *Il Policlinico*, Oct. 1898; G. R. Murray, "Goulstonian Lectures on the Pathology of the Thyroid Gland," *Brit. Med. Jour.*, 11th and 18th March 1899. The literature of this subject is now very extensive.

The thyroid gland follows closely all the variations in a woman's organism. To so marked an extent is this the case that Meckel long ago remarked that the thyroid is a repetition of the uterus in the neck. The fact that the neck swells in women in harmony with the sexual organs seems to have been an observation made in very early times. The thyroid swells at the first menstruation, and not uncommonly it increases to some extent at every menstruation; at its final suppression also the thyroid may swell, while Simpson, Engelmann, and other gynæcologists have observed enlargement of the thyroid as an accompaniment of uterine disorder. In the dog, cat, sheep, goat, and deer it has also been observed that the thyroid enlarges during rut. Catullus refers to the influence of the first sexual intercourse in causing swelling of the neck, and it is a very ancient custom to measure the necks of newly-married women in order to ascertain their virginity. This custom has not yet quite died out in the south of France. Heidenreich found that a similar swelling occurs in men at the commencement of sexual relations. Democritus refers to the swelling of the neck during pregnancy, and in recent days Tarnier, Lawson Tait, and others have confirmed this ancient observation. Freund finds that congestion of the thyroid is almost constant during pregnancy (in 45 out of 50 cases), and further, that it increases in volume at the birth of the child, and sometimes also continues in this condition during lactation.[1] In rare cases there is visible and obvious swelling of the thyroid in association with emotional states, even in men.

Nearly all the diseases of the thyroid gland are more frequent in women than in men. Goitre—or simple enlargement of the gland—is decidedly more common in women; the proportion varies in different localities from one man to two women to one man to

[1] Hermann Freund, *Deutsche Zeitschrift für Chirurgie*, Bd. xxxi., p. 446.

fifteen women.[1] Cretinism—or idiocy resulting from disease of the thyroid gland—appears to be usually rather more common in males, but it is stated that in this country sporadic cretinism is more common in females. Myxœdema—a closely-allied physical and mental disorder dependent on degenerative disease of the thyroid—is chiefly found in middle-aged women. Exophthalmic goitre (Graves' disease or Basedow's disease) is a somewhat more complicated disorder, and has been termed a neurosis of the emotional nervous system (Burney Yeo). But goitre is usually a characteristic feature, and this disease is possibly a primary affection of the thyroid gland.[2] Its symptoms present a picture which is the reverse of that presented in myxœdema, and are probably due to excess of thyroid secretion, as myxœdema undoubtedly is to defect of thyroid secretion. All authorities are agreed that it is more common in women than in men; the proportions given differ from one to two to one to eight, some finding it almost exclusively in women.

The appearance of the patient suffering from this disease—the staring protruded eyes, the breathlessness and rapid heart, etc.—suggests a person suffering from terror, and it is remarkable that fright has often formed the starting-point of the disease; a number of cases, for example, occurred in Alsace and Lorraine after the Franco-German war. Dr. H. W. G. Mackenzie, who has made a careful study of this disease

---

[1] This prevalence of goitre among women is not merely found in the Pennine valleys in England and in the other parts of Europe where it is endemic, but, it would seem, in nearly all parts of the world where the disease is found. Thus Munson, who made a collective investigation concerning goitre among American Indians, found that fully 80 per cent. of the cases occurred in females, the disease tending to appear at puberty; when found in men it was a much less serious disease. From Kafiristan, to the north of India, the same report is made. "Goitre is a common disease," Sir G. S. Robertson writes in The Kafirs of the Hindu-Kush, "but is almost exclusively confined to women; Bashgul men and women live under the same conditions of life, drink from the same streams, and eat more or less the same kind of food;" yet the women alone are affected.

[2] See Professor Greenfield's Bradshaw Lecture on the Thyroid Gland, Brit. Med. Journal, Dec. 9, 1893.

("Clinical Lectures on Graves' Disease," *Lancet*, Sept. 1890), has some very interesting and suggestive remarks on the resemblance between exophthalmic goitre and terror which may here be quoted:—

"Fright, intense grief, and other profound emotional disturbance have been recognised as causes of the pathological condition, but I do not think that sufficient attention has been paid to the very close connection between the chronic symptoms of Graves' disease and the more immediate effects of terror. The descriptions given by Darwin and Sir Charles Bell of the condition of man in intense fear might almost have been written in regard to one of the patients we have been considering. The heart beats quickly and violently, so that it palpitates or knocks against the ribs. There is trembling of all the muscles of the body. The eyes start forward, and the uncovered and protruding eyeballs are fixed on the object of terror. The surface breaks out into a cold clammy sweat. The intestines are affected. The skin is flushed over the face and neck down to the clavicles. The hair stands erect. 'Of all emotions fear notoriously is the most apt to induce trembling.' The symptoms of terror are common to man and the lower animals. There are one or two of the minor symptoms of Graves' disease whose independent occurrence under the influence of emotions is well known. These are pigmentary changes in the skin and hair, falling out of the hair, and epistaxis.

"Such being the condition resulting from severe terror, we have only to imagine the condition to become prolonged by a failure of the nervous system to recover its balance and to right itself, and we have a more or less complete clinical picture of Graves' disease. We have all the well-known symptoms—trembling, palpitation, flushing, sweating, exophthalmos, relaxation of the bowels. There is no information that I know of in regard to the enlargement of the thyroid gland under the influence of profound emotional disturbance. All one can say on that point is that the enlargement which takes place in those cases where the symptoms develop rapidly after such disturbance makes it probable that this is actually the case. If this be so, we have had associated with one another, probably as long as the human race and its ancestors have existed, the symptoms which we find in Graves' disease. The existence of a certain abnormal condition of the nervous system having been once established, we know how in time it becomes dissociated from its exciting cause, rises to independence as a disease in its own right, and may require only a minimal incitement to set it off. In many cases the disease is started anew by severe mental shock; probably in a good many more it is the expression of the unconscious memory of the individual of some such shock in an ancestor.

"Such is what I would suggest to you as the origin and development of this very curious disease. It is likely that the alteration of the function of the thyroid body, whose importance in connection with nutrition and the transmission of nerve-force has been amply demonstrated, has a good deal to do with many of the secondary symptoms to which I have called attention, but the real disease is a widely distributed derangement of the emotional nervous system."

The Larynx and the Voice.—Something may here be said of the functions of the larynx, an organ in close proximity to the thyroid, although perfectly distinct.

In the lower human races generally the larynx is comparatively undeveloped, and the voice is usually inclined to be high and shrill. It is in Europe that both larynx and voice are most highly developed; all great singers are of European race, and the European voice is the most sonorous; the Tartars are, however, said to possess the loudest and most powerful voices, the Germans coming next.[1] On the whole, it may probably be said with truth that the tendency of evolution is in the direction of the enlargement of the larynx and of the deepening of the voice.[2]

Up to puberty the sexual differences in the larynx and in the voice are not marked, but at this epoch they become considerable. The boy's larynx enlarges to a greater degree than the girl's, while his voice "breaks" and becomes deeper. The woman's larynx and voice retain more nearly the characteristics of the child's. While the growth of the male glottis at puberty is as 5 to 10, that of the female glottis is only as 5 to 7 (C. Langer).

In castrated persons, however, the larynx remains puerile, although perhaps slightly larger than in women. The old

---

[1] Sir Duncan Gibb, "The Character of the Voice in the Nations of Asia and Africa, contrasted with that of the Nations of Europe," *Mem. Anthrop. Soc.*, vol. iii., 1870, p. 244.

[2] This is the conclusion reached by Gaëtan Delaunay in an interesting and ingenious discussion of this point in his *Études de Biologie Comparée*, 2e Partie, pp. 97-110.

Italian custom of castrating boys to preserve their youthful singing voices bears witness to the close connection between the voice and the organs of sex. Delaunay remarks that while a bass need not fear any kind of sexual or other excess so far as his voice is concerned, a tenor must be extremely careful and temperate. Among prostitutes, it may be added, the evolution of the voice and of the larynx tends to take a masculine direction. This fact, which is fairly obvious, has been accurately investigated at Genoa by Professor Masini, who find that among 50 prostitutes 29 showed in a high degree the deep masculine voice, while the larynx was large and the vocal cords resembled those of man; only 6 out of the 50 showed a normal larynx; while of 20 presumably honest women only 2 showed the ample masculine larynx. (*Archivio di Psichiatria*, vol. xiv., Fasc. 1-2, p. 145.)

The position of the larynx in adult normal women

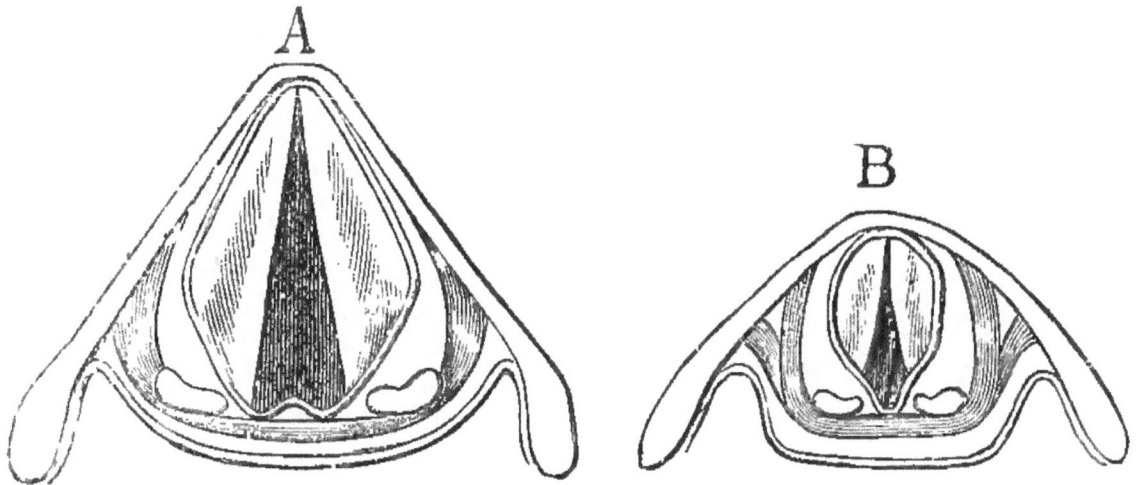

A. HORIZONTAL SECTION OF MALE GLOTTIS.
B. FEMALE GLOTTIS. (*Langer.*)

is somewhat higher in the neck than in men; in this, as well as in the character of the larynx generally, women approach children. In nearly every dimension man's larynx is larger, the entire male larynx being about one-third larger than the female. But while in the transverse diameter there is comparatively little sexual difference, in the antero-posterior diameter there is great difference. The vocal cords are considerably longer in men.[1]

[1] A detailed account of the anatomical differences in the larynx will be found in the Art. "Larynx" by Béclard, *Dict. ency. des Sci. Méd.*, pp. 554-565; see also Professor K. Taguchi (of Tokio), "Beiträge zur

The difference in voice is one of the most obvious of the human secondary sexual characters. The higher and shriller voice of woman, Delaunay remarks, seems to have determined the nature of the grammatical feminine endings of words, and the sharper quality of the feminine endings may be well studied in the French language. This sexual vocal difference is by no means peculiar to Man: in most animals the female has a shriller and weaker voice than the male, as the hen, bitch, and mare, for example; and Buffon observed that the she-ass has a clearer and more piercing voice than the male. Darwin, discussing the loud voices of male animals at the breeding season, came to the conclusion that the most probable view is that "the frequent use of the voice, under the strong excitement of love, jealousy, and rage, continued during many generations, may at last have produced an inherited effect on the vocal organs."[1] It is scarcely possible yet to speak more definitely as to the cause of this secondary sexual character, or its utility. That the deeper voice of a man, and the gentler but higher-pitched voice in woman, have their effect in heightening the pleasure of the sexes in each other's person is a well recognisable fact.

Among the lower animals it is nearly always the males that are most vocal. This is not the case in the human species. Women are both readier and more accomplished than men in the use of the voice. Thus Monroe found in America that at all ages girls surpass boys in ability to sing the scale, and also, though to a less degree, in memory for tones.[2]

The Thoracic Viscera.—The heart at an early age

topographischen Anatomie des Kehlkopfs," *Archiv für Anat. u. Phys.*, 1889, heft. v.-vi. The accompanying diagram shows roughly the main difference between the typical male larynx and the typical female larynx.

[1] *Descent of Man*, Part II., Chap. xviii. This conclusion is not universally accepted.

[2] W. Monroe, *Psych. Rev.*, March 1903, p. 155.

is as large in the female as in the male, or even larger. According to Boyd's tables, it is still absolutely larger in girls between the ages of fourteen and twenty, but from that age on it keeps about two ounces smaller; the maximum weight is only attained at a mature age. In Russia Falk found the heart larger in boys up to twelve years, and from then to fifteen larger in girls. According to F. W. Beneke, the child has a relatively large arterial system, but at puberty this relation is changed; "the larger the heart relatively to the vessels the higher the blood pressure, and the earlier this becomes the case the earlier, stronger, and more complete is the development of puberty."[1] According to Vierordt's tables, the male heart from birth onwards increases its original weight fully thirteen times, the female heart less than twelve times. Hypertrophy of the heart is about twice as common in men as in women, while atrophy is somewhat more frequent in women.

The right lung, according to Boyd, is absolutely larger in the female child at birth, but between the ages of twenty and thirty the male lung has become by as much as a third of its weight heavier than the female.[2]

It is not easy to ascertain the normal weights of the lungs and heart, as these are so frequently increased or diminished through disease. It seems probable, however, that there is a tendency in early life for the heart and lungs in the female child to develop faster than in the male. If so, it may be another case of precocity resulting in diminished final attainment, for there is reason to think that in women these organs are relatively somewhat smaller than in men. This result is in harmony with what

[1] F. W. Beneke, *Die anat. Grundlagen der Constitutionsanomalien des Menschen*, Marburg, 1878.

[2] Boyd's "Table of Weights of the Human Body and Internal Organs," founded on the results of 2600 post-mortems, *Philosophical Transactions*, 1861.

we know of the size of the thorax in women, and of their marked inferiority in vital capacity and in muscular efforts.

The Abdominal Viscera.—The stomach appears to be relatively larger in women than in men. Thus, according to Boyd's tables, it is the same size in both sexes at birth; between the ages of 14 and 20 it is still of equal size in both sexes, or indeed somewhat heavier in girls, although the tota average weight of the boys is five pounds more than of the girls. At the age of 20 to 30 it is still nearly the same size in men and women, although the preponderance of men in total weight has by this time become much greater.

It is stated by Burdach and other old writers that the intestinal canal is longer in women than in men.

Women are said by Burdach and others to digest more rapidly than men. Delaunay found on making inquiries from the matrons of orphan asylums that little girls become hungry much oftener than little boys, and he also found that in almshouses for the aged where there are three regulation meals a day, the old women often put aside a portion of their meals to eat during the interval. The need for food at frequent intervals is common among the young.

At the same time women eat less than men. In prisons and hospitals, according to Burdach, women take nearly one-fifth less food than men. A London vegetarian restaurant-keeper said that the average price a man pays for a vegetarian dinner is tenpence, while the women only average sixpence. It would probably be easy to add proofs of the small appetite of women, but it must be added that when women work, are under good conditions, and not forced to economise, the sexual difference is by no means marked.

It has often been said that gluttony is more common in women than in men. Delaunay, who has a curious discussion on the frequency of gluttony in various classes of the community,[1] came to this conclusion as the unanimous result of his inquiries; he found it was most marked during menstruation and pregnancy. Brillat Savarin thought that women are inclined to be *gourmandes*, the reason being that they know it is

---

[1] *Études de Biol. Comp.*, "Physiologie," pp. 16-25.

favourable to beauty. I should be inclined to say that women are *friandes* rather than *gourmandes*, loving special foods, chiefly sweets, sometimes acids; such a conclusion is quite in accordance with the facts given by Delaunay. And it may be added that if women were as much addicted as men are to the use of tobacco their *friandise* would probably no longer be observable. The taste for tobacco and the taste for sweets seem usually to be mutually exclusive.

The liver is relatively very large at birth, and according to Vierordt it is proportionately somewhat larger in women.[1] Boyd's figures tend on the whole to show the same result. According to Gegenbaur, however, the liver represents 28 per cent. of the weight of the body in men, and only 26 per cent. in women. Wiesener's figures show that it varies very greatly through life, and at birth is larger in the female. On the whole, it is difficult to speak definitely regarding so variable an organ, but it seems probable that if there is any sexual difference at all it is in favour of women.

The spleen, according to Boyd's tables, is, on the average, absolutely larger in the female, if prematurely stillborn, if stillborn at full time, or if born alive. Up to three months it is the same size in both sexes, and after that it is of about equal size in both sexes proportionately to body-weight. The maximum weight of the spleen in proportion to the body, according to Gaston and Vallée, who have specially studied the organ, it may be mentioned, is attained at the age of eight;[2] it is therefore essentially an organ of childhood. Blosfeld of Kasan and Gocke of Munich have both found the spleen (according to Vierordt) absolutely larger in women by about 12 grs.; Vierordt himself does not find much sexual difference.

The kidneys in infancy are relatively very large. In early life, according to Boyd's tables, they are in absolute figures slightly smaller in the female, the

[1] H. Vierordt, "Das Massenwachsthum der Körperorgane des Menschen," *Arch. f. Anat. u. Phys.*, 1890.
[2] *Revue Mensuelle des Maladies de l'Enfance*, September 1892.

difference increasing in the adult. Sappey has found the average length, breadth, and thickness equal in the sexes, and therefore relatively greater in women. While the absolute weight is somewhat less in women, proportionately to body-weight there seems to be little sexual difference.

The bladder is relatively small in infancy, and its shape is at this time inclined to be fusiform; in men it is ovoid, and in women ellipsoid, or rounder. It is also relatively larger in women, with a tendency to lateral expansion, and more dilatable; the majority of cases of enormous distension of the bladder have been found in women. It may perhaps be said, therefore, that the bladder is more highly evolved in women than in men.

There has been considerable controversy as to the relative size of the male and female bladders. Cruveilhier stated that it is larger in women. Sappey, as well as Hoffmann, on the other hand, claim a vesical predominance for men, and conclude that when in women the viscus is large it is simply due to unnatural habits of distension, the result of social causes. Charpy, who attributed much importance to sexual differences of size in the bladder, found that it was anatomically smaller in women, but of greater physiological capacity. Heitzmann and Winckel (who has made a special study of the female bladder) find it larger in women. Hart and Barbour find that, relatively to body-weight, it is more capacious in women. This result is doubtless correct.

The question of the dilatability of the bladder has been carefully studied by Genouville ("Etude Comparative des Organes de Miction dans les deux Sexes," *Archives de Tocologie et de Gynécologie*, Mai 1893). This investigator, examining the bodies of 25 men and 25 women after death, found that on an average

Male bladder without pressure contained 88 gr.
Female   ,,   ,,   ,,   58 gr.
Male bladder with   ,,   ,,   238 gr.
Female   ,,   ,,   ,,   337 gr.

So that while without pressure the female bladder only contains about two-thirds of the amount contained in the male, with pressure the proportion is almost reversed; the male bladder with a pressure of om. 20 height of water contained nearly three times what it contained before, the female bladder nearly six times what it contained before. (It must be remembered that the results without pressure do not correspond to what is normally found during life, the pressure of the muscular tonicity of the sphincter in life, as Hache has pointed out, making a greater difference between the dead and living bladder in women than in men.) Duchastelet in the living subject also found that the tolerance of the female bladder on injecting water is much greater than of the male. And Duchastelet also found, like Mosso and Pellacani, that the desire to urinate always makes itself felt at the same pressure; the threshold of desire is not determined by the amount of urine, but by the energy with which the bladder walls contract on that amount, and this threshold is constant in any one individual. Genouville considers that habit may possibly have something to do with the greater dilatability of the bladder in women, but that it is certain that the female bladder is predisposed to this, and possesses a native dilatability. It is less heavy and muscular than that of men. The child's is even less dilatable than that of men. The anatomical capacity of the bladder (*i.e.*, after death), Genouville concludes with Charpy, is greater in men; the physiological capacity is greater in women.

On the whole, this glance at the viscera seems to show that the thoracic organs somewhat predominate in men and the abdominal in women. Our knowledge is imperfect and the fallacies are so considerable that we can scarcely hope to attain very accurate information. Such results as we see, however, are in harmony with what we have already found as to the sexual differences in the thoracic and abdominal cavities. They are in harmony, also, with the opinions of the older writers, who attributed abdominal predominance to women. The muscular energy which is so marked a characteristic of men depends largely on the strength of the heart and lungs.

It is not possible to say much at present of the viscera as organs of emotion, although there is reason to believe that the organic basis of emotion is largely to be traced here. A very ancient and widespread psychology has placed the seat of the manly virtues of courage and endurance in the breast, and the womanly virtues of love and pity in the belly.　Cœur-de-lion is emphatically a manly title of honour; the liver was formerly regarded as the organ of love, and the Hebrew and other races, even as far off as the Pacific, have found the seat of compassion in their bowels.

CHAPTER XI.

THE FUNCTIONAL PERIODICITY OF WOMEN.

THE PHENOMENA OF MENSTRUATION—ORIGIN—THE THEORY
THAT WOMEN ARE NATURAL INVALIDS—THE CYCLIC
LIFE OF WOMEN—ITS RECENT DISCOVERY—ILLUS-
TRATED BY THE OBSERVATION OF VARIOUS FUNCTIONS
—THE HEART, THE EYE, ETC.—THE SPECIAL PHYSICAL
AND PSYCHIC PHENOMENA OF THE MONTHLY CLIMAX
— THESE ARE INTENSIFIED IN ILL HEALTH — THE
LEGAL, SCIENTIFIC, AND SOCIAL IMPORTANCE OF
WOMEN'S PERIODICITY OF FUNCTION.

THE fact that from the evolution of puberty onwards
during the years of sexual life, with periods of inter-
mission caused by impregnation, women are subjected
to a monthly loss of blood has incidentally come
before us several times. The amount of blood lost
every lunar month may be said to be between 100
and 200 grammes; the period of flow lasts from three
to five days, and on an average recurs on every
twenty-eighth day;[1] and the age at which it first
appears is usually between fourteen and sixteen,
though it may be earlier or later.

The tables of Guy and Tilt indicate that for London the
average age of first menstruation is 15; Whitehead at Manchester found it a few months later. It is possible that climate,

---

[1] Osterloh in Dresden (quoted by Näcke, *Archiv f. Psych.*, 1896,
heft 1) found that among 3000 women in good general and sexual
health, the regular period of four weeks occurred in 68 per cent.; in
2000 cases the flow lasted from one to five days.

race, habits of life, social position, the influence of towns, as well as constitution and health, may all have an influence in modifying the age. For a summary of the facts bearing on these influences see Ploss, *Das Weib*, 7th ed., 1901, vol. i. pp. 362-381. So far as the North American Continent is concerned, the question has lately been very thoroughly investigated by an eminent gynæcologist, Dr. G. J. Engelmann, who has succeeded in accumulating a vast amount of data. He finds that while the average age of first menstruation in Europe is 15.5, in the American Continent it is 14, with a range from 13.5 in the case of girls of refinement and education, to 14.5 in the case of American-born labouring-class girls of Irish and German parentage. Engelmann considered that in America climate has had practically no influence, race very little, mentality, surroundings, education, and nerve stimulation being the main factors of American precocity. It is curious that in this respect the American girl resembles the American Indian who matures at an earlier age than the girls of any other land in the temperate zone. (G. J. Engelmann, "The Age of First Menstruation," *Trans. Am. Gynecological Soc.*, 1901.)

This periodic flux exists in all races, and some traces of it may be found among the higher mammals, such as the mare and cow, as Aristotle remarked; it is found also in the bitch; and among monkeys and apes in their wild condition there is a well-marked menstrual discharge. In the higher apes, when they do not suffer from captivity, the flow is said to be sometimes quite as copious as in women; some monkeys become swollen and brilliantly pigmented, so that tomato-like, vermilion-tinted masses render their condition conspicuous.[1] On the whole, however, it may be said that menstruation in its fully-developed form is a human character.

---

[1] Some of these facts were ascertained by the late Dr. Wiltshire; see his valuable lectures on "Comparative Physiology of Menstruation," *Brit. Med. Journal*, 1883. During recent years the whole question has been greatly elucidated by the researches of Walter Heape: "Menstruation of Semnopithecus Entellus," *Trans. Royal Soc.*, 1894; "Menstruation and Ovulation of Macacus Rhesus," *id.*, 1897; "The Menstruation of Monkeys and the Human Female," *Trans. Obstet. Soc.*, 1898; "The 'Sexual Season' of Mammals," *Quarterly Jour. Microscop. Soc.*, 1900 (the last Paper contains a useful bibliography). See also Havelock Ellis, "Sexual Periodicity," *Studies in the Psychology of Sex*.

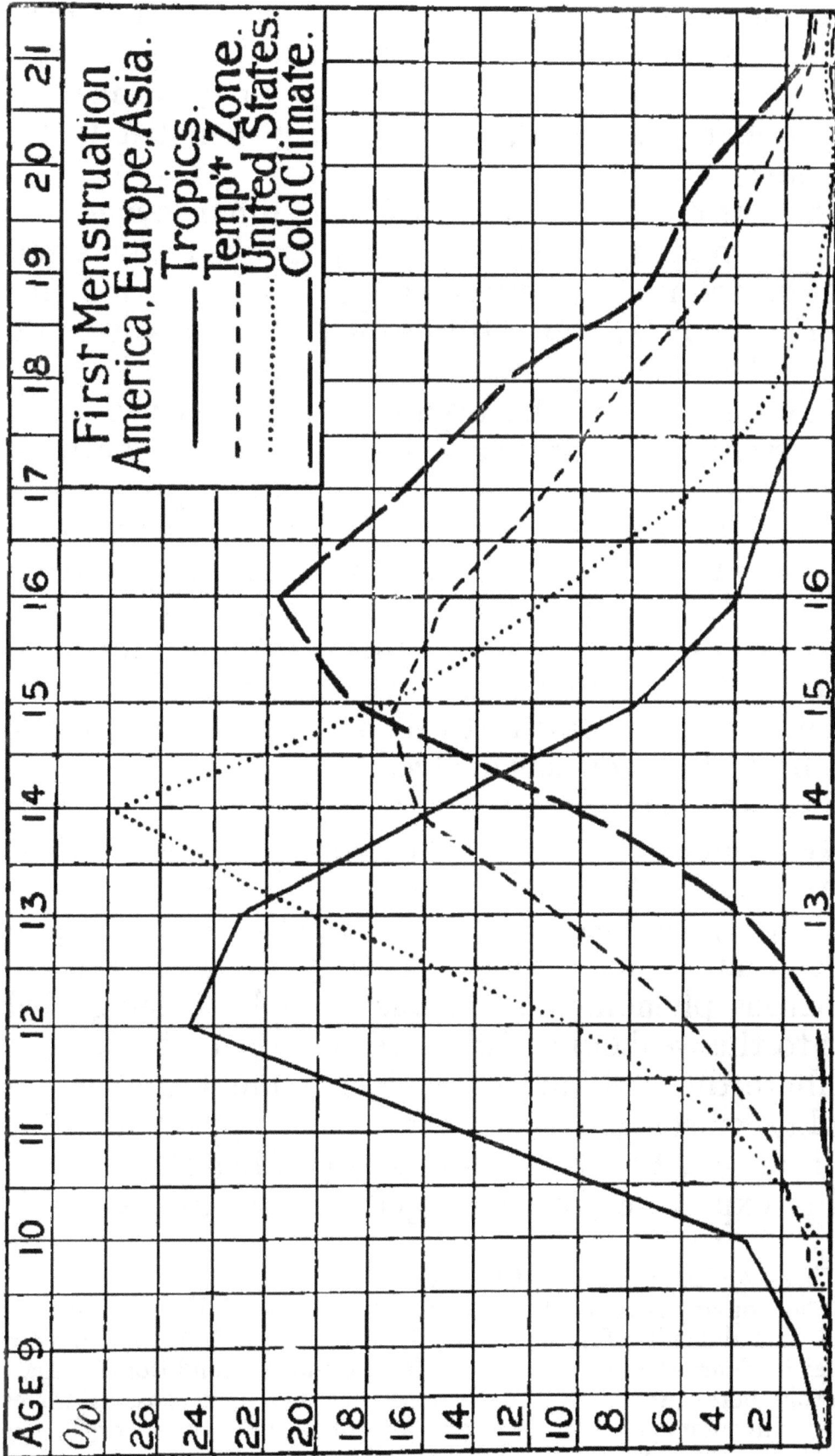

AGE OF FIRST MENSTRUATION IN 57,000 CASES. (*Engelmann.*)

Not only is the flow more copious generally as the animal approaches Man, but among the lower human races it is less pronounced than among the higher races; American Indian women, for instance, as Dr. Holder has found, usually only menstruate for two days.

The curious resemblance to the lunar cycle was long ago noticed. More recently Darwin suggested that the connection between physiological periodicity and the moon was directly formed at a very remote period of zoological evolution, and that the periodicity then impressed on the organism has survived until the present day. Creatures living near low or high water-mark would have their nutrition profoundly modified by their position, and the fortnightly cycles they pass through would lead to a general tendency to periodicity.[1] He did not, however, so far as I am aware, directly connect this particular function with the tides, and there is perhaps a difficulty on account of the comparatively recent period during which the function has evolved.[2]

The fact that women are thus, as it were, periodically wounded in the most sensitive spot in their organism, and subjected to a monthly loss of blood, is familiar, and has been used, legitimately or illegitimately, as we have indeed already seen, to explain numerous phenomena. It has even been suggested that to the weakening influence of this cause we must attribute the early arrest of development of girls in height, muscles, larynx, etc. In support of this position, Dr. Fothergill, for example, has stated that, in his experience, a prolonged menstrual period is

---

[1] *Descent of Man*, Part I., Chap. vi.

[2] The non-appearance of any corresponding periodic cycle in men is less of a difficulty, for, as we shall see (Chap. XV.), men have a greater tendency than women to vary from primitive conditions. Apart from this there is some reason to believe that men may possess traces of a rudimentary menstrual cycle, affecting the whole organism. (Havelock Ellis, "Sexual Periodicity," *Studies in the Psychology of Sex.*)

more common in small than in well-developed girls, and that sometimes when this heavy expenditure has been checked growth has continued.[1] On the whole, however, there does not seem any real ground for this supposition; among all mammals, as well as among many other kinds of animals fairly high in the morphological scale, the male is more highly developed than the female, frequently to a very much greater extent than in Man. There are also so many advantages gained by the precocious and slighter development of women that we cannot legitimately regard the character of feminine development as merely the fortuitous and pathological result of a periodic function.

It is not difficult to see how the menstrual function has given origin to the erroneous notion that women are natural invalids. Thus Galiani, in his *Dialogue sur les Femmes*, describes woman as "un animal naturellement faible et malade." "At first she is an invalid," he remarks, "as all animals are until they have attained their full growth; then come the symptoms so well known in every race of man, and which make her an invalid for six days during every month on an average, which makes at least a fifth part of her life; then come pregnancies and lactations which, properly considered, are two troublesome disorders. Women, therefore, only have intervals of health in the course of a continual disease. In character they show the influence of this almost habitual condition: they are caressing and engaging as invalids usually are, although, like invalids, *brusque* and capricious at times; quickly irritated, they are promptly appeased. They seek for distraction; a mere nothing amuses them, like invalids. Their imagination is always in play: fear, hope, joy, despair, desire, disgust, succeed each other rapidly in their heads, and disappear with equal rapidity. . . . And then we—yes, we seek to cure them by causing them perhaps a new disease." Michelet, the historian, in his book *L'Amour* (1859), expounds the same idea that women are invalids; "woman is for ever suffering," he says, "from the cicatrisation of an interior wound which is the cause of a whole drama. So that in reality for 15 or 20 days out of 28 [in any case, an extremely exaggerated estimate, it may be remarked]—one may almost say always—woman is not only invalided

---

[1] J. Fothergill, *West Riding Reports*, vol. vi.

but wounded. She suffers incessantly the eternal wound of love." Quite recently a woman has sought to revive the idea that women are normally in a pathological condition, owing to this function, the cause of which she finds, in some unexplained way, in the brutality of men. It is scarcely necessary to point out that a pathological condition can scarcely be called normal. A function which affects half the human race cannot be dismissed as a mere symptom of ill-health.

Other writers have gone to the opposite extreme, and have asserted that this function, normally and even generally, has no effect whatever on the health or general physical condition of women. Thus Miss Frances Power Cobbe has made this assertion in reply to Michelet. Mrs. Fawcett, again, has more recently made a similar assertion in replying to Mr. Frederick Harrison:—"He says, 'all women,' with very few exceptions, are 'subject to functional interruption absolutely incompatible with the highest forms of continuous pressure.' This assertion I venture most emphatically to deny. The actual period of childbirth apart, the ordinarily healthy woman is as fit for work every day of her life as the ordinarily healthy man." Mrs. Fawcett appears to attribute this to a marvellous improvement in the health of women, brought about in recent years by attention to hygiene (*Fortnightly Review*, September 1891). Unfortunately there is ample evidence to show that this rose-coloured view is scarcely justified, although no one doubts that it is fairly true concerning a certain proportion of women. The question is, as we shall see: What proportion of women are "ordinarily healthy"?

While this periodic loss of blood has always attracted attention, and has furnished a more or less hazardous basis for various poetic and scientific suppositions, it is only within recent years that it has come to be recognised that menstruation is not an isolated phenomenon. It is but the outward manifestation of the climax of a monthly physiological cycle which influences throughout the month the whole of a woman's physical and psychic organism. Whatever organic activity we investigate daily with any precision we find traces of this rhythm. While a man may be said, at all events relatively, to live on a plane, a woman always lives on the upward or downward slope of a curve. This is a fact of the very first importance in the study of physiological or

psychological phenomena in women. Unless we
always bear it in mind we cannot attain to any true

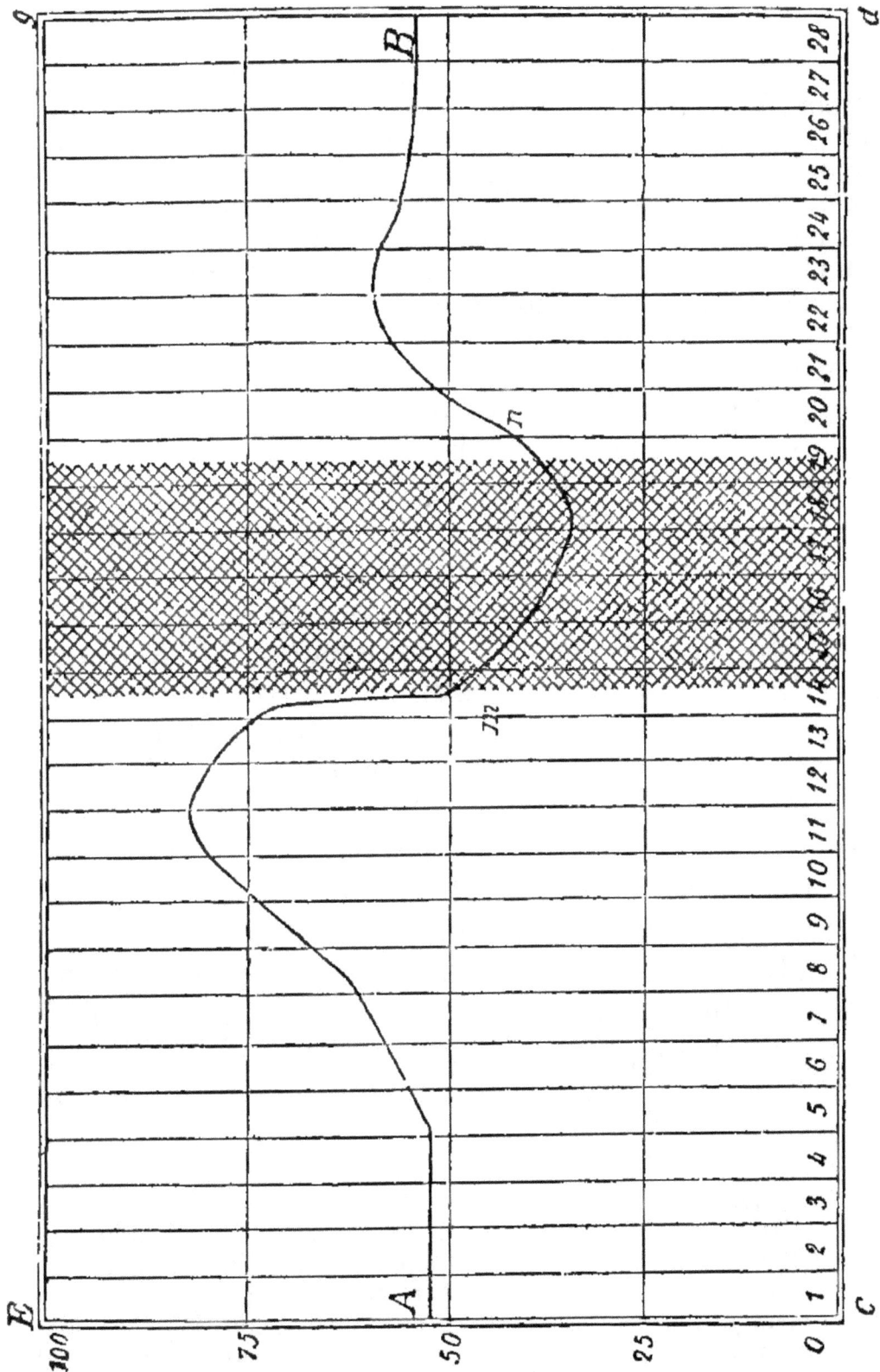

CHART OF THE MONTHLY CYCLE. (*Van Ott.*)

knowledge of the physical, mental, or moral life of
women.

Our knowledge of the physiological and psychological periodicity of women is chiefly owing to Goodman, "The Cyclical Theory of Menstruation," *American Journal of Obstetrics*, 1878, p. 673; Dr. Mary Putnam Jacobi, *The Question of Rest for Women during Menstruation*, New York, 1877; Stephenson, *American Journal of Obstetrics*, 1882, p. 287; Reinl, Volkmann's *Sammlung*, No. 243; Professor Ott (of St. Petersburg), "Des Lois de la Périodicité de la Fonction Physiologique dans l'Organisme Féminin," *Nouvelles Archives d'Obstétrique*, Paris, 25th September 1890. There are several interesting chapters discussing "The Monthly Rhythm" in Dr. H. Campbell's *Differences in the Nervous Organisation of Man and Woman*, 1891. I have not been able to see all these papers.

In order to give a fairly correct general view of the monthly physiological curve in women I here reproduce a diagram, prepared by Professor Ott, which sums up a very large number of daily observations carried on during 68 monthly cycles on about 60 healthy women. The observations concerned temperature, muscular force, vital capacity, and reflex action. While this curve represents the average result, the period of maximum excitability (usually attained, it will be seen, nearly three days before the onset of menstruation) may sometimes be delayed until the appearance of the flow. The line A, B represents the curve of physiological oscillation during the twenty-eight days of the cycle (noted at bottom of the diagram); the degree of intensity of the functions investigated is represented along the line E, C; the actual period of menstruation (somewhat more prolonged than we usually find it in this country) corresponds to the shaded portion of the diagram.[1]

[1] Various investigators have prepared charts of the menstrual wave, but Van Ott's probably remains the most accurate. Engelmann remarks (*Trans. Am. Gynecol. Soc.*, 1900) that it is "thoroughly in accord with my own observations with reference to the physical and psychical changes during the monthly periods, characterising the menstrual wave in all its phases. It is almost equally correct for morbid nervous symptoms as characterised by the hystero-neuroses. During pregnancy and labour we have similar conditions but of longer duration and much greater intensity."

The heart and the tension of the vascular system have most frequently been observed with reference to this monthly periodicity. Cullen long ago maintained that the pulse-rate rises at the approach of the periods. Stephenson found a monthly cycle as regards arterial tension and pulse-rate. Dr. Mary Jacobi concluded, as the result of her investigations with the sphygmograph, that "in women exists a rhythmic wave of plenitude and tension of the arterial system, at all events perceptible in the radial artery, which begins at a minimum point, from one to four days after the cessation of menstruation, and gradually rises to a maximum, either seven or eight days before menstruation, or at any day nearer than this, or even during the first day of the flow."[1] Giles's observations show the greatest blood-pressure on the first two days of menstruation and the day preceding. Dr. Clelia Mosher finds that the fall of blood-pressure, as measured by Mosso's sphygmomanometer, occurs most frequently just before (occasionally during) the menstrual flow, the maximum fall being coincident with the onset of the flow.[2] This process involves an active engorgement of the thyroid, parotid, tonsils, and other organs also, during the period of the flow. The temperature is also at its highest point a few days before actual menstruation, as has been shown by Jacobi, Ott, Giles, and others; and, according to Silva, the alkalinity of the blood is reduced, and the vasomotor system reacts to stimuli in the same way as in states of fever.[3] The curve in the excretion of urea and urine I have referred to already (p. 247). The highest points of activity in the sexual organs also correspond to the general maximum, and in

[1] *The Question of Rest*, etc., pp. 148-161.
[2] Mosher, "Normal Menstruation," *John Hopkins Hosp. Bull.*, Ap. 1901.
[3] *Il Policlinico*, 15th Feb. 1896, summarised in *Brit. Med. Jour.*, 24th March 1896.

most healthy women the sexual emotions are strongest at the maximum before the period, and at the lesser maximum after it. That the intellectual vigour is also greatest at the same points is somewhat less easy to prove, but is extremely probable. That the mental energy, as well as the muscular strength and dexterity, even in the strongest, healthiest, and most determined women, are usually somewhat impaired during the menstrual period itself is a fact that is familiar to most women; I am not, however, aware of any data showing a maximum during the intermenstrual period.

There can be little doubt that a daily examination of any of the senses would show a monthly rhythm. I am, however, only acquainted with one series of observations on this point, those of Finkelstein of St. Petersburg, carried out on the eye, under the superintendence of Professor Mierzejewski. Finkelstein studied the functional activity of the eye during menstruation in twenty healthy women, aged between nineteen and thirty-three. He found that during the period there is a concentric narrowing of the field of vision, beginning one, two, or three days beforehand, reaching the greatest intensity on the third or fourth day of menstruation, and gradually disappearing on the seventh or eighth day after its appearance. The narrowing is more pronounced in those women in whom menstruation is associated with *malaise*, headache, cardiac palpitation, and other nervous symptoms, as well as in those who lose large quantities of blood. Not only the field of vision for white but also the visual fields for green, red, yellow, and blue undergo a regular diminution. Perversion of perception of green (which is seen as yellow) is observed fairly often (in 20 per cent. cases). Central vision is but slightly impaired, and rapidly returns to the normal standard after the period, and refraction remains intact.[1] There can be little doubt that observation of the other sense organs would yield similar proof of monthly periodicity.

As soon as the climax of vital activity is reached, or a day or two afterwards, the menstrual flow begins. Even in perfectly healthy women this affects the whole organism to a more or less marked degree. There is a general feeling of tension in the pelvic organs; the breasts also are slightly enlarged, and may consequently be somewhat tender and painful. The same congestive tendency shows itself in the enlarged thyroid. The temperature, even under strictly physiological conditions, may rise 0.5° Fahr. The surface blood-vessels tend to be fuller than usual, so that there may be flushing of the face. There is increased nervous tension and greater muscular excitability; reflex action is more marked, and there may be slight twitchings of the legs; also yawning and stiffness in the neck, and sleep is heavier than usual. There is loss of appetite and a certain amount of digestive and intestinal disturbance with a tendency to flatulence. Thirst may be present, and urination more frequent than usual. There is a fall of urea and an increase of uric acid. There is a tendency to pigmentation; the pigmented circle around the nipple usually becomes somewhat darker, the complexion is changed, losing its clearness, and a dark ring may sometimes be perceptible around the eyes; these pigmentary changes are more especially observed in brunettes, and, like many other disturbances of menstruation, during pregnancy they become still more marked. In many women the breath and also the skin exhale an odour (quite distinct from that due to the discharge) of a peculiar aromatic and not unpleasant character. The voice also may undergo some change; there is a tendency

[1] Summarised in *Ophthalmic Review*, 1887, pp. 323-326. The influence of normal menstruation on the eye is also dealt with by Salmo Cohn, *Uterus und Auge*, 1890, pp. 13-19.

to hoarseness, and singers sometimes lose the brilliancy of their high notes, so that at this period (as is generally recognised on the Continent) it is not desirable for public singers to appear.[1]

With reference to the influence of normal menstruation on the voice, Lennox Browne, a well-known specialist, wrote to me as follows:—"With regard to singers, I believe that the pitch of the voice is often lowered at the menstrual epoch, although I have not found this to be universally admitted by patients to whom I have spoken on the subject. Many have told me that they have a disposition to sing flat, and in two cases in my recollection the patients, who suffered from dysmenorrhœa, told me that they sang sharp, of which they were conscious— probably from information, for of course you know that those who sing sharp are not generally sensible of the defect. It is, however, generally agreed that the *timbre* and tone-quality is impaired, the voice being decidedly thinner and poorer during the epoch.

"On this point you may like to know that in all Continental engagements with female singers provision is made for suspension of duty during the menstrual period, but this does not obtain in English contracts, although the *impresario* is in practice obliged to recognise it. It would be well were this concession made universal, not only in grand opera, but in smaller lyric ventures in which the *artiste* sings every night in the week, and continuously for many months."

Most of these physical signs may exist in women whom we must consider to be in a state of good health, although we need not expect to find them all in the same person; to a skilled observer it is often easily possible to detect the presence of the monthly period. On the psychic side, even in good health, there is another series of phenomena. There is greater impressionability, greater suggestibility, and more or less diminished self-control; Burdach stated that at this time women are more under the influence

---

[1] Dr. Robert Barnes has specially drawn attention to some of the points in the above picture. (*Brit. Med. Journal*, 2nd March 1889.) In Tilt's *Uterine and Ovarian Inflammation*, 1862, Chaps. i.-xiv., there is a full account of menstruation, giving facts and statistics regarding the various nervous and other normal characters of this function. See also the works on menstruation by Brierre de Boismont, Krieger, etc.

of mesmerism, and there can be no doubt that at this time all the phenomena which may be termed hypnotic become more prominent in women. It is at this time, in those women who are at all predisposed, that sudden caprices, fits of ill-temper, moods of depression, impulses of jealousy, outbursts of self-confession, are chiefly liable to occur. In turning over the pages of a young woman's diary, Icard remarked, very little skill is required to detect those written during the monthly period.

The psychic condition during the menstrual period in ordinary health is well summarised by Dr. Clouston:—"It has a psychology of its own, of which the main features generally are a slight irritability or tendency toward lack of mental inhibition just before the process commences each month, a slight diminution of energy or tendency to mental paralysis and depression during the first day or two of its continuance, and a very considerable excess of energising power and excitation of feeling during the first week or ten days after it has entirely ceased, the last phase being coincident with woman's period of highest conceptive power and keenest generative nisus." (*Mental Diseases*, 1887, p. 480.) It seems to me very probable that the superstitions regarding the evil influences exercised by women at their periods on the food, etc., they prepare may be supported by an actual decreased success in such operations at this time, due merely to a physiological decrease in energy and skill.

" Mental energy and acumen," remarks Engelmann (*Trans. Am. Gynecol. Soc.*, 1900), " are, as a rule, diminished during the first days of the flow at least, as is affirmed by perhaps 65 per cent. of the many questioned, who state that mental exertion and study at that time is more difficult and wearing, and requires greater effort, precisely as the working girl—only in a larger proportion of cases, 75 per cent.—expresses impaired ability for work, saves herself, and relies upon her mates to complete some part of her task."

Clelia Mosher found (*John Hopkins Hosp. Bull.*, 1901) that a curve constructed on the subjective observations of the sense of well-being corresponded to the menstrual wave of blood-pressure, the sense of maximum efficiency corresponding to the period of high pressure and lessened efficiency to the period of low pressure. The period of low pressure appeared to be one of increased susceptibility to morbid influences.

So far I have been careful to speak only of those

phenomena of the menstrual cycle which can fairly be regarded as strictly normal and physiological. It is instructive to glance at the cases in which menstruation produces abnormal and diseased conditions, because what we see under such conditions is simply an exaggeration of what takes place under ordinary conditions. There may be so high a degree of physical pain and disability that the woman is really an invalid for several days every month. All sorts of slight visceral affections, of a congestive character, may be directly due to menstruation, and recur periodically.[1] On the mental side the irritability or depression may be so pronounced as to amount to insanity. Migraine is a disorder common at this period; hysterical and epileptic fits often occur.[2] Erotomania, dipsomania, and kleptomania are also specially liable to be developed at this time, and of all forms of insanity melancholia is the most liable to occur. Whenever a woman commits a deed of criminal violence it is extremely probable that she is at her monthly period; it is unfortunately difficult to give precise figures, as there is often neglect to ascertain this point. Lombroso, however, found that out of 80 women arrested for opposition to the police, or for assault, only 9 were not at the menstrual period.[3] Legrand du Saulle found that out of 56 women detected in theft at shops in Paris, 35 were menstruating. There is no doubt whatever that suicide in women is specially liable to take place at this period; Krugelstein stated that in all cases (107) of suicide in a woman he had met with, the act was committed during this period, and although this cannot be accepted as a general rule (especially when we bear in mind the frequency

[1] See a paper by Plicque on "Visceral Affections of Menstrual Origin," *Gazette des Hôpitaux*, 19th Oct. 1893.

[2] Thus Dr. Fisher found that out of 60 epileptic women, in 16 the menstrual period was either the only time at which the attacks took place, or they were much increased in frequency at that time. (*New York Med. News*, November 1891.

[3] *La Donna Delinquente*, p. 373.

of suicide in old age), Esquirol, Brierre de Boismont, Coste, Moreau de Tours, R. Barnes, and many others have noted the frequency of the suicidal tendency at this period.[1] In England Wynn Westcott has stated that in his experience as a coroner, of 200 women who committed suicide, the majority were either at the change of life or menstruating;[2] and in Germany Heller ascertained by post-mortem examination of 70 women who had committed suicide that 25 (or in the proportion of 35 per cent.) were menstruating, a considerable proportion of the remainder being pregnant or in the puerperal condition.[3] Women in prison, again, are apt to exhibit periodic outbursts of unmotived and apparently uncontrollable violence: these "breakings out," as Nicolson and others have observed, are especially liable to occur at the menstrual epoch.[4] Among the insane, finally, the fact is universally recognised that during the monthly period the insane impulse becomes more marked, if, indeed, it may not appear only at that period. "The melancholics are more depressed," as Clouston puts it, "the maniacal more restless, the delusional more under the influence of their delusions in their conduct; those subject to hallucinations have them more intensely, the impulsive cases are more uncontrollable, the cases of stupor more stupid, and the demented tend to be excited." These facts of morbid psychology are very significant; they emphasise the fact that even in the healthiest woman a worm, however harmless and unperceived, gnaws periodically at the roots of life.

We see, therefore, that instead of being an isolated and temporary process, menstruation is a continuous

---

[1] A full and careful statement of the present state of knowledge regarding the mental condition of women during the menstrual period will be found in Icard, *La Femme Pendant la Période Menstruelle*, Paris, 1890.

[2] *Lancet*, 11th Aug. 1900.

[3] *Münchener Med. Wochenscrift*, 1900, No. 48.

[4] See Havelock Ellis, *The Criminal*, third edition, pp. 172 *et seq.*

process, and one which permeates the whole of a woman's physical and psychic organism. A woman during her reproductive life is always menstruating, as Dr. Harry Campbell puts it, just as the moon is always changing. "Souvent femme varie," it may be said, is a physiological fact; it is not the result of wilful caprice. The fact is one of considerable importance, not only to the physician and the medico-legal expert, but to the man of science generally, to the sociologist, and indeed to the whole community. In the investigation of any fact in a woman's life or organism, we ought to know its exact position in the woman's cyclic life. If we have to investigate the comparative reaction of a man and a woman to any scientific test, we have to recognise that the woman lives on a curve, and that her exact position on the curve at a given moment may affect her superiority or inferiority to the man. In trials of skill or strength among women (as in a swimming match, for instance) everything may depend on a woman's position in her monthly cycle; her full possession of strength, nerve, and dexterity will depend to some extent, even if she is in perfect health, on the time of month, and a few days sooner or later may even make it impossible for her to engage in the contest; it is needless to add that this fact opens the door to considerable intrigue. Again, whenever a woman has committed any offence against the law, it is essential that the relation of the act to her monthly cycle should be ascertained as a matter of routine; it is a fact that control is physiologically lessened at the menstrual period even in health, while it is very much more lessened in the neurotic and unbalanced; it must be clearly recognised that guilt also is lessened.

The existence of the monthly cycle is, lastly, a factor which cannot be entirely ignored in considering the fitness of women for any business position. It is found at the Post-office and elsewhere, where men and women are employed, that the women are more often absent from work than the men, owing to "slight indisposition." This fact cannot be altogether disregarded, but it must be remembered that there is no ground for supposing that an ordinarily healthy woman needs any absolute rest from ordinary healthy work at any period of the month. The fact that so large a proportion of women do need such rest is due to the fact that, from one cause or another, so few are "ordinarily healthy." Brierre de Boismont, in France, found that among 360 women, 278 (or 77 per cent.) suffered some slighter or greater degree of pain at their monthly periods; 82 (or only 23 per cent.) had complete immunity. Dr. Mary Jacobi, in America, by a more careful investigation, out of 268 women found 94 (*i.e.*, 35 per cent.) who never suffered any pain or weakness during the flow; of these 25 per cent. were married, though of those who do suffer only 11 per cent. are married. Dr. Jacobi concludes that, normally, rest is not necessary. "It remains true, however," she adds, "that in our exciting social conditions, 46 per cent. of women suffer more or less at menstruation, and for a large number of these, when engaged in industrial pursuits or others, under the command of an employer, humanity dictates that rest from work during the period of pain be afforded whenever practicable."

This question has recently been studied on a large scale in the United States by Dr. G. J. Engelmann. "To obtain satisfactory results," Dr. Engelmann states, "we must record not individual observations or professional experience, which deals with pathological conditions alone, but we must obtain the facts as found among the representatives of American girlhood and young womanhood under the varying conditions of modern day life, and this could be done only in institutions of learning and in large business organisations.

"It seemed to me important that the girl in study and in work should be represented, from the advent of puberty through the period of adolescence until maturity, when a more stable, less impressionable condition is attained: from the fifteenth to the twenty-sixth year. This means High and Normal School, College, and business house, as representing respectively mental and physical labour, and, between the two, the Normal School for physical training approximating mental labour, and the Training School for Nurses nearing physical labour, the average age being in the High School 16; in Normal School and College, 19 to 20; in Physical Training, 22.6; the Nurse 26, and the working girl from 15 to 30." The results are summarised in the following table:—

Group.	Number.	Class.	Percentage of sufferers.	
			During school or college.	Before entering.
College	100		95 per ct.	90 per ct.
In business	800		83.3 ,,	71.5 ,,
College -	50	Freshman	74 ,,	69 ,,
		Higher Classes	80 ,,	60 ,,
Nurses -	169		73 ,,	69.1 ,,
State Normal School	105		81 ,,	70.5 ,,
,, ,, ,, -	100		77 ,,	76 ,,
Norm. Sch. of Gym. -	98		71.4 ,,	66 ,,
Norm. School, City	306	{ Less hrs. gym.	67.1 ,,	57.4 ,,
		{ More hrs. gym.	64.7 ,,	58.2 ,,
	1000	Freshman	66 ,,	
	125		60— ,,	60+ ,,
College - - -	223		57.84 ,,	
	45		57 ,,	67 ,,
	103		56 ,,	
Normal School, City	539	{ Junior	54.10 ,,	
		{ Senior	53.02 ,,	
High School -	100	{ Junior	42 ,,	
		{ Senior	32 ,,	

"The numbers are high," Dr. Engelmann remarks, "owing to the fact that I have included moderate pain in this group, suffering of every degree and kind save the more trifling discomforts, suffering being classified as severe, some, none, severe and some being here combined, and the result verified by a second question as to kind of suffering, languor, headache, or pain; languor or headache alone, usually about 15 per cent., is not here considered as suffering. It may be well to note the fact that severe suffering exists in from 11 per cent. to 18 per cent.—i.e., one-fifth to one-fourth of those experiencing discomfort during the period suffer severely. The very high percentage of suffering (95 per cent.) in one of the higher institutions of learning is rather surprising, and can only be explained by the fact that all discomfort has here been considered, but the figures are correct, as this investigation was made with the utmost care by one of the medical officers of the institution.

"As is to be expected, great suffering is likewise found in the business woman, averaging in the class here considered 83 per cent., but this varies, even in the same class of business, with the character of the work.   The girl behind the counter, who is on her feet most of the day, with but little space for change of position, shows 91 per cent.; those who sit, bookkeepers and stenographers, show 82 per cent.; and those who have a certain freedom of motion—floor-walkers, cash girls, packers—are noted with only 78 per cent.

" For the pupils of the Nurses' Training Schools (73 per cent.) the numbers are as yet small and the records less perfect than those of any other class; but the results, such as they are, demand investigation, since we know that only women in perfect health are admitted.

" That pupils in the Normal School for physical training should appear with 71 per cent. would seem inexplicable, as these are young women under the best possible conditions, with an apparently most favourable combination of mental and physical work.   A better state of functional health is to be expected, and we should certainly find very different conditions were it not for the fact that girls already broken down frequently undertake this course for the purpose of restoring health wrecked in previous occupations.   As a consequence they enter under most unfavourable conditions.

" In school and college we find too large a proportion of sufferers—from 40 to 70 per cent.—and I must call attention to a Normal School in which one-half of the pupils devote but two forty-five minute periods weekly to gymnastic exercises, while others allow four and more.   Among those devoting more time to physical exercise we find 64 per cent. of suffering, as compared with 67 per cent. in the other group.   The lowest percentage is found in one of the Normal Schools and in a High School.   Almost invariably the percentage of suffering is greater in the more exacting work or the study of more advanced classes than it was before in years of greater freedom; yet we find that from 65 to 70 per cent. enter the higher institutions of learning—Normal School, College—and business with menstrual suffering of some kind, and, as a rule, this suffering increases in the mental and physical occupations here considered, with some few exceptions in those educational institutions where marked attention is given to physical training.   Thus we find in one of the Normal Schools 54 per cent. in the junior and 53 per cent. in the senior class, the first having entered with 66 per cent. and the second with 71 per cent.; but the most marked exception is in the very youngest class in one well-conducted High School with an admirable system of physical training, where we find the most pliable and impressionable condition—the menstrual function barely established and the slight irregularities which may have arisen yielding readily to excellent surroundings and judicious management. Here we find 42 per cent. in the junior class and only 32 per cent. in the same girls at the close of their senior year, some eighteen months after the first record. We have seen an aggravation of suffering with advancing grade, as much as 10 per cent., and yet in school and college a certain number record their general health as better, and this is as it should be, owing to the often improved habits of life and greater regularity. It must be noted that while the percentage of suffering is greater, severe suffering, as a rule, grows less. In one institution 18 per cent. suffered severely before and only 10 per cent. during or after entering upon the course. This is especially marked in the pupils of physical training schools. In the working girl, however, severe suffering increases, most so in the girl behind the counter, who stands most of the day. The percentage of suffering may appear high, but it is nevertheless correct, as the figures are based upon large numbers." (G. J. Engelmann, "The American Girl of To-day," *Trans. Am. Gynecological Soc.*, 1900.)

It may be added that Dr. Clelia Duel Mosher, of the John Hopkins Hospital, who has made a special study of the physiology of menstruation, points out that so-called "menstrual suffering" is very largely "simply coincident functional disturbance in other organs, induced, possibly, by the favouring conditions of a lower general blood pressure occurring near or at the time of menstruation." (C. D. Mosher, "Normal Menstruation and some of the Factors Modifying It," *John Hopkins Hosp. Bull.*, Ap. 1901.) This is no doubt the case, but suffering occurring at the menstrual period, whether directly or only indirectly due to the menstrual process, is quite properly described as "menstrual suffering."

One point at all events is clear: it is no longer possible to regard the physiological periodicity of women, and the recurring menstrual function, as the purely private concern of the woman whom it affects.

CHAPTER XII.

HYPNOTIC PHENOMENA.

THE VARIOUS PHENOMENA HERE INCLUDED UNDER THIS TERM — SOMNAMBULISM — HYPNOTISM —ECSTASY — TRANCE—CATALEPSY—MAGICAL PHENOMENA—WOMEN HAVE PLAYED A LARGER PART IN NEARLY ALL.

DREAMS—WOMEN AS DREAMERS AMONG PRIMITIVE RACES —IN THE MIDDLE AGES—IN MODERN TIMES—RESULTS OBTAINED BY HEERWAGEN, JASTROW, AND CHILD.

HALLUCINATIONS IN THE SANE—SIDGWICK'S INVESTIGA-TIONS—GREATER PREVALENCE AMONG WOMEN.

THE ACTION OF ANÆSTHETICS—NITROUS OXIDE—SILK'S OBSERVATIONS—ABNORMAL ACTION UNDER ANÆSTHESIA OCCURS ON THE WHOLE CHIEFLY IN WOMEN.

METEOROLOGIC SENSIBILITY — SUICIDE — INSANITY — CON-CLUSION AS TO SEXUAL DIFFERENCE DOUBTFUL—PERIODICITY IN GROWTH.

NEURASTHENIA AND HYSTERIA—DESCRIPTION OF NEUR-ASTHENIA—DEFINITION OF HYSTERIA—ITS CHARACTER-ISTICS—SUGGESTIBILITY—RELATIVE FREQUENCY IN THE SEXES.

RELIGIOUS HYPNOTIC PHENOMENA—NATURE OF THE PART PLAYED BY WOMEN IN RELIGIOUS MOVEMENTS—SHAKERS — THEOSOPHISTS — DANCING MANIA — CAMI-SARDS—MODERN HYSTERICAL RELIGIOUS EPIDEMICS—CHRISTS—SKOPTSY—HYPNOTIC RELIGIOUS PHENOMENA AMONG UNCIVILISED RACES—NATURE AND CAUSATION.

WE may use the term "hypnotic phenomena" as a convenient expression to include not merely the condition of artificially-produced sleep, or hypnotism in the narrow sense of the term, but all those groups of psychic phenomena which are characterised by a decreased control of the higher nervous centres, and increased activity of the lower centres.[1] These groups of phenomena are closely related, and are all marked by diminished consciousness of the subject, or diminished power of control, or both. Taken altogether they constitute the phenomena which have often been called "super-human," but which, as Chambers long ago remarked, may quite as truly be called "sub-human." The best known of such phenomena is that which we have all experienced during ordinary sleep, which is perhaps the most primitive and fundamental form of consciousness.

That modified kind of sleep, the condition of ordinary somnambulism or sleep-walking, in which the motor centres are awake and respond to ordinary stimuli while the higher centres are asleep and fail to control the responses of the more automatic centres, is fairly common to a slight degree, or at rare intervals, especially among children.[2] There are no exact statistics, so far as I am aware, as to its frequency among adults; the majority of those who have occupied themselves with the subject seem to regard it as more common in women, or have at all events found the worst and most persistent cases in women. Although this is probable, it is not yet clearly established.

The phenomena of mesmerism, animal magnetism, etc., now usually grouped under the head of hypnotism, have always been specially identified with

---

[1] It may not be superfluous to remark that what in nervous physiology are termed the "lower" centres are by no means "low" in the sense of being unimportant; on the contrary, they are the most fundamental.

[2] Dr. E. von der Stein (*Ueber den natürlichen Somnambulismus*, Heidelberg, 1881) found by investigating orphan asylums in Baden that out of 1000 children 17 (or 1.7 per cent.) showed somnambulistic phenomena; there were not necessarily any signs of neuropathic constitution.

women. Women have most easily fallen under their influence, and the chief advances in our knowledge of hypnotism have come through investigations on women. One or two enthusiasts have declared that most persons, taken at random and irrespective of sex (80 per cent. according to Liébault), are hypnotisable. It is probably true that, with the exercise of sufficient skill and patience, the phenomena might be elicited in every one possessing a fair degree of mental health (for it is notoriously difficult to hypnotise the insane even with the exercise of very considerable skill and patience), but it remains true that, in the experience of the most skilful investigators, women more easily fall into the hypnotic condition, and exhibit the phenomena in a more marked form. In every hypnotic *clinique* we find women in a great majority. Thus Pitres, a chief authority, finds that with the greatest possible persuasion two-thirds of hysterical women, and only one-fifth of hysterical men, can be hypnotised.[1] Again, Bérillon, an enthusiastic and at the same time judicious believer in hypnotic therapeutics, during 1890 and the early part of 1891 (as he stated at the Berlin International Medical Congress), treated 360 patients by hypnotism; of these 265 were women, 45 were children, only 50 were men—a statement agreeing with my own recollections of Dr. Bérillon's *clinique* at about the same period. These figures do not necessarily indicate the sexual proportion of hypnotisable persons among the general population, but they at least show that a comparatively small proportion of men can be treated by hypnotism with any chance of success. It may be added that children may easily be put into the hypnotic state: Beaunis found that out of 100 children between seven and fourteen years of age, 55 are hypnotisable, and Bérillon considers that this is below the truth, as he finds that most children

[1] *Lecons cliniques*, etc., tom. ii. p. 404; cf. Grasset, *L'Hypnotisme et la Suggestion*, 1902, p. 93.

above the age of seven, provided they are not idiots, may easily be hypnotised.[1]

The allied phenomena of ecstasy, trance, and catalepsy, it is generally agreed, are more frequent in women, and it may be added that the most remarkable cases on record, with few exceptions, occurred in women.   In catalepsy the subject's mental functions are largely or altogether suspended as regards the external world; the muscles are passive and retain any position in which they may be placed.   In ecstasy, which cannot be very clearly distinguished from trance, there is not the same absence of muscular control, and the subject's mental functions, instead of being suspended, are actively employed in seeing visions; during the trance the subject's countenance expresses inspired illumination of a more than earthly character, and on awaking he is able to recall his visions, which have played a considerable part in the world's spiritual history.   Both catalepsy and ecstasy are allied to hysteria, but are not necessarily identical with it.[2]

All the phenomena which of old were termed "magical" come under the group here termed "hypnotic," and they have always been regarded as especially connected with women.   Pliny tells us that women are the best subjects for magical experiences.   Quintilian was of the same opinion.   Bodin estimated the proportion of witches to wizards as not less than 50 to 1.[3]   The oracles, which in various

[1] Dr. E. Bérillon, *Hypnotisme et Suggestion*, Paris, 1891, p. 37.

[2] The short articles, "Catalepsy," "Ecstasy," and "Trance," by Dr. Hack Tuke in the *Dict. Psych. Med.*, may be consulted; also the excellent articles (though written some years ago) by Dr. Chambers on "Ecstasy," "Somnambulism," and "Catalepsy" in Reynolds' *System of Medicine*, vol. ii.; for an elaborate study from the modern point of view of the differences between catalepsy, ecstasy, lethargy, somnambulism, etc., regarded as typical and mixed forms of hypnosis among the hysterical, see Pitres, *Leçons cliniques sur l'Hystérie et l'Hypnotisme*, 1891, tom. ii. pp. 117-142.

[3] Millingen, *Curiosities of Medical Experience*, 1857, vol. i. p. 225; and see Lombroso and Ferrero, *Donna Delinquente*, pp. 203-208; also J. Grimm, *Teutonic Mythology* (translation), pp. 1038-41.

religions are given out in a more or less hypnotic state, usually emanate from women. This was not only the case among the Greeks but also among the ancient Babylonians and Assyrians.[1]

It is interesting to find that magical phenomena corresponding to those to be found in remote districts to-day in England (where witches—white and black—still flourish, and "ill-wishing," though not always avowed, is firmly believed in) existed in a substantially similar form six thousand years ago in the oldest historical civilisation. It was a widespread and apparently already very ancient belief among the Babylonians and Assyrians that certain human beings possessed demoniac powers, and could exercise them for evil on whomsoever they pleased. Such sorcerers could be either male or female, but they were mostly female. These witches, Jastrow remarks, are so closely associated with demons in the Babylonian incantation texts that we may regard the witch as merely the person through whom the demon has manifested himself. From the basis of this identity the witches reached a stage through which they could control the demons, though the demons could not control them. The Babylonian witch's "evil-eye" had great power, as had also her "evil word" (or magic formula) and her potions made from poisonous herbs. We also find that all the more indirect devices of what may fairly be called modern witch-craft were well known to the Babylonian woman. By sympathetic magic she could strangle her victim by tying knots in a rope, or by making an image of him in clay, pitch, honey, or fat. She could symbolically burn, torture, bury, or drown him.[2]

The hypnotic and "magical" aptitude of women is chiefly a fact of their organisation. But its development in the past has certainly been favoured by the wonder excited by the physical

---

[1] In a series of eight oracles addressed to Esarhaddon, Professor Morris Jastrow records that six were given out by women.

[2] Morris Jastrow, *Religion of Babylonia and Assyria*, 1898, p. 266.

mystery of womanhood, to which reference was made in Chapter I. Women in savage and barbarous stages of existence are believed to have a strange influence over the whole of nature. Thus Pliny (*Natural History*, Book vii. c. 13) tells us that "on the approach of a woman in this state [the menstrual], meat will become sour, seeds which are touched by her become sterile, grafts wither away, garden-plants are withered up, and the fruit will fall from the tree beneath which she sits," etc. At Bordeaux and on the Rhine women must still avoid entering wine-cellars during their periods. (A. Bastian in the "Vorwort" and notes to his *Inselgruppen in Oceanien*, Berlin, 1883, has collected a large number of similar beliefs.) It was not only when in this state that a woman possessed this magical influence; in another part of his work (Book xxviii. c. 23) Pliny writes:—"Hailstorms, they say, whirlwinds, and lightning even, will be scared away by a woman uncovering her body while her monthly courses are upon her. The same, too, with all other kinds of tempestuous weather; and out at sea a storm may be lulled by a woman uncovering her body merely, even though not menstruating at the time. At any other time, also, if a woman strips herself naked while she is menstruating, and walks round a field of wheat, the caterpillars, worms, beetles, and other vermin will fall from off the ears of corn." Many of these beliefs survive in Italy (and in other parts of the world) up to the present day; thus at Belluno, according to Bastanzi, it is customary for a priest and for a naked young girl to go (separately as a rule) early in the morning into the fields to drive away the caterpillars. (The introduction of the priest is merely an example of the way in which Christianity has sought to sanctify the Pagan rites it could not eradicate.) Similar customs may be found all over the world. Thus the wonder excited by women has in the past, if not in the present, powerfully reinforced the influence they have gained through what I have here broadly termed "hypnotic phenomena." (Many facts bearing on the prevalence of the belief in the magical aptitude of women, both in ancient and modern times, are brought together by Ploss and Bartels, *Das Weib*, 7th ed., Bd. ii. pp. 663-680; these authors believe that these phenomena are of universal extension and probably constitute a fundamental human belief.)

A large part of the fascination which women possess for men lies in their liability to such hypnotic explosions as we have here to consider. It has been a mystery which men have never grown tired of contemplating, and which has left an ineffaceable mark on the literature produced by men.

The mystery has been sympathetically described by Diderot, who himself combined the man's temperament and the woman's, in his rhapsodical fragment *Sur les Femmes:*— "It is especially in the passion of love, the attack of jealousy, the transports of natural tenderness, the instincts of superstition, the way in which they share popular epidemic emotions, that women astonish us, beautiful as Klopstock's seraphim, terrible as Milton's angels of darkness. I have seen love, jealousy, superstition, anger in women carried to heights which man has never reached. . . . A man never sat at Delphi on the sacred tripod. The part of Pythia only suited a woman. It needs a woman's head to feel seriously the approach of a god, to become exalted and agitated, dishevelled, foaming, to cry out: 'I feel him, I feel him, the god is come!' and then to repeat truly his words. A woman carries within her an organ capable of terrible spasms, which do as they will with her and excite in her phantoms of all kinds. In her hysterical delirium she sees the past over again, she is projected into the future, all times are present to her. Nothing closer together than ecstasy, vision, prophecy, poetry, and hysteria. . . . Madame Guyon, in her book of *Torrents*, has lines of an eloquence which knew no models. It was Saint Theresa who said of the devils, 'How unhappy they are! they do not love!' It was a woman who walked barefooted through the streets of Alexandria, with a torch in one hand and a pitcher in the other, saying: 'I will burn heaven with this torch and extinguish hell with this water, so that man may love his God only for Himself.' Such a part belongs only to a woman. But this fiery imagination, this temper which seems incoercible, may be abashed at a word. . . . More civilised than men outside, within they have remained true savages, and they are all of the sect of Machiavelli, more or less. The symbol of woman in general is that of the Apocalypse, on the forehead of which was written Mystery."

DREAMS.

Among primitive peoples the dreams of women often play an important part. In the Lake Shirwa district of Central Africa, for example, very sacred functions are performed by the prophetess. It is to her that the gods or ancestral spirits make known their will, and this they do in dreams. The prophetess, who is frequently one of the chief's wives, dreams her dreams and then gives forth oracles at intervals, according to the exigencies of the case; they are usually delivered in a frenzied state.[1]   It seems clear, however, from the description given of the emotional and other phenomena accompanying the delivery of these oracles that they are largely manifestations of hysteria.   Nor, if we take savage races generally, can it be said that these phenomena are more common among women; we find them fully developed among men.

It is not until we turn to races which have reached a high degree of barbarism that we find clear evidence concerning the relative frequency of dreaming in the sexes.   The old French epic cycles furnish us with interesting material for the study of this question in mediæval Europe; and the dreams of the Arthurian and Karolian epics have been carefully studied by Mentz.[2]   Dreams are represented throughout these cycles as of great importance and significance; they are visions from God.   Heroes and princes were great dreamers; heathens rarely or never.   The greatest dreamer of all was Karl the Great, though only when he was young and vigorous.   But women dreamed much, and Mentz argues from this that they must have been highly thought of.   "These poets have with special preference attributed dreams to women, and this is shown not only by the number of examples of women dreaming, but by some very remarkable cases.   For example, when any common misfortune overtakes a married couple or two lovers, it is always the woman who receives information of the misfortune."   After giving numerous examples, Mentz adds: "I have not found a single case in which, on such an occasion, the dream has come to the father or the husband; the dreamers are always

---

[1] James Macdonald, "East Central African Customs," *Journal of the Anthropological Institute*, Aug. 1892, p. 105.

[2] Richard Mentz, *Die Träume in den altfranzösischen Karls- und Artus-epen*, 1888. (Stengel's *Ausgaben und Abhandlungen aus dem Gebiet der romanischen Philologie*, lxxiii.)

women. Women's parts are filled with dreams, which otherwise are only imparted to heroes and princes."

In modern times dreams have lost all divine significance, although they have acquired a new scientific value as helping to furnish the key to many psychological problems of the past and the present. There can be no doubt whatever that women are greater dreamers than men. While men, as they reach adult age, usually find that their dreams become rarer and less vivid, receding into a dim background where they can with difficulty be perceived, though doubtless always present, in women dreams usually remain frequent and vivid. This fact is familiar to all who have inquired into psychological phenomena, and it has often been confirmed by statistical investigation. Thus Heerwagen[1] found that women dream more than men, whilst male students stand as a class between other men and women. Sante de Sanctis, in his valuable study of dreaming, *I Sogni*, found that only 13 per cent. men dream always as against 33 per cent. women. Dreaming reaches its maximum intensity at from 20 to 25 years of age. Married women, according to Heerwagen, dream less than the unmarried. A dreamful sleep, Heerwagen found, is in women more likely to be prolonged than a dreamless sleep; but it is not so in men. Men, it may be added, sleep more soundly than women, while sleep is soundest in childhood.

Professor Jastrow, in an interesting study of the dreams of the blind,[2] gives statistical information as to the dreams of 183 blind persons. There is reason to believe that the blind are not, on the whole, such good dreamers as the sighted, but the sexual difference probably remains un-

[1] Friedrich Heerwagen, *Statistische Untersuchungen über Träume und Schlaf*, Wundt's Philosophische Studien, v. 2. I have only seen abstracts of this investigation.

[2] "The Dreams of the Blind," *New Princeton Review*, Jan. 1888.

impaired. While of the males 54.5 per cent. dream seldom, 19.2 per cent. frequently, and 7.1 per cent. every night, similar numbers for the females are 29.8, 26.2, and 8.3 per cent.—*i.e.*, the females include more " frequent " and fewer " occasional " dreamers. Professor Jastrow remarks: " This favours the view that it is the vividness of the emotional background elaborated by the imagination that furnishes the predominant characteristic and tendency to dreams; for it is in the development of just these qualities that women excel men; the same view is favoured by the prevalence of dreams to age. In my tables there is a loss of the total amount of dreaming in passing from the period of five to nine years to that of from ten to fourteen years. A slighter decrease is noted in passing from the latter period to that of the next five years, and this very gradual decrease seems to continue from then on. Childhood, the period of the lively imagination and highly tinged emotional life, brings the richest harvest of dreams."

As to sexual differences in the character of dreams and the modes of dreaming, we possess at present little definite evidence. I will only allude to a study of " The Statistics of 'Unconscious Cerebration'" (*American Journal of Psychology*, Nov. 1892, vol. v. No. 2), by Mr. Charles M. Child of Wesleyan University, U.S.A. This investigation, carried out under the superintendence of Professor A. C. Armstrong, was made on 200 college students (151 men and 49 women). It does not refer exclusively to dreaming, but various points bearing on dreams came within its scope. Thus it was found that only 12 per cent. of the women remember having any logical or connected train of thought in a half-sleep, but the general percentage is twice as large. The low percentage of the women here may be connected with the fact, which was also brought out in this investigation, that a very large percentage of women wake directly. On the other hand, 24 per cent. of the women reach results which are at least fairly accurate, this being rather above the general percentage (17). The percentages for different ages do not vary much, nor with any regularity. It was found that the dreams of women are more affected by position than those of men, and that a larger percentage of women than of men are conscious of a moral sense when dreaming. Possibly the greater vividness of women's dreams may account for this. After 30 years of age consciousness of moral sense in dreams diminishes. Persons under 25 are least affected by position, probably because at this age dreaming is a more constant and normal phenomenon. There was found to be a continuous decrease with age in the number of those who dream, although sexual differences in the number of students who dream (apart from the vividness, etc., of the dreams) was found to be trifling, a result which is fairly in accordance with Heerwagen's conclusions. The figures show a slightly larger proportion of men than of women who talk in their sleep, but the percentage of women who answer questions when asleep is much larger than that of men (56 per cent. as against 32 in men). While the men can usually only answer questions on the subject they are talking about, the women can more often answer questions on any subject. The percentage of those who talk in their sleep is much higher under 25 years of age than above, and the ability to answer questions also diminishes with age.

HALLUCINATIONS IN THE SANE.

Hallucinations of the senses occurring under ordinary conditions, when the subject is in fair health and otherwise sane, are very closely allied to the dreams that occur during sleep.[1] Their occasional occurrence has often been recorded, more especially in men of genius or in persons under mental stress.[2] They may also be produced as a kind of embryonic hypnotic suggestion in ordinary life, and Professor Jung has found that such hallucinations are more easily produced in women, children, and the uneducated, although by no means exclusively in them.[3]

Our chief source of statistical information at present concerning their frequency in the general population is the inquiry into the nature and frequency of hallu-

---

[1] Parish in his acute and elaborate study, *Hallucinations and Illusions*, 1897, has shown that these phenomena tend to appear on the borderland of sleep.

[2] See, for instance, Lombroso, *Man of Genius*, pp. 56, 57.

[3] "Des Hallucinations suggérées à l'état de veille," *Rev. de l'Hypnotisme*, 1889.

cinations of the senses occurring to sane persons, conducted by Professor Henry Sidgwick.[1] As the affirmative or negative experiences of 17,000 persons (comprising men and women in nearly equal proportions) are recorded in Professor Sidgwick's tables, they carry considerable weight. It was found that 656 (or 7.8 per cent.) of the men and 1033 (or 12.0 per cent.) of the women affirmed that they had at some time experienced a hallucination. It is probable that this proportion approximates to the facts; at the same time it is quite possible that women are more easily persuaded than men that they have experienced a hallucination, and also that women are more ready to confess to such an experience. Some deduction may perhaps have to be made on this account from the feminine percentage, but a greater liability to hallucination in women is in harmony with the greater prevalence of other allied phenomena in the same sex. A classification of the answers according to the competence of the collectors strengthens rather than weakens the preponderance of women, for if we separate 1649 answers which were obtained by scientific inquirers only, psychologists or medical men, we find that the percentage of women is nearly double that of the men—*i.e.*, 9.0 per cent. men against 17.1 per cent. women.

It may be added that the persons investigated were chiefly English, or at least English-speaking, but there were a certain proportion of foreigners, more especially nearly 600 Russians and 200 Brazilians, and the differences according to nationality were considerable. Thus, if we take the English-speaking alone, we find that 7.3 per cent. men and 11.4 per cent. women give affirmative answers. If we take the Russians, we find that 10.2 per cent. men and 21.4 per cent. women give affirmative answers. And if we take the Brazilians, we find that 23.0 per

[1] " Report on the Census of Hallucinations," *Pro. Soc. Psych. Research*, Aug. 1894.

cent. men and 27.7 per cent. women give affirmative answers. Hallucinations, therefore, taking these three nationalities, appear to be least prevalent among the English, most prevalent among the Brazilians; while the Russians show the maximum, and the Brazilians the minimum sexual difference.

THE ACTION OF ANÆSTHETICS.

The physiology of anæsthesia, as produced by chloroform, nitrous oxide, and other anæsthetics, is not yet fully understood. Nitrous oxide is the anæsthetic that is probably best understood, and what is here said will chiefly apply to that anæsthetic. In both the brain and spinal cord there appears to be first a period of excitement with increased pulsation of blood-vessels; then a period of disordered action; and finally a period of sedative action. The highest centres are most rapidly lulled; in the lower centres there is a greater tendency to excited action. The spinal centres are liberated, perhaps stimulated. There is usually dilatation of the pupils, which always indicates either paralysis of the higher or stimulation of the lower centres; and this dilatation, especially in the anæmic or hysterical, may be considerable even at a very early stage of anæsthesia.[1]

Such being the influence of anæsthesia on the nervous system, it is easy to observe its intimate connection with the phenomena here called hypnotic. Such phenomena involve the comparative quiescence of the highest centres, or else their inco-ordination, leading to disordered action. It is precisely to such a result that an anæsthetic like nitrous oxide leads. We may therefore regard it as an easily controllable agent for the production and study of hypnotic phenomena. If the administration of nitrous oxide

---

[1] See, for instance, J. F. W. Silk, *Manual of Nitrous Oxide Anæsthesia*, London, 1888; also Dudley Buxton, "A Note on Ankle-Clonus," *Brit. Med. Journal*, 24th Sept. 1887.

for dental purposes were carefully observed and recorded on a large scale, we should possess a valuable
and exact key for the study of many of the most
important sexual nervous differences, for during the
evolution of the anæsthetic process we have the secret
mechanism that underlies psychic action laid bare in
an objective manner which we can never under any
circumstances hope for during the subject's conscious
life.

It can scarcely be said that the importance of this
field for such research has yet been adequately
realised. There are, however, certain observations
and results recorded by scientific investigators which
throw considerable light on our present inquiry.

It is usually considered that women yield rapidly
to the influence of anæsthetics generally; pregnant
women take them well; and although they yield so
rapidly, there is no reason to suppose that women are
more exposed to danger from anæsthesia; it seems
more probable that they are less exposed. Children
also fall rapidly and deeply under chloroform and other
anæsthetics; but they bear them well and recover
with equal facility.[1] A committee appointed by the
Odontological Association found the following average times for nitrous oxide anæsthesia:—

	Time going off.	Duration.	Time from com-mencement to recovery.
Males	I min. 21 secs.	24 secs.	I min. 55 secs.
Females	I ,. 16 ,,	28 ,,	2 ,,
Children (under 15)	I ,, 3 ,,	22 ,,	I ,, 40 ,,

The exact duration of anæsthesia is not, however,
easy of very exact determination.

[1] D. W. Buxton, *Anæsthetics*, London, 1892; Maurice Perrin, Art.
"Anésthésie," *Dict. ency. des Sci. Méd.*

We have seen that the effect of an anæsthetic such as nitrous oxide is practically to lull the higher nervous centres and to give the lower nervous centres the opportunity of indulging in an orgy. Is it the nervous system of men or of women that most readily takes advantage of this opportunity?

It has frequently been noted, as a general observation, that various phenomena which may occur during anæsthesia are more common in women. Thus chloroform, ether, nitrous oxide, cocaine, and possibly other anæsthetics, possess the property of exciting the sexual emotions. Women are especially liable to these erotic hallucinations during anæsthesia, and it has sometimes been almost impossible to convince them that their subjective sensations have had no objective cause.[1] Those who have to administer anæsthetics are well aware of the risks they may thus incur. It has also been noted (as by Perrin) that women are more liable to dream under anæsthesia. General muscular excitement, both in the earlier and in the later stages of nitrous oxide anæsthesia, have been observed to be more common in women. Among girls and women, especially if of hysterical temperament, Dr. Silk remarks that during the usually quiet early stage of anæsthesia "every variety of antic may at times be indulged in, of which singing and kicking are the most common;" while just as they are passing fully under the influence of the gas, girls who have hitherto been quiet may begin to scream and kick in a manner that is usually entirely reflex and automatic; "during the stage of recovery, too, the period of excitement is often very marked, especially in females. Hallucinations with a desire to go somewhere or do something are very common; there may be also more or less violent screaming,

---

[1] See, for instance, D. Buxton, *Anæsthetics*, p. 204. Dr. Silk remarks that sexual emotions during anæsthesia are "rarely observable in men."

beating of the feet, jactitations, etc., followed by hysterical crying.[1]

Definite figures are of much greater value than general observations, and these on the whole fully confirm the general impressions already recorded. Thus Mr. Gunn has found that females are much more liable to vomit after anæsthetics than males; of about 2000 males and nearly 2000 females who were anæsthetised at Moorfields Ophthalmic Hospital 51 per cent. of the females and 40 per cent. of the males were sick;[2] it must be added that Dr. Silk finds vomiting, both in childhood and adult age, more common in males, though he also finds that excessive evolution of intestinal flatulence under anæsthesia occurs almost exclusively among women. It is to Dr. Silk that we owe the most valuable contribution yet made to the precise knowledge of sexual differences as revealed by anæsthetics.[3] Of his 1000 cases 240 were in men, 760 were in women; the average age in each sex was 24 years. It is the tendency to muscular movement which may be most easily observed. Rhythmic movements, such as swinging the legs, beating time to music with the hands, etc., were observed 27 times; it is impossible to say in what class of patients such movements are to be expected; 6 (or 2.5 per cent.) of Dr. Silk's male cases showed such movements; 21 (or 2.8 per cent.) of the female cases. The excess of females is here scarcely perceptible; it is much more marked in regard to rigid muscular contractions of an opisthotonic character; they were noted in only 17 (or 7.1 per cent.) males, but in 89 (or 11.7 per cent.) females. A tendency to opisthotonos was observed in 7 males (or 2.9 per cent.) and in 44 females (or 5.8 per cent.).

[1] J. F. W. Silk, *Manual of Nit. Ox. Anæsthesia.*

[2] R. Marcus Gunn, *Brit. Med. Journal*, July 21, 1883.

[3] J. F. W. Silk, "An Analysis of a Series of 1000 Nitrous Oxide Administrations Recorded Systematically," *Trans. Odontological Soc.*, June 1890. I am indebted to Dr. Silk for further elucidations regarding several points, and also for additional figures.

Erotic symptoms were found by Dr. Silk to have undoubtedly occurred in six cases out of the whole series, and always in women, with one exception in young unmarried women under the age of 24. Involuntary micturition occurred ten times, invariably in females; twice in children under 14 (which was, relatively, a large proportion, *i.e.*, 20 per cent.), the remainder in women between that age and 40.

I take these results chiefly from the published paper already mentioned, but recently Dr. Silk has been good enough to place in my hands the general results of a very much larger number of cases—not less than 5119, of whom 1719 were males, 3400 females; 889 were children under the age of 15. The anæsthetic used was chiefly, although not exclusively, nitrous oxide. The results of this larger investigation confirm, while at the same time to some extent modifying, the results founded on the smaller number of observations. It was found that there was a decided excess of vomiting among males; defecation and rhythmic movements were about equal in the two sexes; in all other respects females were in a majority, and usually in a very large majority. Thus the tendency to opisthotonos occurred 74 times instead of 46 times, as it should have done in order to agree with the male ratio. Erotic phenomena occurred 18 times, but only once in a man; to preserve the male ratio they should only have occurred twice among the women. Micturition occurred 23 times in women, instead of 8 times, which would have been in the same proportion as among the males, in whom it occurred only 4 times. If we separate the children (under 15) from the adults, we find that rhythmic movements occur almost exclusively in adults; intestinal rumbling occurs almost exclusively in adult women. Of the 4 male cases of micturition only one was in an adult, but of the 23 female cases 16 were in adults; the erotic phenomena were of course exclusively in adults.

The evidence furnished by the human organism under the influence of anæsthetics, which abolish conscious and voluntary action, is peculiarly reliable, and the figures here given, which include a sufficient number of cases to ensure trustworthy results, all point more or less plainly to one conclusion: hypnotic phenomena are more frequent and more marked in women than in men; the lower nervous centres in women are more rebellious to control than those of men, and more readily brought into action.

METEOROLOGIC SENSIBILITY.

This is not, strictly speaking, a form of sensibility at all, and it has no connection with any of the sense-organs. It is really a form of what we shall later on be concerned with as "affectability," and is therefore allied to emotional states. It may perhaps be fairly considered among hypnotic phenomena.

Atmospheric changes are announced, some time in advance, by modifications of the electric, barometric, thermic, hygrometric, and possibly magnetic conditions, and by a number of other physical changes, to which, for the most part, civilised people have become insensitive.

Animals, however, of all kinds—sheep, pigs, fish, ducks, grouse, etc.—can perceive these changes, and understand what they foretell. It has indeed been said by an acute observer of animal life that "there are few animals which do not afford timely and sure prognostications of changes in the weather."[1]

In man, although the meteorologic sense, as Beaunis calls it, is not universal, it is by no means uncommon to find individuals who are very sensitive to the approach of atmospheric disturbances, more especially to storms. This sensibility may be exhibited by varying phenomena—heaviness of the head, general discomfort, a sense of oppression, vague pains, etc.

[1] St. John, *Wild Sports of the Highlands*, chap. xxxiii.

Thus a snowstorm may be invariably preceded by gastric disturbances, nervous irritability, mental and general depression a day or two in advance; and rheumatic subjects often experience pains in their bones with barometric certainty. Beaunis states (as also Gavarret had previously stated) that such sensibility is more common in women and in children, and any one whose attention has been called to this point will probably have observed the greater frequency of meteorologic sensibility in women. The best subjects are of nervous or neurotic temperament.

Meteorologic sensibility has been carefully studied in America by Professor E. G. Dexter on the basis of a large amount of data obtained from schools, police and prison records, etc.[1] He finds that such sensibility is in many respects more marked in children than in adults, and that among children at school boys seem to be more susceptible than girls; this was indicated both by the actual curves of data, so far at least as heat, cold, and wind are concerned, and by the opinions of the teachers. It is suggested that this may be due to the fact that the boys are often under less disciplinary control than the girls, and one teacher remarks that the girls are greater adepts both at restraining and at concealing their impulses to mischief. Among adults, however, the same tendency is not seen. Dexter found that wherever there was any clear sexual distinction it was in the direction of a greater meteorological sensibility on the part of the women. This accorded with the experience of several principals of schools accustomed to deal with teachers of both sexes. The sexual distinction was very marked in regard to the New York police records for assault. The hot weather increases the pugnacity of women to a very much greater extent than that of men. Starting at the lower temperature with a deficiency much greater than that for males, the

---

[1] E. G. Dexter, *Conduct and the Weather*, Monograph Supplement, *Psych. Rev.*, No. 10, 1899; *ib.*, *Popular Science Monthly*, Ap. 1902.

curve indicates a somewhat gradual increase to an excess of 100 per cent., or double the expected number, for the temperature groups 80° to 85°, at which point it makes a drop to 33 per cent. (due to the exhausting and devitalising influence of great heat). The curve for males shows neither extreme so far from the expected result, nor is the drop at the end so marked.

Sensibility to the influence of seasonal changes is shown in a marked manner by the prevalence of insanity and suicide during the spring and summer months.[1] Suicide by no means necessarily implies insanity; it involves, however, a similar condition of mental instability, and it is largely subject to the same cosmic laws.

Morselli, in his monograph on *Suicide*, notes in women the quicker development of suicidal tendency during the summer season or the first warmth of spring. "The greater proportion of suicides among women," he remarks, "is manifest, whether during the whole season (Italy, Prussia, and Saxony) or in the warmest months of June (France) or July (Bavaria). In Italy and Saxony is to be noted the same prevalence of suicides among women in the months of April and May, while the proportion offered by women in certain warm months (as July in Bavaria) largely exceeds the highest monthly average of men." Turning to the question, "What is the monthly average of suicides through mental disease in the two sexes?" Morselli found from the data he collected that "among women violent deaths through madness are proportionately more numerous in those months which, by reason of their average temperature, operate fatally—that is, in April, when the first heat, though not intense, is felt exceedingly by the cerebral organism not yet accustomed to it,

---

[1] Durkheim in his sociological study, *Le Suicide*, 1897, ch. iii., regards these seasonal phenomena as really social, and due to the greater length of the day in summer.

and in July, when the average monthly temperature reaches the maximum of the year."

It must be added that some slight examination of the suicide rates that I have been able to make, considering them not by month but by season, do not altogether confirm Morselli's conclusions. In Saxony, for example, during the years 1876-79, I find that while 28.5 of the total male suicides took place in the spring, only 26.1 of the female suicides were committed during that season. And if we group together the Teutonic and Scandinavian countries —Prussia (1869-72), Saxony (1876-79), Denmark (1874-78), Norway (1866-70), Sweden (1833-51)—it will be found that out of a total of 18,836 male suicides 28.3 per cent. occurred in spring, and out of a total of 4,815 female suicides 28.2 occurred in spring; while 30.3 per cent. of the male suicides and 29.3 per cent. of the female suicides were committed in summer; 22.5 per cent. male suicides and 23.6 per cent. female suicides were committed in autumn, and precisely the same percentage of 18.9 male and female suicides took place during the winter. This shows no marked sexual difference, and the preponderance of women in the autumn is almost exactly balanced by the preponderance of men in the summer. Morselli's conclusions cannot be accepted unreservedly without further investigation.

As to the varying incidence of insanity, month by month, in the two sexes, I do not possess much evidence. So far as I am aware, the question of any sexual difference in this respect has not been raised. Figures of 2669 admissions to asylums in France, supplied by Parchappe to Bucknill and Tuke,[1] seemed to show that men were more affected by season than women. The result is different, however, if we turn to the very much larger figures (nearly 40,000) sup-

[1] *Manual of Psychological Medicine*, 1858, p. 249.

plied by Scotch asylums during eighteen years.[1]   Per
1000 men during the years 1865-74 the excess of
admissions during the spring and summer over the
autumn and winter was 54, and during the years
1880-87 it was 58.   For women during the first
period the excess in spring and summer over autumn
and winter was 66, and during the second period 76.
During the three spring months the proportion of
male insane admitted was 27.1 per cent., that of
females 27.5 per cent.   Or, expressed in another way,
while in the months of January during these years
the admissions of men and women were nearly equal,
being 1493 men to 1481 women, in May there were
1669 men admitted to 1952 women, being a large
excess of women.   The greater sensitiveness of
women to this seasonal influence is therefore in
Scotland fairly constant and well marked.   In New
York Dexter has lately found that the yearly curve
of the incidence of insanity is more marked in females
(though his numbers are hardly sufficiently large); a
chief climax in May and minor climaxes in March
and September were all more marked in the females.

Daily observations of the pulse-rate, temperature, etc., all
furnish a fruitful field for the investigation of the various monthly,
yearly, and other physiological rhythms, which has at present
been very little exploited. (I may refer, however, to the interesting observations of Mr. F. H. Perry-Coste, " The Rhythm
of the Pulse," *University Mag.*, Feb. 1898; cf. Havelock Ellis,
" Sexual Periodicity," *Studies in the Psychology of Sex*, vol. i.)
   There is also an interesting connection between meteorologic
sensibility and seasonal influences on the rate of bodily growth.
The investigations of Wretlind in Sweden, and of Wahl and
especially Malling-Hansen in Denmark, have shown that season
exercises a very marked influence on the rate of growth of
children.   It is not yet quite clear to what extent this seasonal
influence is connected with the influence of holidays, but there

---

[1] *Reports of Board of Commissioners in Lunacy, Scotland*, 17th
Report, p. 26, and 31st Report, p. 28. Quoted, with many observations on the physiological influence of season, in Leffingwell's *Influence of Seasons upon Conduct* (Social Science Series), 1892, pp. 101,
157.

is no doubt that it is very largely a genuine and regular physiological phenomenon. Malling-Hansen has shown that from the point of view of body-growth there are three seasons in a child's year:—(1) from the end of November or beginning of December until the end of March or beginning of April; during the whole of this period, development, both as regards height and weight, is at a low ebb; (2) from March-April until July-August; during this period there is great development in height but no increase in weight, even some loss; (3) from July-August to November-December; this is the period of growth in weight; the daily increase is at this time three times as great as during the winter, but increase in height is at a minimum.

There are slight independent oscillations in growth, chiefly depending on changes in temperature; thus Malling-Hansen shows that even an elevated temperature lasting only a few days will produce an increase in growth. It is of great interest to observe that the period of physical quiescence corresponds almost precisely with the period of emotional quiescence, as shown by the comparative infrequency of insanity, suicide, murder, and offences against chastity. I have not seen Malling-Hansen's original memoir, and cannot say whether his figures show any marked sexual differences.

NEURASTHENIA AND HYSTERIA.

Neurasthenia and hysteria are probably the typical nervous disorders of women. Our attention is called to them here because in their main outlines they exhibit the characteristics common to hypnotic phenomena generally.

Neurasthenia, as it is now generally called,—or spinal irritation, nervosism, etc., as it was formerly called,—is not a modern complaint. It is at least as old as Hippocrates, the Father of Medicine, although it was not until the last century that—owing chiefly to Beard in America and Bouchut in France —it was fully described. Even now, however, neurasthenia is only a large collection of vague nervous symptoms which not all authorities can reckon as a definite disorder; thus Schüle and Mendel are inclined to class a large number of such cases as hypochondriasis, while others would consider them as mild examples of melancholia, hysteria, etc. It is of no interest from our present point of view how the phenomena are classified or what they are called. There is general agreement that under any name they are much more common in women. In the experience of some authorities as many as fourteen out of every fifteen cases are women, though this is no doubt an excessive proportion. The symptoms are, generally speaking, a weakness of the nervous system—including both brain and spinal cord—due partly to insufficient or inappropriate nutrition and partly to faulty development, showing itself by a tendency to over-action and irritability of the nervous system, morbid sensibility, and mental anxiety. It may present all degrees of intensity, and although it is not a definite organic disease, the neurasthenic condition is the soil on which organic nervous diseases may grow.

The study of neurasthenia throws so much light on the nature and on the beginnings of the nervous and hypnotic conditions which are especially common in women, that it seems worth while to indicate its chief outlines. I will especially follow the admirable and precise account given by Professor Rudolf Arndt of Greifswald in his article on "Neurasthenia" in the *Dictionary of Psychological Medicine*. The distinct peculiarities of neurasthenia are negative rather than positive. We are sure to find either hypochondriacal or paralytiform or epileptoid or hysteroid symptoms, but they are not sufficiently developed to enable us to say that hypochondriasis or melancholia or general paralysis, epilepsy or hysteria or locomotor ataxy, is really present, although any of these diseases may possibly emerge ultimately; it must be remembered that there is no function without an organ, and therefore no functional disorder without an organic basis which may develop into a definite disease. Although in neurasthenia there is really deficient nervous power, there appears, in accordance with a well-recognised law of nerve-stimulation, to be an increase of nervous energy. This is because there is a decrease of nerve-resistance, and the nervous system responds too readily and too emphatically to a slight degree of stimulation. This exaggerated excitability, which is characteristic of neurasthenia, is therefore closely associated with that loss of complete control which we have found to be an essential element in all hypnotic phenomena.

At a later stage this increased excitability rapidly decreases; the nerve becomes blunted or paralysed, and fails to respond adequately even to strong stimulation.

Sensory nerves being normally more excitable than motor, hyperæsthesia, or morbid sensibility, appears somewhat earlier than muscular weakness: these two symptoms—hyperæsthesia and muscular weakness—are the chief characteristics of neurasthenia. No objective foundation can be found for the hyperæsthesia, which is the most common phenomenon, so that it is often regarded as imaginary, although it is far from imaginary to the patient, and may cause misery during the greater part of life. All kinds of unpleasant sensations and pains are felt in all parts of the body, and, as in all sensations and pains the brain must take part, we have in neurasthenia an element of what has been called cerebral irritation. This cerebral irritation is often shown by all sorts of morbid dreads which may find a kind of basis in the abnormal sensations. Thus we may have agoraphobia or the fear of open spaces claustrophobia or the fear of enclosed spaces, anthropophobia or the fear of being with others, rupophobia or the fear of being dirty, nyctophobia or the fear of night, and a vast number of other fears to which it is not worth while to give names. (A vivid literary picture of such morbid obsession is to be found in a chapter of Borrow's *Lavengro;* it is undoubtedly taken from life.) Obsessions are much more common in women; Pitres and Régis found 154 cases in women to 96 in men ("Obsessions et idées fixes," *Comptes-rendus du XII. Congrès Int. de Med.*, Moscow, 1897, vol. iv., part i., p. 45; these ideas have been studied in women with very great care by Janet). In the simplest and most elementary form these fears may be called natural; in their most pronounced form, and carried beyond all control of reason, they belong to the domain of insanity; in neurasthenia we have them in an intermediate stage.

The abnormal motor phenomena correspond to the sensory. At first they are excessive, as they are in all varieties of hypnotic phenomena; spasmodic cramps and twitchings are present with great frequency, but languor and immobility may also be present. The pupils are dilated or unequal; the tendon reflexes are exaggerated; yawning is often frequent, and there is a tendency to blush, which Beard and other authorities consider as a very characteristic symptom of neurasthenia.

Neurasthenia is a general condition of agitation of the nervous system, and it is not surprising that we find it with especial frequency in both men and women who overstrain their brains, in artists and writers and those who are over-strenuous in social movements. Hysteria, which is one of the chief of the more definite diseases to which neurasthenia may lead, has no necessary connection of this kind with mental tension. It occurs with much greater frequency among those whose nervous activities are unemployed.

Although one of the greatest of the old English physicians, Sydenham, laid our knowledge of hysteria on a sound and scientific basis, the word has too often been used in a loose and inaccurate sense, or even as a mere term of abuse, and it is only within recent years that it has been somewhat more rigidly defined and its nature more precisely investigated in detail. This advance is very largely owing to the initiative of Charcot and to the brilliant and painstaking students of nervous disease who grew up around him at the Salpêtrière.[1]

Hysteria is a disease which affects the whole nervous system, and more especially the brain; it is, as Charcot taught and is now usually agreed, essentially a psychic disease.[2] If we try to make clear to ourselves the broad general character of the mental phenomena in hysteria, we shall find that they may be summed up in one word—suggestibility.[3] Response to suggestion is a fundamental normal character of all nervous tissue. Even among bees it is said that when a band of brigand bees enter a strange hive to despoil it of honey, the owners of the hive are themselves sometimes so carried away by the contagion of rapine that they will even go over to the robbers' side and assist in destroying the result of their own labours. The

[1] For a clear and judicious summary of the present position of knowledge regarding hysteria, see Gilles de la Tourette, *Traité clinique et thérapeutique de l'Hystérie, d'après l'enseignement de la Salpêtrière*, Paris, 1891. For a discussion of the definitions of hysteria, see the articles by Pierre Janet in the *Archives de Neurologie*, vol. xxv., 1893.

[2] Charcot, *Leçons du Mardi*, t. i. p. 205, 1887.

[3] See the admirable chapter on the mental condition in hysteria in Gilles de la Tourette's *Traité clinique*, etc., 1891, pp. 486-555.

same irrational suggestibility is found among healthy human beings, at all events in an incipient state. An English prison matron confessed that sometimes when she heard the women under her care "break out" (as it is called) and commence smashing and destroying everything they could get hold of, it was as much as she could do to restrain herself from joining in; and many persons have experienced a similar impulse. In hysteria this tendency is so heightened that it becomes irresistible, and may be aroused by the faintest suggestion from without, and also from within. Thus there is what Huchard, who belongs to a somewhat older school, calls moral ataxy.[1] And Féré, in allusion to this almost uncontrollable response to stimuli, has called the hysterical subject "the frog of psychology."

Dr. Conolly Norman (who considers that "weakness, with irritability, is the fundamental note of the hysterical character") has the following observations on "hysterical mania," a form of insanity which is combined with hysteria:—"The sufferer from hysterical mania is exceedingly emotional. The pain of melancholia is unknown, the appearance of depression is very shallow. A trifling and passing depressive emotion is responded to by instant tears, perhaps with loud outcry and by a great display of grief, but the feeling is quite temporary. There is a certain hyperæsthesia showing itself by a too quick response to every emotional irritation without any permanent substratum of painful feeling. In a similar way there is a sharp irritability of temper without the constant state of anger which will sometimes occur in other forms of mania. The entire emotional state is unstable in the extreme, and the expression of emotion bears a peculiar whimsical and uncertain character, such as is also seen in the entire conduct of the patient. Impulse is very apt to be translated into action with alarming rapidity. Impulse and whim sometimes rise almost to the dignity of ruling motives in a mind incapable of forming any fixed resolution." (Art. "Mania, Hysterical," in *Dict. of Psych. Med.*)

This mental mobility, emotional facility, and uncontrollable response to stimuli have frequently led to charges of wanton deception and simulation against the hysterical. Such charges

---

[1] Huchard, "Caractère, mœurs, état mental des Hystériques," *Arch. de Neurologie*, 1882, p. 187.

are quite unfounded. "The real deceiver," as Gilles de la Tourette well remarks (*Traité clinique*, etc., p. 527), "is an active and reasoning being; the hysterical, when they deceive, are not conscious of the deception; they are passive beings, photographic plates which register and show forth their impressions as they have received them, sometimes amplified, indeed, but always with the good faith of unconsciousness. 'Deception' is a word which has been abused beyond measure in hysteria, so as to have been made the characteristic of a morbid species. It must be added that this has been largely due to ignorance."

Clouston has defined hysteria as "the loss of the inhibitory influence exercised on the reproductive and sexual instincts of women by the higher mental and moral functions." (*Edinburgh Med. Journal*, June 1883, p. 1123.) The loss of the complete control exercised by the higher centres is undoubtedly an essential character of hysteria as of hypnotic phenomena generally, but it is not usually accepted that there is necessarily any sexual element in hysteria. Formerly the sexual element in hysteria was somewhat exaggerated; there is now a tendency to unduly minimise it. (Havelock Ellis, "Auto-Erotism," *Studies in the Psychology of Sex*, vol. i.) Sexual irritation in any crude form, or any gross disease of the sexual organs, is certainly not essential in hysteria, but many of the symptoms of hysteria can be traced back to a sexual origin. It is noteworthy also that, as Lombroso points out (*La Donna Delinquente*, p. 613), the criminal offences of the hysterical very largely revolve round the sexual functions. There is often some perversion of the sexual emotion, so that, though the hysterical may crave for love and tenderness from the opposite sex, normal sexual relations may be indifferent or repulsive. Both among the "possessed" of former days and in modern times it has been noted that erotic dreams are very frequent in the hysterical, but that they are often painful rather than pleasurable. The mistake of supposing that there is some special connection between hysteria and the sexual organs has probably arisen from the undoubted fact that in women the organic sexual sphere is of greater extent than in men. When, therefore, the higher controlling centres are to some extent paralysed we must expect to find all sorts of phenomena traceable to a sexual origin more prominent in women. It is not so in hysteria only, but in nearly all varieties of nervous and mental disorder.

It is necessary to say a word as to the relative frequency of hysteria in the two sexes. Up till within about twenty years it was always supposed that hysteria was enormously more frequent in women than in men. Sydenham recognised hysteria in men, especially among those of studious and sedentary habits (no doubt including what we should now call neurasthenia), but hysteria in the male had always been regarded as a rarity. Briquet, the chief authority on hysteria during the middle of the last century, found one man to twenty women. In Germany Bodenstein has found in the polyclinique of Eulenburg and Mendel one man to ten women. But Pitres at Bordeaux finds one man to two women, and at Paris Gilles de la Tourette found that among Charcot's cases there was also one man to two women. It is no longer possible, therefore, to assert that hysteria in men is rare. At the same time there is excellent reason for believing that it is scarcely so frequent as these recent statistics would lead us to think. It is generally agreed that hysteria in men usually occurs among the poor and ill-nourished classes who frequent hospitals, while in women it occurs chiefly among the idle and well-to-do, whose numbers do not swell hospital statistics. Again, it has been found by Charcot and others that hysteria in the male is a more serious and obstinate affection, while in the female mild cases are much more usually seen; this also tends to vitiate the statistics of the frequency of hysteria according to sex, as it is only the serious cases which prominently attract medical attention. We may safely conclude that while hysteria in men is more frequent than was once supposed, it is much more common in women. Such a conclusion is in harmony with the opinions of the greatest masters in the science of morbid psychology, from Sydenham, who asserted that there are very few women (except those leading a hard and laborious life) who are entirely exempt from some trace of hysteria, down to Tonnini, in whose vigorous phrase the hysterical person is the colossal image of all that is most peculiarly feminine—*la gigantessa della feminilità*.

There is an interesting parallelism, and probably a real deep-lying nervous connection, between the suggestibility of women and the special liability of female butterflies, birds, and mammals to be mimetic in coloration, etc. Mimicry, or suggestibility, is an adaptation to the environment, ensuring the protection of the sex that is less able to flee or to fight.

RELIGIOUS HYPNOTIC PHENOMENA.

There is a very intimate connection between hypnotic phenomena—understood in the broad sense in which I have here used the term—and the phenomena of religion. The part played by women as religious leaders is by no means so large as the large proportion of women in religious movements would lead us to expect, but it is considerable, and it has been most conspicuously exercised in that part of religion which covers the field of hypnotic phenomena. As " prophetesses," women, who seem to have fallen into the trance state and seen visions or heard dogmas, which they subsequently declared, have often been of the greatest service to religious leaders, and conspicuously helped to draw disciples by the charm of the supernatural. Apelles, the founder of the Apellæans of the second century, was powerfully assisted by the prophetess Philumene. Montanus, who was himself similarly affected, was closely associated with the prophetesses Priscilla and Maxi-milla, who were subject to ecstasy, during which they had visions that seem to have influenced Tertullian, one of the greatest of the Latin Fathers. The Quintilians, led by the prophetess Quintilia, were a branch of the Montanists, and their virgins in public assembly wore white robes and exercised prophetic functions; they asserted that women are entitled to exercise all the sacerdotal and episcopal functions. Petersen, a visionary Millennarian of the eighteenth century, was aided by his wife, who was also a visionary, and with them was associated an inspired countess, who was also honoured with visions. It would not be difficult to multiply examples of women playing an important part in religious movements who have exhibited hypnotic phenomena in a high degree. A very large proportion of the most eminent female saints who led a conventual life were in the highest degree hysterical. It will, however, be sufficient to refer to two religious sects which have both been founded or led by women, and which have both been intimately identified with (non-hysterical) forms of hypnotic phenomena. The Shakers were not founded by a woman, but by a man and a woman in conjunction, James Wardley, a Quaker tailor, and his wife; their most distinguished and successful leader was, however, Anne Lees, of Manchester, who transferred the sect to America, where, under her guidance and by means of her missionary zeal, it grew and flourished. The community was founded on a communistic basis, and the property was admirably managed; the religious characteristics of the sect, in which women always took a very prominent part, lay in their worship, in which music and singing were especially conspicuous, the ministry as ordinarily understood being entirely abolished; they held that the history of the return of the prodigal justified their adoption of music and dancing as leading parts of public worship, for it was the elder son, representing the natural man, who condemned these soul-reviving practices. Their religious exercises, we are told, consisted chiefly of "*Shaking* and trembling, singing and dancing, leaping and shouting, and prophesying and speaking with new tongues." Hypnotic phenomena, less crudely muscular in character, but not less well marked, form the chief distinguishing characteristics of the Theosophists. It is instructive to note that this is at once both the only modern religious sect of any importance founded and led by women, and the only modern sect established on "magical" and esoteric doctrines and practices. It is thus of profound interest to the student of history, as it enables him to understand how "magical" and esoteric sects—in which, again, women played a conspicuous part—sprang up and flourished under eastern influence on the decay of the Roman Empire.

There is another great class of religious movements in which the various hypnotic phenomena, especially those of a contagious character, play so large a part that nearly every intellectual element disappears. Such religious movements, which are unquestionably morbid in character, are very largely and sometimes exclusively manifested in women, and they rarely possess any prominent leader. They are often saltatory in character, and are in some cases varieties of that epidemic nervous disorder called hysterical chorea. The Dancers, a religious sect of the fourteenth century, which arose at Aix-la-Chapelle and spread throughout Belgium, present an admirable example of religious hypnotic phenomena in which women played a prominent part. The Dancing Mania began immediately after the pagan midsummer orgies of St. John the Baptist's Day in 1374. Men and women seemed to have lost all self-control. Suddenly, whether in public or private, they would begin dancing, while holding each other's hands, and would continue dancing with extreme violence until they fell down exhausted; during these periods of muscular agitation they were insensible to outward impressions, and were favoured with wonderful visions.[1] The Camisards, or prophets of the Cevennes, who arose in Dauphiné and Vivarais in the seventeenth century, and met with much success in France and England, exhibited a variety of hypnotic phenomena, in which, as usual, women were prominent adepts. These people were subject to ecstasy, and, as they considered it, the inspiration of the Holy Ghost. "They had strange fits," we are told, "which came upon them with tremblings and faintings, as in a swoon,

---

[1] Hecker, *Epidemics of the Middle Ages*, "The Dancing Mania," Chap. i.

which made them stretch out their arms and legs, and stagger several times before they dropped down. They struck themselves with their hands, they fell on their backs, shut their eyes, and heaved their breasts. The symptoms answer exactly to those produced by inspiring nitrous oxide, and were the fact then discovered we should have been tempted to suspect imposture. They remained a while in trances, and coming out of them declared that they saw the heavens open, the angels, paradise, and hell. Those who were just on the point of receiving the spirit of prophecy dropped down, not only in the assemblies, but in the fields, and in their own houses, crying out *Mercy*. The least of their assemblies made up to four or five hundred, and some of them amounted to even three or four thousand. The hills rebounded with their loud cries for mercy, and with imprecations against the priests, the Pope, and his anti-Christian dominion; with predictions of the approaching fall of popery. All they said at these times was heard and received with reverence and awe."[1] This is an admirable picture of a religious orgy of the uncontrolled hypnotic activities of the human organism.

In the convulsive religious epidemic of Redruth, at the beginning of the past century, which spread with extreme rapidity over a considerable region from Helston to Camborne, and which was marked by uncontrollable movements of all parts of the body, no age or sex was exempt, but girls and women were the most frequent victims. The religious nervous affection of the Shetland Islands, which belongs to about the same period, was almost identical in character, and almost exclusively affected young women.[2]

---

[1] *A Dictionary of All Religions*, Art. "Camisars," in which references are given to original authorities.

[2] Hecker, *Epidemics*, "The Dancing Mania," Chap. iv. and Appendix v. The hysterical phenomena witnessed during the great religious

At Morzine, a little village in the Haute-Savoie, during 1861-65 there was a hysterical religious epidemic in which gentle young girls during the paroxysm replied judiciously to questions in various languages, uttered abominable blasphemies, were subject to hallucinations, climbed trees with marvellous agility, and gave forth prophecies which were sometimes realised. They knew nothing afterwards of what had gone on. The epidemic seems to have been confined to young girls, and the population generally regarded the phenomenon as supernatural. The ecclesiastical authorities attempted exorcism in vain, but the civil authorities, with a brigade of gendarmerie and isolation of the affected individuals, were more successful. A somewhat similar outbreak also took place some years ago at Verzegnis, a mountain village in Friuli, after a mission preached by a Jesuit father among a superstitious population predisposed to hysteria. The phenomena were those of profound hysteria of demoniac form, chiefly or exclusively in women, and they were dissipated with great difficulty by somewhat the same means as those adopted at Morzine.[1] A few years ago the little town of Alia, near Palermo, became famous on account of the religious enthusiasm of its female inhabitants; insanity, epilepsy, and hysteria abounded, and the town fell into great moral and physical misery.[2]

Russia is the only country to-day in which it is possible to study all the various forms of hypnotic religious phenomena, and here indeed they may be studied in their most intense manifestations and on a very wide scale. The strong religious instincts of the people, the primitive conditions of their life, their semi-pagan beliefs, and the suffering and oppression

revival of 1859 in Ireland have been very well studied in a pamphlet of great interest by Archdeacon Stopford, "The Work and the Counter-work," Dublin, 1859.

[1] Pitres, *Leçons cliniques sur l'hystérie*, vol. i. pp. 40-44.
[2] "La Psychopathie religieuse d'Alia," *L'Encéphale*, 1881.

to which they are subjected, all tend to heighten the play of hypnotic religious emotion. During the past century a number of religious sects have been founded, or have developed, which have practised dancing, leaping, flagellation, even castration, although some of them have been at the same time of a practical and rationalistic character. In all these sects women play a very prominent part; in some the majority of the members are women; a few have been founded by women. It is not surprising that in these Russian sects women enjoy a position of freedom equal to that of the men. The sect of Christs (or Khlysts) believe that every person contains, or may contain, a portion of the divinity, and is worthy of adoration. Amid dancing and sobbing, which play a very important part in Russian mystical sects, the Holy Spirit descends. It is a wild and giddy dance which begins at midnight, after long hours of prayers and psalm-singing and religious discussion. Then the Christs rise, both men and women remove all their garments and put on long white shirts and white cotton stockings. Candles are lighted, and after singing a monotonous chant a few begin to leap and to dance. Gradually the others join, and they beat time with their feet, the men in the direction of the sun, and the women in the opposite direction. Their movements increase in rapidity, and their sobs become more violent. Each Christ begins to revolve, the men to the right, the women to the left, with such rapidity that the face cannot be distinguished. They leap, they contort themselves, they run after each other, they flagellate each other. In the midst of mad laughter, of cries and sobs, loud shouts are heard: "It is coming! It is coming! The Holy Spirit is coming!" Then the excitement of this strange *danse macabre* of shouting, half-naked, white-garmented figures—which produces a tremendous effect on the novice—begins to culminate. Men and women tear off their garments, go about on all fours, ride on one another's backs, and give way to the sexual erethism which had been exalted to the highest point. The Christs reject marriage, and generally practise asceticism, but at such moments they are carried beyond themselves, and they feel that the physical emotions they experience are sanctified. There are a great many women among the Christs; at one of their resorts the police, in 1845, found nearly one hundred young girls. Women among them enjoy great honour, as well as equal rights with men. At their religious ceremonies some strong, beautiful, and intelligent young woman is often chosen for special adoration as the personification of divinity and the emblem of generative force; they call her the Virgin Mary, and they identify her with the Earth Goddess. She is their priestess; they prostrate themselves before her; she bears on her head a sacramental plate of grapes, and solemnly distributes them to the worshippers. Among the Skoptsy, a sect related to the Christs, the same observances and the same worship of women are carried to a still higher point; the castration or mutilation of both men and women is practised in their rites; they sometimes worship a naked young girl, cover her with kisses, and when she has reached the necessary pitch of reckless exaltation she allows them to communicate in her blood. It has sometimes been found among groups of Skoptsy that more than half the members are women.[1]

Religious movements of this epidemic character find their chief adepts among persons in whom the inhibiting influences of the higher intellectual centres are in but a lowly stage of development. The com-

[1] These and other semi-Christian mystical and rationalistic sects are described in the interesting work of N. Tsakni, *La Russie Sectaire*, 1888. The Christs or Khlysts have lately been studied by Dr. Paul Jacoby of Orel (*Arch. d'Anth. Crim.*, 15th Dec. 1903); he finds that their leaders are often hysterical or insane, and that their practices resemble those of Finnish shamanism.

paratively rare cases in which individuals of more than average mental culture are attracted in any number to a religious movement of this kind seem to belong to periods of over-strenuous intellectuality, during which a number of individuals are forced to adopt a rationalistic asceticism for which they are unfitted; at last the rationalistic fetters fall off, and the suppressed hypnotic centres explode with immense satisfaction. This is the most important key to the psychology of "conversion."

It is natural that we should find hypnotic phenomena most highly developed among primitive races, and the *shaman*, who is nearly everywhere the priest or priestess of savage races, presents the perfected type of hypnotic phenomena devoted to religious service and carried to the highest point of development.[1]

Among the numerous religious movements of hypnotic nature in somewhat primitive races may be mentioned that exhibited by the Russian *klikuschi* ("screaming women possessed"). The *klikuschi* were women attacked by severe paroxysms of hysterical religious emotion, which usually lasted for a short time only, but might continue for a day or more. These women were persecuted and tortured in the Middle Ages. An allied form of hypnotic religious emotion is the *ikota*, which is found among the Samojed women of Siberia. It occurs almost exclusively in married women, and in its milder forms is characterised by listlessness, with occasional outbursts of anger, and in its more developed forms by brief outbursts of maniacal excitement.

---

[1] At the present day in Siberia, among the tribes whose religion is shamanistic, besides the male shamans there are also very frequently female shamankas. Solovieu states that the shamankas are regarded as inferior to the shamans, except in the cure of mental diseases. Gmelin saw, however, among the Yakuts a shamanka, twenty years of age, who was much respected even by old shamans, and among the Tunguses he found that shamankas are sometimes superior to shamans (*Jour. Anth. Inst.*, Nov. 1894, p. 129).

In Abyssinia, again, at the beginning of the last century, the *tigretier*, as described by Nathaniel Pearce, an uneducated but reliable witness, closely resembled the mediæval Dancing Mania, and was especially common among women, though "men are sometimes afflicted, but not frequently." In Abyssinia to-day the women are very subject to hysteria.

One more form of hysterical hypnotic emotion, propagated by imitation, is the *lata* found among the Javanese, and in an allied form called *lattah* in Malacca. It chiefly occurs among native women, both of higher and lower social rank, and is marked by paroxysmal outbursts of involuntary movement with rapid ejaculation of inarticulate sounds, corresponding to the "speaking with tongues" found among Christian sects. There is temporary loss of consciousness, but the mental powers are intact except during the paroxysm. Lata assumes many forms, but in most of them, as in the Tarantism of the Middle Ages, and indeed in nearly all hypnotic manifestations, there is an irresistible tendency to imitation, a boundless suggestibility. The case is mentioned of a woman who appeared to be quite normal, but on any one throwing off a coat in her presence she would suddenly pass into a state of frenzy, strip herself of her clothes, and conduct herself in other indecent ways, whilst all the time she kept abusing the instigator of what she regarded as an outrage. Again, the ship's cook of one of the local steamers, a pronounced sufferer from the disease, was dandling his baby on the deck. One of the men noticing this, picked up a billet of wood, and, standing in front, commenced nursing it in the same way. Presently he began tossing the billet up to the awning, the cook imitating his motions with the baby. Suddenly the sailor opened his arms, and the billet fell to the deck; the unfortunate cook did the same, and the child, falling on the planking, was instantly killed. In other respects the subjects of *lata* are mentally quite sound.[1]

It is impossible here to deal at all adequately with the fascinating subject of religious psychology;[2] but it will probably be sufficiently obvious that all the various forms and stages of hypnotic phenomena (as here understood) go to make up religious exaltation in its most characteristic forms. This fact is patent even to the devout historian of the Camisards, who, as we have seen, is struck by the close resemblance between the religious phenomena presented by that sect and the phenomena of anæsthesia by nitrous oxide, the lowest and least intellectual of the hypnotic states. The general characteristic of all the various hypnotic forms may be expressed by saying that there is lessened control by the higher intellectual centres and increased activity of the more spontaneous and automatic motor and visceral centres. Or, if we prefer, we may say that the more highly co-ordinated action of the nerve centres gives way to their more inco-ordinated action, and therefore the presence of hypnotic phenomena indicates a somewhat lower degree of mental integration.[3] In catalepsy and anæsthesia there may be complete quiescence of the higher modes of action; in dreaming, ecstasy, and hypnotism proper, they are taken into comparatively uncontrolled spheres; in hallucinations they remain in the normal sphere, but are perverted; in neurasthenia and hysteria there is merely a slightly lessened control of the higher

[1] Art. "Klikuschi," "Ikota," "Lata," "Tigretier," *Dict. Psych. Med.* For several of these and allied hypnotic affections, occurring chiefly or exclusively in women, see Max Bartels, *Medicin der Naturvölker*, pp. 215-218.

[2] Professor Starbuck's detailed study, *The Psychology of Religion*, in which due attention is given to sexual differences, may be consulted with advantage.

[3] "As we ascend the animal scale," Ferrier remarks (*Functions of the Brain*, 1886), "the centres of which the cerebro-spinal system is composed become more and more intimately bound up and associated with each other in action."

centres; while the increased activity of the lower centres may be intertwined with a considerable degree of intellectual activity in the modes of religious exaltation.

It is not necessary here to discuss the causation of hypnotic religious phenomena. To do so would be to open up many interesting questions which are still scarcely ripe for solution. Tylor (*Primitive Culture*, 3rd edit., 1891, vol. ii. pp. 128-142, and pp. 410-421) has briefly discussed in his usual masterly manner the evolution of what I have here called hypnotic religious phenomena, from the earliest savage times to the revivals of the present day. He insists on the importance of fasting in their development: "Bread and meat would have robbed the ascetic of many an angel's visit; the opening of the refectory door must many a time have closed the gates of heaven to his gaze." The importance of fasting in the evolution of visions is certainly great. It must be added that sexual abstinence has played a very prominent part in producing the more typical motor phenomena. Continence is enjoined on the adepts of nearly all religions. It is only among a few sects, and at the climax of religious excitement, that the sexual emotion has been regarded as sanctified. Its repression has usually been necessary to assist in elaborating the process of religious auto-intoxication. But the final explosion of the suppressed sexual instincts is often violent. Having been, as it were, diverted into a foreign channel, and their impetuosity at the same time increased, they finally break violently back into their normal channels. Anstie, an acute observer of some of the intimate details of the emotional life, has remarked ("Lectures on Diseases of the Nervous System," *Lancet*, Jan. 11th, 1873): "I know no fact in pathology more striking and even terrifying than the way in which the phenomena of the ecstatic state—which have often been seized upon by sentimental theorisers as proofs of spiritual exaltation—may be plainly seen to bridge the gulf between the innocent fooleries of ordinary hypnotic patients and the degraded and repulsive phenomena of nymphomania and satyriasis." At the time when Anstie wrote the connection between spiritual exaltation and organic conditions was not so plain as it is at present, but he had clearly perceived the especial facility with which the ecstatic condition passes over into disordered sexual emotion. Since then the almost constant connection between ecstasy and sexual excitement has become fairly well recognised. (See, for instance, Conolly Norman, Art. "Mania," *Dict. Psych. Med.*) The phenomena of the religious life generally are to a large extent based on the sexual life, and the majority of conversions

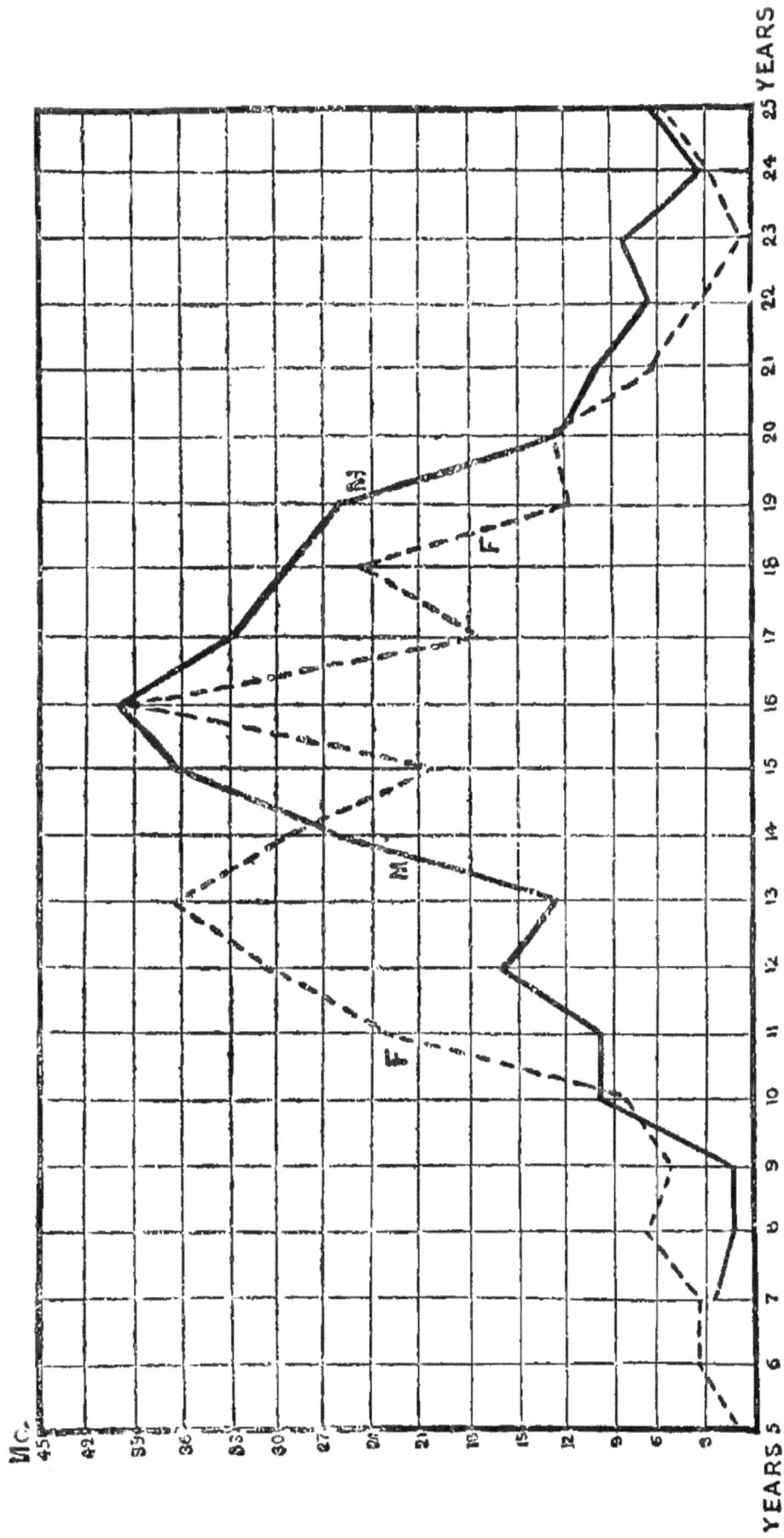

CURVES SHOWING THE FREQUENCY OF CONVERSIONS IN VARIOUS YEARS. (*Starbuck.*)

——— = Males.   – – – = Females.

(about 80 per cent.) take place during adolescence. (See a suggestive paper by A. H. Daniels, B.D., "The New Life: A Study of Regeneration," *Am. Journal Psych.*, 1893, vol. vi., No. 1; Krafft-Ebing, *Psychopathia Sexualis*, 8th edit., 1893, pp. 8-11; and especially Starbuck, *The Psychology of Religion*.) Starbuck found that in each sex conversion tends to occur within a year after the establishment of puberty; the average age of puberty being reckoned as 13.8 years for girls and 15.6 for boys; the average age for conversion was 14.8 for girls and 16.4 for boys.

It must be remembered that hypnotic phenomena are strictly physiological, although they are liable to be increased or modified to a degree that is distinctly morbid; an individual in whom the action of the higher centres had largely abolished the stirrings of the lower hypnotic centres would be morbid to a still greater degree. Hypnotic phenomena form, with the allied vaso-motor movements, the chief physiological basis of what we more generally call "emotion." When, therefore, we conclude that women are more liable than men to present hypnotic phenomena, we have but discovered in a more definite and fundamental manner that women are more "emotional" than men. We have now to define more precisely what is meant by the "emotionality" of women.

CHAPTER XIII.

THE AFFECTABILITY OF WOMEN.

WHAT IS AN EMOTION?—READIER RESPONSE OF THE VASO-MOTOR VASCULAR SYSTEM IN WOMEN—PHYSIOLOGICAL AND PATHOLOGICAL EVIDENCE—THE HEART —THE CONVULSIVE TENDENCY OF WOMEN—EPILEPSY— BLUSHING—THE REFLEXES—TICKLISHNESS—LAUGHTER AND TEARS — FACIAL EXPRESSION — THE IRIS — THE BLADDER—SUSCEPTIBILITY TO FRIGHT—MENTAL SUGGESTIBILITY — OBSESSIONS — EMOTIONAL CAUSATION OF DISEASE PREDOMINATES IN WOMEN—DESTRUCTIVE TENDENCIES—"BREAKINGS OUT"—THE SOURCE OF THESE—THE CONGENITAL EXHAUSTIBILITY OF WOMEN —THE ADVANTAGES OF WOMEN'S AFFECTABILITY— ANÆMIA AND AFFECTABILITY—THE GREATER AFFECTABILITY OF WOMEN TO SOME EXTENT THE RESULT OF CIRCUMSTANCES, TO SOME EXTENT ORGANIC.

WOMEN respond to stimuli, psychic or physical, more readily than men. This general statement, though it may be modified or limited in certain respects, is uncontested. By what word we may best describe this characteristic of women's nervous constitution is less clear. We may call it with perfect correctness a greater "irritability," or "plasticity," or "suggestibility." All these terms are legitimate, but on the whole I prefer to use an old word, approved by Laycock,[1]—sufficiently colourless to be unobjectionable, while it indicates both the quick psychic and

[1] Laycock, *Nervous Diseases of Women*, p. 76.

the quick physical response to stimuli,—and to speak of the greater "affectability" of women.

In considering the preponderance of "hypnotic" phenomena in women—the tendency, that is, of the more primitive nervous centres to be stronger than the more recent centres, and to rise up in revolt against them—we were approaching on its most obscure side the greater emotionality of women. We are now approaching the emotionality of women from a somewhat less obscure side.

What is an emotion? We shall more easily gather the drift of the facts if we understand this at the out-set. It was formerly supposed, and is no doubt still supposed by many people, that an emotion is a purely mental phenomenon, and that anger or love may go on in the brain somewhat in the same way as an arithmetical calculation. This is not the case. It is conceivable that, if the head could be removed from the body at will, the brain when isolated could per-form a mathematical calculation; it is no longer possible to believe that it could feel anger or love, or any other emotion, save in the most remote and intellectualised form. If it were found by the appli-cation of delicate physiological tests that a man's vascular and muscular systems were working at their usual normal tension, it could probably be affirmed that that man was not feeling emotion. No amount of self-control over the coarser expressions of emotion alters the case, for even to unscientific inspection the passion of the self-controlled man reveals itself by some quiver of muscle, some sudden pallor, some quickening of heart-beat. Just as it may be said: no muscle, no motion; so it may equally be said: no muscle, no emotion.

Bocalosi, an Italian writer of the eighteenth century, in his book *Della Fisionomia*, seems to have had a glimmering of the truth that emotion depends on physical organisation. Its full and precise statement has had to wait for the delicate investigations initiated during recent years by the great Italian physiologist,

Angelo Mosso, of Turin. Mosso has shown, largely by means of various ingenious instruments, such as the plethysmograph and the balance, which he had himself devised, that the whole organism—especially the whole vaso-motor vascular system—responds at every psychic or physical stimulus, at a word or at a touch, and has brought evidence to show how every muscular movement and every intellectual effort produce an entire redistribution of blood in the body; so that the heart, the whole circulatory system, and all the viscera and glands form, as it has been said, a kind of sounding-board, against which every change in consciousness, however slight, at once reverberates. (For a charming and popular exposition of many of his results, see Professor Mosso's little book on fear.) The slight changes never reach consciousness again, but at a certain threshold of intensity they return to consciousness, and emotion is attained.

The fact that the vaso-motor system—the neuro-muscular ruler of spontaneous organic life—responds more readily to stimulus in women than in men is embodied in the familiar saying that woman's heart is tender. This, as Mosso remarks, is only another way of saying that the nervous mechanism of women's hearts is excited, so causing them to beat more quickly, under the influence of stimuli by which men's hearts in a state of health are unaffected.[1] A proof of the greater excitability of women's hearts is found in the fact, which has been noted by several observers, that there is a distinctly greater increase in the number of pulsations on awaking from sleep in women; the excitement of waking life affects the hearts of women (and also of children) to a greater extent than those of men.[2] Even the complex phenomena of hysteria have been defined by Rosenthal as ultimately resolvable into a weakness of resistance, congenital or acquired, of the vaso-motor system. And Féré quotes with approval the remark of Marshall Hall that hysteria is "very much a disease of emotion; the same organs, the same functions are affected." It is also worthy of note that the special tendency of women to be affected by the disease of the eyes

[1] Mosso, *La Peur*, p. 84.
[2] Bertin, Art. "Sommeil (Physiologique)," *Dict. ency. des Sci. Méd.*

called glaucoma, which is accepted by nearly all authorities, is also referred by Priestley Smith to the greater instability of the vaso-motor system in women, and particularly to the disturbances of circulation which emanate from the generative organs.[1]

Women are more liable than men to convulsive manifestations. This special convulsive tendency is expressed in the greater frequency in women of epilepsy, which may be roughly defined as a vaso-motor and neuro-muscular spasm of extreme violence, affecting primarily the brain, and secondarily the whole body. As Gowers points out, it is based on an abnormal readiness for action, or in other words an undue affectability.

It was formerly supposed in England that epilepsy is somewhat more common in men than in women. This was due, as Gowers and others have shown, to the confusion with true epilepsy of convulsive conditions caused by syphilitic brain disease and other physical disturbances. It is only in adult age (when these syphilitic conditions are most likely to intervene) that "epilepsy" is found more common in males. In France epilepsy has always been recognised as more common in females, and Esquirol placed the proportion as 3 to 2. Gowers in London finds it to be 108 females to 100 males, but, as he himself points out, at the hospital where he gathered most of his observations, the male patients are in excess. The greater prevalence of true epilepsy in women is indicated by the much greater frequency with which in males extraneous exciting causes can be assigned for the disease, and Gowers further points out that even in the first year of life there are nearly twice as many epileptic female infants as males. The chief period of life for the manifestation of epilepsy is in both sexes puberty and adolescence, and Gowers finds that the maximum of cases in males is reached at the age of twelve, in females at the age of sixteen. It is not until after the age of twenty-nine that epilepsy begins to occur more frequently in males. The prognosis is slightly better in males than in females, who are also rather

---

[1] P. Smith, *Pathology of Glaucoma*, 1891, p. 132. Wagner has found in his practice at Odessa that among over 1200 cases of glaucoma, 38 per cent. were in men and 62 per cent. in women; the predominance of women was marked at all ages, except under twenty, when the disease is extremely rare. *Comptes-rendus XII. Congrès Int. Med.* (Moscow), 1897, vol. vi. p. 180.

more likely to suffer from mental defect (Sir W. R. Gowers, *Epilepsy*, 2nd ed., 1901; this book embodies the mature work of a clinical observer of extreme acuteness and penetration). In its greater severity and frequency in women, and less precocious development at puberty, epilepsy may be said to reverse the usual sexual difference in grave disease, and may thus be regarded as a more peculiarly feminine disease. It must also be regarded as especially associated in both sexes with the efflorescence of sexual life; in some cases it is only during the menstrual period that the attacks take place, and in others they are aggravated at that time. So marked is the tendency for epilepsy to appear in early life that Sir William Broadbent goes so far as to say that when it appears in adult life we must always seek for some contributory cause, or even suspect that we are not dealing with true epilepsy at all (*Brit. Med. Jour.*, 4th Jan. 1902). Of the immediate causes of epilepsy the most generally assigned are psychical,—excitement, anxiety, and above all (more especially in early life) fright. These are causes which are specially operative in woman, being part of her greater affectability. It may be noted that the chief feature in the ordinary conduct of epileptics is their irritability and tendency to impulsive acts, frequently associated with religious or erotic ideas. The temperament of the epileptic declares itself before the fits actually appear. "When one has known these epileptics in childhood," Voisin remarks (Art. "Epilepsie," Jaccoud's *Nouveau Dict. de Med.*), "before the disease had developed, one found them quarrelsome, indocile, restless, very sensitive, falling into suffocating attacks of anger, growing pale in moments of ill-humour, making sudden movements. They are feeble in appearance and rather sad. I have several times noticed that epileptics were so timid in childhood and youth that they could not be left alone in the dark." All these signs—which cannot, however, be found in every case—are those of affectability.

The general convulsive tendency of women in its broadest aspects has been admirably discussed by an eminent gynæcologist, Dr. Robert Barnes, in his Lumleian Lectures on the convulsive diseases of women. Women's special proclivity to convulsive nervous diseases, he remarks, depends upon the reproductive functions, the great convulsive disorders of women being almost entirely limited to the period of reproductive activity. It is in the breeding season that the nervous excitability of the frog attains such a height that slight irritation of the skin will produce almost tetanic convulsions; "it is easy to perceive analogous phenomena, sometimes quite as pronounced, in the human female, at the advent of puberty, at the periods of ovulation, during gestation, and eminently during the act of labour." Labour, he observes, is a series of convulsions, and during a labour pain, "the resemblance to epilepsy is, for the moment, so close that the two conditions can hardly be distinguished." It is scarcely necessary to refer, further, to the ancient observation, "Coitus brevis epilepsia," and many physicians have noted that coitus may cause epileptic fits. In short, "an energy which may be compared with, if not identical in nature with, convulsion is an essential element in the leading acts of the generative function." The very periodicity of the sexual life in women, Barnes points out, indicates an accumulation of nerve force ready to use when the periodic occasion arises, or to burst out tumultuously. Barnes clearly realised the intimate association between the convulsive proclivity of women and their proclivity to emotion, which takes a large part in every act or process of the generative function. "In short, emotional affectability is the measure of convulsive liability." (R. Barnes, "The Convulsive Diseases of Women," *Brit. Med. Jour.*, April 1873.)

Blushing, which Darwin called the most human of all expressions, is a vaso-motor nerve storm of spontaneous and uncontrollable character. Its much greater frequency in women affords evidence that needs no insistence, of the greater affectability of the vaso-motor system.[1] Partridge found that in those cases in which he had data as to age, there was a chief maximum between the ages of fifteen and eighteen (more especially at the earlier age), and a secondary maximum at twelve; this corresponds curiously with the maxima for the appearance of epilepsy, and clearly indicates the intimate connection of blushing with the sexual life.

One of the bases of the affectability of women, and the convulsive tendency, is to be found in the reflexes. To say that women are more affectable than men, and more emotional, means in part to say that reflex action is more developed than in

---

[1] The physiology and pathology of blushing have been investigated by Darwin, *Expression of the Emotions*, and Dr. H. Campbell, *Flushing and Morbid Blushing* (1890). Tilt found that flushes occurred in 244 women out of 500. Partridge (*Pedagogical Seminary*, April 1897) has carefully studied the phenomena of blushing in 120 cases (of which 84 were females) and of flushing in 134 cases, of which nearly all were women, or girls who had reached the age of adolescence. Blushing refers to the objective phenomena of this vaso-motor storm, and flushing to its subjective phenomena.

men and less under control of the higher centres. In other words they are, in the widest sense of the term, more ticklish. Dr. Gina Lombroso has examined a large number of persons, children and adults, normal and abnormal, of both sexes as regards the reflex responses of those parts of the body most sensitive in this respect, especially the abdomen and the soles of the feet. She found these very marked in children and in young people from fifteen to eighteen, but much diminished in adults; while the results as regards adults are not very clearly presented, it would appear that marked responses, as regards both abdominal and plantar reflexes, were distinctly more frequent in the women than in the men.[1] Francotte of Liège has studied the radio-bicipital reflex in over 500 individuals of both sexes divided into various normal and abnormal groups. In all groups its absence was much less frequently found in women than in men. Its exaggeration, showing undue reflex hyperexcitability, was especially found among anæmic and neurotic subjects.[2] The reflex wink, or the response of the eyelids to a sudden stimulus presented to the eyes, has been studied by Partridge among 1100 school children at Worcester, Mass. He tested ability to inhibit the wink when a visual and auditory stimulus was presented to the eyes on the other side of a piece of plate glass. The control of the wink was gained much more speedily with increase of age. In boys this increase with age was rapid and regular; with girls it was less rapid and more irregular, with a marked regression at the age of eight, a slight one at ten, and a very marked regression, almost falling back to the level of the age of six, at twelve years. Partridge refers to " the fuller neuro-muscular training which the average boy receives from his freer life," but he cannot explain the regression of girls at

---

[1] *Compte-Rendu Cong. Int. d'Anth. Crim.*, Amsterdam, 1901, p. 295.
[2] *Jour. Ment. Science*, April 1897, p. 389.

twelve; it would be interesting to know if the plantar and other reflexes show a similar deviation at this age. Irrespective of age the average number of winks was 19 for a boy and 34 for a girl.[1] Allied evidence of the convulsive tendency in women is furnished by the facility with which they yield to tears and laughter. Tears are defined by Sir B. W. Richardson[2] as "the result of a nervous storm in the central nervous system, under which there is such a change in the vascular terminals of the tear-secreting glands that excretion of water from the glands is profuse;" he points out that tears are not produced by pain even when amounting to agony, but occur when the sympathetic nervous system is most developed and most impressionable, and the great emotions of fear, grief, and joy most active, and that hence it is that women are more given to tears than men. As regards laughter, Dr. Louis Robinson[3] has suggested that it has its basis in the reflex phenomena of tickling. Pouting, again, is a characteristically childlike method of automatic response to external stimuli which is rarely seen in its most emphatic form in adults, except sometimes during insanity; in a very slight but still quite perceptible form it is, however, fairly common in women, especially as the unconscious indication of an offended dignity which cannot find expression in words.

Women's faces are more expressive than men's, or, rather, it would be better to say, they are more mobile; that is to say, that there is greater neuro-muscular affectability. If we watch the faces of the

[1] Partridge, "The Control of the Reflex Wink," *Am. Jour. Psych.*, Jan. 1900.

[2] Richardson, Art. "Tears, Psychology of," Tuke's *Dict. of Psych. Med.*

[3] Robinson, Art. "Ticklishness," Tuke's *Dict. of Psych. Med.* "The Psychology of Tickling" has been studied in a very interesting and suggestive manner by Stanley Hall and Arthur Allin, *Am. Jour. Psych.*, Oct. 1897. Numerous studies of laughter have recently appeared, especially in France.

men and women in the streets of London, or of any other crowded city, where people think themselves sheltered by numbers from inquisitive observation, it will be seen that while the men more usually have a fixed immobile expression, the women's faces are more usually in actual movement, the mouths twisting and the foreheads wrinkling, seeming to indicate an early stage of physiological distress. It cannot strictly be said that the women's faces are more expressive; for if the men's stereotyped features may express a mood that is past, the fluctuating and evanescent muscular movements on the women's faces have not yet become co-ordinated into the expression of a definite mood. They are for the most part the play of a neuro-muscular mobility still submerged beneath the level of consciousness. Children's faces are extremely mobile. Dr. Francis Warner, who has examined 100,000 school children, finds that the signs of undue nervous mobility are more common in girls, and that "defective expression" is much more rarely met with in girls.[1] In insanity women's faces usually express in a much higher degree than men's the apparently constant presence of intense emotional conditions. The mobility of women's faces is due to their affectability to stimuli both from within and from without; in the latter form it is closely related to suggestibility, which is indeed but one of the forms of women's affectability. A woman instinctively responds more easily than a man to influences from without, even in spite of herself. A young woman, especially if her nervous control is at all defective, involuntarily changes when an individual of the opposite sex approaches; however indifferent he may be to her personally, she cannot

---

[1] F. Warner, *Report of a Committee as to Average Development and Condition of Brain Function among Children*, 1888; Milroy Lectures on Physical and Mental Condition of School Children, *Brit. Med. Journal*, 1892; also a suggestive article by the same author on "Expression, Facial," in *Dict. of Psych. Med.*

prevent the instinctive response of her vaso-motor and muscular system, and becomes at once shyer and more alive. Again, a man's rigid facial expression does not respond as a woman's does to the faces it encounters. I have noticed the haggard face of a young woman whose child had just died break out momentarily into a pleasant automatic smile in response to the smile of an acquaintance; this could scarcely have happened to a man. A large portion of the "tact" of women has the same basis. This affectability has often been brought as a reproach against women, even by their own sex, but we must remember that to a large extent it is physiological.

The affectability of the involuntary muscular system is shown in ways that are not easily open to inspection, or which are not obvious. The pupil of the eye dilates involuntarily to all sorts of slight stimuli. Not only is it affected by light as well as in association with accommodation and convergence of the visual axes, but the irritation of almost any cutaneous nerve, as by pinching or pricking the neck, arm, or leg, and the stimulation of some of the nerves of special sense, such as by a loud noise, and various emotional conditions, all produce dilatation of the eyes. This result, according to Moeli and others, is much more constant in women and children than in men. The bladder, although its affectability to faint stimuli is not easily demonstrated, is, as Mosso and Pellacani have shown, an even more delicate æsthesiometer than the iris, and is probably the most delicate in the body. Mosso and Pellacani found that contraction of the bladder follows directly on the slightest stimulation of any sensory nerve, and also that all the varying conditions of the organism which raise the blood-pressure and excite the respiratory centres produce an immediate and measurable effect upon the bladder. These investigators found by experiments upon several young women, that when a plethysmograph was brought into connection with the bladder, even a slight touch with the finger on the back of the subject's hand produced a notable contraction of the bladder, and whenever the subject spoke, was spoken to, or made the slightest mental exertion, there was a similar contraction.[1]   These reactions are much more delicate than those of the blood-vessels, and cannot be paralleled by any other part of the organism.   The bladder, as Born puts it, is the mirror of the soul; it would be equally correct to say that to some extent the soul is the mirror of the bladder.   The fainter vesical contractions cannot be said to play a recognisable part in emotion, but when they attain a somewhat higher degree of intensity they play a well-recognised part; "a nervous bladder," as Goodell puts it, "is one of the earliest symptoms of a nervous brain."   Contraction of the bladder plays a part in the constitution of various emotional states of fear, anxiety, and suspense.   In its extreme spasmodic form, as incontinence of urine, it is very common in children, and by no means uncommon in young women, quite apart from pregnancy or the results of pregnancy, though rare in men.[2]

No doubt other organs, if we could examine them with equal precision, would furnish similar evidence to that furnished by the heart, the iris, and the bladder.   The comparatively larger size of the abdominal and some other organs in women, and the comparatively greater range of their physiological action, furnish a visceral basis for the greater affectability of women.

[1] These experiments are briefly summarised in Art. "Urinary Bladder," by H. Ellis, *Dict. of Psych. Med.*

[2] Stevenson, "Enuresis," *Lancet*, 10th January 1891. It may be objected that this phenomenon is simply due to the shorter and broader urethra of women. Maurice Hache, however, one of the chief authorities on the bladder, states that the force required to produce expulsion is almost equal during life in men and women, though after death there is much less resistance in women's bladders. (Hache, Art. "Vessie," *Dict. ency. des Sci. Méd.*)

Fright is an emotion in which the phenomena I have been speaking of play a conspicuous part, and fright is an emotion which is seen in women far more than men. Among the lower social ranks more especially it is noteworthy how the women will start and call out in the presence of any unexpected phenomenon, although men of the same class are quite unmoved. Some Prussian statistics of suicide among school children show that while "fear of punishment" caused 19 per cent. of the suicides among the boys, it was responsible for 49 per cent. among the girls. This characteristic has probably been fostered by both men and women, since it leads to displays of strength and protection on the part of the man towards the woman which are equally gratifying to both parties. Fright is a frequent origin of nervous disease in children and in women, but rarely in men. In the causation of epilepsy, according to Gowers, it is equally effective in each sex during childhood; at puberty it is most effective in girls; after twenty it is seldom traceable in men, but is still a relatively frequent cause in women. Chorea, again, or St. Vitus's dance, is a disease which is frequently caused by fright (in 27 per cent. cases, according to the Collective Investigation Committee of the British Medical Association), and simulates the defective muscular control and inco-ordination of fright; it is sometimes caused by imitation, and is altogether a disorder to which females are predisposed. On the whole, about three females are affected for one male; the preponderance of girls, as we should expect, is least marked in childhood; after sixteen, when the disease falls markedly in frequency, it is rarely seen in boys, and between the ages of twenty and thirty it is practically confined to women. It may be added that all nervous diseases are in women largely due to emotional causes. Hammond is inclined to think that moral and emotional insanity without marked intellectual aberration is more common in girls than in boys.[1]   Pitres found that emotion is influential in causing nervous disease in 54 women out of 69, but in only 8 men out of 31.[2]   It is due to their suggestibility that women are more liable than men to be affected by communicated insanity or *folie à deux*.[3]

It is owing to the great suggestibility of women that nearly everywhere hysterical manifestations in women have from time to time tended to take on an imitative character, so that the women thus affected have simulated the actions and especially the cries of various animals—dogs, cats, sheep, doves, etc.   The prevalence of such manifestations of vocal hysteria in women has been noted for two thousand years.[4] Obsessions which, as we have seen, are much more frequent in women, are a special form of morbid emotivity, and are most usually caused, on a predisposed mental soil, by strong moral emotions, religious or sexual preoccupations, terror, or even horrible dreams; Pitres and Régis found that it is at puberty, between 11 and 15 years of age, that obsessions most usually begin to take root in the mind, and that it is between 26 and 30 (also a somewhat critical age in women) that they most usually develop.   It is the same suggestibility that causes women to be less subject to nostalgia, or home-sickness, than men, and more adaptable to changes of habit and new impressions.[5]   In a similar manner, as is frequently seen, the wife of the " self-made man " is often much better able than her husband to adapt herself to the manners and customs of the new circles in which she moves.

Some recent experimental results in psychology

[1] Hammond, *Insanity*, p. 96.

[2] *Leçons cliniques sur l'hystérie*, etc., t. i. p. 36.

[3] Hack Tuke, Art. " Communicated Insanity," *Dict. Psych. Med.*

[4] F. Houssay, " Imitation Hystérique des cris d'Animaux," *Rev. Mens. de l'Ec. d'Anth.*, 1898, p. 209.   We are here brought near to manifestations more or less identical with those hypnotic phenomena we encountered in Chap. XII.

[5] Widal, Art. " Nostalgie," *Dict. ency. des Sci. Méd.*

indicate that the affectability of women shows itself even in comparatively unemotional departments, and exercises a disturbing influence on their sense-judgments. Thus Gilbert found that in experiments devised to show the influence of size in affecting judgments as to weight, among 2000 school children between the ages of six and seventeen, except at the age of nine when both sexes are equal, girls are throughout more suggestible than boys to the deceptive influence of size, girls being most inferior to boys during the last three years.[1] Triplett found also that 60 per cent. girls, and only 40 per cent. boys, were deceived by the pretence of throwing a ball into the air.[2]

Irascibility—"irritability" in the more homely sense of the word—is a form of affectability which has in all ages, and perhaps quite legitimately, been attributed to women.[3] As Terence said—

" Mulieres sunt fermè, ut pueri, levi sententia;
  Fortasse unum aliquod verbum hanc inter eas iram conciverit."

In its most extreme form this tendency shows itself in reckless and uncontrollable outbursts of purposeless destruction. This may best be studied, although not exclusively, in the prison and the lunatic asylum. In prisons spasmodic "breakings out" of wild destructive violence are in England usually regarded as peculiar to the woman's side.[4] The greater obstreperousness of the female patients in lunatic asylums is well recognised; as Dr. Clouston remarks, "there is ten times as much noise in the female wards as there is in the male wards;"[5] and, as

---

[1] *Studies Yale Psychological Laboratory*, vol. 2, 1894, p. 61.

[2] *Am. Jour. Psych.*, July 1900, p. 111. It should be added that Dresslar (*Am. Jour. Psych.*, June 1894) testing illusions of weight due to size, among a small group of children, found the boys more suggestible; he also found that the most intelligent children were the most suggestible.

[3] See, for example, Lombroso and Ferrero, *La Donna Delinquente*, pp. 147-148.

[4] See, for example, H. Ellis, *The Criminal*, pp. 142-152.

[5] *Journal of Mental Science*, April 1893, p. 314.

the same authority also points out, in the insanity of puberty a destructive tendency in the female seems to take the place of pugnacity in the male.[1] The greater noisiness and talkativeness of insane women is by no means confined to one race. It has been noted by Raggi in Italy, and among so calm a people as the Russians I noted during a visit to the Alexiev Municipal Asylum in Moscow some years ago that it was found necessary to confine a few noisy women in solitary rooms, while on the men's side, the assistant physician informed me, all was quiet. Dr. Näcke of Hubertusburg, dealing with women who were at once both criminal and insane, found that among 53 individuals as many as 41 showed extreme irritability; 23 were violent and liable to attack the attendant or the doctor, more especially at the menstrual epoch; most of these, although not all, were destructive, and in their wrath would destroy furniture, bed-clothes, their own garments, and especially window panes; of the latter several destroyed about forty per annum each; the ground of these outbursts is said to lie in the extreme irritability and unbounded egotism of the women. The "breaking out," or *Zuchthausknall*, in its most sudden, violent, apparently unmotived, and almost epileptic form, was found by Näcke to occur in 12 cases.[2] One reason why women love dancing is because it enables them to give harmonious and legitimate emotional expression to this neuro-muscular irritability which might otherwise escape in more explosive forms. Music, in a slighter degree, satisfies the same craving, for in a muffled but harmonious manner it exercises the whole of the emotional keyboard.

In a thoughtful and interesting paper on "The Sexes in Lunacy" (*St. Bartholomew's Hospital Reports*, vol. xxiv. 1888), Dr. T. Claye Shaw discusses many of the points we are concerned with here. His paper is so full of instruc-

---

[1] Clouston, Art. "Developmental Insanities," *Dict. Psych. Med.*
[2] Näcke, "Verbrechen und Wahnsinn beim Weibe," p. 78.

tion regarding the affectability of women generally—which in insanity is seen in its most unrestrained form—that I venture to quote from it at some length, more especially as it is published in a somewhat inaccessible manner. After remarking that women are less willing to work in asylums than men, and that they "give infinitely more trouble than men and cause much more anxiety" (although, at the same time, it must be remembered, insanity is much less serious in women, as they far more frequently recover than men), he continues: "The number of women in an asylum who require extra supervision and consequent deprivation of liberty far exceeds that of the men. It is only epilepsy and drink that reduce men to the same condition as women. . . . Destructiveness is a very dangerous and troublesome symptom, and it must be said that it prevails to a far greater extent among women than among men. A look at the airing-grounds of an asylum is as good a test of this statement as can be got. On the male side the damage done is comparatively trifling, but on the female side the gardener is driven to despair, for broken trees, torn-up flowers, and trodden-down plants proclaim the presence in its exaggerated and insane form of the spirit that animated the occupiers. . . . In the matter of clothes, too, the female patients are more destructive than the men. . . . I have been up to now speaking more of aimless destruction, but when we come to purposed destruction the women have much the more unfavourable account. Impulsiveness shows itself in glass-smashing or crockery-breaking, probably because these are the readiest ways in which they can vent their superabundant energy; and though men will at times do this, they never approach the other sex in their attempts in this direction. It would seem as if brain-action in women is quicker than in men, and that their proverbial rapidity in forming a conclusion is partly due to their natural excitability or proneness for discharge, and partly also to the natural education of life." Taking governesses, for example, Dr. Shaw finds that those who had themselves received only an ordinary "ladies' school" education, with the merely superficial emotional training which is usual, are troublesome, destructive, uncontrollable patients; those who had been trained *ab initio* to be high-class governesses, in a thorough-going methodical way (like many German governesses), though originally they may have been of ardent temperament, are able to some extent to control their emotional effervescence even when insane. "From my experience the Germans and the Scotch form the quietest and most reasonable patients; the Irish are, as a rule, very noisy and excitable: but for downright vindictiveness and unreasoning awkwardness I have never met the equals of the women who come from the parishes of the East of London. . . . To many people the most striking difference between the sexes in asylums is in the language, and here the women hold the palm for volubility, abuse, and foul-mouthedness. There is no difference in this respect between the barefaced virago from the lowest parts of the town and the fashionable woman from the best quarter. . . . Certain it is that noise, filthy conduct, and sexual depravity, both by speech and act, are much more common on the female than on the male side of an asylum. I no more expect to find quiet and unobtrusive mania among women than I should hope to see Niagara without hearing the roar of it. . . In all forms of acute insanity the sexual element is more prominently shown in women than in men—a fact not to be wondered at, considering the important part the physiology of the reproductive organs plays in the life of the woman, causing her whole life to be instinctively blended with ideas more or less traceable to the rearing of offspring." The comparative frequency with which, as we have seen (pp. 313-315), sexual excitement occurs in women under the influence of anæsthetics is another proof of the predominant sexuality of women. Dr. Shaw points out finally how the natural impulsiveness and affectability of women are increased by her training in life:— "Women in acute states of insanity are abusive, indiscriminately violent, impulsive, obscene, and wayward out of all proportion to what men are, because they are fulfilling the condition that has been allowed to them in ordinary circumstances. Men have received their abuse with levity, and they think that they will still do so. When in their sane rage they have broken the furniture or used foul language and have been only laughed at, is it not natural that they should think that the same immunity from punishment will attend them in other circumstances? When they have pouted and sulked until their wish has been gratified, is it not natural that they should do the same when through disease placed among strangers? Women have been treated in the same way as animals—they have been petted or cuffed according to the fancy of the moment; and because men have found it easier to let them talk than to argue with or contradict them, they (women) fancy that their surest way of success is by keeping themselves constantly *en evidence*, by never taking 'yes' or 'no' for an answer, and, in short, by never ceasing to worry until they have gained their ends." But all the same, even when insane, women have charm for those whose duty it is to care for them, and Dr. Shaw concludes by saying that in insanity, as well as in ordinary life, " das ewig-weibliche zieht uns hinan."

In this connection mention may be made of the extravagant exaltation of obscenity and cruelty, far surpassing that of men, to which women have been carried in times of popular epidemics of passion and excitement; this has been pointed out by Diderot, Despine, and others (see, for instance, Lombroso and Ferrero,

La Donna Delinquente, p. 76), and Zola has given an artist's picture of it in *Germinal.* There is physiological ground for the saying that every woman carries a slumbering *petroleuse* in her bosom.   Lombroso has pointed out that while women generally take a very small part in revolutions, they take a large part in revolts.   I may mention a typical instance, which occurred when I was in Barcelona during the revolt of the workers in 1901, and excited general comment.   A young Catalan woman of the people placed herself at the head of a large body of strikers, mostly men, and displayed immense energy in organising and leading them.   Nobody knew who she was, and when martial law was proclaimed in the city and the revolt subsided, she silently retired into the obscurity from which for a moment she had emerged.

The evidence I have brought together in this chapter will help to make clear the statement made in the chapter on " The Senses," that a quick response of the vaso-motor and muscular organism to stimuli, from within or from without, has no connection whatever with delicacy and precision of response in the sense-organs.   It remains to point out that the results here reached are in harmony with those we have reached when considering other groups of phenomena.

In considering " Motion " I referred to the interesting experiments of Riccardi, showing how women, in making muscular exertion with the dynamometer, tend to reach their maximum power at the first effort, while men more often only attain their maximum power at the second or third effort.[1]   The fact thus clearly brought out has a distinct bearing on the affectability of women.   As Féré expresses it, women exhibit a congenital exhaustibility, and, as among children, savages, and nervous subjects, their motions and their emotions are characterised by a brevity and violence which approach to reflex action.[2]   To some extent affectability is simply a tendency to fatigue.

[1] It may be added that Riccardi has been confirmed by Wissler in New York (*Psych. Rev. Monographs*, vol. iii. No. 1); Wissler found that 80 per cent. women reach their maximum strength with the dynamometer at the first effort, but only 61 per cent. men.

[2] Féré, *Pathologie des Emotions*, 1892, pp. 398, 480.   Dr. Mary Jacobi makes a similar statement, *Question of Rest*, etc., p. 204.

Mr. Galton once carried on an interesting investigation among teachers as to the signs of fatigue. Summarising the results of answers received from 116 teachers, he found that nervous fatigue is chiefly revealed by involuntary muscular twitchings of the face, fingers, etc., grimace, frowning, compression of lips, tendency to nervous laughter, and general muscular unsteadiness. There are also vaso-motor symptoms, pallors, flushings, and various alterations in the colour of the face and ears; also depression and hyperæsthesia of the senses. These are all manifestations of "irritability," which in its common mental form the teachers acknowledge to be "perhaps the commonest sign of incipient mental fatigue."[1] Lack of "staying power" is the popular way of expressing the neuro-muscular exhaustibility of women, and, as we have previously seen (p. 208), this is everywhere found to characterise the work of female clerks in the Post-office, etc.; under ordinary circumstances the women are equal to the men, but they cannot work under pressure. It is sometimes said that women are more easily distracted from their work; thus Mr. Valentine, of Valentine & Son, photographers, of Dundee, remarked, in addressing his workpeople, that "a man could talk and work at the same time, but when a girl talked she stopped work;"[2] if there is an element of truth in this, we must connect it with this congenital exhaustibility of women. It may be added that this quick exhaustibility of women is not due to the special conditions of civilised life, but is also found among savages. Thus Landor, among the Ainos, noted that most of the hard work is done by the women, who surpass the men in muscular strength, and at all events as regards manual labour in endurance. But at the same time he found that they

---

[1] F. Galton, "Mental Fatigue," *Journal Anthrop. Institute*, 1889, p. 157.

[2] *Photographic News*, Feb. 17th, 1893. Cf. *ante*, p. 177.

could not compete with men in work leading to severe and prolonged fatigue; in walking and running a woman was as good as a man for one day's journey, but not for longer distances. The same characteristic marks savages as compared with Europeans; thus the Rev. W. Grey, who is himself accustomed to manual labour, writes of the natives of Tanna:— "In steady pick and shovel work the natives could do more than I could the first day. We were about equal the second day. On the third day they fell far behind me." [1]

It may seem that this characteristic of women's neuro-muscular energy is an unmitigated disadvantage, but this is by no means the case. Not only is it associated with the greater readiness of women, but it is an extremely valuable safeguard. Men are able to undergo far more prolonged and intense exertion than women, but they purchase this capacity at a price; the resulting collapse, when it comes, is more extreme and more difficult to recover from. Women yield to the first strain, but for that very reason they quickly recover. Energetic women, who are able to disregard physiological warnings, naturally suffer from more serious collapse, as men would. As a rule, their affectability protects women from the serious excesses of work or of play to which men are liable. The frequency and comparative triviality of nervous disorders in women, their much greater seriousness and fatality in men, largely finds its explanation here. That women are more often attacked by most zymotic diseases than men, but more rarely die from them, seems to be a fact belonging to the same group.

The neuro-muscular exhaustibility of women is no doubt in some measure due to the fact—which we encountered when considering "Metabolism"—that the blood of women is more watery than that of men; in women, at all events as women exist to-day, a

[1] *Jour. Anth. Inst.*, Aug. and Nov. 1898, p. 128.

certain slight degree of anæmia may be regarded as physiological.[1] But anæmia increases affectability; in an anæmic woman a very slight stimulus or exertion produces too strong a reaction; to live healthily she must live at a very low and slow rate of tension.

As Dr. Foxwell, pointing out how dangerous sudden transitory toil is for the anæmic, remarks:—"Continuous toil, mental or physical, is an impossibility to the anæmic patient. But anæmic people who are up and about and trying to do their work in the world, have a certain standard of speed and persistence set them by the healthy people they see around them. This standard they try to attain; they therefore start off with the vigour of a healthy person, but their feeble muscle or nerve cells soon pull them up and they have to rest, starting off again in a few minutes with more than normal vigour, to make up for lost time, but only the sooner to be rearrested by helpless debility. Their work is therefore done in jerks, the toil during the jerk being far beyond their strength. They might perhaps do just as much in the aggregate without injury to themselves if they worked from beginning to end at a steady, slow rate commensurate with their strength; but the forces of imitation and emulation are too strong for them, and they persist in exhibitions of normal energy with subnormal bodies. But even had they perfect control of themselves, how can they avoid sudden efforts of high pressure? The anæmic school-girl standing up in class has to concentrate her brain power to answer with costly speed the question rapidly passed down from one to another, or has to work sums for marks against time. The house-maid is bound to run upstairs quickly to answer her mistress's bell, to carry trays full of food, and scuttles full of coal. This quickness of answer, these trays and scuttles have been formed for healthy persons; to them they would act but as a sturdy developmental stimulus, but to the anæmic they become a breathless and exhausting labour. If anæmics held sway over toil there would be no quickness of performance, no strenuous effort allowed. Luckily for the world's progress, but unluckily for them, they have to play a very subordinate part on life's stage, and to be content with things as they find them." (A. Foxwell, "Ingleby Lectures on Condition of the Vascular System in Anæmic Debility," *Brit. Med. Journal*, 16th April 1892.)

---

[1] See Dr. Stephen Mackenzie's Lettsomian Lectures on Anæmia, *Brit. Med. Journal*, 1891, vol. i., for evidence showing that the physical characteristics of the anæmic are an exaggeration of those of women generally. Cf. *ante*, p. 225.

The question still remains how far the affectability of women is natural and organic, how far it is the mere accidental result of external circumstances. Is the greater emotionality of women a permanent and ineradicable fact? There can be no doubt that to a very large extent emotionality may be modified. Hypnotic phenomena, perhaps as common in men as in women among savages, are rare among civilised men. The men of to-day are not as emotional as the men of the thirteenth century; the modern English gentleman does not talk and behave like the English gentlemen who killed Thomas à Beckett. The woman of to-day, again, is less emotional than her great-grandmother a century ago; she is not subject to vapours and swoons on trivial occasions to anything like the same extent. The mere fact of the immense difference on the whole which exists as regards emotionality between women of different social classes (and which, as we have seen, is removed when the restraint of sanity is removed), suggests that emotion, in its coarser manifestations at all events, is to an immense degree educable. The attention that is now, fortunately, beginning to be given to the physical culture of women will undoubtedly tend to strengthen and develop the neuro-muscular system. Just as we have sure reason to believe that sensibility may by training be increased, so there is still greater reason to believe that affectability may by training be decreased.

That there is, however, a limit to this sexual equalisation of affectability remains extremely probable. The comparatively larger extent of the sexual sphere in women and of the visceral regions generally, —for in women at puberty, as Dr. Campbell puts it, a new keyboard and a fresh series of pipes are added to the instrument,—the physiological tendency to anæmia, and the existence of inevitable periodicity of function in women, conspire to furnish a broader basis for the play of emotion which no change in environment or habit could remove. Affectability in women may be reduced to finer and more delicate shades; it can scarcely be brought to the male standard.

This result is by no means to be regretted. We have seen that the affectability of women ensures to them certain solid advantages, and assists to safeguard them against evils from which men are specially prone to suffer. Beyond this, if men and women were more on the same level as regards emotionality, they would lose very much of their power to help one another. They would certainly, also, lose very greatly their power to charm one another. The man of facile emotions makes little impression on a woman; the woman who is lacking in emotionality leaves a man cold. As long as this is so we may be perfectly sure that—even if the greater affectability of women had a less firm organic basis—men and women will never be equal in emotionality.

The affectability of women exposes them, as I have had occasion to point out, to very diabolical manifestations. It is also the source of very much of what is most angelic in women—their impulses of tenderness, their compassion, their moods of divine childhood. Poets have racked their brains to express and to account for this mixture of heaven and hell. We see that the key is really a very simple one; both the heaven and hell of women are but aspects of the same physiological affectability. Seeing this, we may see, too, that those worthy persons who are anxious to cut off the devil's tail might find, if they succeeded, that they had also shorn the angel of her wings. The emotionality of women, within certain limits, must decrease; there are those who will find consolations in the gradual character of that decrease.

CHAPTER XIV.

THE ARTISTIC IMPULSE.

THE INDUSTRIES AROSE IN WOMEN'S HANDS, THE ARTS IN
MEN'S—POTTERY—TATTOOING—PAINTING—SCULPTURE
—MUSIC—WHY WOMEN HAVE FAILED IN MUSIC—
METAPHYSICS—MYSTICISM—POETRY—FICTION—WHY
WOMEN HAVE SUCCEEDED IN FICTION—THE SUPREM-
ACY OF WOMEN IN ACTING—THE ARTISTIC IMPULSE
GENERALLY IS MORE MARKED IN MEN—THE CAUSES
OF THIS.

PRIMITIVE women have in their hands all the
industries, and, in consequence, the rudiments of
most of the arts. But when we get beyond the
rudiments the position begins to change, and when
we reach fully differentiated arts, even among
savages, we find that they are almost exclusively
in the hands of men.

The making of pottery is an industry which
develops almost insensibly into an art. In nearly
every part of the world pottery has at the outset
been entirely, or almost entirely, in the hands of
women, and so long as it remained in their hands
the potter's industry has usually retained a severely
practical character. It is sufficient to quote the evidence of one observer who possessed a peculiarly
intimate acquaintance with the lowest stages of
primitive culture. Miklucho-Macleay, speaking of
Papuan art in North-east Guinea, remarks:—" I have
been struck by the absolute absence of ornament on

the pottery, the clay easily lending itself to all sorts of ornamentation; this lack of ornament is due to the fact that the manufacture of pottery is exclusively confided to women, who are not usually very artistic by nature. I have found confirmation of this ancient and just observation even among Papuan women. I am able to state that I have never seen the slightest ornament invented or executed by a woman. During a visit to the island of Bibi-Bibi, where pottery is manufactured for all the neighbouring villages, when observing a dozen women and young girls fashioning pottery, I saw several women doing nothing; as they had in front of them a mass of pots without the slightest ornament, I asked why they did not ornament them. 'What is the good? It is not necessary!' were the replies they gave. But this did not prevent two young boys from finding pleasure in imprinting with their nails and a pointed stick a sort of ornamental border on some of the pots." [1]

Tattooing is in many parts of the world chiefly in the hands of women. Thus among the Nagas of Assam it is " often performed by old women of the chief's household, and as a matter of right." [2] Among the Aino, also, tattooing is done by women, and at present indeed it is the women alone who are tattooed. [3] Again, among the Songish or Lkungen Indians of Canada the tattooing is done by women, who introduce charcoal beneath the skin by means of a needle held horizontally. [4] It must be remembered, however, that tattooing is by no means the pure outcome of the art impulse, but a social and religious rite of a traditional character. Such semi-ritual art

---

[1] *Bull. Soc. d'Anthropologie*, 19th Dec. 1878. Andree has brought out the same point.

[2] Peal, "On the Morong," *Journ. Anth. Institute*, Feb. 1893, p. 247.

[3] MacRitchie, Supplement to *Internationales Archiv für Ethnographie*, Bd. iv., 1892.

[4] *Brit. Assoc. Report on the North-Western Tribes of Canada*, by Dr. Boas, 1890.

may be in the hands of either men or women; thus among the Papuans (according to S. J. Hickson) the designs on houses and praus are wrought by old men or priests of the village to keep off the spirits of storms.

If we turn to the pure artistic impulse, as manifested in the higher stages of culture, we find that the supremacy of men in painting is unquestionable. There have been thousands of women painters, but only the men have been remembered; it would be unkind to make a comprehensive list of famous women painters. Even the great central situation of Christianity, as of life—the relation of the mother to her child—which appeals so strongly to a woman's heart, has never received memorable rendering at a woman's hand. In sculpture, also, it is scarcely necessary to add, the great names are all men, from Phidias to Donatello, from Michael Angelo to Rodin. That there have been two or three women whose names deserve honourable mention is the most that can be said.

In the evolution of music women have played a very small part. It does not appear that a woman has ever invented any well-known musical instrument, and there is not in any part of the world an instrument that is peculiar to women or chiefly played by them; it is rarely even that they perform on men's instruments. In aboriginal America Professor Otis Mason remarks that musical instruments are never played by women, though they beat time on various objects and may now and then use the rattle, as well as join in certain choruses.[1]

Mr. Henry Balfour, of the University Museum, Oxford, has brought forward a few exceptions to the general rule from the South Pacific. "In the South Pacific the 'nose-flute' is very generally, though by no means exclusively, played upon by

---

[1] *Nature*, 13th Oct. 1892; *ib.*, *Woman's Place in Primitive Culture*, ch. viii.

women. In the account of the voyage of Captains Cook and King there is in one of the plates a figure of a woman of the Tonga Islands seated under a hut playing upon a 'nose-flute.' A similar figure of a woman playing upon a 'nose-flute' may be seen in plate 28 of Labilladière's *Voyage de La Perouse*, in the representation of a Tongan double-canoe. Melville (*Four Months' Residence in the Marquisas Islands*, p. 251) mentions playing upon the 'nose-flute' as being 'a favourite recreation with the females.' In Wilkes' *U.S. Exploring Expedition*, iii. p. 190, there is a description of this instrument as used in the Fiji Islands, and it is stated that 'no other instrument but the flute ["nose-flute"] is played by the women as an accompaniment to the voice.'

" Turning now to another genus of primitive instruments, viz., the 'musical bow,' we find a peculiar local form, the 'Pangolo,' occurring at Blanche Bay, New Britain. There are specimens of this at Berlin and Vienna. This instrument is stated by Dr. O. Finsch (*Ann. des K. K. Naturhist. Hofmuseums*, suppl. vol. iii., Pt. 1, p. 111) to be only played upon by women of Blanche Bay. Guppy too (*Solomon Islands*, p. 142) says that the women of Treasury Island produce a soft kind of music by playing, somewhat after the fashion of a Jew's-harp, on a lightly-made fine-stringed bow about 15 inches long.

" It cannot, I believe, be said that any of these instruments have been *invented* by women, and it is undoubted that women in savagery but seldom figure as performers upon musical instruments. It would certainly be interesting to collect all the instances recorded."—*Nature*, 17th Nov. 1892.

Among barbarous and civilised races in all parts of the world women have been trained profusely to play on musical instruments; but the position of the sexes has remained relatively the same as among savages. The players of music have often been women; the makers of music have nearly always been men. Unless we include two or three women of our own day whose reputation has perhaps been enhanced by the fact that they are women, it is difficult to find the names of women even in the list of third-rate composers.

There is, I believe, no difference of opinion whatever on this point. Mr. G. P. Upton, in his intelligent and sympathetic little book, *Woman in Music* (Chicago, 1886), endeavours to magnify the part that women have played in music, but he

recognises that none of the masters in music have been women.
He gives a list of forty-eight women musicians who lived during
the seventeenth, eighteenth, and nineteenth centuries and left com-
positions, but none of them rose above mediocrity.   How small
this number of noted women musicians is we may realise by re-
calling that Italy alone (as Lombroso remarks in his *Man of
Genius*) has produced not less than 1210 musicians of more or less
note.   Mr. Upton has, I think, very felicitously expressed one chief
reason why women have failed in music, though they have had
nearly equal advantages with men :—" Conceding that music is
the highest expression of the emotions, and that woman is
emotional by nature, is it not one solution of the problem that
woman does not musically reproduce them because she herself
is emotional by temperament and nature, and cannot project
herself outwardly, any more than she can give outward expression to other mysterious and deeply-hidden traits of her nature ?
The emotion is a part of herself, and is as natural to her as
breathing.   She lives in emotion, and acts from emotion. . . .
Man controls his emotions, and can give an outward expression
of them.   In woman they are the dominating element, and so
long as they are dominant she absorbs music.   Great actresses
may express emotion because they express their own natures ;
but to treat emotions as if they were mathematics, to bind and
measure and limit them within the rigid laws of harmony and
counterpoint, and to express them with arbitrary signs, is a
cold-blooded operation possible only to the sterner and more
obdurate nature of man."   He adds that it is significant that
while a man who has once learned to play on an instrument
rarely ceases to delight in it, a woman's love for music ceases
with age ; it is not an æsthetic but an emotional influence.
Rubenstein, in his book on *Music and its Masters*, has some
remarks which well supplement Mr. Upton's, though they are
somewhat less precise :—"This increase of the feminine
contingent in music, both in instrumental execution and in
composition (I except the department of singing, in which they
have always excelled), begins with the second half of our
century.   I regard it as one of the signs of musical decadence.
Women lack two prime qualities necessary for creating—
subjectivity and initiative.   In practice they cannot get beyond
objectivity (imitation), they lack courage and conviction to rise
to subjectivity.   For musical creation they lack absorption,
concentration, power of thought, largeness of emotional horizon,
freedom in outlining, etc.   It is a mystery why it should just
be music, the noblest, most beautiful, refined, spiritual, and
emotional product of the human mind, that is so inaccessible
to woman, who is a compound of all those qualities ; all the
more as she has done great things in the other arts, even in the
sciences.   The two things most peculiar to women—love of a

man and tender feeling for a child—have found no echo from them in music. I know no love duo or cradle song composed by a woman. I do not say there are none, but only that not one composed by a woman has the artistic value that could make it typical."

Music is at once the most emotional and the most severely abstract of the arts. There is no art to which women have been more widely attracted, and there is certainly no art in which they have shown themselves more helpless.

It cannot be said that literature is an art. It is merely a method of recording very diverse manifestations of psychic aptitude and artistic impulse. It is enough to mention four of these—metaphysics, mysticism, poetry, fiction.

It is remarkable that although women are so strongly drawn to religion, they have done almost nothing to give classic expression to that mysticism which is the kernel of religion everywhere. The great manuals of devotion which have fed so many thousand souls, and which all say the same thing with a few verbal differences—the manual of Lao Tze, Marcus Antoninus's *Meditations*, Epictetus's *Encheiridion*, the gospel of St. John and the Epistles of St. Paul, the *De Imitatione Christi*, the *Deutsch Theologie*, much of the writings of Schopenhauer— are the work of men, although they have probably found, on the whole, at least as many readers among women as among men. St. Theresa is, so far as I know, the only woman who can be put in the first rank, but it must be added that there is an element of unquestionable morbidity in her work which cannot be said to characterise any of the great mystics I have named, not even St. Paul or Schopenhauer. Madame Guyon's name occurs, but she belongs to the second rank of mystics, which numbers a vast army of men.

The art of metaphysics belongs almost exclusively to men. Even in the third rank of metaphysicians the names of no women can yet be very clearly discerned. The philosopher's art consists in building up an ideal and conjectural world on the basis of his own psychic organism; it is of all arts that in which emotion is most highly intellectualised, and the material most abstracted from the practical and concrete. Whether women's failure here means the condemnation of metaphysics or the condemnation of women is a problem which every one will decide according to the basis of his own temperament.

In poetry women have done much more than in either mysticism or metaphysics. The strong emotional poetic energy, chiefly lyrical in form, which in English is perhaps best represented by Mrs. Browning, has been expressed by the women of many lands. At the same time it has had a tendency to be either rather thin or rather diffuse and formless. Strong poetic art, which involves at once both a high degree of audacity and brooding deliberation, is very rare in women. We have a Sappho and a Christina Rossetti—one representative of each of the great poetic nations of Europe—but it is difficult (I will not say impossible) to find women poets who show in any noteworthy degree the qualities of imagination, style, and architectonic power which go to the making of great poetry.

Mr. Edmund Gosse has made some remarks worth quoting as to the place occupied by women in the poetic literature of the world:—"That Shakespeare should have had no female rival, that the age in which music burdened every bough, and in which poets made their appearance in hundreds, should have produced not a solitary authentic poetess, even of the fifth rank, this is curious indeed. But it is as rare as curious, for though women have not often taken a very high position on Parnassus, they have seldom thus wholly absented themselves. Even in the iron age of Rome, where the muse seemed to bring forth none but male children, we find, bound up with the savage verses of Juvenal and Persius, those seventy lines of pure and noble indignation against the brutality of Domitian which alone survive to testify to the genius of Sulpicia.

"It is no new theory that women, in order to succeed in

poetry, must be brief, personal, and concentrated. It was recognised by the Greek critics themselves. Into that delicious garland of the poets which was woven by Meleager to be hung outside the gate of the Gardens of the Hesperides he admits but two women from all the centuries of Hellenic song. Sappho is there indeed, because, 'though her flowers were few, they were all roses,' and, almost unseen, a single virginal shoot of the crocus bears the name of Erinna. That was all that womanhood gave of durable poetry to the literature of antiquity. A critic, writing five hundred years after her death, speaks of still hearing the swan-note of Erinna clear above the jangling chatter of the jays, and of still thinking those three hundred hexameter verses sung by a girl of nineteen as lovely as the loveliest of Homer's. Even at the time of the birth of Christ, Erinna's writings consisted of what could be printed on a page of this magazine. The whole of her extant work, and of Sappho's too, could now be pressed into a newspaper column. But their fame lives on, and of Sappho, at least, enough survives to prove beyond a shadow of doubt the lofty inspiration of her genius. She is the type of the woman-poet who exists not by reason of the variety or volume of her work, but by virtue of its intensity, its individuality, its artistic perfection." (Edmund Gosse, "Christina Rossetti," *Century Magazine*, June 1893.)

In fiction women are acknowledged to rank incomparably higher than in any other form of literary art. Thus in England, at all events, in Jane Austen, Charlotte and Emily Brontë, George Eliot, we possess four story-tellers who, in their various ways, are scarcely, for the artistic quality and power of their work (although not for quantity and versatility), behind our best novelists of the male sex. In France, it is true, where the novel has perhaps reached the highest degree of artistic perfection, women, owing to a variety of circumstances, have produced little fiction of artistic value; but in many countries of Europe at the present day, both in the north and in the south, there are one or two women who stand in the first rank. It is only when (as in the work of Flaubert) the novel almost becomes a poem, demanding great architectonic power, severe devotion to style, and complete self-restraint, that women have not come into competition with men. But fiction in the proper sense makes far less serious artistic demands than poetry, inasmuch as it is simply an idealised version of life, and may claim to follow any of the sinuous curves of life. What it demands is a quick perception of human character and social life, coloured by a more or less intense emotional background. A vivid perception of social phenomena—of the interaction of men and women which is the basis of fiction—is natural to all women, who are, in a sense, more close to the social facts of life than men. They are, too, more receptive of detailed social impressions and more tenacious of such impressions.[1] In the poorest and least cultured ranks the conversation of women consists largely of rudimentary novelettes in which "says he" and "says she" play the chief parts. Every art, one may say, has an intellectual and an emotional element: women have done so well in fiction because they are here organically fitted to supply both elements. In fiction women possess a method of self-expression which is artistically well within their grasp.

On the whole, however, even when we take fiction into account, it cannot be said that women have reached the summits of literature, although literature is of all methods of expression that which has been most easily within their reach. There are doubtless many reasons why this should be so, although at present these reasons do not easily come within the

---

[1] This social impressionability of women must still be admitted, even though we accept the statements of Groos and Durkheim, that in the deeper sense women are less socialised than men. Groos remarks (*Spiele der Menschen*, p. 438) that women possess in a much less degree than men the sense of rigorous subordination to abstract law, and illustrates this by their greater willingness to cheat in various departments of life. He associates this characteristic with the absence of the discipline involved in the exercise of the male combative instincts. Durkheim (*Le Suicide*, p. 442) finds that women are nearer to nature, less the product of society than men, whose activities, tastes, and aspirations have to a greater extent a collective origin; in woman's less degree of socialisation he sees the explanation of various sociological phenomena, though he does not regard it as a final and ultimate fact.

region of exact research. It is possible, for instance, that one factor may be found in that quick affectability and exhaustibility which we have seen to characterise the nervous energy of women. In whatever direction a woman exerts her energies they are all swiftly engaged and no reserve is left. The qualities of Aphra Behn and of Emily Brontë have never been combined in one woman. Yet to be at once gay and profound—a combination supremely exemplified in Shakespeare—is part of the fascination and the power of nearly all the finest literature. Women have achieved complete success in letter-writing, and in love-letters they are supreme,[1] for here their special characteristics become of the first importance; but they have not on this basis wrought any literature of the highest order. In Montaigne we have a great writer who may be said to have set out with the literary methods of a woman—spontaneity, carelessness of form, a very personal and intimate frankness—yet we cannot even conceive a feminine Montaigne.

There is, however, one art in which women may be said not merely to nearly rival but actually to excel men: this is the art of acting. In a land and in an age prolific in dramatic ability, Bachaumont wrote in his *Mémoires* in 1762 that perhaps none of the great actors of his day were so transcendent as its four great actresses—Clairon, Dumesnil, Gaussin, and Dangeville. Half a century later Roussel wrote that there were more good actresses than good actors.[2] The same may probably be said at the present day; during recent years, at all events, Sarah Bernhardt and Eleanora Duse have had no male rivals. And if we look back at the history of the stage during the

[1] "Thousands of women's letters," truly remarks Mantegazza, "that lie in the cabinets of lovers, and are eventually burnt, would, if they could be published, convince us that Madame de Sévigné has many rivals."

[2] P. Roussel, *Système de la Femme*, Partie I., chap. iv.

last two hundred years, against every famous actor whose name survives it seems usually possible to place a still more famous actress. With women's success as actresses may be associated their perhaps equally undoubted success as singers, singing being in part vocalised dramatic art. It is not difficult to find the organic basis of woman's success in acting. In women mental processes are usually more rapid than in men; they have also an emotional explosiveness much more marked than men possess, and more easily within call. At the same time the circumstances of women's social life have usually favoured a high degree of flexibility and adaptibility as regards behaviour; and they are, again, more trained in the vocal expression both of those emotions which they feel and those emotions which it is considered their duty to feel. Women are, therefore, both by nature and social compulsion, more often than men in the position of actors. It is probable also that women are more susceptible than men to the immediate stimulus of admiration and applause supplied by contact with an audience. In the allied art of dancing women are also supreme.

It is worth remarking, in connection with the superiority of women in acting, that it has frequently been found that women are also better readers. Thus Mr. Bryce, in a report on the state of education in Lancashire, remarks in regard to reading:— "This is one of the few things in which girls' schools are markedly better than boys'. There does not seem to be much more direct training in the one case than in the other, so it is left us to suppose that the superiority of the girls is due to their more correct ear, their quicker perception of the meaning of what they read, and that more perfect harmony which seems to exist between their intelligence and its expression in voice, feature, and gesture. Even where they have no special training, they are free from that plodding awkwardness which generally belongs to a Lancashire boy's reading. And in several schools, where the mistresses had accustomed their pupils to read aloud, and had carefully checked any tendency to affectation, the reading was everything that could be desired in point of grace, variety, and expressiveness." And Mr. Fearon, reporting on schools on the East Coast, also refers to the superiority of girls in reading; he found that even in mixed schools girls read better than boys. (D. Beale, *Reports issued by the Schools' Inquiry Commission*, pp. 55 and 136.)

Legouvé, who had a long and intimate connection with the stage, has some remarks on the success of women in acting in his charming and acute though scarcely scientific *Histoire Morale de la Femme*, 6th ed., 1874 (p. 345):—"Whether actor or singer, the interpretative artist needs above all a talent for observing details, flexibility of the organism to follow the movements of thought, and above all, that mobile, ardent, and varied impressionability which multiplies in an almost incredible degree the sensations and signs which represent it. For this reason the dramatic faculty is more native to women than to men. All great cantatrices, as experience shows, reach the supreme height of their talent before the age of twenty, that is to say, after four years of study; a man to be a great singer requires eight years." (See also a chapter in Upton's *Woman in Music* on "Woman as the Interpreter of Music.")

On the whole, there can be no doubt whatever that if we leave out of consideration the interpretative arts, the artistic impulse is vastly more spontaneous, more pronounced, and more widely spread among men than among women. There is thus a certain justification for Schopenhauer's description of women as the unæsthetic sex. Even in the matter of cooking we may see how emphatic is the tendency for an art to fall into the hands of men. All over the world cooking, as an industry, is women's business, yet wherever cooking rises from an industry to become something of an art it is nearly always in the hands of a man.

When we consider the proportion of women, as compared to men, who obtain even moderate fame, we find that it is even at the present day extremely small. As regards literature, Mantegazza examined the *Dizionario biografico degli Scrittori Contemporanei* and found that among over 4500 writers only 4.1 per cent. were women. In my own study of British genius from the earliest period to the end of the nineteenth century (based on the *Dictionary of*

National Biography), I found that among the most eminent British persons in all departments, 1030 in number, only 5.3 per cent. were women, and it has at the same time to be admitted that a minor degree of ability sufficed to ensure the inclusion of the women.[1]

Galton found, in investigating nearly 900 individuals, that 28 per cent. males and 33 per cent. females showed artistic tastes—*i.e.*, were fond of music, drawing, etc. That is to say, that notwithstanding all that our education does to bring out artistic tastes in women, the sexes remain nearly equal.[2] If we go back to early times. we may be perfectly sure that the rough drawings of men, animals, and other natural objects which are found on primitive implements and on rocks are the work of men. At the present day the impulse to scribble, draw, and carve—the artistic impulse in its most primitive form—is very much more marked in boys and men than in girls and women. Both in colleges and prisons this difference is decided. It may thus probably be said that women are less imaginative than men. In her study of young children's fears, Katharine Fackenthal found that the boys showed much more originality than the girls, and a larger proportion of the objects of their fear were imaginary, though at this early age the sexual differences were slight.[3] If this difference is real it is not without significance, for it is on their fears and their desires that men's art is founded. Insanity, again, which is so instructive in the terrible clearness with which it brings to the surface the most fundamental impulses, reveals in women a singular imaginative poverty. The delirious ideas of women, remarks Toulouse,[4] one of the subtlest psychological students of insanity,

---

[1] Havelock Ellis, *A Study of British Genius*, chap. i.
[2] F. Galton, *Natural Inheritance*, chap. ix.
[3] *Pedagogical Seminary*, Oct. 1895, p. 322.
[4] Quoted in *Arch. d'Anth. Crim.*, Feb. 1903, p. 122.

are few in number and simple in nature; "the insane woman is altogether lacking in invention in the conception of delirious ideas; she shows nothing of the wealth of extravagance manifested by men." The characteristic ideas of grandeur which so often affect men are rare in women, and then usually of a feeble and pedestrian sort, Toulouse remarks, for the most part confined to the region of the toilet, or playing around a supposed secret legacy.

The assertion of Möbius[1] that the art impulse is of the nature of a male secondary sexual character, in the same sense as the beard, cannot be accepted without some qualification, but it may well represent an approximation to the truth.

Ferrero has sought the explanation of the small part played by women in art, and their defective sense for purely æsthetic beauty, in their less keen sexual emotions.[2] This is doubtless an important factor. The sexual sphere in women is more massive and extended than in men, but it is less energetic in its manifestations.[3] In men the sexual instinct is a restless source of energy which overflows into all sorts of channels. At the same time, the rarity of women artists of the first rank is largely due to another cause which we shall be concerned with later on—the greater variational tendency of men.

[1] P. J. Möbius, *Stachyologie*, 1901.
[2] G. Ferrero, "Woman's Sphere in Art," *New Review*, Nov. 1893.
[3] H. Ellis, "The Sexual Impulse in Women," *Studies in the Psychology of Sex*, vol. iii.

CHAPTER XV.

MORBID PSYCHIC PHENOMENA.

SUICIDE—FACTORS THAT INFLUENCE ITS FREQUENCY— SEXUAL PROPORTIONS IN EUROPE—THE INFLUENCE OF AGE—THE CAUSES OF SUICIDE—METHODS OF SUICIDE — MEN PREFER ACTIVE, WOMEN PASSIVE METHODS—RACIAL SEXUAL DIFFERENCES.

INSANITY—IN VARIOUS PARTS OF THE WORLD—CAUSES OF INSANITY—FORMS OF INSANITY—ALCOHOLIC INSANITY AND GENERAL PARALYSIS INCREASING AMONG WOMEN —GENERAL PARALYSIS AS A TYPICALLY MASCULINE INSANITY—INSANITY AND CIVILISATION.

CRIMINALITY—DIFFICULTIES IN THE WAY OF THE STUDY OF SEXUAL DIFFERENCES — WHY WOMEN ARE LESS CRIMINAL THAN MEN — THE SPECIAL FORMS OF WOMEN'S CRIMINALITY—CRIMINALITY AND CIVILISA- TION.

SUICIDE.

THE suicidal impulse is not necessarily morbid. But there can be no doubt that in the majority of cases suicide implies a considerable degree of psychic abnor- mality, whether the lack of mental balance is the result of a sudden shock or is simply the last stage in a slow disintegration. Suicide is rarely the result of a deliberate weighing of evidence resulting in the decision that, as Marcus Antoninus expresses it, the house is smoky and must be quitted. The philo- sophers who have given this advice have rarely them- selves found that the house was smoky. And the proceedings at coroners' inquests show that in a very large proportion of cases suicides are the eccentric, the perverse, the highly strung, and the mentally unbalanced, who—under circumstances when all may have thought of suicide—have not preserved the mental integrity which enables men to see that beyond these circumstances life is still tolerable. The morbid nature of suicide, as it usually exists among us to-day, is shown by its curious parallelism with the phenomena of insanity.[1]

There are, it is well known, many cosmic, racial, and social factors influencing the frequency of suicide. The maximum of suicide, as of insanity, occurs during the early heat of summer. Among Europeans suicide is more frequent than among negroes and other lower races; and in Europe it is more prevalent among the Teutonic than among the Latin races; in America these racial differences are to a large extent persistent. There are more suicides in towns than in the country; the rate is much higher in manufacturing than in agricultural centres; among soldiers and sailors than among civilians; the liberal professions yield a higher proportion of suicides than any other class of occupations; they are only exceeded, and that greatly, by those who have no occupation at all.[2] The unmarried, whether men or women, commit suicide more often than the married, this immunity of the

---

[1] The morbid character of suicide is usually recognised by juries in England, although it is not easy to justify the usual formula of "temporary insanity," but the English law (and even the latest project for its reform), with that curious conservatism which makes English law so interesting to archæologists, continues to regard the attempt to commit suicide as a crime. The man who succeeds in committing suicide is innocent; the man who fails is a criminal. As Sir Frederick Pollock remarks (*Oxford Lectures*):—"In our existing polity the latest mechanism of elaborate legislation may be found side by side with relics of a period of legal culture not less archaic than that of the twelve tables at Rome."

[2] Westergaard points out that the economic factor in suicide is especially well marked in England and Wales, the suicide-rate rising whenever the amount of imports and exports per head falls. (*Grundzüge der Theorie der Statistik*, Jena, 1890, p. 14.)

married being especially marked when there are children; young widowers and widows kill themselves twice as often as the married of the same age, and in old age the suicidal tendency of the widowed is still more marked. The aged generally commit suicide far oftener than the young.

Suicide in Europe is from three to four times more frequent in men than in women. This was first shown in the last century by the famous alienist, Esquirol. The chief variations in different countries during recent times will be found in the following table, which presents the proportions of the sexes per hundred suicides:—[1]

	M.	F.		M.	F.
France (1827-80) .	77	23	Baden (1865-83) .	85	15
„ (1849-54) .	80	20	Bavaria (1844-47) .	75	25
„ (1870) .	81	19	Austria (1876-77) .	83	17
„ (1886) .	79	21	Hungary (1851-54) .	72	28
Paris (1849-54) . .	68	32	Switzerland (1876-83)	86	14
London (1858-59) .	69	31	Canton of Geneva		
„ (1891) . .	76	24	(1838-55) . .	82	18
England (1858-59) .	73	27	Belgium (1865-83) .	84	16
„ (1861-88) .	74	26	Holland (1875-79) .	78	22
„ (1891) .	75	25[2]	„ (1880-82) .	81	19
Ireland (1874-83) .	73	27	Denmark (1835-56) .	75	25
Scotland (1877-81) .	70	30	„ (1861-86) .	78	22
United States (1860).	79	21	Copenhagen (1835-56)	70	30
„ (1897-1901)	78	22	Norway (1866-73) .	76	24
Connecticut (1878-82)	70	30	„ (1876-82) .	79	21
New York (1870-72) .	78	22	Sweden (1865-82) .	78	22
Victoria (1865-70) .	82	18	Finland (1878-83) .	81	19
Prussia (1850-52) .	82	18	Russia (1870-74)	80	20
„ (1872) . .	80	20	Italy (1867) .	81	19
„ (1887) . .	80	20	„ (1874-83) . .	80	20
„ (1889) . .	79	21	Spain	71	29
Saxony (1865-83) .	80	20			

[1] I have compiled this table, making numerous additions, from Maurice Block, *Statistique de la France*, and Legoyt, Art. "Suicide," *Dict. ency. des Sci. Méd.*

[2] From 1858 to 1883, for equal numbers living, and having similar age-distribution, the male suicide-rate was to the female suicide-rate, according to Ogle, as 104 to 39, or 267 to 100. The varying annual proportion of suicides per million persons living during the years 1861-

It will be seen that Spanish women are more inclined to suicide than the women of any other country, the proportion being about 1 woman to 2.5 men. Morselli attributes this aptness of Spanish women to suicide to "the force of their passions, which brings them nearer to the male sex." It will be noted, however, that the proportion of women is almost equally high in Hungary and Scotland.[1] In Switzerland the proportion of women suicides to men is lower than in any other European country, being (according to Morselli's figures) 12.2 per cent., as against 28.8 per cent. in Spain. It appears that the oscillations are greater in the female than in the male sex. It will be seen from the table that there is a decided tendency for the proportion of women suicides to decrease; or, one should rather say, women have taken a smaller share than men in the modern development of suicide.[2] We may note that this is the case in France, England, and Norway, though not in Prussia, where suicide is decreasing in relation to population, but woman's share seems slightly on the increase, as is woman's share in criminality. On the whole, however, the proportion of male to female suicides is far more constant than the general proportion of suicides to the population; thus in Saxony, both in 1867 and in 1877, there were 18 female suicides to 82 male, but while in the former year suicides were 312 per million of the population, in the latter they were 394. In Italy again, in the year 1877, for example, suicides were only 41 per million of the population, but the sexual ratio was

1888 will be found in the very interesting and comprehensive article, "Suicide," by Dr. Hack Tuke, *Dict. Psych. Med.* While the rate per million has for males risen from 100 to 124, for females it has only risen from 35 to 39.

[1] It is of interest to note that towards the beginning of the last century, when insanity was nearly everywhere more common in men, in Spain (according to Esquirol) and in Scotland there was an excess of female lunatics.

[2] This was observed some years ago by Legoyt, *Ann. Med. Psych.*, March 1870, p. 325.

still the same as in Saxony, 80 to 20. This seems to hold good of European countries generally.[1]

Suicide among women appears to be everywhere more precocious than among men. In England the relative number of female suicides, very high at the age of 10, is almost equal to or greater than that of men at the ages of 15 to 20. Then for a few years the female rate sinks, to rise again, however, more especially about the age of 45; as old age comes on there is a much stronger tendency to suicide amongst males than amongst females. This is shown in a table, drawn up by Ogle, which exhibits the proportion of the male suicide-rate to the female suicide-rate (reckoned as 100) at successive age-periods:—[2]

Age-period.	Female Rate.	Male Rate.
10-	100	133
15-	100	87
20-	100	182
25-	100	236
35-	100	282
45-	100	263
55-	100	333
65-	100	349
75-	100	360
85-	100	491

With reference to the marked predominance of female suicides over male suicides in the 15-20 age-period, Ogle remarks that this is also "the only period in which the general death-rates, as shown in the Registrar-General's returns, is higher in the former sex, and also is marked, as the census returns for 1881 show, by an exceptionally higher rate of lunacy

[1] Harald Westergaard, *Die Grundzüge der Theorie der Statistik*, Jena, 1890, p. 13.
[2] W. Ogle, "On Suicide in Relation to Age, Sex, etc.," *Journal Statistical Society*, 1886.

(exclusive of idiocy or imbecility) for females than for males."

In France, from the ages of 7 to 16, suicide is equally frequent in both sexes; but of 100 women in France who commit suicide (taking the years 1876-80), 9 have not yet reached their 21st year, while out of 100 male suicides, only 4 are below 21.[1] In Prague, according to Morselli, six-tenths of all the female suicides are by women under 30. That suicide is comparatively so frequent among girls at about the age of 15 is a noteworthy fact. It is difficult not to connect it with the stress resulting from the precocious physical development of girls, which is just completed at this age. Probably an often hidden factor in the frequency of female suicides in early life generally is shame at the prospect of becoming a mother. In France, the chief age at which men commit suicide is from 40 to 50, while for women it is between 15 to 30; for women, however, there is comparative quiescence between the ages of 20 and 35 and from 65 to 75, after the epoch of the closing of sexual life has been safely passed. In England, during the last half century there has been a marked increase of suicide at all ages except for women above 65 years of age.

It would be of interest to compare the sexual ratio of suicide in Europe with that in extra-European lands and in inferior races, but statistics here are not so easy to obtain. In India the ordinary European ratio is nearly reversed, being, according to Chevers, 5.5 males to 8 females. And Surgeon-Major M'Leod, after stating that in round numbers the proportion is 100 males to 150 females, adds that it is probable the excess of females is even greater. "The survival of the *Sati* [widow-burning] feeling in the country, the low social position of women, their ignorance and want of education, render them more prone to commit suicide than men."

The causes of suicide correspond very nearly in sexual difference with the causes of insanity. Mental disorders, passions, and domestic troubles are much commoner causes

---

[1] Legoyt, Art. " Suicide " in *Dict, ency. des Sci. Méd.*

of suicide in women; overstrain and financial troubles are commoner in men; while physical disease is about equal. (See Morselli's *Suicide*, pp. 309-310; also Lombroso and Ferrero, *La Donna Delinquente*, Part iv., Chap. 7.) If we turn to the Prussian statistics, for example in the year 1883, we find that passion is set down as accounting for 1.9 per cent. of the male suicides, but for 6.4 of the female, and in 1887 the percentages are respectively 2.5 and 6.5. Shame and remorse are set down as responsible for 7.6 of the Prussian male suicides in 1883, and for 9.2 of the female, not a great disproportion. It is not possible, however, to attach much value to official statistics of the causes of suicide.

Differences in the methods of accomplishing suicide throw a curious side-light on sexual psychology, and may be studied with more certainty than official records as to the causes of suicide. Throughout Europe the law, roughly stated, is that men hang themselves and women drown themselves, although a very large proportion of male suicides drown themselves, and a very large proportion of female suicides hang themselves.[1] With modifications this rule probably holds good all over the world. In India, for example, it is modified through both sexes showing a greater preference than in Europe for drowning; according to Chevers, six out of seven women in India who commit suicide prefer the water, while men resort to drowning and hanging in about equal numbers. In Europe the great majority of boy suicides hang themselves, while the girls drown themselves. The greatest divergences in England between men and women are in the use of weapons and poison, men preferring the former, women the latter. Women also choose falls from heights, about twice as many women as men adopting this method, but on the other hand a much smaller number of women than of men throw themselves before trains.

Ogle prepared the following table showing the

---

[1] In Denmark, for example, during the years 1861-86, 82.9 per cent. of male suicides hanged themselves, 56 per cent. of the female suicides.

various methods adopted per 1000 suicides during the years 1858-83:—

Method.	Males.	Females.
Hanging and Strangulation . . .	417	240
Drowning	152	264
Cut or Stab . . .	207	129
Poison	79	145
Gunshot . . .	67	2
Jump from Height . . .	21	36
Railway Trains . .	24	8
Otherwise	33	176

It may be said, generally, that while men prefer to adopt *active* methods of suicide, which are at the same time usually more deliberate and more repulsive, women prefer more *passive* methods, which are at the same time usually more decorous and require less resolute preparation. The only exception is in regard to the passive method of suicide by being run over by a train. About three men resort to this for one woman. The reason probably is that, though a passive method of self-destruction, it requires considerable resolution to face, and offends against women's sense of propriety and their intense horror of making a mess; women usually avoid committing suicide in public. If it were possible to find an easy method of suicide by which the body could be entirely disposed of, there would probably be a considerable increase of suicides among women. The sexual preferences in regard to active methods of suicide (hanging, shooting, cutting the throat) and passive methods (drowning, poison, being run over by train, fall from height) is very decisively shown if we sum them up. I take, for instance, the year 1888 in Prussia, selecting a country in which women show a more marked preference than is usual for the masculine methods of hanging and the use of the knife. In this year only 11 per cent. of the male suicides adopted passive methods, as against 89 per cent. who adopted active methods; not less than 57 per cent. of the women adopted passive methods, 43 per cent. adopting active methods.

There is a constant change of opinion going on in the community as to the most desirable methods of committing suicide. This change, at all events in England, is remarkably rapid. I have selected for comparison the years 1858 and 1891. The results are shown in the following table, dealing exclusively with the four chief methods of suicide:—

	Male.		Female.	
	1858.	1891.	1858.	1891.
Weapons and implements .	27.9	35.4	19.0	15.5
Hanging	52.4	33.8	36.0	21.8
Drowning	12.2	20.4	28.2	36.8
Poisoning	7.5	10.4	16.8	25.9

The tendency of change in regard to weapons is anomalous; this is emphatically a masculine method of suicide, rare among women; while increasing among men, it is decreasing among women. In the progress of all three of the other chief methods of suicide a common tendency is visible: hanging has become much rarer in both men and women, while drowning and poisoning have become commoner in both. That is to say, that women have become more womanly than ever in their preferences for the passive methods of suicide, while men have become less manly in their suicidal preferences by exhibiting a growing dislike for active methods of suicide, only 69.2 having adopted active methods in 1891, in spite of the growing taste for firearms, against 80.3 in 1858. It is impossible to regard these figures as purely fortuitous, and I believe that they possess a certain significance with reference to the trend of civilisation.

There is another factor to be taken into consideration when dealing with methods of suicide—the factor of racial preferences. I am unable to throw any light on these, but Morselli has some interesting remarks on the point:—"We find that those who exceed others in hanging amongst men are the Danes, Russians, inhabitants of Würtemberg, and the Austrians; amongst women, Russians with a number equal to the men, the Slavo-Croatians of the Military Frontiers, the Austro-Hungarians, and the Scandinavians. Hence it is evident that in women the Slavic origin betrays itself in a strong tendency towards hanging. On the other hand, drowning is at its maximum amongst the Celto-Latin nations, France, Italy, Belgium, and in Sweden and in Switzerland; whenever the Slavic element comes into play the choice of water falls to its minimum. The largest proportion of suicide by firearms is that of the Slavo-Croats of the Frontiers, and it is to be remarked that the numbers among the women are equally above the average. As to poisoning, its highest proportion is found amongst the Swedish and Austrian women. Among French women those who prefer firearms are hardly 6 per 1000; amongst Italian women 35 per 1000. It is curious that the strong tendency of Italian women as opposed to French women to use the knife or the pistol should be shared by the English and Americans, although the Anglo-Saxon habits are so different from the Italian."

Is the comparative immunity of women from the suicidal impulse real or only apparent? This question has sometimes been raised. It appears that those occupations which "by habit, physical and mental, bring women near to men," considerably raise the suicide-rate among women.[1] Association with men has a similar influence in increasing insanity and criminality. It is obvious that the more nearly women are placed under the same conditions as men the more closely their actions will approximate to men's. This fact tells us nothing with regard to

[1] *Journal of Mental Science*, vol. xxxi. p. 95.

the special psychology of women, and it is evidently not the only factor, for while women's work to-day more nearly resembles men's than it did fifty years ago, we have seen that on the whole women's tendency to suicide as compared to men's is decreasing. Male preponderance in suicide has been explained by saying that women are more sheltered in the struggle for existence, that they are more adaptable, more self-sacrificing, more resigned, more influenced by religious scruples and public opinion, and less given to alcoholism. One writer on the subject believes that the sexual disproportion would not be so great if we could take into account all those who contemplate suicide—*i.e.*, who are suicidal. "Many more women than men desire, or think they desire, but have not the courage to cause their own death."[1] Dr. Harry Campbell also thinks it "probable that the idea of suicide more frequently presents itself to the woman than to the man, because women so much more frequently suffer from the minor forms of melancholia," but he does not think that women have less courage than men, but rather more resignation and a stronger sense of duty; he believes that the sexual difference in the rate largely depends upon external circumstances.[2] That external circumstances, save in a very general way and to a limited extent, have any marked influence in altering the sexual incidence I do not believe; the very slight variations in the sexual incidence throughout Europe make this unlikely. That women very often contemplate suicide is probable, and it may be added that a very large number of women fail in their attempts at suicide. If in determining the suicide-rate we could include unsuccessful attempts at suicide, it is probable that women's share would be larger. The passive methods of self-destruction are

[1] *Journal of Mental Science*, July 1885, vol. xxxi., p. 218.
[2] H. Campbell, *Nervous Organisation of Man and Woman*, pp. 217-218.

not always available, and they are also liable to miscarry; moreover, when a woman adopts a more energetic method of self-destruction she is more likely than a man to miscalculate from ignorance, violent methods of destruction being more within man's province. These circumstances doubtless do much to minimise the influence of the melancholic depression to which women are often subject. On the whole, however, there seems every reason to believe that the suicidal impulse, in European races at all events, is somewhat stronger in men than in women.

Since the above summary was written, an important study of suicide from the sociological standpoint has been published by Durkheim (*Le Suicide*, Paris, 1897); the question of sexual differences is suggestively discussed in the work (see especially pp. 38, 185, 189, 231, 389, 442). It has not seemed necessary to replace the statistics here given by more recent figures as no change can be detected over a few years. When, indeed, we consider very large masses of population of fairly similar racial and social composition, the differences become small. This is strikingly shown by F. L. Hoffman, who finds that if we take 10,000 cases of suicide in various American States and 400,000 cases of suicide in Europe, the percentage of females for both sections of the world is exactly the same, namely 21.6 per cent. ("The Sex-Relation in Suicide," *Publications of American Statistical Ass.*, March-June 1894.) Yet, as the same writer points out, in smaller areas racial and religious conditions maintain a persistent influence, and in Canada, for instance, while in Ontario the proportion of female suicides is 21.8 per cent., in the Catholic French province of Quebec it is only 12.5.

INSANITY.

Aretæus, the Greek physician of the first century, and Cœlius Aurelianus, a writer of uncertain age and country, taught that men are more subject to insanity than women. Esquirol, who appears to have been the first to apply statistics to the matter, showed elaborately that more women are insane than men,

the proportion being 38 women to 37 men.[1]   Georget,
Haslam, and others confirmed this conclusion.   Bur-
rows, even before Esquirol, had said more women
were insane than men in large towns, but that it was
not so in the country.   Parchappe made an important
step in advance by pointing out that in order to form
an accurate estimate of the sexual incidence of insanity
we must consider the admissions to asylums, and not
the actual number of inmates, which is affected by
the varying rates of mortality and recovery in the
two sexes.   He considered the admissions to various
large asylums (Bethlem, Bicêtre, Salpêtrière, Charen-
ton, Turin, etc.), and found that with the very marked
exception of Bicêtre and Salpêtrière, the admissions
of men exceeded those of women.   He concluded
that the solution of the question was still doubtful.[2]
A few years later Thurnam made a more accurate
and decisive investigation than any that had gone
before.[3]   He showed that the probability of recovery
is greater in women than in men, the recoveries of
women exceeding those of men by from 4 to 28 per
cent.   He showed also that there is a still greater
difference in the rate of mortality, the mortality of
men being 50 and sometimes nearly 90 per cent.
greater than that of women—i.e., nearly double.   In
24 asylums out of 32 (including a total of 71,800
admissions), Thurnam found a decided excess of men
among admissions, the average excess being 13.7 per
cent.   There was, however, no such excess of men
in the admissions to London asylums.   Thurnam
also observed that a larger proportion of women
become insane relatively to men among the lower
classes than among the higher.   He concluded
that "in nearly all points of view women have

[1] *Maladies Mentales*, 1838.
[2] *Recherches statistiques sur les Causes de l'Aliénation Mentale.*
Rouen, 1839.
[3] *Observations and Essays on the Statistics of Insanity.*   London,
1845.

an advantage over men in reference to insanity; for not only do they appear to be less liable than men to mental derangement, but when the subjects of it, the probability of their recovery is on the whole greater, and that of death considerably less. On the other hand, the probability of a relapse, or of a recurrence of the disorder, is somewhat greater in women than in men." Dr. Jarvis, a few years later, after examining the statistics of asylums in Great Britain, Ireland, France, Belgium, and America, came to the similar conclusion that "males are somewhat more liable to insanity than females."[1]

If we look only to the gross number of lunatics in the various countries of Europe, we shall find on the whole that the women are more numerous than the men. There are, however, notable exceptions; male lunatics are more numerous in Germany, Denmark, Norway, and Russia. In Italy in 1888 there were 11,895 male lunatics to 10,529 female, being 78.1 males per 100,000 of the population, and 70.1 females. There is a proportionately greater increase among the men in Italy than among the women, but to a very slight extent.

On the whole, therefore, in this country, and it may probably be said nearly everywhere else, men have hitherto been more liable to insanity than women, any excess of insanity in women being apparent only. There is, however, a change taking place, at all events in Great Britain. For several years not only has there been in our asylum population an excess of women over men, but there has been an excess of women in the admissions to the asylums. Medical statisticians, when the change in the sexual incidence of insanity was pointed out,[2]

[1] *On the Comparative Liability of Males and Females to Insanity*, 1850.
[2] This was done by the present writer: Art. "Sex, Influence of, in Insanity," *Dict. of Psych. Med.*, 1892.

were on examination able to verify it. The Lunacy Commissioners have admitted the change in the figures, and stated that they were not aware of any fallacy underlying them. It must, therefore, be accepted that in this country men are no longer markedly more liable to insanity than women.

This increased liability of women to insanity is, moreover, not an accidental variation. It is the outcome of a gradual change which may be traced back in this country for more than a century. During the latter half of the eighteenth century there was an obvious excess of male over female lunatics, but that excess was tending to diminish. At the middle of the last century Thurnam found it necessary to analyse the figures carefully in order to show the greater liability of men to insanity. In the early days of the Lunacy Commissioners (fifty years ago) the rate of increase of insanity to population, as Mr. Noel Humphreys pointed out, was greater among males than among females; in more recent years the rate of increase among females has slightly exceeded that among males. During the ten years 1878-87 the total number of admissions of women to the public and private asylums of England and Wales was 69,560 as against 66,918 men. There is here an obvious excess of women, but if we take into account the excess of women in the general population, the liability of the sexes to insanity is found to be almost equal. During later years, however, the excess of women, although slight, has become clearly marked, even when allowance is made for the excess of women in the general population. When we turn to the admissions to the public and private asylums of England and Wales for 1890 we find that 10,025 women were admitted against 9,109 men. The exact proportion of admissions per 100,000 of the population during the years 1888-90 is as follows:—[1]

---

[1] Art. "Statistics of Insanity," by Dr. Hack Tuke, *Dict. of Psych. Med.*

				M.		F.
1888	...	...	...	5.23	...	5.24
1889	...	...	...	5.21	...	5.37
1890	...	...	...	5.55	...	5.71

In the United States of America and in the English colonies (as in foreign countries generally) there is an excess of male lunatics. The statistics for the United States are still very imperfect, but in Pennsylvania, where they receive most attention, the excess is very clear; thus, during 1889, an average year, there were 1017 admissions of men to 836 of women. In New South Wales the number of insane persons on the official registers at the end of the year 1890 was 1906 men and 1196 women. At the Cape, at the same time, the European and coloured inmates of the asylums numbered 335 men and 240 women, the excess of men being nearly as well marked among the white as among the black population.

The sexual variations in the age at which insanity first appears have been studied by Marro at the Turin Asylum during the years 1886-95.[1] He was careful to include only those cases in which the age at the first appearance of insanity was definitely known. (His results are presented in a graphic form on p. 394.) Before the appearance of puberty there is little insanity, and it is then usually due to some arrest of development (idiocy, imbecility, cretinism, moral insanity, etc.). There is a rapid rise at puberty, taking place earlier in girls and subsiding later. During mature life men are more liable to insanity, but at the period of the change of life in women they again become more liable to insanity, while in old age there is little sexual difference.

The study of sexual differences in the causes of insanity is not very satisfactory. Alcoholic excess (which, however, needs further analysis) is usually both in England and France set down as the chief cause in men, followed by bodily disease and pecuniary troubles; while in women, love, pecuniary troubles, domestic misfortunes, religion, and jealousy are usually set down as the chief causes.

[1] Marro, *La Pubertà*, p. 233.

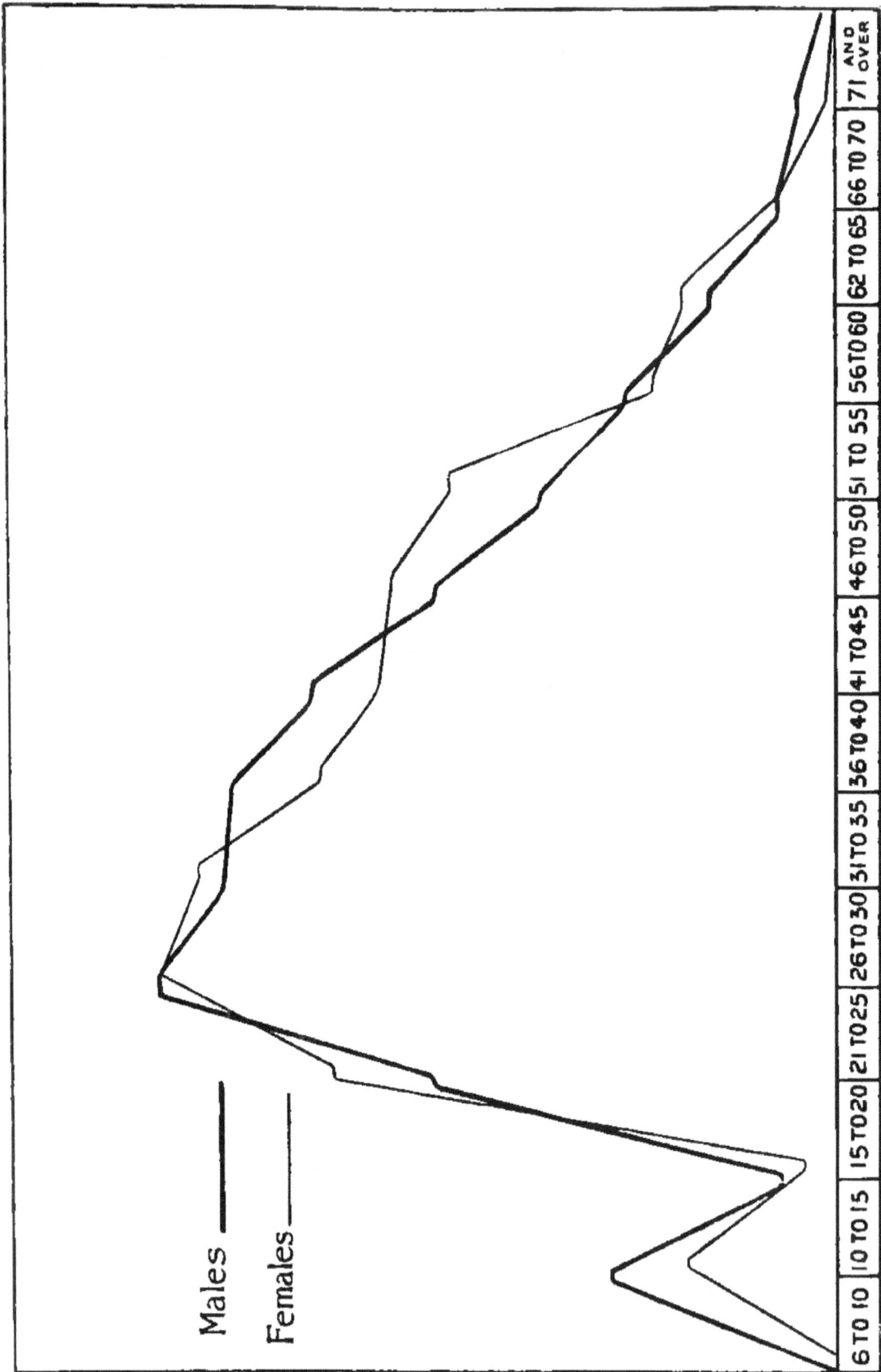

AGE AT FIRST APPEARANCE OF INSANITY IN 2900 CASES, NORTH ITALY. (*Marro.*)

During the ten years 1878-87, 136,478 persons (66,918 men and 69,560 women) were admitted into all classes of asylums in England and Wales. If we consider the causes of their insanity, the proportion per cent. to total number admitted during the ten years was stated to be as follows:—

	Male.	Female.
Alcoholic intemperance . . .	19.8	7.2
Various bodily diseases and disorders .	11.1	10.5
Domestic troubles (including loss of relations and friends)	4.2	9.7
Adverse circumstances (including business anxieties and pecuniary difficulties) .	8.2	3.7
Parturition and the puerperal state .	—	6.7
Mental anxiety, "worry," and over-work .	6.6	5.5
Accident or injury	5.2	1.0
Religious excitement . . .	2.5	2.9
Love affairs (including seduction) .	0.7	2.5
Fright and nervous shock . .	0.9	1.9
Sexual intemperance . . .	1.0	0.6
Venereal disease .	0.8	0.2
Self-abuse (sexual) . .	2.1	0.2
Over-exertion . .	0.7	0.4
Sunstroke	2.3	0.2
Pregnancy . .	—	1.0
Lactation .	—	2.2
Uterine and ovarian disorders	—	2.3
Puberty	0.2	0.6
Change of life . . .	—	4.0
Fevers	0.7	0.5
Privation and starvation . .	1.7	2.1
Old age	3.8	4.6
Other ascertained causes existed in	2 3	1.0
And the causes were unknown in .	21.3	20.1
There had been previous attacks in .	14.3	18.9
Hereditary influence was ascertained in	19.0	22.1
Congenital defect was ascertained in	5.1	3.5

On the whole, it may be said that causes acting on the brain are more common in men; moral and emotional causes are more common in women; excesses, both intellectual and sensual, are more common causes in men.

If we turn to consider sexual variations in the incidence of different forms of insanity, somewhat more reliable results are obtained, but we meet with the difficulty that the nomenclature is not yet uniform. Taking the admissions for this country for one year (1889), the proportions per cent. were divided as follows between the forms of mental disorder recognised by the Lunacy Board:—

	Male.	Female.
Mania	46.1	52.1
Melancholia	21.1	28.6
Dementia { Ordinary .	13.9	8.3
{ Senile	4.7	3.4
Congenital insanity (including idiocy and other mental defects from birth or infancy)	6.3	4.2
Other forms of insanity . .	7.9	3.4
	100	100

Garnier[1] gives the following result of his experiences at the Paris Préfecture de Police as to the relative frequency of various types of insanity in men and women during the years 1886-88. He adopts Magnan's classification, and is dealing with 8139 persons (4831 men and 3308 women). I have arranged them in the order of frequency for both sexes, and reduced the figures to percentages. In making any comparison with the English figures it must be remembered that we are here dealing with an urban population.

[1] *La Folie à Paris,* 1890.

	Male.	Female.
Alcoholism (acute, sub-acute, chronic) .	37.5	11.4
Mental degeneration (idiocy, imbecility, psychic debility, hereditary degeneration)	17.0	19.5
General paralysis	14.8	8.7
Intellectual enfeeblement (due to hæmorrhage, softening, or tumour) .	11.3	13.3
Melancholia . . .	3.7	15.4
Mania . .	4.3	9.7
Epilepsy	6.1	5.1
Senile dementia	3.1	8.7
Progressive systematic insanity, or paranoia	2.2	8.2
	100	100

States of exaltation, speaking generally, belong to early age; "mental exaltation," as Clouston remarks, "is perfectly natural in childhood. It is, in fact, the physiological state of brain at that period;" states of depression belong to a somewhat more advanced age, when mania is extremely rare. Among negroes, also, manias are largely in excess of other forms of insanity.[1] It seems to be generally agreed that, as shown in the tables already given, mania is more common in women than in men. Mendel finds that out of over 800 patients 5.2 of the males are maniacal, 9.6 per cent. of the females, or nearly double.[2] In its most extreme form, also,—acute delirious mania,—it is more common in women, and

[1] Winter, " Insanity in the Coloured Race," *Alienist and Neurologist*, Jan. 1891. There are various minor racial differences. Thus Kurella remarks, in a note to the German translation of the present work, that in his experience cheerful exaltation predominates among insane young women in the Polish and mixed Slavo-German districts of East Prussia, while in the Prussian maritime districts to the west, where the population is mainly of Low German race, depressive forms predominate in women and girls.

[2] Mendel, *Die Manie*, Wien, 1881, p. 141

in women at the same time there is better hope of recovery.[1]

While mania is more common in women than in men, melancholia is, relatively, still more common in women. It is worthy of note that while mania is an insanity of the young, the uncivilised, and the savage, melancholia is an insanity of the adult and civilised. "To get a fine type of melancholia," says Clouston, "you must get an educated brain." Among the educated, he remarks, there are more cases of melancholia, of "monomania," of paralysis of will power, of *folie circulaire*. It is remarkable that these typical examples of the insanities of the educated are all more common in women than in men. The greater prevalence of melancholia and of systematised delusional insanity (formerly called "monomania," and now more frequently called "paranoia") may be seen in the tables already given; paralysis of will-power, in its chief form, for example, which is called *folie du doute*, is also more common in women, and circular insanity is found (according to Jules Falret) in the proportion of about one man to four or five women. On the other hand, the graver and more incurable forms of insanity, which chiefly prevail among paupers, such as epileptic insanity, are much more frequent in men. We must not, however, generalise too hastily from these facts.

The forms of insanity which are now most rapidly increasing amongst women are those which have hitherto been more especially predominant in men— alcoholic insanity and general paralysis. Inebriety, as is now happily beginning to be recognised, is something more than a mere taste for drink; it is in a large number of cases the sign of a deep-rooted disorder of the nervous centres. Inebriety is not only an increasing cause of insanity among women, it is in great part responsible for the increase of recidivism

---

[1] R. Percy Smith, Art. "Acute Delirious Mania," *Dict. of Psych. Med.*

among women criminals in various countries. In
Paris, as Garnier has shown, alcoholic insanity among
women has more than doubled in fifteen years,
though, it must be added, the rate of increase in men
is very little less.

General paralysis has been called the *maladie du
siècle*. It is the disease of excess, of vice, of prolonged
worry; it is especially the disease of such urban
centres as Newcastle and Cardiff.[1] It is rare in
Norway; it is rare among the sedate Arabs, and rare
among lower races generally; it is very rare among
priests and monks, also among Quakers. General
paralysis was formerly rare among women, and
sixty years ago it was even doubted whether it ever
occurred in women. Now, in all the great centres of
civilisation in England (as calculated by Mickle from
the lunacy blue books), there is one female general
paralytic for every four males.

Its increase among men in England, and its
proportionately still greater increase among women,
have been noted by many alienists; and Savage
remarks that it is specially apt to occur among
middle-class women who are taking the places of
men. In Germany the growing proportion of women
among general paralytics has been noted by Mendel,
Sander, and others; the proportion was formerly
1 woman to 5 men; it is now 1 to 3. Siemerling,
who does not consider that the statistics of the

[1] See an interesting article by R. S. Stewart, "The Increase of
General Paralysis," *Jour. Ment. Sci.*, Oct. 1896. Greidenberg in the
Crimea has also noted the special increase of general paralysis among
both sexes in flourishing sea-ports. I may remark that I am not disposed to question the fundamental part played by syphilis as one of the
causes of general paralysis, as also of the allied disease of tabes dorsalis
(or locomotor ataxy). Byrom Bramwell states (*Brit. Med. Jour.*, 27th
Dec. 1902, p. 1952) that syphilis is a cause in at least 75 per cent. cases
of both diseases, and this estimate is probably sound. But it must be
remembered that by no means all syphilitics are general paralytics; a
selection is operated; only certain kinds of syphilitic persons become
general paralytics. The presence of a hereditary element is shown by
the investigations of Näcke (*Allgem. Zt. Psych.*, vol. 58, 1902) into the
marked prevalence of internal abnormalities among general paralytics.

Charité, in Berlin, show any real increase of general paralysis in women, admits it for men; he finds a sexual difference in the symptoms, which are on the whole quieter in women, with a tendency to delusions, often of a sexual character. In France the increase of general paralysis in both sexes is well marked. Lunier and Dumesnil pointed out its increase among women in the asylums of the Seine between 1864 and 1874. Garnier finds that in Paris it has nearly doubled in men during fifteen years, and in women considerably more than doubled during the same period; so that there is 1 woman to $2\frac{1}{2}$ men. Greidenberg comes to the conclusion, on a general survey of the question, that there has been a real increase of this disease in women, and to a relatively greater extent than among men.[1]

We may regard general paralysis as a typically masculine disease, and it is therefore of some interest from our present point of view to analyse it more minutely. It is fundamentally a gradual disorder and paralysis of the finer movements of the muscular system and a blunting of the senses, coming on at first imperceptibly, or only betrayed to observation by a peculiar slow tremulousness of speech. There is some resemblance to the early stage of drunkenness. Concomitantly with the slight paralytic symptoms appear equally slight emotional and intellectual disorders; there is a general coarsening and exaggeration of the thoughts, feelings, and conduct, corresponding to the lack of sensory and motor delicacy of discrimination, and at first there is often great over-activity, associated with, and due to, loss of control. There are very frequently ideas of grandeur, and Baudelaire's muse, as described by Swinburne, with "deep division of prodigious breasts," is the characteristic goddess of the general paralytic.

General paralytics, and those who are predisposed to general paralysis, seem to have to a certain extent a general common character. This has been admirably described in detail by

---

[1] "Progressive Paralyse bei Franen," *Comptes-Rendus XII. Congrès Int. Méd.* (Moscow, 1897, vol. iv., part i., p. 136). In this instructive summary Greidenberg discusses the various sexual differences in general paralysis. He considers that in both sexes the struggle for existence is the most general predisposing cause of this disease, preparing the soil for the action of more specific causes.

Dr. G. R. Wilson, whose account, which is instructive from our present point of view, I will here summarise (*Journal Mental Science*, January 1892).

They often belong to large families, and not infrequently one or both parents have lived rather too freely. At school they are usually fairly active and intelligent, and are apt to leave early and to show considerable determination and ambition in choosing a career which they very often change, for they are of restless spirit and they cannot stand the humdrum life of the country; they usually rush to the towns. What the occupation is makes very little difference; "he will live like a general paralytic whether he be a mason's labourer or a barrister." It cannot be said that they show any uniformity in physical type; that is a matter of race; but they possess certain general physical characters. "As a rule they are well-nourished, and not of a neurotic, phthisical, or otherwise delicate appearance. On the contrary, they are spoken of as men of 'strong constitutions,' full-blooded and vigorous, well-favoured men. In short, they are good animals." They have good nerve and great power of endurance. But they are not generally athletic; they usually eschew all kinds of sports, and seldom possess the play-instinct.

"An inquiry into the life-history of these men brings out an important and almost constant characteristic. Their view of life is rarely, if ever, that of men commonly called 'good.' It is essentially a selfish, non-moral view. They are described as men who 'would do nobody a bad turn,' 'kind-hearted,' 'generous,' 'hard-working,' sometimes even 'conscientious.' But none of the men whose history I have got have been men with any religious interests or of any great moral ambition. The characteristic general paralytic is a man with a large belief in himself, restless, ambitious, and with a relentless desire for the good things of this life." He is sociable, and is often brilliant in society; anxious for the world's good opinion; and his fits of depression or of quick temper are soon over. Unusually strong sexual impulses are among the fundamental characteristics of these patients, and often bring them into trouble; this characteristic seems also to lead to a considerable degree of resemblance in the wives they select. Dr. Savage says he has been struck by "the frequency of the occurrence of general paralysis in the husbands of some women of voluptuous physique," and Dr. Wilson remarks that it is frequently possible to pick out the general paralytic's wife in the visitors' room.

"Such, in the rough," Dr. Wilson concludes, "are the fundamental characteristics frequently, though by no means invariably, associated in the victims of general paralysis. Regarded as a whole, the type is characteristic as much in what it lacks as in what it possesses. General intelligence and common-sense, ambition and energy, sociability and a large capacity for enjoyment, a firm belief in one's self, and a preference for handsome women, are all eminently sane characteristics according to our present standard. On the other hand, some admirable qualities are notably wanting— qualities which make for a higher control to temper the tendency to excess, the selfishness, and the restlessness. I cannot refrain from mentioning Mr. R. L. Stevenson's beautifully drawn character of 'Will of the Mill' as a typical contrast to these restless general paralytics, exhibiting some of their characteristics, and many more besides which they conspicuously lack."

It is worth while to compare this masculine insanity with the description of neurasthenia (p. 322), a disorder which is typically feminine.

It would be quite possible to take in detail the diseases of the brain and spinal cord generally, and to discuss their sexual incidence. I refrain from doing so, because although the difference in sexual incidence is often very marked, its significance cannot be said to be clear in detail. On the whole, the more serious diseases which produce very gross lesions of the nervous centres are more common in men; the slighter and so-called "functional" disorders are more common in women. For this reason insanity and nervous diseases generally are much more fatal in men; women tend to recover easily, although they may again relapse. These facts are connected with a general sexual difference which we have met with already and shall meet with again.

A disease which involves the nervous system though it may not be itself of primarily nervous character, and which shows interesting sexual differences, is gout. Gout, though not very uncommon in women, is an essentially masculine disease, and among men it tends to occur in most pronounced form in those individuals who are of the most pronounced masculine type and habits, and on this account probably is much rarer in its acute form now than it was in the days when England was called "the classic land of gout." Sir Spencer Wells (*Practical Observations on Gout*, 1854, p. 156) remarks that in its pronounced form it tends to occur in masculine women, and that in Southern Europe, where the habits and constitutions of the men are more feminine "acute regular gout is almost as rare as among British females," though "suppressed gout" is very common both among South European men and British women.

On the whole, we see that while, as a rule, men are more liable to insanity than women, there is a tendency for women to come into rank with men in this respect, and in England they have even shown a tendency to surpass men. This increase may be compared with the varying frequency of criminality among women. Roughly speaking, both tend to go together, and to reach a maximum in the restless industrial centres of civilisation; everywhere insanity and criminality follow in the wake of progress and prosperity, though insanity is probably a more certain and well-marked sign of the tension of civilisation than criminality. In France they are both on the increase, but the upward curve of both, so far as women are concerned, has been less well marked during the last few years. In Italy, where there is little crime among women, male lunatics greatly preponderate over female. Even a century ago the greater tendency of urban life to produce insanity in women could be traced in England. This increased tendency to insanity and to criminality is a tax—at the present moment unduly heavy—which women pay for the privilege of taking part in our civilisation. If English women are to be as free from insanity as Italian women, and as free from crime as Greek women, they must be content to take a back place in the forward movement. If at present there is a tendency for women to suffer to an undue extent, this is owing to external obstacles which will probably disappear. The present evil is that while obtaining their share of work women are not at the same time acquiring an adequate control of that work, and of the conditions under which it is carried out. They are forced to carry it out under conditions which were made for men by men, or—little, if at all better—by men for women. Hence women are subjected to an undue stress. What we see here is not the result of work upon women, but the result of work under unwholesome and unnatural conditions which they have not themselves controlled. It has been repeatedly shown that the four chief evils from which the workers of to-day suffer—long hours, low wages, irregular employment, insanitary conditions—in every case press more heavily on women; apart from the fact that, as childbearers, women workers are already handicapped. The indications of this barometer of insanity need not therefore be received with undue alarm. They are merely the outcome of the stress of imperfect adjustment to new conditions, warning us that certain readjustments are necessary.

CRIMINALITY.

I do not propose to give more than a glance at the question of sexual differences in criminality. I have elsewhere said whatever I have to say on the general question, inclusive of feminine criminality.[1] Moreover, during the last few years the sexual relations of criminality have been studied in various countries so thoroughly, and from so many different points of view, that it is difficult either to bring any new contribution to the subject, or to present it more clearly.[2]

[1] H. Ellis, *The Criminal*, third edition, 1901; see especially pp. 261-268.

[2] Lombroso e Ferrero, *La Donna Delinquente, la Prostituta, e la Donna Normale*, Turin and Rome, 1893, is the largest and most comprehensive work; it has been translated into French and German, and there is an incomplete translation of a portion of the book in the English Criminology Series under the title of *The Female Offender*. Reference may also be made to Näcke, *Verbrechen und Wahnsinn beim Weibe*, 1894; R. de Ryckere, *La Femme dans les Prisons et Devant la Mort;* a chapter on "Sex, Age, and Crime" in W. D. Morrison's *Crime and its Causes*, 1891; Proal, *Le Crime et la Peine*, Paris, 1892; a chapter on "La Criminalité Féminine" in Joly's *Le Crime*, 1888; Kellor, "Sex in Crime," *Int. Jour. Ethics*, 1898; A. Bosco's very careful and able statistical study, *Studio della Delinquenza*, Rome, 1892. For a convenient summary of the main international statistical facts regarding sexual differences in criminality see Roncoroni,

It must also be added that the study of the sexual differences in criminality is very complicated and fallacious, much more so than in the case of suicide, or even in the case of insanity, which is at all events recognised by all as within the scientific province. Laws vary so greatly, the severity with which they are upheld is so uncertain a quantity, judicial and police proceedings are so unreliable, police statistics often so peculiar, that our conclusions would be doubtful, even if we were sure that the criminal was caught, that he was indeed the culprit, and the sole culprit. This also we can by no means be sure of, and there can be no doubt that our ignorance often shields women who, although in the background, have either morally shared the responsibility for the crime, or have assisted in a subordinate capacity.

Whatever deductions, however, have to be made, and however great may be the difficulties in arriving at precisely accurate results, there can scarcely be doubt that the criminal and anti-social impulse is less strong in women than in men.[1] In Europe generally the crimes committed by women, according to Hausner, who has made a special study of the subject, are 16 per cent. of all crimes. We should be inclined to suspect this, in the absence of definite facts, from what we know of the nature of women. Not only are women by their maternal functions more organically tied to the social relations of life, but their affectability renders an anti-social and unusual course of life much more organically difficult. Their physiological timidity—for, as we have seen, the timidity of women has a neuro-muscular basis— makes the impulse to crime more difficult even by the very vaso-motor perturbation the impulse produces.

"La Criminalità Femminile all' Estero," *Archivio di Psichiatria*, vol. xiv., Fasc. ii.-iii., and more especially a valuable study by Hugo Hoegel, "Die Straffälligkeit des Weibes," *Archiv für Kriminal Anthropologie*, vol. v., 1900.

[1] This has, however, been denied, and by so eminent a sociologist as Professor Durkheim, *Le Suicide*, p. 389.

The impulse is expended in emotion before it becomes a deed. The abnormal woman has much greater encouragement to become a prostitute, an occupation which is only incidentally connected with crime, and which is not viewed with the same unmitigated reprobation. The forms of criminality into which women most easily fall are the subtlest (like poisoning), and also the more domestic forms. Murders, assaults, burglaries, thefts, commercial crimes—as well as the so-called political crimes— are comparatively rare among women. In Italy, for 100 men who commit any one of these offences the proportion of women is from six to below one.

Poisoning, on the other hand, is a characteristically feminine criminal method. In Greek days Euripides makes Medea say that poison is the way of murder in which women excel, and they have retained that pre-eminence ever since.[1] In France the proportion is about six women to three or four men: so that about two-thirds of detected cases of poisoning are by women. In Italy, for every 100 men found guilty of poisoning there are 123 women. Infanticide is the crime in which women stand out in greatest contrast to men; in Italy, for example, for every 100 men guilty of infanticide there are 477 women. This must be so; immense social pressure is put on a woman to induce her to destroy or abandon the infant which all her natural instincts prompt her to cherish; and the man who commits this crime is usually doing it for the sake of a woman. Women, as Quetelet long since remarked, are domestic criminals; this is simply because the home occupies so large a field in their life generally; even against their own children, and apart from infanticide, mothers commit crimes somewhat more frequently than fathers. This has, for instance, been the experience of the Society for the Protection of Children, which in one year (1891)

[1] On the frequency of poisoning among women in lower races, see Lombroso and Ferrero, *La Donna Delinquente*, pp. 208-210.

obtained convictions against 347 fathers and 356 mothers. The crimes of women are usually more marked by cruelty than those of men. Bosco has pointed out that women are relatively more often guilty of aggravated than of simple homicide, and that this is a general fact, which can be demonstrated in England as well as in Italy, in Spain as in Germany, in France as in Hungary. De Ryckere, writing as a magistrate, says in his study of feminine criminality that the crimes of women tend to take on characters that are " more cynical, more cruel, more brutal, more depraved, and more terrible than those of men."[1] It must be said that beside this element of cruelty in women, we have the element of compassion which is founded on the maternal instinct.

In most respects, physical and psychic, as we have had occasion to see, women are more precocious than men. It is not so in respect of criminality. While in men the maximum is attained usually about the twentieth year or soon after, in women it is not usually attained until the thirtieth year or soon after. This to some extent explains the fact, which has often been pointed out, that more women criminals are married than men criminals. It would be instructive to unravel the causes of this later development of criminality in women, but it is not easy to do so at present. To some extent the apparent increase of crime in women as age increases is due to the simple fact that in the advanced periods of life women are in a decided majority. Recidivism, it may be added, is in most countries distinctly less marked in women than in men. In France, for example (1876-80), 53 per cent. of male committals were of recidivists, but only 21 per cent. of the female committals. In Germany, twenty years ago, recidivism was also more common in men, but there has been a gradual change, and now it is at least as common in women. In drunken-

<hr />

[1] Ferrero has an interesting chapter on the cruelty of women; Lombroso and Ferrero, *La Donna Delinquente*, pp. 67-78.

ness, as Kerr pointed out, recidivism is commoner in women than in men, and it is probable that the tendency to the increase of recidivism among women is largely due to the increase of drunkenness. In any case the recidivism of women is very marked. In England, for instance, during the year 1900, we find that if we take the number of persons committed to prison for the first time there were over 19,000 men to less than 6000 women; but among those who had already been in prison more than twenty times there were only 4000 men to 6,500 women.

Even to a greater extent than in suicide or in insanity, there is a social factor in criminality, and it is determined very largely by the differences between town and country. Towns modify the nature of crimes; thus the women who commit infanticide in the country practise abortion in towns. This influence is still more marked in increasing the total amount of crime. This is especially so where we find women working in factories, and, above all, working for low wages and without any organisation. It is largely to this cause, doubtless, that, so far as women are concerned, Scotland occupies the position of being (except some parts of Germany) the most criminal country in Europe. The bad record of Glasgow, for instance, as regards feminine criminality is notorious. In Glasgow (notwithstanding its municipal energy in many directions) women workers are ill organised, and are only able to earn half as much as the women workers of Lancashire in the same industries. If we turn to the United States we find, as Dr. F. H. Wines, the chief American authority on criminal statistics, has recently shown, that there is a remarkable preponderance of feminine criminality in the North Atlantic group of States as compared with the rest of the country. Taking the white population only, it is found that in the nine States comprised in New England, New York, New Jersey, and Connecticut, the number of female prisoners is 12 per cent.

of the total; in the remaining thirty-five States they furnish only 4 per cent. The only explanation seems to be that the North Atlantic corner of the country is the oldest and most highly civilised; it is the region of cities and of factories, employing immense numbers of women, who in the rest of the country are more home-living. If we take Europe generally we find that feminine criminality is very high in Scotland, and generally in Germany; high also in England and Belgium and Holland and Italy and Denmark and Norway; somewhat lower in Ireland and France and Austria; very low in Russia and Spain, and probably reaching a minimum in Greece. It will be seen that the energetic, independent, industrial Teutonic races stand at the head as regards feminine criminality, Russia and Spain, on the other hand, are the two great predominantly agricultural countries in Europe, having in this, as in some other respects, much in common; in Greece women may almost be said to have no activities outside their homes. We have clearly to recognise that the tendencies of modern life are developing the criminality of women, notwithstanding that the organic tendencies of woman's nature restrain her to a considerable extent from the commission of crime. There is, however, nothing fatal in these tendencies of modern life, and, in a very large degree, they are assuredly within our control.

CHAPTER XVI.

THE VARIATIONAL TENDENCY OF MEN.

MOST ABNORMALITIES MORE COMMON IN MEN—THE IN-
FLUENCE OF THE PELVIS ON THE SIDE OF MEDIOCRITY
—STILL-BORN CHILDREN—SEXUAL PROPORTION OF
CONGENITAL MALFORMATIONS—MUSCULAR ABNORMAL-
ITIES—THE EAR AND ITS ABNORMALITIES—PSYCHIC
ABNORMALITIES, IDIOCY, GENIUS, ETC.—THE PRIMITIVE
RACIAL ELEMENTS IN A POPULATION PERHAPS MORE
CLEARLY REPRESENTED BY WOMEN—WOMEN MORE
DISPOSED THAN MEN TO PRESERVE ANCIENT CUSTOM
AND ANCIENT METHODS OF THOUGHT—THE ORGANIC
CONSERVATISM OF WOMEN — ADVANTAGES OF THIS
SEXUAL DIFFERENCE.

IT was at one time supposed that women are more
variable than men and more liable to exhibit congenital
malformations. John Hunter, it is true, who first
touched on the matter from a biological standpoint,
vaguely indicated that males are more variable than
females; but Meckel, on the contrary, came to the
conclusion, on pathological grounds, that in the
human species females show a greater degree of
variability, and he thought that since man is the
superior animal and variation a sign of inferiority
the conclusion was justified. "We may state as a
principle," Meckel wrote ninety years ago at the
outset of his manual of descriptive and pathological
anatomy, "that anomalies are more common in the
female. This phenomenon seems to depend on the
eighth law [Meckel's 'law of development,' according

to which woman is more primitive than man] since the organisation of the female results from development being arrested at an inferior degree." But while he regarded deviations as on the whole more common in woman he admitted certain exceptions, and more especially instanced the heart and the bladder as more variable in man.

Meckel was a profound student of anatomy, but not a very luminous thinker. It by no means follows, even if we accept his law as to the greater primitiveness of the female, that anomalies should therefore be more frequent in women; the opposite inference would, indeed, be equally plausible. Some years later Burdach took up the question in his *Physiologie.* That great biologist at once raised the problem to a higher level, realised its wider bearings, and cleared away the prejudices which had surrounded it. He recognised that in some respects women are more variable than men, but pointed out that, contrary to Meckel's opinion, this was no indication of woman's organic inferiority. He showed from the statistics of the Anatomical Institute of Königsberg that we must distinguish between different kinds of abnormality. Further, he referred to the facts that indicate that woman is more childlike than man, but, he added, "it is a very common but a very gross error to consider age as a scale of perfection and to regard the child as absolutely imperfect as compared to the adult. It is not imperfection but simply certain childlike characteristics that women preserve;" and, he pointed out, it is in decrepitude that women take on the characteristics of the so-called superior sex. His general conclusion was that the nature of man and the nature of woman are both excellent, but there are wider variations in men, more genius and more idiocy, more virtue and more vice.

Darwin turned his attention towards this point, and accumulated data. In the *Descent of Man* he brought together many of the chief facts then known concerning variation in man and woman. All the evidence that he could find pointed in the same direction, and he concluded (Part II., ch. 8) that there is a "greater general variability in the male sex." It cannot, however, be asserted that all the implications of this fact are yet clearly recognised.

The tendency of men to be abnormal has, so far as size is concerned, to contend at an early period of life with a very powerful force on the side of equality and mediocrity. This, as we have already seen (p. 71), is the narrowness of the maternal pelvic outlet, which probably allows boys to pass through less readily than girls. Still-born children are much more frequently boys than girls, the proportion in this country being about 140 males to 100 females. If it were not for this levelling influence there can be little doubt that the proportion of men remarkable for exceptional physical or mental qualities would be even larger than it actually is. Thus Boyd's tables have shown that the average brain-mass in the children who are born dead at full time is larger than in those who live; and that while the average new-born living male child at full time has a total brain-mass only about $1\frac{1}{2}$ ounces heavier than the female (and the maximum brain-weight in a living child was actually found by Boyd in a female), among the still-born the maximum male brain is nearly seven ounces larger than the maximum female brain, although the minimum still-born male brain is only a little over an ounce larger than the minimum female brain. Statistics of English and Scotch infants collected by the Anthropometric Committee of the British Association showed that while the range of height in the male infants was 10 inches, in the female infants it was only 8 inches. Exceptional weight in new-born children is most usually found among the males; in France, for weights above 3500 grammes there are 29 boys to only 19 girls.[1]

[1] Depaul, Art. "Nouveau-né" in *Dict. ency. des Sci. Méd.*

It is because of the selective action of the pelvis, and the influences of later life, which there is good reason to believe do not act equally on both sexes, that we are not entitled to introduce the factor of size in discussing the incidence of variations in men and women.[1] There is good reason to believe that so far as size is concerned men are not more variable than women, and probably less so.[2] This appears to be the result of unequal selective influences during life, and has no necessary bearing on the primary incidence of variations.

Abnormalities of most kinds having their origin in some arrest of development, or unknown pathological accident at an early period of embryonic growth, are for the most part more common in males than in females. This is shown both by the Registrar-General's Reports and the surgical records of any large hospital; while among 50,000 English children Warner found the percentage with main classes of defects was 18.04 boys and 14.71 girls;[3] and among 1000 American children Macdonald found that nearly every class of abnormality is more frequent among boys.[4] Hrdlicka, also, in an elaborate investigation of 1000 children in the New York Juvenile Asylum, found that both among the white and the black children abnormalities were more frequent in the boys.[5]

If we consider the deaths per million from congenital defects we find, taking the five years 1884-88

[1] This point is further emphasised in the Appendix, "Professor Karl Pearson on Variation in Man and Woman."

[2] K. Pearson, "Variation in Man and Woman," *Chances of Death*, vol. i.; also Giuffrida-Ruggeri, "La Maggiora Variabilità della donna dimostrata col metodo Camerano," *Monit. Zoolog. Ital.*, 1903, No. 12; and Frassetto, "La Variabilità del Cranio umano," *Atti. Soc. Rom. Antrop.*, 1901, p. 155.

[3] "Mental and Physical Condition among Fifty Thousand Children," *Jour. Statist. Soc.*, March 1896, p. 137. Cf. *Report of British Association on Mental and Physical Deviations from the Normal among Children*, 1900.

[4] *Education Report*, 1897-98, pp. 1032, 1087.

[5] A. Hrdlicka, *Anthropological Investigations of One Thousand Children*, 1899.

(as Campbell has pointed out), that the average is 49.6 for the male sex, 44.2 for the female.[1] Surgical experience among the living gives a similar result. Thus at St. Thomas's Hospital, if we take, for instance, the years 1881-87, we find that hare-lip, for example, was found in 43 males to 20 females. Bryant's note-book (according to Braxton Hicks) showed 44 males to 20 females, almost the same proportion, while Manley[2] found 27 males to only 6 females. Double hare-lip is almost exclusively found in males. Hare-lip with cleft palate is always more frequently found in males; according to Bryant, in 17 males to only 4 females. Cleft-palate alone is, however, more often found in females; in 58 females to 37 males, according to the experience at St. Thomas's. Spina bifida is also usually slightly more common in females; 13 males to 17 females, according to Bryant, though the records at St. Thomas's appear to show a majority of males. Nearly every other important form of malformation is found more frequently in males than in females. Congenital absence of the fibula seems to occur almost exclusively in males. Talipes equino-varus, the most important form of club-foot, usually indicates an arrest of development, as it represents the normal position of the foot in the apes and in man before birth; it is much more frequent in males, the proportions being (according to experience at St. Thomas's Hospital) 44 males to 26 females; while, if we include all forms of club-foot, the proportion is 80 males to 53 females. If we take larger figures we find, according to Duval, that 364 males exhibit congenital club-foot as against 210 females, while the acquired forms are also more common in males.[3]

---

[1] H. Campbell, *Nervous Organisation of Man and Woman*, p. 133.

[2] *International Med. Mag.*, April 1893.

[3] Infantile palsies, acquired in early years, and involving various deformities of the foot, were found by Muirhead to affect the sexes almost equally. But they were more often severe in the boys, and more often affected both limbs. (*Brit. Med. Jour.*, 1st Sept. 1900.)

Imperforate anus, meningocele, ectopia vesicæ (1 female in 10 cases, according to John Wood), abnormality of the vermiform appendix[1] are all more common in males. Congenital dislocation of hip is a marked exception, the proportion being about 4 or 5 females to 1 male, and another exception (according to J. H. Morgan) is furnished by macrostoma congenitum or fissure of the cheek; both these defects, like those which are more common in males, are probably due to arrest of development. It is not yet quite clear that we can generalise concerning the developmental defects most common in males and in females, though this may be possible when our knowledge is more complete.

Supernumerary digits are much more frequently found in males than in females. Supernumerary nipples are also much commoner in men; among several hundred persons Mitchell Bruce found that 9.1 per cent. men and only 4.8 per cent. women possessed an extra nipple, so that it is nearly twice as frequent in males.[2] Although goitre is much commoner in women than in men, it is remarkable that congenital goitre occurs much more frequently in males. The majority of cases of transposition of viscera (in which the heart and the stomach are found on the right side and the liver on the left) are found in males. An additional (eighth) true rib is an interesting anomaly which has been especially studied by Professor Cunningham; he finds it to occur twice in a male to once in a female; it is normal among the lower apes and in the chimpanzee, and may therefore be regarded as a reversion.[3]

The majority of muscular abnormalities are found

[1] We may perhaps connect this fact with the much greater frequency of appendicitis in men, less than 20 per cent. cases being in women. There may, however, as Woods Hutchinson indicates (*Human and Comparative Pathology*, p. 52), be other factors at work.

[2] *Journal of Anat.*, vol. xiii. p. 432.

[3] D. J. Cunningham, "Occasional Eighth True Rib in Man," *Journal of Anat.*, October 1889.

in male subjects. It would be of little interest to consider in detail the results reached by Wood, Schwalbe, Macalister, Wenzel Gruber, and others, but on the whole there seems to be little doubt of the fact, although there are exceptions as regards certain muscles, and Testut is of opinion that the sexes may be regarded as about equal in this respect.

The following remarks by Professor Macalister concerning muscular anomalies are worth quoting:—" Varieties are probably more common in males than in females; those of fission and suppression occur more frequently in the latter, as they usually possess a weaker muscular system. Anomalies of duality, altered course and attachment, and coalescence most frequently are to be found in males. New muscular germs are more frequently developed in the male sex, although an exception has been claimed for some." The muscle germs are muscles usually found in other animals, not in Man. To this class belong also cases of muscular duality, depending on vegetative repetition, and some cases of suppression; while muscle-fission and some cases of suppression depend on deficient growth, and are associated with weakness; and coalescence is dependent on exuberant growth and is associated with strength. (Alexander Macalister, " Further Notes on Muscular Anomalies," *Proc. Roy. Irish Academy*, vol. x., 1867, p. 121.) Schwalbe and Pfitzner (" Varietäten-Statistik," *Morphologische Arbeiten*, Bd. iii., heft 2) have shown the marked prevalence of varieties of muscular suppression among females.

The sexual differences in abnormality are somewhat complex. We may, for example, take the anomalies of the ear, which have been carefully studied by numerous investigators in various countries. It is pretty generally agreed that, as Ranke states, the ear in women is more finely modelled and less subject to abnormality than in men, though Schaeffer is of opinion that this difference is apparent only, and is merely due to the ear in women being smaller and defects less obvious. Schwalbe argues that the male ear is much closer to that of the apes than the female ear: " We are here concerned," he says, " with a very remarkable fact, that the female sex here does *not* exhibit the more primitive forms, as, for example, in the formation of the sexual organs, but the derived form." He shows that in various respects the ear in women is further removed from the apes than the ear in men, more especially as regards the Darwinian tubercle; thus, taking chiefly Alsatians, he finds that among 109 men and 102 women 73.4 per cent. of the male ears showed the tubercle, and only 32.8 per cent. of the female ears; while more than three-fourths of the men and nearly three-fourths of their ears, collectively, exhibited the Darwinian tubercle, hardly half the women and only a third of their ears showed it. Schaeffer found it in 47 per cent. women; while in men it varied greatly in different regions, but was usually more frequent; he considers the peculiarity especially common in England, and very unusually so among English women; while he found it in only 22 per cent. ears in Swabia and Upper Bavaria, he found it in 55 per cent. English ears; in Jewesses, on the other hand, abnormal ears are rare. Gradenigo finds the ear normal in 56 per cent. men, in 66 per cent. women; he finds every abnormality, even adherent lobule, more common in men. Vali has found every abnormality with the exception of adherent lobule more common in men. Warner, in an extensive investigation of English school children finds abnormal ears very much commoner in boys than in girls. Lannois's investigations show the proportion of normal ears to be 28 per cent. in men and 41 per cent. in women. The prominent outstanding ear (*ad ansa*) is everywhere more common in men (11 per cent. males and 3 per cent. females, according to Gradenigo); it is usually associated with a large mastoid process. Wildermuth's ear (antihelix projecting beyond helix) is usually found to be more frequent in women; Lannois found it in 27 per cent. women, 20 per cent. men; Gradenigo in 20 per cent. women, 7 per cent. men. Adherent lobule is also more common in women in the experience of most observers. Laycock many years ago considered that the lobule and also the helix are both relatively and absolutely smaller in women; in men of feminine character he found the helix and lobule like those of women, and he thought that active instincts and appetites are often associated with large lobules. (J. Ranke, *Der Mensch;* Schwalbe, "Beiträge zur Anthropologie des Ohres," *Rudolf Virchow Festschrift*, Berlin, 1891, Bd. i.; Laycock, "Lectures on Physiognomical Diagnosis," *Medical Times*, 22nd March 1862; Lannois, "Pavillon de l'Oreille chez les Sujets Sains," *Archives de l'Anth. Crim.*, Juillet, 1892; Oscar Schaeffer, "Ueber Ohrentwickelung und Ohrformen," *Archiv für Anth.*, Bd. xxi., 1892; Kurella, *Naturgeschichte des Verbrechers*, Stuttgart, 1893, pp. 75-84, 270.)

If we turn to those congenital variations which are very closely allied to mental characters we still find, and in an even more marked degree, that men have a greater tendency to abnormality than women. Left-handedness was found by Ogle to be twice as common in men as in women. Colour-blindness, which has been discussed in a previous chapter, is an interesting instance of a congenital variation markedly more frequent in men than in women. It may be added here that albinism, or congenital absence of pigmentation, is another typical variation which appears to be everywhere more prevalent among men than among women;[1] in Europe there are three males to two females; among many savages the proportion of females is still smaller. There are nearly everywhere more male than female deaf-mutes; thus in Scotland 100 men are deaf-mutes to 79 women, and if we take the proportion to population for Great Britain generally the sexual difference is still more marked; in Germany the proportion is 100 males to 85 females; and in Norway, according to Uchermann, for every 100 deaf-mute males there are only 78 females. Only about 50 per cent. cases of deaf-mutism are of congenital origin, but the male preponderance is equally marked both in congenital and acquired cases. Idiocy and imbecility probably possess very great significance as forms of congenital mental variability, and are probably to some extent mixed up with other forms of mental variability with which they are far from having any obvious relationship. Idiocy is almost everywhere recognised as more common in males than in females; Mitchell estimated the proportion as 100 males to 79 females in Scotland.[2] The Prussian census shows that precisely the same proportion of idiots are born in that country; in France the proportion is 100 males to only 76 females. Langdon Down some years ago found that the ratio in which the sexes are afflicted is 2.1 to .9, and this is about the proportion in which the sexes are found in idiot asylums to-day in England—a somewhat larger proportion of males than among idiots in the general population. Endemic cretinism, a particular form of idiocy in

[1] Seligmann, *Lancet*, 20th Sept. 1902, p. 804.
[2] *Edin. Med. Journal*, vol. xi. p. 639.

which there is degeneration of the thyroid gland, is also more common in males, in the proportion, according to Lunier, of 5 to 4, varying, however, according to the region. Criminality and insanity and the tendency to suicide I have dealt with in another chapter; they all usually arise on a basis of congenital mental abnormality, and are all on the whole more prominent in men than in women. That form of insanity which is sometimes called "moral insanity," or perhaps more properly "moral imbecility," and which is almost identical with what is now frequently called congenital or instinctive criminality, is a truly inborn abnormality, and is far more common in males than in females.[1] The "mattoid" or "crank," again, whose whole life pursues an eccentric and futile orbit of its own, is a congenitally abnormal person, although his abnormality may not develop until late; the mattoid is very rarely a woman, although that very mild mattoid, the "faddist," is perhaps quite as usually a woman as a man; this fact is doubtless part of the general affectability of women under the influence of minor stimuli (referred to elsewhere), and according to which, for instance, while women more often suffer from indigestion than men, the latter much more often suffer from cancer of the stomach.

To turn to a somewhat higher but still undoubtedly congenital form of mental abnormality, we may take arithmetical prodigies; Dr. Scripture has studied these with some fulness.[2] Taking into account all those of whom we have record, from Nikomachus

---

[1] Sexual perversions, again, are more common in men than in women. I find that of 198 cases recorded in detail by Krafft-Ebing, only about 11 per cent. are women (*Psychopathia Sexualis*, Stuttgart, 1893). Although there may be some fallacy here, and it is probable that minor anomalies of the sexual instinct are fairly common in women, there can be no doubt that the more developed perversions, congenital or acquired, are usually met with in men.

[2] E. W. Scripture, "Arithmetical Prodigies," *Am. Journal Psych.*, April 1891.

down, he finds not less than twenty-one men to one woman—Lord Mansfield's daughter, who almost equalled Colbourn. The only calculators of the first rank who have appeared since Scripture wrote, Inaudi and Diamandi, serves to increase the male proportion. While a few distinguished men, like Ampère and Gauss, are to be numbered among arithmetical prodigies, this abnormality is by no means due to education, and is sometimes found in uneducated persons who are almost idiots. Scripture gives further references to extraordinary memory for figures, though not strictly of calculation. All the examples given are men.

The arithmetical prodigy leads us up to the most interesting and important of all forms of psychic abnormality, that which we usually call "genius." We must regard genius as an organic congenital abnormality (although the evidence in proof of this cannot be entered into here), and in nearly every department it is, undeniably, of more frequent occurrence among men than among women.[1] The statement of this fact has sometimes been regarded by women as a slur upon their sex; they have sought to explain it by lack of opportunity, education, etc. It does not appear that women have been equally anxious to find fallacies in the statement that idiocy is more common among men. Yet the two statements must be taken together. Genius is more common among men by virtue of the same general tendency by which idiocy is more common among men. The two facts are but two aspects of a larger zoological fact—the greater variability of the male.

"There are no women of genius; women of genius are all men." This saying of Goncourt's has been quoted far more

---

[1] See *ante*, p. 375. If we may trust Macdonald's studies among Washington school children, the greater variability of male intelligence would appear to hold good even within the range of ordinary school experience; he found (*Education Report*, 1897-98, p. 1046) that girls show higher percentages of average ability and therefore less variation.

frequently than it deserves to be. It is only imperfectly true, since many women of genius have been of entirely feminine organisation, and in so far as it is true it is without point, for the reason that while many women of genius have shown masculine qualities, very many men of genius have shown feminine qualities. The real truth is conveyed in the wider statement that in persons of genius of either sex there is a tendency for something of the man, the woman, and the child to coexist. It is not difficult to understand why this should be so, for genius carries us into a region where the strongly-differentiated signs of masculinity or femininity, having their end in procreation, are of little significance.

From an organic standpoint, therefore, women represent the more stable and conservative element in evolution. It is a metaphorical as well as a literal truth that the centre of gravity is lower in women and less easily disturbed. In various parts of the world anthropologists have found reason to suppose that the primitive racial elements in a population are more distinctly preserved by the women than by the men. Lagneau has remarked with reference to the Saracenic element in France, to the Basques and to some other races, that the women seem to preserve ethnic peculiarities better than the men. Dally has some observations to the same effect.[1] Jacobs remarks:—" I seem to observe that Jewesses have more uniformly what we term the Jewish face than Jews have."[2] The men of Arles —of old, the Gallic Rome—are of very ordinary physical character; the women of Arles, on the contrary, are famous for their beauty; they are like Italians, with pale faces, black hair, and noble carriage; it is probable that they recall the characters of the population of Arles when that decayed and crumbling place was a city of palaces.[3] In the same way the infusion of Spanish in the Flemish,

[1] E. Dally, Art. " Femmes," *Dict. ency. des Sci. Méd.*
[2] J. Jacobs, " On the Racial Characteristics of Modern Jews," *Journal Anth. Inst.*, 24th Feb. 1885.
[3] And see Elisée Reclus (*La France*, p. 507) for some remarks on this point, and references.

due to Spanish domination during the sixteenth century, is, Coucke remarks, best seen in the hair, eyes, complexion, and hips of some of the women near Bruges.[1]   It may be said generally that traces of the primitive Mongoloid elements in the so-called "Celtic" race are everywhere more apparent in the faces of the women than of the men; various observers have noted this in Brittany, Morvan, etc.,[2] and I myself have observed it in Savoy and in Cornwall.   Mantegazza has remarked that at Cortona and Chiusi the women recall the ancient Etruscans, and at Albano the ancient Romans, more than do the men.   Major Sykes says of the gipsies of Persia that "the men cannot easily be distinguished from the surrounding peasantry, but the women dress differently, while their features are certainly not those of the Persian peasant."[3]   The Giao-Chi, an ancient race regarded by the Annamites as their ancestors, are remarkable for the position of the big toe, set at a considerable angle to the foot, and almost opposable to the other toes.   Notwithstanding a very large amount of mingling with other races, this atavistic peculiarity is still met with in the Tonquin delta, says Dumoutier, more especially among the women.[4]   There can be little doubt that the smaller size of women as compared to men is connected with the preservation of a primitive character.   Zoologists believe that the early or ancestral members of a group are of small size, and that the study of the smaller members within given groups of animals promises the best results as to their phylogeny.   Women by their smaller size approximate to the probably smaller stature of Man's ancestors.

---

[1] *L'Humanité Nouvelle*, Oct. 1902, p. 83.
[2] G. Hervé, *Rev. Mens. de l'Ec. d'Anth.*, 1898, p. 204.
[3] Sykes, "Anthropological Notes on Southern Persia," *Jour. Anth. Inst.*, 1902, p. 344.
[4] "Notes Ethnologiques sur les Giao-Chi," *L'Anthropologie*, Nov. 1890.

On the psychic side women are more inclined than men to preserve ancient customs and ancient methods of thought. In Russia spells and other primitive methods of solving the difficulties of life are in the hands of women who have a recognised position as witches and soothsayers. (Gregor Kupczanko, "Krankheitsbeschwörungen bei russischen Bauern in der Bukowina," *Am Ur-Quell*, 1891, p. 12.) In Sardinia, Sicily, and the remote valleys of Umbria many ancient beliefs and pagan rites, which are perhaps of even prehistoric character, are still preserved by women. (Lombroso and Laschi, *Il Delitto Politico*, vol. ii. p. 8.) In the island of Lewis Sir A. Mitchell (*Past in the Present*, p. 27) found that *craggons* (globular pots of very primitive shape) were still made by women, working with their hands, in the prehistoric manner. Archæologists carrying on excavations in remote districts of the north of Scotland have repeatedly found that the women, still inspired by pagan feelings, have dissuaded their male folk from giving assistance. In some parts of France artificial deformation of the skull still persists. It appears that in Normandy, Limousin, Languedoc—wherever the custom persists at all—boys wear the bandages for but a short time; with girls and women the custom is life-long. (Delisle, "Sur les Déformations artificielles du crâne," *Bull. Soc. d'Anth. de Paris*, Série III., t. xii. p. 649.) All forms of astrology are now chiefly supported by women, although at one time they were equally sought after by both sexes; Mr. Edgar Lee, who has answered nearly thirteen thousand astrological queries, found that 70 per cent. of the inquirers were women who wished to know if they were going to be married; it should be added that they belonged chiefly to the middle and upper classes. (E. Lee, "Astrology Fin de Siècle," *Arena*, Nov. 1892.) Lombroso and Ferrero have also given various examples of the conservatism and misoneism of women, *La Donna Delinquente*, pp. 163-165. The circular dancing and singing games of children (such as "Nuts in May"), which are believed to be survivals of primitive sacred dances once performed chiefly by men, are now preserved by girls alone. (Groos, *Spiele der Menschen*, p. 452; Haddon has a full and interesting discussion of these games in reference to their primitive character, *Study of Man*, chaps. xi.-xv.)

The same tendency is well shown by the conservatism of women's garments. The dalmatic, the special ecclesiastical robe of a deacon, was once the ordinary garment of Dalmatian peasants, though afterwards adopted as a fashion at Rome, to become part of consular and senatorial dress; it has long ceased to be a masculine garment outside the Church, but it is still worn as an overcoat by the Dalmatian women of Clissa and other country places in the neighbourhood of Spalato. (T. M. Lindsay, *Good Words*, June 1898.) "Feminine fashions in Burmah" (writes E. D. Cuming, *In the Shadow of the Pagoda*, 1893) "are as permanent and lasting as the Pagoda itself. . . . On the other hand the man is always ready to adopt the latest creation in giant checks, and the European merchant employs a Burman designer to evolve novelties in this direction for the guidance of the manufacturer at home." In connection with the conservative tendency of woman's dress, the following passage, though somewhat lengthy, may be quoted from a paper by Professor Patrick:—"Among the women of the most civilised communities the idea of dress has only partly given place to that of clothing. The flowing and, upon occasions, even the trailing robe still persists. The hair is uncut and fantastically arranged with bits of shell or metal, and sometimes decorated with ornaments of shell, silver, or gold, or imitations of these. Feathers are still worn upon the head-dress, and the head-dress itself is purely for adornment, affording little or no protection for the head, and in inclement weather is sometimes left behind for safety or exchanged for a simpler kind. Upon the streets of European towns peasant women in the morning are usually seen with uncovered heads, and in America neighbourly women are often so seen passing from house to house, but never upon state occasions. Furs are still worn by both sexes in winter, but much more commonly by women. The use of striking colours, such as red, yellow, blue, green, and purple, is still frequent in the dress of women and children, but much less so in men's dress, where the blacks, greys, and browns prevail. Survivals of the primitive custom of leaving parts of the body entirely exposed and unprotected are still seen in women's evening dress, showing how little the idea of display has given place to that of utility. The use of rare metals and stones as ornaments for the ankles, wrists, fingers, ears, nose, lips, and neck persisted in the dress of women long after it became extinct with men. Rings in the ears were commonly worn by women within the memory of many of us, and rings and stones upon the wrists and fingers are still very common. Survivals of the neck ornaments are still seen in the various forms of pins and necklaces. Beads, so highly prized by the lower races, still persist to some extent in the bead trimming of women's dress. The use of paint to decorate the person is now practically extinct with both sexes, but as a means of decorating the face was practised by women within comparatively recent times. In respect to various powders and perfumes, the evolution has not been so rapid, and they are still in use among women to some extent. Mutilations of the body for ornamental purposes are all but extinct, but among women certain mutilations, such as piercing the ears, unnatural constriction of the waist, and pinching of the feet, have persisted almost to the present time. In countries like China, where the last of these is still practised, the practice is confined to women.   In certain other trifling matters there is in women's dress a suggestive survival of primitive customs.   The dress of the primitive man was loosely and irregularly attached to the body, and was fastened with strings or thongs or afterwards with pins of metal.   Later these pins were attached to the garment and bent into the form of hooks.   Buckles, and finally buttons, took the place of the primitive pins and hooks. But women still use the metal pins, and the primitive lack of definite correspondence between the dress and the body is seen, for instance, in the hat or bonnet which does not fit the head, and must be fastened on with strings or pins.   This retarded development and absence of differentiation in women's dress is curiously illustrated in the case of shoes.   Only a few decades ago girls' and women's shoes were made straight and worn indiscriminately on either foot, while men's shoes were uniformly made rights and lefts.   But the most striking case of retarded development in women's dress is seen in the persistence of the idea that dress is not so much a protection for the body as a symbol of the wealth of the wearer or the wearer's family. . . . It is not urged that the dress of men is perfect or free from savage elements, or that the æsthetic motive common to the dress of the primitive man and civilised woman is not a worthy one, but only that in the evolution of dress there is a definite progressive movement from the primitive conception of display and expenditure to the modern conception of utility and comfort, and that in this movement woman's dress has been retarded or arrested at a primitive stage." (G. T. W. Patrick, "The Psychology of Woman," *Pop. Sci. Monthly*, vol. 47, 1895.)

We have, therefore, to recognise that in men, as in males generally, there is an organic variational tendency to diverge from the average, in women, as in females generally, an organic tendency, notwithstanding all their facility for minor oscillations, to stability and conservatism, involving a diminished individualism and variability.[1]

[1] On the psychic side it is sometimes said, as long since by Burdach, that when women vary, they tend to vary more intemperately than men.   Thus Dr. Barnardo, as a result of long experience, remarks that in regard to depraved habits and depraved talk "the girls are always much worse than the boys.   I have had no such degree of depravity with boys as with girls."   Inebriety, again, according to Norman Kerr and other authorities, is more curable in men than in women.   Cruelty, again, as well as pity, seems more marked in women than in men. These and similar phenomena are not, however, strictly speaking, manifestations of any variational tendency, but simply the results of the greater affectability and exhaustibility of women.

Men show a more marked variational tendency than women, and this fact is closely allied with the fact, to which I have had to call attention in another chapter, that men exhibit more marked pathological characters; for, as Virchow insists, every deviation from the normal type must have its foundation in a pathological accident. It may not be out of place to add that in emphasising the variational tendency in men, the conservative tendency in women, we are not talking politics, nor throwing any light whatever on the possible effects of women's suffrage. It is undeniably true that the greater variational tendency of the male is a psychic as well as a physical fact, but zoological facts cannot easily be brought within the small and shifting sphere of politics. Organic conservatism may often involve political revolution. Socialism and nihilism are not, I believe, usually regarded by politicians as conservative movements, but from the organic point of view of the race, they may be truly conservative, and, as is well known, these movements have powerfully appealed to women. Women opposed the French Revolution. "If it were not for women," it was said, "the Republic would be safe;" but, on the other hand, the establishment of Christianity, the most revolutionary movement that has ever been seen in Europe, was to a considerable extent furthered by women. It is difficult to argue from zoological facts to an order of facts which is of purely local and temporary character. The mistake is often made, and it is, therefore, not out of place to refer to it here.

A large part of the joy that men and women take in each other is rooted in this sexual difference in variability. The progressive and divergent energies of men call out and satisfy the twin instincts of women to accept and follow a leader, and to expend tenderness on a reckless and erring child, instincts often intermingled in delicious confusion. And in women men find beings who have not wandered so far as they have from the typical life of earth's creatures; women are for men the human embodiments of the restful responsiveness of Nature. To every man, as Michelet has put it, the woman whom he loves is as the Earth was to her legendary son; he has but to fall down and kiss her breast and he is strong again. Woman is more in harmony with Nature than man, as Burdach said, and she brings man into harmony with Nature. This organically primitive nature of women, in form and function and instinct, is always restful to men tortured by their vagrant energies; it was certainly with genuine satisfaction that the tender and sympathetic Diderot wrote of women that "they are real savages inside." It is because of this that the ascetics, those very erratic and abnormal examples of the variational tendency, have hated women with hatred so bitter and intense that no language could be found strong enough to express their horror. They knew that every natural impulse of a woman is the condemnation of asceticism. All true lovers of the artificial and perverse find woman repulsive; "Woman is natural," it is written among the sayings of Baudelaire, "that is to say abominable." But for most men and women this sexual difference has added to the charm of life: it has also added to the everlasting difficulty of life.

CHAPTER XVII.

NATALITY AND MORTALITY.

THE BIRTH-RATE OF MALES HIGHER THAN OF FEMALES—
THEIR DEATH-RATE STILL HIGHER—CAUSES OF THE
GREATER MORTALITY AMONG MALES—THE RESISTANCE
OF WOMEN TO DISEASE—AS ILLUSTRATED BY SCARLET
FEVER, SMALL-POX, INFLUENZA, ETC. — RECENT IM-
PROVEMENTS IN THE DEATH-RATE HAVE SPECIALLY
BENEFITED WOMEN—GREATER LONGEVITY OF WOMEN
—THE CHARACTERISTIC SIGNS OF OLD AGE LESS
MARKED IN WOMEN—THE GREATER TENDENCY TO
SUDDEN DEATH IN MEN—THE GREATER RESISTANCE
OF WOMEN TO DISEASE AND DEATH PERHAPS A ZOO-
LOGICAL FACT.

IN turning to the birth-rates and death-rates to seek
what light they may have to throw on the organisation of man and woman, we are entering the region
of demography. It requires a skilful statistician to
reach any assured results here, and I propose to touch
very lightly on the matter. From the most reliable
investigations into sexual differences in natality and
mortality, however, emerge certain results which have
a very distinct bearing on the points we are here
mainly concerned with. It is necessary at all events
to point out this bearing, however briefly.

It is well known that while in England, and in
most other old countries, there is an excess of females
in the adult population, at birth there is an excess

of males nearly everywhere.[1] There are more boys than girls born among the Germans, French, English, and the other most civilised European races; there are equally more boys than girls born among the Veddahs of Ceylon, one of the lowest of human races.[2]

According to a Report prepared for the Italian Government in 1884, the proportion of male births to 100 female births is in various countries as follows:—

Russian Poland	. 101	Sweden	.	105
England and Ireland	. 104	Denmark	.	105
France	. 105	European Russia	.	105
Scotland	. 105	Vermont	.	105
Prussia	105	Rhode Island	.	105
Bavaria	. 105	Italy	.	106
Saxony	. 105	Ireland	.	106
Thüringia	. 105	Austria	.	106
Würtemberg	. 105	Croatia	.	106
Baden	. 105	Norway	.	106
German Empire	. 105	Servia	.	106
Alsace-Lorraine	. 105	Massachusetts	.	106
Hungary	. 105	Spain	.	107
Switzerland	. 105	Connecticut	.	110
Belgium	. 105	Roumania	.	111
Holland	. 105	Greece	.	112

The great excess of male births in Greece is notable, and it may be added that Greece is perhaps the only European country in which males are in marked excess among the adult population; at the census of 1889 there were 107.6 males to 100 females. But even in Greece, after the age of 85, an

[1] Such demographic data as we possess concerning extra-European populations point in the same direction; thus Karl Ranke (*Correspond.-Blatt Deutsch. Gesell. Anth.*, Nov. 1898) found among the Indians of Brazil 1000 men to 879 women, the excess of males being most marked in early life, and giving place after the age of forty to a slight excess of females. There is considerable reason to conclude that the same excess of males is found among at all events a large number of the lower animals; see, for example, Darwin, *Descent of Man*, Part II., chap. viii.

[2] Deschamps, "Les Veddas," *L'Anthropologie*, 1891, No. 3.

excess of females in the population becomes more and more marked. Among Russian Jews it appears that no fewer than 129 boys are born to every 100 girls.[1] Among Jews everywhere the male birth-rate is higher than among Christians. It is also note-worthy that the proportion of male births in England is decreasing; while, about fifty years ago, it was 105.3 males for every 100 females, it is now 103.6. On the whole the variations from year to year are not very great, as the following table, which presents the number of boys in 1000 children at birth in various countries, clearly shows:—[2]

	Italy.	Scotland.	Ireland.	Saxony.	Rhode Island.
1878 .	516	514	511	513	519
1879 .	516	512	516	514	511
1880 .	515	512	515	514	511
1881 .	515	513	515	509	517
1882 .	514	512	514	512	514
1883 .	515	513	514	512	504

It is unnecessary to accumulate figures, but it may be added that in most countries there is some differ-ence in this respect between legitimate and illegitimate births, the preponderance of boys being less among the illegitimate births than among the legitimate by 1 or 2 per cent., notwithstanding the fact that, accord-ing to Bertillon, a woman's first children are more likely to be boys than girls.[3]

In England and Wales, according to the Report of the Registrar-General for 1891, if we take the births for thirty years as a basis, the proportion of male infants to 1000 female infants varies from 1032 to 1033 in some counties to 1055, 1056, and 1058 in others. He adds some suggestions as to the possibility of the variations being due to racial difference. "It may be noticed that the registration counties with the highest

[1] Leinenberg, *Int. Klin. Rundschau*, 15th Sept. 1889.
[2] Westergaard, *Theorie der Statistik*, p. 11.
[3] Bertillon, Art. "Natalité," *Dict. ency. des Sci. Méd.*

proportions are Cumberland, Cornwall, and North Wales, while South Wales, though it has not the next highest proportion, comes only a little way down in the list, its proportions being 1046, and considerably above the average for the whole country. . . . The Celtic character of the areas mentioned above as having the highest proportions of male infants suggests the idea that not impossibly race has some influence in the matter; a surmise which is not inconsistent with the fact that the proportions are invariably much higher both in Ireland and in Scotland than in England." I question if this suggestion will bear examination.

If we turn to the adult population, we find usually that, in very varying degrees, there is a marked excess of women. It exists independently of emigration; and while it may be said to be excessive in most European countries (and especially in Great Britain and Sweden), in new countries it usually does not exist at all.

How are we to explain this discrepancy between the sexual proportions at birth and at adult age?

It was formerly supposed that war and the exposure of men in dangerous occupations were alone sufficient to account for the greater mortality of men. That they are the chief factors seems to admit of little doubt; an exact analysis does not now permit us to conclude that they are the sole factors.

War and occupation can only come in as working factors during youth and adult life; and the same may be said, on the whole, even of men's tendency to indulge in excesses,[1] which is sometimes brought in as a factor, though it is probably to a large extent a factor of organic rather than of merely accidental social character. It is during the very earliest period of life and at the latest that the greater mortality of males is most clearly marked.[2] Bertillon

---

[1] I do not attach much importance to this, as against it must be set the depressing influences, lack of air and nourishment, etc., under which women's lives are frequently passed.

[2] The greater mortality of new-born males is found in all countries where precise statistics exist. In some countries, in Sweden, for instance, but not in England, the male mortality is greater than the female at every age. (Bertillon, Art. "Mortalité," p. 762, *Dict. ency. des Sci. Méd.*)

showed, many years ago, that while the proportion of living children born is 100 girls to 105 boys, the proportion of all births, living and dead, is 100 girls to 106.6 boys; the proportion of still-born children in Belgium during 1860-65 was 100 females to not less than 136 males; so that still-born children are much more frequently males than are living children.[1] Girls, owing to their smaller size, possess at the out-set a better chance of slipping safely into the world. For some little time after birth the same factor is operative. Collins, of the Rotunda Lying-in Hospital, Dublin,[2] showed that within half-an-hour after birth only 1 female died to 16 males; within the first hour only 2 females to 19 males, and within the first six hours only 7 females to 29 males.

The larger size of the male head can, however, only be a factor at birth, and for a short time afterwards, but there is still a greater male mortality; male children under one year of age are very liable to die, and this, as Sir G. Humphry remarks in his study of *Old Age*, is alone enough to suggest, though by no means to prove, that the superiority of females in this respect is not due to their comparative freedom from exposures and to their greater temperance. Dr. Longstaff also considers that the great mortality of males during the first year of life "must depend on some constitutional difference." During the first dentition male children are much more apt to die of diseases of the nervous system than female children. From the third until towards the thirty-fifth year there does not appear to be great sexual difference in mortality; this is no doubt due to the great mortality of males at the beginning of life; only the more robust out of a large number being left to compete with the smaller but apparently more vigorous

[1] Bertillon, Art. "Mort-né," *Dict. ency. des Sci. Méd.*
[2] As quoted by Braxton Hicks, "Croonian Lectures on the Differ-ences between the Sexes in regard to the Aspect and Treatment of Disease," *Brit. Med. Journal*, 1877.

females; after the development of puberty in women, from the fifteenth to the twentieth years, the female mortality is usually greater than the male; this is the period of special danger for women. After the thirtieth or thirty-fifth years there is a difference in favour of women which steadily increases. Four-fifths of the excess of women in this country consists of widows.[1]

The farther we proceed towards the extreme limit of life, and the more we are able to eliminate all but the inherent constitutional factors of vitality, the more marked is the preponderance of women. Sir G. Humphry, in his *Old Age*, found opportunities for the detailed study of 36 female centenarians as against only 16 males. The Registrar-General's Reports show that of those persons who at death are supposed to have died over the age of 100, only a small proportion are males.[2] In England in 1891, at the age of 85 and upwards, 8,291 women died to only 5,320 men; between 75 and 85, it is worth noting, the excess of women is by no means so great (24,506 men to 28,785 women). The last census shows more than twice as many women as men over the age of 90 in England and Wales. In France, from 1866 to 1885, the yearly average of deaths of centenarians has been 27 men to 46 women.[3] Among the more primitive human races it is not so easy to obtain definite statistics, but it is probable that the same relation holds good as in civilisation; thus among

[1] Longstaff, *Studies in Statistics*, p. 8. The accompanying diagram (p. 435), reproduced from the *Studies* by Dr. Longstaff's permission, shows in a graphic form the sexual differences in mortality from all causes in England and Wales during the years 1871-80.

[2] It is probable that not only are women in a majority among centenarians, but that the absolutely most extreme cases of longevity occur in women. The familiar cases of Thomas Parr and Henry Jenkins are now regarded as mythical, but there is no doubt about the case of Mrs. Hanbury, who was born in 1793 and died in 1901 at the age of 108, while T. E. Young (*Centenarians*, 1899) cites 15 trustworthy cases of women living to ages between 100 and 106, and only 7 of men.

[3] Turquan, "Statistique des Centenaires," *Revue Scientifique*, 1st Sept. 1888.

the Nicobarese Islanders, according to Man, of those who survive the sixtieth year fully two-thirds are women.[1] It may be added that, if we take a broader zoological view, the same truth seems frequently to hold good.

If we turn to consider the bearing on this point of the mortality from definite diseases, the impression given by a glance at the birth-rate and death-rate as a whole is confirmed. If, for instance, we take the zymotic group of infectious diseases which chiefly affect young children, we find nearly always that the advantage is on the side of the female. Whooping-cough and diphtheria only are more fatal in the female, a result which has been attributed to the smaller larynx of girls, and to their customs of frequent kissing, sharing sweets, etc. Even when we take statistics which show on the whole a greater liability to in-fection in women, the mortality is not equally great. Thus if we take the figures of the Metropolitan Asylums Board Hospitals during the years 1871-91, as given by Dr. Whitelegge, we find :—[2]

		Cases.	Deaths.	Case Mortality.
Scarlet fever	Males ...	19,887 ...	2,051 ...	10.3
„	Females...	22,224 ...	1,982 ...	8.9
Enteric fever	Males ...	4,041 ...	676 ...	16.7
„	Females...	3,674 ...	662 ...	17.3
Typhus	Males ...	964 ...	216 ...	22.4
„	Females...	1,175 ...	217 ...	18.5
Diphtheria	Males ...	1,360 ...	478 ...	35.2
(1888-91) „	Females...	1,715 ...	555 ...	32.4

So that, except in enteric, if we take into account the number of individuals attacked, the mortality of females is not greater than that of males. This small fatality with considerable susceptibility is what we see in brain disease also in a marked character; nervous disease of a slight and non-fatal character is extremely prevalent among women; nervous disease of a grave

[1] *Journal Anth. Institute*, May 1889, p. 385.
[2] Whitelegge, " Milroy Lectures on Changes of Type in Epidemic Disease," *Brit. Med. Journal*, March 18th, 1893.

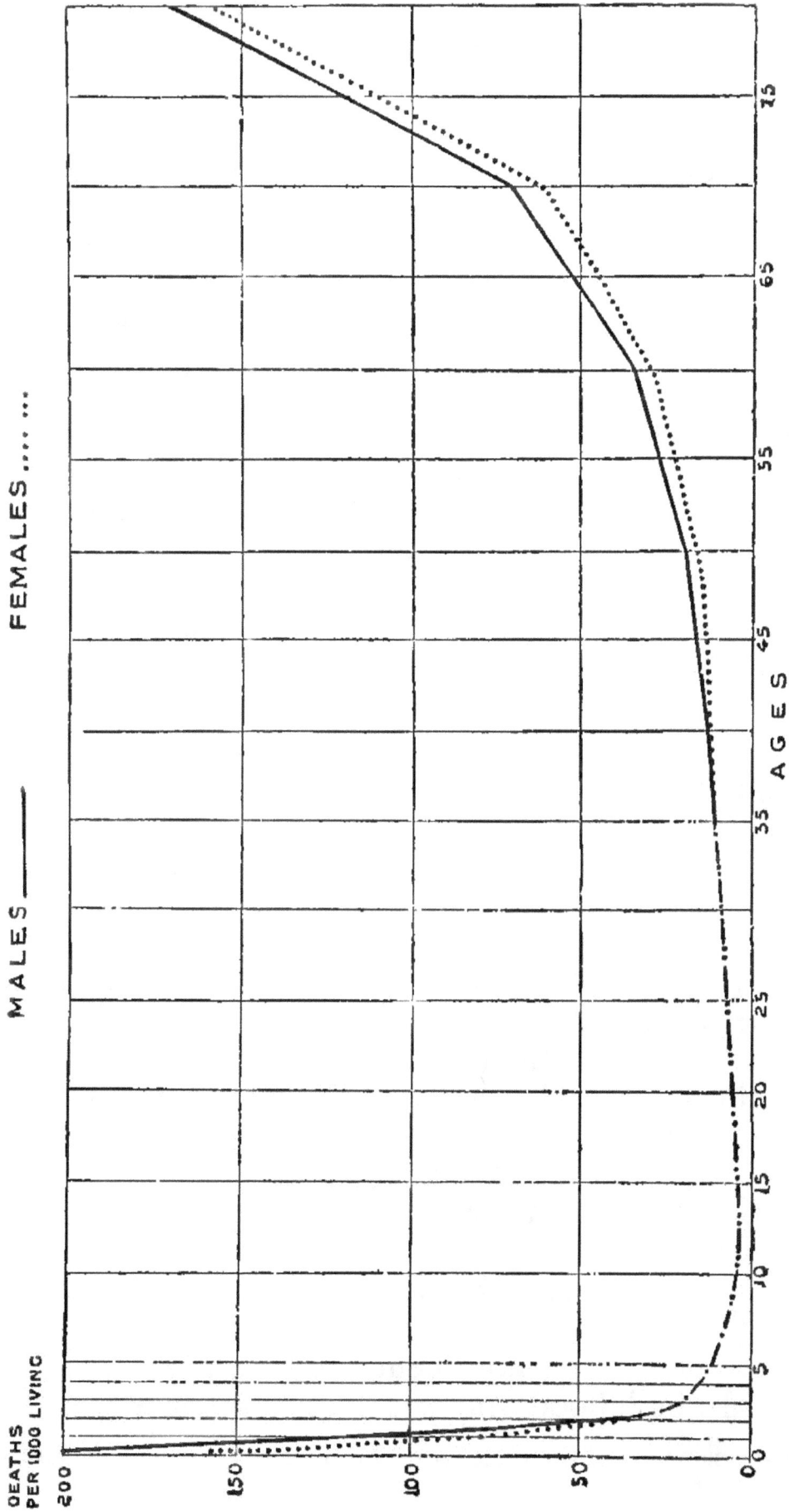

CHART OF SEXUAL DIFFERENCES IN MORTALITY. (*Longstaff.*)

character is comparatively rare. This is probably another aspect of the affectability of women.

An analysis of the phenomena of one of the most important of the zymotic diseases, scarlet fever, brings out the characteristic sexual differences. From the Registrar-General's Reports for 1859-85 it appears that the highest mortality from scarlet fever occurs in both sexes in the third year of life, and diminishes with each successive year-period. Up to the end of the tenth year of life the mortality among males considerably exceeds that among females, but in all subsequent periods the reverse is the case—*i.e.*, women remain nearer to children than men. On the whole, the liability of males to a fatal result is considerably greater than that of females. But though the attacks in males are more likely to end fatally, the female sex throughout life, with the possible exception of the first year, is more liable to be attacked by scarlet fever than the male sex.[1]

Small-pox is more fatal to males than to females throughout nearly the whole of life, except during the years from ten to fifteen. Cholera attacks women more often than men, but less often fatally; during the epidemic of 1854 the mortality for males was 8.02, for females 7.78. Influenza, according to most observers, attacks women more frequently than men, but the mortality among men is much greater than among women, being as 1 to 2; children are more rarely affected, and suffer but slightly. It would be easy to show by the examination of other groups of disease that while women are frequently, as in the zymotic group, more susceptible, men usually suffer more severely.

It is an interesting fact, as pointed out by Dr. Longstaff, that recent improvements in the death-rate have on the whole benefited women more than men. In childhood and youth girls suffer more than

---

[1] For a summary of the statistics of this disease, see *Sanitary Record*, 16th January 1888.

boys from phthisis, whooping-cough, diphtheria, and heart disease, which are all diminishing in fatality. On the other hand, boys suffer more than girls from violence, kidney disease, brain disease, "all other causes," lung disease, and to a less degree from diarrhœal diseases, small-pox, measles, and scarlatina. Of these, lung and kidney disease are increasing in fatality, the rest declining; the net result being that girls gain more than boys in the proportion of 7 to 6. During adult life it is only from cancer that women suffer more than men—the loss here being more than double—but the rate of increase in cancer is greater in males than in females. The net results show that females gain more than males in the proportion of 7 to 3. So in old age; the mortality of both old men and old women is increasing, but the death-rate of old men three times as fast as that of old women. "It is quite plain," Dr. Longstaff concludes, "that the recent fall in the death-rate favours the accumulation of surplus women, if one may be allowed such an expression, and should the change of mortality go on in the same direction the rate of accumulation will be increased."[1]

The greater tenacity of life in women and their great constitutional youthfulness are shown also in the less frequency with which they exhibit the characteristic signs of old age. Baldness is rare in women; it is equally rare among the less civilised races; for example, among the Nicobarese Islanders, with whom baldness in men is not uncommon. Degenerative disease of the arteries is less common in old women than in old men. Sir G. Humphry found among his centenarians that the elasticity of the thorax, as evinced by the condition of the costal cartilages, and its capacity for dilatation during inspiration, are better preserved in women than in men. He also found (as may, indeed, be stated to be the rule) that the *arcus senilis* in the eye, a very characteristic

[1] G. B. Longstaff, *Studies in Statistics*, pp. 248-251.

indication of old age in men, is less marked in old women. The specific gravity of the blood, also, as Lloyd Jones has found, is higher in old women than in old men. The mental derangements of old age, again, are commoner in men than in women; thus Wille finds 10 per cent. males to only 6 per cent. females.[1] There is also some reason to believe that old age produces relatively less loss of brain tissue in women than in men.

One other fact may be brought forward in proof of the greater tendency of men to die. The majority of sudden deaths from internal or pathological causes are in men. French statistics show a very considerable difference in the frequency of sudden death from the sexual point of view. Devergie gives 39 cases in men to only 5 in women, a proportion of males equal to 88.7 per cent. Tourdes, among 88 cases, found 59 men—i.e., 67.3 per cent. Lacassagne, consulting the archives of the Lyons Morgue, found that from 1854 to 1880, out of 459 cases of sudden death 365 were men—i.e., 79.6 per cent. Out of 62 cases under the observation of Lacassagne, Coutagne, and P. Bernard, there were 41 men—i.e., 66.1 per cent. We may conclude that about three-fourths are men. It is rare among children, and commonest between the ages of 50 and 60.[2] It should be added that a greater liability to sudden death may to a considerable extent be regarded as the manifestation of a greater liability to degenerative disease of the arteries.

All the evidence brought together or referred to in this chapter points, with varying degrees of certainty, to the same conclusion—the greater physical frailty of men, the greater tenacity of life in women.[3]

[1] Ludwig Wille, Art. "Old Age and its Psychoses," *Dict. of Psych. Med.*

[2] Paul Bernard, *Arch. de l'Anth. Crim.*, 15th March 1890.

[3] An independent collection of data on the same subject will be found in Dr. H. Campbell's *Nervous Organisation of Man and Woman*, pp. 121-128. He concludes that women possess "a greater innate recuperative power."

We must not too rashly assume that this result is ultimate and unanalysable; but we are justified in holding it provisionally. Although such a conclusion may not be altogether in harmony with the popular notion, it is in harmony with many other groups of facts, some of which are elsewhere dealt with in this book. It is in harmony also with the impression that we obtain on glancing across the zoological field. The female is the mother of the new generation, and has a closer and more permanent connection with the care of the young; she is thus of greater importance than the male from Nature's point of view. We therefore find that the female—notwithstanding her greater affectability by minor stimuli—is more resistant to adverse influences and longer lived than the male.

CHAPTER XVIII.

CONCLUSION.

THE KNOWLEDGE WE HAVE GAINED DOES NOT ENABLE US DEFINITELY TO SETTLE SPECIAL PROBLEMS—WHAT IT DOES ENABLE US TO DO—WOMEN ARE NEARER TO CHILDREN THAN ARE MEN—BUT WOMAN IS NOT UNDEVELOPED MAN — THE CHILD REPRESENTS A HIGHER DEGREE OF EVOLUTION THAN THE ADULT— THE PROGRESS OF THE RACE HAS BEEN A PROGRESS IN YOUTHFULNESS—IN SOME RESPECTS IT HAS BEEN A PROGRESS IN FEMINISATION—ABSURDITY OF SPEAK-ING OF THE SUPERIORITY OF ONE SEX OVER ANOTHER —THE SEXES PERFECTLY POISED—BUT SOCIAL RE-ADJUSTMENTS MAY STILL BE NECESSARY—WE MAY FACE ALL SUCH READJUSTMENTS WITH EQUANIMITY.

WE have examined Man and Woman, as precisely as may be, from various points of view. It is time to pause, as we do so bringing together a few general observations suggested by the multifarious facts we have encountered.

It is abundantly evident that we have not reached the end proposed at the outset. We have not suc-ceeded in determining the radical and essential characters of men and women uninfluenced by external modifying conditions. Sometimes a suffi-ciently wide induction of facts (as in the question of the alleged sexual differences in respiration) suffices to show us what is artificial and what is real; at other times (as in the question of differences in sensibility) the wider our induction of facts the more complex and mobile become our results. We have to recognise that our present knowledge of men and women cannot tell us what they might be or what they ought to be, but what they actually are, under the conditions of civilisation. By showing us that under varying conditions men and women are, within certain limits, indefinitely modifiable, a precise knowledge of the actual facts of the life of men and women forbids us to dogmatise rigidly concerning the respective spheres of men and women. It is a matter which experience alone can demonstrate in detail. If this is not exactly the result which we set out to attain, it is still a result of very considerable importance. It lays the axe at the root of many pseudo-scientific superstitions. It clears the ground of much unnecessary verbiage and fruitless discussion, and enables us to see more clearly the really essential points at issue. The small group of women who wish to prove the absolute inferiority of the male sex, the larger group of men who wish to circumscribe rigidly the sphere of women, must alike be ruled out of court. Nor may we listen to those would-be scientific dogmatists who on *a priori* grounds, on the strength of some single and often doubtful anatomical fact, lay down social laws for mankind at large. The ludicrous errors of arrogant and over-hasty brain anatomists in the past should alone suffice to teach us this caution. The facts are far too complex to enable us to rush hastily to a conclusion as to their significance. The facts, moreover, are so numerous that even when we have ascertained the precise significance of some one fact, we cannot be sure that it is not contradicted by other facts. And so many of the facts are modifiable under a changing environment that in the absence of experience we cannot pronounce definitely regarding the behaviour of either the male or female organism under different conditions. There is but one tribunal whose sentence is final and without appeal. Only Nature can pronounce concerning the legitimacy of social modifications. The sentence may be sterility or death, but no other tribunal, no appeal to common-sense, will serve instead.

Yet there are certain general conclusions which have again and again presented themselves, even when we have been occupied in considering very diverse aspects of the physical and psychic phenomena of human life. One of these is the greater variability of the male; this is true for almost the whole of the field we have covered, and it has social and practical consequences of the widest significance. The whole of our human civilisation would have been a different thing if in early zoological epochs the male had not acquired a greater variational tendency than the female. Another general conclusion of an equally far-reaching character is the precocity of women, involving greater rapidity of growth and its earlier arrest than in men. The result of this precocity is that women, taken altogether, present the characters of short men, and to some extent of children. The whole organism of the average woman, physical and psychic, is fundamentally unlike that of the average man, on account of this fact alone. The differences may often be of a slight or subtle character, but they are none the less real, and they extend to the smallest details of organic constitution. We have found over and over again that when women differ from men, it is the latter who have diverged, leaving women nearer to the child-type The earlier arrest of development in women is thus connected with the variational tendency of men. And all these sexual differences probably have their origin in the more intimate connection of women with offspring.

Further evidence regarding the infantile diathesis

of women, as we may call it, is found in pathological statistics. It is difficult to find diseases that are common in children and men and rare in women, and still more difficult to find diseases that are rare in children and men and common in women. On the other hand, it is very easy to find diseases which are common in children and women and rare in men, and diseases which are rare in children and women and common in men.

Asthma is a well-ascertained example of a disease which is common in children and men and rare in women; Salter gives the proportion as two men to one woman in England, and Sée agrees with Naumann that in France and Germany it is as much as six times more common in men than in women. The case of asthma does not, however, possess much significance, as it is a symptom rather than a disease. Typhlitis (or appendicitis) is also common in children and in men but rarer in women, while chyluria seems to be a disorder that is rare in childhood but commoner in females than in males.

There are a large number of important and fully-studied pathological conditions which reveal children and women in association for good or for ill. As an example of those in which they are associated for good may be mentioned angina pectoris, which is extremely rare in women, while very few cases in children are recorded. Diabetes, again, is essentially a disease of adult life, occurring chiefly between the ages of 40 and 50, but in women somewhat earlier, between 30 and 40. It is much more frequent in men than in women; in England from 1850 to 1870 there were nearly twice as many deaths of men as of women from diabetes; Oppolzer, at Vienna, found the proportion to be four cases in men to one in women; while in France, Lécorché, uniting various statistics, found 117 women to 310 men. Diabetes, it may be added, is a disease of towns rather than of the country, and is therefore increasing, though well known to both Greeks and Romans at the commencement of the Christian era; among the highly-educated and non-flesh-eating inhabitants of India it is very prevalent, as well as among the Jews, but the yellow and black races are almost entirely free from it (R. Saundby, *Lectures on Diabetes*, 1891). Dupuytren's contraction of the fingers is an interesting example of a pathological condition to which there is undoubtedly strong hereditary predisposition, but which is almost unknown in childhood; in 800 children no trace of the disease was to be found, and among 203,000 soldiers between the ages of seventeen and thirty-five only three cases came under treatment; it is not until late middle

life that an appreciable percentage of cases can be found, and
of these only half are women, or, according to one authority,
only a fifth (W. Anderson, " Lectures on Contractions of the
Fingers and Toes," *Lancet*, July 4, 1891). Bright's disease is a
disease of middle life, rare in childhood, and it affects about
twice as many males as females. Sciatica, again, is an affection
of mature life which is much commoner in men; thus Gibson,
at Buxton, in 1000 cònsecutive cases found 88.4 per cent. in
men, 11.6 per cent. in women. Hay-fever rarely attacks
children, and among adults it affects about three men to one
woman; it is a disease of the town rather than the country, and
is chiefly found among the refined and educated. Aneurism is
much commoner in men than in women, and is very rare in
children, but carotid aneurism is about equally common in
men and in women, and appears to be found at a somewhat
earlier age than other forms of aneurism. Some of the
diseases that are common in men and rare in women and
children, it can easily be seen, owe their discrepancy in
sexual incidence merely to the greater exposure of men to
excesses and strains of various kinds. The predominantly
masculine diseases are thus often associated with high mental
or physical development; they are also very often diseases
that are on the increase, and that are favoured by town life
and by civilisation.

If we turn to the group of diseases which tend to affect both
children and women, we find that scarlet fever, as Sanné concludes (Art. "Scarlatine," *Dict. ency. des Sci. Méd.*), is almost
equally common in both sexes up to about twenty years of age,
while after that women are more liable to it. Subungual
exostosis is common in early life, and more frequent in girls.
Scleroderma (or hide-bound disease) is much commoner in
women than in men (at least three women to one man), and
while it attacks all ages, is very frequently found among the
young. Herpes zoster is as common in children above the age
of two as in adults, and is much more frequent in females than
in males. Aphtha of the mouth, which is chiefly found in infants,
is, among adults, more often found in women than in men.
There are two important pathological conditions of the heart,
one affecting the mitral valve, the other the aortic valve.
Mitral disease is comparatively common in children; aortic
disease is very rare in children. But among adults it is
universally agreed that mitral disease is much commoner in
women, and aortic disease in men; Bamberger found aortic
insufficiency three times as frequent in men as in women, and
mitral stenosis, according to various authorities, is found to be
from two to four times more frequent in women than in men.
It is scarcely necessary to add that not all these sexual differences correspond to radical organic differences.

This general character of woman's organic development has long been recognised.[1] Its significance has by no means been so clearly recognised. To assume, as Herbert Spencer and many others have assumed, that on this account woman is "undeveloped man," is to state the matter in an altogether misleading manner. That the adult man diverges to a greater extent from the child-type than the adult woman is on the whole certainly true—though even this is not entirely true of the more primary sexual organs and functions—and, so far as it is true, it is a fact not merely of human life, but of animal life generally. To add, however, that woman is undeveloped man is only true in the same sense as it is to state that man is undeveloped woman; in each sex there are undeveloped organs and functions which in the other sex are developed. In order to appraise rightly the significance of the fact that women remain somewhat nearer to children than do men, we must have a clear idea of the position occupied by the child in the human and allied species. In Chapter II. I alluded to the curious fact that among the anthropoids the infant ape is very much nearer to Man than the adult ape. This means that the infant ape is higher in the line of evolution than the adult, and the female ape, by approximating to the infant type, is somewhat higher than the male. Man, in carrying on the line of evolution, started not from some adult male simian, but from the infant ape, and in a less degree from the female ape. The human infant bears

[1] Thus Topinard considers that, structurally, woman is intermediate between the child and the adult man; this is not strictly correct, however, as in some respects women are farther removed from the infantile state than are men. Dr. H. Campbell (*Nervous Organisation of Man and Woman*, chaps. viii., ix.) has an interesting discussion of this question. Giuffrida-Ruggeri (*Monit. Zoolog. Ital.*, 1903, No. 12), criticising my conclusions on this point, argues that the infantile characteristics of women are " coincidences." It is legitimate so to regard them, provided we recognise that they are highly significant coincidences.

precisely the same relation to his species as the simian infant bears to his, and we are bound to conclude that his relation to the future evolution of the race is similar.[1] The human infant presents in an exaggerated form the chief distinctive characters of humanity—the large head and brain, the small face, the hairlessness, the delicate bony system. By some strange confusion of thought we usually ignore this fact, and assume that the adult form is more highly developed than the infantile form.[2] From the point of view of adaptation to the environment it is undoubtedly true that the coarse, hairy, large-boned, and small-brained gorilla is better fitted to make his way in the world than his delicate offspring, but from a zoological point of view we witness anything but progress. In Man, from about the third year onwards, further growth—though an absolutely necessary adaptation to the environment—is to some extent growth in degeneration and senility. It is not carried to so low a degree as in the apes, although by it Man is to some extent brought nearer to the apes, and among the higher human races the progress towards senility is less marked than among the lower human races. The child of many African races is scarcely if at all less intelligent than the European child, but while the African as he grows up becomes stupid and obtuse, and his whole social life falls into a state of hide-bound routine, the European retains much of his childlike vivacity. And if we turn to what we are accustomed to regard as the highest human types, as represented in men of genius, we shall find an approximation to the child-type. "You Greeks are always children;" such was the impression

---

[1] It may be argued, in explanation of the phenomena, that the ape has descended from a more human ancestor, but there is no ground for such an assumption.

[2] The confusion has, however, often been pointed out. "It is a gross error," remarked Burdach, whose intuitions were rarely wrong, "to suppose that increase in age is increase in the scale of perfection." (*Phys.* i. p. 383.)

given by the ancient people whom we are taught to regard as the highest type the world has reached. According to the formula of an old mystic, the reign of the Father gave place to the reign of the Son, which must be succeeded by the reign of the Holy Ghost. It might be said that this formula corresponds to a zoological verity. The progress of our race has been a progress in youthfulness.[1]

When we have realised the position of the child in relation to evolution we can take a clearer view as to the natural position of woman. She bears the special characteristics of humanity in a higher degree than man (as Burdach pointed out), and led evolution in the matter of hairiness (as Darwin, following Burdach, pointed out), simply because she is nearer to the child. Her conservatism is thus compensated and justified by the fact that she represents more nearly than man the human type to which man is approximating. This is true of physical characters: the large-headed, delicate-faced, small-boned man of urban civilisation is much nearer to the typical woman than is the savage. Not only by his large brain, but by his large pelvis, the modern man is following a path first marked out by woman: the skull of the modern woman is more markedly feminine than that of the savage woman, while that of the modern man has approximated to it; the pelvis of the modern woman is much more feminine in character than that of the primitive woman, and the modern man's pelvis is also slowly becoming more feminine.

We may note also that, as many investigators have found, the student (to whose type the modern man has approximated) occupies, both physically and mentally, a position intermediate between that of women and ordinary men. Throughout the whole course of human civilisation we see men following

[1] The facts encountered in our consideration of the cephalic index in Chapter V., for example, are interesting from this point of view.

women and taking up their avocations, with more energy, more thoroughness, often more eccentricity. Savagery and barbarism have more usually than not been predominantly militant, that is to say masculine, in character, while modern civilisation is becoming industrial, that is to say feminine, in character, for the industries belonged primitively to women, and they tend to make men like women. Even in quite recent times, and in reference to many of the details of life, it is possible to see the workings of this feminisation; although, it is scarcely necessary to caution the reader, this is but one tendency in our complex modern civilisation. I have pointed out (p. 386) how, even during very recent years, there appears to have been a movement amongst men in favour of adopting feminine methods of committing suicide. We have, again, but to compare the various conveniences of our streets and of locomotion to-day with the condition of the streets of a large city a century ago, or even in many respects thirty years ago, to realise the progress that has been made in affording equal facilities for women with men, and in so doing to make life easier for men as well as for women. St. Clement of Alexandria was of opinion that women should be allowed to wear shoes; it was not, he said, suitable for their feet to be shown naked; "besides woman is a tender thing, easily hurt. But for a man bare feet are quite in keeping."[1] To-day a man also is a "tender thing," and there is less and less inclination to recognise any distinctions of this kind. It would not be difficult, had it been part of my task, to multiply examples of the ways in which women are leading evolution. In the saying with which Goethe closed his *Faust* lies a biological verity not usually suspected by those who quote it.

Any reader who has turned to this book for facts or arguments bearing on the everlasting discussion regarding the "alleged inferiority of women," and

[1] *Pædagogus*, Bk. II., Chap. xii.

who has followed me so far, will already have gathered the natural conclusion we reach on this point. We may regard all such discussion as absolutely futile and foolish. If it is a question of determining the existence and significance of some particular physical or psychic sexual difference a conclusion may not be impossible. To make any broad statement of the phenomena is to recognise that no general conclusion is possible. Now and again we come across facts which group themselves with a certain degree of uniformity, but as we continue we find other equally important facts which group themselves with equal uniformity in another sense. The result produces compensation. Thus we find that the special liability of women to be affected by minor vital oscillations is balanced by a special resistance to more serious oscillations; that against the affectability of women we must place their disvulnerability. Again, the greater variability of men, while it produces many brilliant and startling phenomena, also produces a greater proportion of worthless or even harmful deviations, and the balance is thus restored with the more equable level of women. In the intellectual region men possess greater aptitude for dealing with the more remote and abstract interests of life; women have, at the least, as great an aptitude in dealing with the immediate practical interests of life. Women, it is true, remain nearer than men to the infantile state; but, on the other hand, men approach more nearly than women to the ape-like and senile state. The more clearly and broadly we investigate the phenomena the more emphatically these compensations stand out. It could scarcely be otherwise. A species in which the maternal half exhibited a general inferiority of vital functions could scarcely survive; still less could it attain the somewhat special and peculiar position which—however impartially we may look at the matter—can scarcely be denied to the human species.

From many groups of facts, it is true, one may conclude that the world, as it is naturally made, is a better world for women than for men. Nature, as Humboldt put it, has taken women under her special protection. But so far as this is a fact it is a zoo-logical and not a merely human fact. The female animal everywhere is more closely and for a longer period occupied with that process of reproduction which is Nature's main concern. This is, indeed, more than a zoological fact; it is a biological fact; among plants we find that the stamens soon fall away while the pistil remains. The female retains her youthfulness for the sake of possible offspring; we all exist for the sake of our possible offspring, but this final end of the individual is more obviously woven into the structure of women. The interests of women may therefore be said to be more closely identified with Nature's interests. Nature has made women more like children in order that they may better understand and care for children, and in the gift of children Nature has given to women a massive and sustained physiological joy to which there is nothing in men's lives to correspond. Nature has done her best to make women healthy and glad, and has on the whole been content to let men run some-what wild.

— Men have had their revenge on Nature and on her *protégée*. While women have been largely absorbed in that sphere of sexuality which is Nature's, men have roamed the earth, sharpening their aptitudes and energies in perpetual conflict with Nature. It has thus come about that the subjugation of Nature by Man has often practically involved the subjuga-tion, physical and mental, of women by men. The periods of society most favourable for women appear, judging from the experiences of the past, to be some-what primitive periods in which the militant tendency is not strongly marked. Very militant periods, and those so-called advanced periods in which the complicated and artificial products of the variational tendency of men are held in chief honour, are not favourable to the freedom and expansion of women. Greece and Rome, the favourite types of civilisation, bring before us emphatically masculine states of culture. The lust of power and knowledge, the re-search for artistic perfection, are usually masculine characters; and so most certainly are the suppression of natural emotion and the degradation of sexuality and maternity. Morgan has remarked that the fall of classic civilisation was due to the failure to develop women. But women never could have been brought into line with classic civilisation without transforming it entirely. As a matter of fact, when the feminine element at last came to the front with Christianity and the barbarians, classic civilisation went, and for a long time the masculine element in life also largely went—to reappear in monasteries, there to develop its most characteristic aberrations. The hope of our future civilisation lies in the development in equal freedom of both the masculine and feminine elements in life. The broader and more varied character of modern civilisation seems to render this more possible than did the narrow basis of classic civilisation, and there is much evidence around us that a twin move-ment of this kind is in progress. Still there is con-siderable advance yet to be made. So long as maternity under certain conditions is practically counted as a criminal act, it cannot be said that the feminine element in life has yet been restored to due honour.

It will be seen that a broad and general survey of the secondary sexual phenomena in humanity brings us at last into a very humble and conservative attitude before the facts of the natural world. It could scarcely be otherwise; the sexual adjustment has been proceeding for so vast a period of time, even if we only take Man and his immediate an-cestors into consideration, that the sexual balance has become as nearly perfect as possible, and every inaptitude is accompanied by some compensatory aptitude, even if it has not, as sometimes occurs, itself developed into an advantageous character. An open-eyed, child-like, yet patient study of the natural facts of life can only lead us to be reverent in the face of those facts.

This conclusion must not, however, be misunderstood. A cosmic conservatism does not necessarily involve a social conservatism. The wisdom of Man, working through a few centuries or in one corner of the earth, by no means necessarily corresponds to the wisdom of Nature, and may be in flat opposition to it. This is especially the case when the wisdom of Man merely means, as sometimes happens, the experience of our ancestors gained under other conditions, or merely the opinions of one class or one sex. Taking a broad view of the matter, it seems difficult to avoid the conclusion that it is safer to trust to the conservatism of Nature than to the conservatism of Man. We are not at liberty to introduce any artificial sexual barrier into social concerns. The respective fitness of men and of women for any kind of work or any kind of privilege can only be ascertained by actual open experiment ; and as the conditions for such experiment are never twice the same, it can never be positively affirmed that anything has been settled once and for all. When such experiment is successful, so much the better for the race ; when it is unsuccessful, the minority who have broken natural law alone suffer. An exaggerated anxiety lest natural law be overthrown is misplaced. The world is not so insecurely poised. We may preserve an attitude of entire equanimity in the face of social readjustment. Such readjustment is either the outcome of wholesome natural instinct, in which case our social structure will be strengthened and broadened, or it is not ; and if not, it is unlikely to become organically ingrained in the species.

Our investigation, therefore, shows us in what
state of mind we ought to approach the whole
problem ; it can scarcely be said that it gives us the
definite solution of definite problems. It is not on
that account fruitless. There is distinct advantage
in clearing away, so far as we can, the thick under-
growth of prepossession and superstition which
flourishes in the region we have traversed to a
greater extent than in any other region. It is
something to have asked the right question, and to
be set on the right road. It is something, also,
to realise that we may disregard the assertions, or
even the facts, of those who have not faced all the
difficulties that must be encountered. At the very
least it seems impossible to follow the paths we
have here traversed without gaining a more vivid
and tolerant insight into what for us must always
be the two most interesting beings in the world.

APPENDIX.

—◆◆—

PROFESSOR KARL PEARSON ON VARIATION IN MAN AND
WOMAN.

THE substance of the present Appendix has already appeared
in the *Popular Science Monthly* (Jan. 1903). As will be seen,
it is somewhat polemical in form. Personally I object to
controversy. I have always made it a rule not to take part in
it, and to ignore all attacks, devoting my energies to the task
of making my work as sound as I can. Hitherto I have
adhered to that rule. But there are times when it may be well
to break even a good rule. And I think that any one who will
take the trouble to follow the elaborate assault with which I
have here dealt will agree with me that it may fairly claim
the attention I have bestowed upon it. Moreover, Professor
Karl Pearson has elsewhere attained such notable results in
the application of mathematical procedures to biological data
and thereby achieved such wide fame, that—however alien the
ways of controversy may be to me—it would be both discourteous
and unwise to refuse to meet him with the kind of weapon he
prefers.

It may be said indeed that there are here involved even
wider issues than that of the very interesting question of the
comparative tendency for variations to appear in men and
women. Professor Pearson's paper serves admirably to evoke
many profitable reflections concerning the exact function of the
mathematician in biology, and concerning the still larger
question of the scientific spirit and in what that spirit does, and
in what it does not, consist. It would be out of place here to
more than touch upon these wider issues, and I can but com-
mend to the reader the perusal of Professor Pearson's paper for
the sake of such reflections as it may arouse.

In the course of his illuminating history of Greek thought,
in which special attention is given to its scientific aspects,

Gomperz has some observation on the psychology of the mathematician, and on the almost unavoidable defects of his qualities, aptly fitting the case we are now considering: "The mathematician tends inevitably to dogmatic judgments, a tendency which is doubtless due to the fact that his proofs must either be valid or must fail. He is a complete stranger to nuances of thought, to delicate intellectual refinement, to open-minded pliability." His attitude, he adds, when confronted with probabilities yet undemonstrated, "will depend in a remarkable degree on the accidents of temperament and training."

In the sciences of life we are confronted with a great multitude of various elements, and while we gradually learn to measure precisely some of these elements, the co-ordination and subordination of the various elements cannot be made a mathematical process, but involve a very wide knowledge of the complexity of vital phenomena, and at the same time very much of the same tact, intuition, and sound judgment that are required to deal successfully with the non-scientific affairs of life. It is a matter of weighing and sifting evidence of varying value, and often, on the surface, contradictory.

It is on account of this complexity of the biological sciences that the mathematician can give such valuable aid in weighing the precise value of particular factors. But it is on account of that very complexity that while the mathematician can give he cannot take. Mathematical methods can be employed in the biological sciences and the results embodied, but the biological sciences cannot at present be taken over by the mathematician as a branch of applied mechanics. The mathematician's tendency, which is indeed his virtue, to confine himself exclusively to the deductive consideration of the factor immediately before him, his ignorance of the extreme complexity of biological phenomena, cannot fail sometimes to lead him—as we shall see in the case here to be considered—to strain at gnats with elaborate precision while at the same time he is unconsciously swallowing a camel. A supercilious or intolerant attitude in one who approaches the problems of biology from the mathematical side,—may we not, indeed, say from any side?—is therefore altogether out of place. He who ventures to adopt it must not be surprised if he finds himself in a position not displeasing to those whom he attacks.

In Chapter XV. I have discussed this question of the variational tendency, dealing with it more comprehensively than had previously been done and drawing data from a much wider field, but finding no reason to differ fundamentally from the conclusions of Hunter, Burdach, and Darwin. I could not indeed assert that as regards man the greater variability of the male is "general," but all the facts available since Darwin's day indicated that a greater variability of the male occurred in the majority of the groups of data investigated. And when I considered that this greater organic variational tendency of men is apparently true of psychic variations also—of genius, of idiocy and other mental anomalies having an organic basis—it seemed to me that in the greater variational tendency of man we are in the presence of a fact that has social and practical consequences of the widest significance, a fact which has affected the whole of our human civilisation. Although the greater variational tendency of men is balanced by the more equable level of women, we have to recognise that the existence of the exceptional men who have largely created the lines of our progress is based on natural law. It is a conclusion which does not yet appear to me to be fundamentally affected.

There was, however, one important omission in my statement of this question, and I wish to emphasise the importance of the omission because its significance will subsequently become apparent to the reader. I said little or nothing as to the variability of men and women in *size*, either as regards total stature and weight, or the dimensions of parts of the body. The reason for that omission is clearly indicated in various parts of the volume, and we shall encounter it again in due course.[1]

In 1897, in a volume of miscellaneous essays entitled *The Chances of Death*, Professor Karl Pearson published a lengthy paper entitled "Variation in Man and Woman." This writer started with the assertion that in *Man and Woman* I had "done much to perpetuate some of the worst of the pseudo-scientific superstitions, notably that of the greater variability of the male human being," and that it is the object of his essay "to lay the axe to the root of this pseudo-scientific superstition." In fact, as he is careful to tell us at frequent intervals, before he himself entered the field (a field, be it remembered, occupied by some of the world's greatest biologists) all was "dogma," "superstition," "nearly all partisan," at the best "quite unproven." I am inclined to think that these terms, which spring so easily to Mr. Pearson's pen, are automatic reminiscences of the ancient controversies he has waged with theologians and metaphysicians. They are certainly a little out of place on the present occasion.

In selecting the material for his demonstration, Professor Pearson tells us, he sought to eliminate all those "organs or characteristics which are themselves characteristic of sex,"

---

[1] I did not consider that such evidence must be absolutely rejected—I admitted it in one or two cases—but simply that as it was liable to a discount of unknown extent it could not be placed in the first rank of evidence.

such being, *e.g.*, in his opinion, gout and colour-blindness; he also threw aside all variations which can be regarded as "pathological," on the hypothetical ground that such "pathological" variations may have a totally different sexual distribution from "normal" variations. He decided that size is the best criterion of variability. As to how a "variation" may be defined, Professor Pearson makes no critical inquiry, though such inquiry would very seriously have modified his final conclusions.[1]

"What we have to do," he states, "is to take healthy normal populations of men and women, and in these populations measure the size of organs which do not appear to be secondary sexual characters, or from which the sexual character can be eliminated by dealing solely with ratios." Various kinds of size are therefore selected for treatment, such as that of the skull, chiefly as regards its capacity and length-breadth index, stature, span, chest-girth, weight of body and of various internal organs, etc., all these, it is observed, being various aspects of the one factor of size. It is shown by careful treatment of the available data—the so-called coefficient of variation being accepted as a possible or indeed probable measure of significant variation—that, as far as there is any difference at all, women are, on the whole, slightly more variable than men. Having reached this result, the author leaps bravely to the conclusion, that "accordingly, the principle that man is more variable than woman must be put on one side as a pseudo-scientific superstition."

If a reply has so far not been forthcoming from the writer against whom this elaborate paper was chiefly directed, this has not been either because I admitted the justice of its conclusions, or complacently accepted a damnation to which I had been consigned in very excellent company. The subject lay only on the outskirts of my own field; I could claim no originality in it; all that I had done was to sift and bring to a focus data which had hitherto been scattered, and to show their significance. At the same time I again placed the subject on my *agenda* paper for reconsideration. In the meanwhile it scarcely appeared that Mr. Pearson's arguments met with much acceptance, even among his own friends.[2]

[1] It is true, indeed, that Mr. Pearson remarks that the question "What are the most suitable organs or characteristics for measuring the relative variability of man and woman?" "really involves a definition of variability." But he adds that "the definition given may be so vague as to beg off-hand the solution of the problem we propose to discuss." That suspicion, as we shall see, is not altogether unjustified.

[2] Professor Pearson, following Galton (*Nature*, 10th May 1894), has endeavoured to find an opponent of the greater variational tendency of men in Tennyson, who wrote:

Almost the only attempt to consider them, indeed, which I have met is in a review of *The Chances of Death* by Professor W. F. R. Weldon, in *Natural Science*. This sympathetic critic, with a biologist's instincts, clearly felt that there was something wrong with Mr. Pearson's triumphant demonstration, although as the subject lay outside his own department he was not able to indicate the chief flaws.

There is indeed one initial flaw in Professor Pearson's argument to which Professor Weldon called attention; it could scarcely fail to attract the notice of a biologist. We are told that we must put aside "characteristics which are themselves characteristics of sex," like gout and colour-blindness, since, "without being confined to one sex," they are yet peculiarly frequent in one sex. Thus, we see, characteristics not confined to one sex may yet be characteristic of one sex, and when we seek to find what characters are more frequent in one sex than in the other, we must carefully leave out of account all these characters which are most clearly more frequent in one sex than in the other. Professor Pearson thus sets out with an initial confusion which is never cleared up. His object, he tells us, is to seek such degrees of variability as are "secondary sexual characters of human beings," and we infer from the course of his argument that the desired characters, while not confined to one sex, may yet be peculiarly frequent in one sex. *Yet these are precisely the group of characters ruled inadmissible at the outset!* No definition of secondary sexual characters is anywhere given, or on such premises could be given.

Professor Pearson seems to assume that the conception of a secondary sexual character is too obvious to need definition. As a matter of fact there is considerable difference of opinion. Since Hunter first spoke of the "secondary properties of sex," which he regarded as dependent on the primary, only developing at puberty, and principally, though not entirely, confined to the male, the conception has very much changed; there has been a tendency to throw all sorts of miscellaneous sexual differences into the category. I have suggested that it would be convenient to introduce a group of "tertiary" sexual char-

---

"For men at most differ as heaven and earth,
But women, worst and best, as heaven and hell."

But while Mr. Galton merely used these lines, in a perfectly legitimate manner, to illustrate a tendency to variation in morals, Mr. Pearson seeks to give them a physical meaning which was certainly far from the poet's mind. In a chapter of the present work on the affectability of woman I had already pointed out that the "heaven and hell" of woman are both aspects of her greater affectability; not only does one woman differ from another as "heaven and hell," but the *same* woman may so vary at different times.

acters, keeping the term "secondary" to its original sense and reserving as "tertiary" all those minor differences that are not obvious, which therefore can have no direct influence on mating, and only exist as averages; such are the composition of the blood and the shape of the bones.[1]

It is difficult to correct all the errors and confusions which Professor Pearson falls into at this point. He remarks that we must not regard the greater prevalence of idiocy among men as evidence of greater male variability, unless we count on the other side the greater prevalence of insanity among women. The error here is double. As a matter of fact, although in England and Wales during recent years the incidence of insanity has been as great on women as on men,[2] nearly everywhere else it is markedly greater in the case of men. Indeed even in England and Wales, at the present time, if we may trust the Commissioners in Lunacy in their annual report for 1902, the incidence of insanity as indicated by first admissions to asylums is, *in ratio to the male population*, still slightly greater in the case of men. Professor Pearson has been misled by the greater accumulation of females in asylums, failing to take into consideration the greater longevity of women, which among the insane is specially marked.[3] But even if the facts had been as stated by Professor Pearson, his inference would still have been wrong; idiocy is mainly a congenital condition and therefore a fairly good test of organic variational tendency; insanity, though usually on a hereditary basis, is invariably an acquired condi-

---

[1] Professor Waldeyer, who has done me the honour of critically examining some of the main points in my book (in the form of an address at one of the annual meetings of the German Anthropological Society) is inclined to doubt the value of this distinction since there is no clear line of demarcation between secondary and tertiary characters. That, however, I had myself pointed out, and the objection cannot logically be held by any one who accepts secondary sexual characters and recognises that they merge into the primary. There are many natural groups which, as Galton has well said, have nuclei but no outlines. More recently the conception of tertiary sexual characters in a sense practically the same as that in which I use it has been adopted by a leading French anthropologist, Dr. Papillault (*e.g.*, "L'Homme Moyen à Paris," *Bull. Soc. d'Anth.*, 1902).

[2] It so happens that I was the first to call attention to the fact that towards the end of the last century the number of women admitted to asylums in England and Wales had for the first time begun to exceed the number of men. (Art. "Influence of Sex on Insanity," in Tuke's *Dictionary of Psychological Medicine.*)

[3] How serious this fallacy is may be indicated by an illustration that chances to come to hand almost as I write. I read in a South American medical journal that in the Asylum of Santiago in Chili on the 1st of January 1901, there were 560 men and 655 women, but during the year 539 men were admitted and only 351 women.

tion, dependent on all sorts of environmental influences, so that it cannot possibly furnish an equally fundamental test. Colour-blindness, Mr. Pearson also tells us, is a peculiarly male "disease," and must not be used as an argument for greater variability in men unless we use the prevalence of cancer of the breast in women on the other side. Again there is a double error; not only is a congenital anomaly improperly compared to an acquired disease, but a gland like the breast, which is only functional in one sex, is paired off with an organ like the eye, which is equally functional in both sexes. The prevalence of gout among men is, again, paired off against the prevalence of hysteria among women. Here the error is still more complex. Not only is gout not a truly congenital condition, though, like insanity, it frequently has a hereditary basis, but if we take into account conditions of "suppressed" gout it is by no means more prevalent in men than in women, and even if we do not take such conditions into account, it is still not possible to pair off gout against hysteria, since, although in most countries and social classes hysteria is more prevalent in women, in others (as, according to some authorities, among the lower classes in France) it is found more prevalent in men. But it would be tedious to explore further this confused jungle of misstatements.

From the point of view of sexual differences in variational tendency it is not necessary to exclude rigidly either "tertiary," "secondary," or even "primary" sexual characters, provided we are careful to avoid fallacies which are fairly obvious, and do not compare organs and characters which are not truly comparable. Even secondary sexual characters which are almost or entirely confined to one sex may properly be allowed a certain amount of weight as evidence, especially if we grant that such characters are merely the perpetuation of congenital variations. If, therefore, as is generally agreed, such characters more often occur in males, that fact is a presumption on the side of a greater male variational tendency which there is no reason entirely to ignore. It is not conclusive, but it must receive its due weight. To assume, with Professor Pearson, that a variation has no variational significance because it occurs often in one sex and seldom in the other[1] seems altogether unwarrantable and even absurd.

If, however, Professor Pearson's attempt to discriminate between different kinds of sexual characters from the point of view of sexual variability fails to work out, and is in any case unnecessary, at another point he falls into the opposite

[1] In the case of ordinary gout, which Professor Pearson regards as typical of the tests to be excluded, opinions differ considerably as to sexual liability; according to one leading authority it is 68 men to 12 women.

mistake of making no attempt to discriminate where discrimination is of the first importance. As we have already incidentally seen, it seems to him to be of no importance whether the variational tendency is tested by variations having an organic congenital base, or by variations which may be merely due to environmental influences during life.[1] To him they are all alike "variations," and the most important are those that can most conveniently be caught in the mathematical net. Indeed, he goes further than this. He actually discriminates *against* the more organic and fundamental kinds of variation. It seems to him "erroneous" to take into account congenital abnormalities of any kind when we wish to test the relative variability of the sexes. In determining the variational tendencies of the sexes we must leave out of account the majority of variations!

The ground on which Professor Pearson rejects abnormalities is that they are "pathological," and that it is conceivable that pathological variation might be greater and normal variation less in the same sex.[2] He believes that in regarding the "normal" and the "abnormal" as two altogether different and possibly opposed groups of phenomena he is warranted by "current medical science."

This is very far indeed from being the case. If Professor Pearson means that he has consulted his family doctor on the point, I can well believe that he has received confirmation of his view, for it is quite true that in ordinary clinical work the physician does make such a distinction; it is practically convenient. But the practical convenience of the physician has nothing to do with the scientific question. The problem before us is a specifically pathological problem, and for its elucidation we have to consult the pathologist and not the ordinary medical practitioner. I had thought it sufficient to quote the remark of the greatest of pathologists, Virchow, to the effect that every deviation from the parental type has its foundation in a pathological accident—a statement which Professor Pearson, on the strength of what is really a verbal quibble, contemptuously puts aside as "meaningless." We ought not to say "the parental type," he tells us, we ought to say "a type lying between the parental type and the race type": let us say it, and the state-

---

[1] It is scarcely necessary to remark that the two groups cannot be absolutely separated.

[2] This conception, Professor Pearson remarks, seems never to have occurred to me. In that shape, happily, it has not. But in *Man and Woman* and elsewhere I have repeatedly called attention to the fact that, as regards various psychic and nervous conditions, while gross variations are more frequent in men, minor variations are sometimes more common in women. This seems to cover whatever truth there may be in Professor Pearson's supposition.

ment remains substantially the same so far as the question before us is concerned.[1]

Virchow is by no means the only pathologist of high authority who has distinctly laid down this principle. Thus, as Ballantyne points out,—when remarking that the ancient belief, held even by Simpson, that anomalies and malformations are due to disease, has been supplemented by modern research,—Mathias Duval has emphatically declared that it is not to be thought that the malformation of any part is a result of disease of that part.[2]

Even, however, if we go back to the time of Simpson, and earlier, we find that Meckel—who is sometimes regarded as one of the founders of the study of variations—clearly recognised that the simplest anomalies and varieties pass gradually into monstrosities, and that the same laws apply to both.[3]

Indeed so did Hunter in the previous century. "Every deviation," he wrote at the outset of his almost epoch-marking "Account of an Extraordinary Pheasant," "may not improperly be called monstrous," so that "the varieties of monsters will be almost infinite."

The tendency of scientific pathology is at once to push the frontiers of the normal into regions popularly regarded as belonging to disease, and at the same time, when actual disease comes into question, to refuse to admit that any new laws are brought into operation. "Between any form of disease and health," one of the founders of modern pathology declared a quarter of a century ago, "there are only differences of degree.

[1] Virchow repeatedly emphasised the statement in question, and by no means always in the form that offends Professor Pearson. Thus he remarked in 1894, at the annual meeting of the German Anthropological Society, that whenever "the physiological norm hitherto subsisting is changed" we are in the presence of an anomaly, and that in this sense every departure from the norm is a pathological event, though it is not a disease and may not be harmful, may even be advantageous. In what was perhaps his last utterance on the subject (*Zeitschrift für Ethnologie*, 1901, p. 213) he repeated that pathology as well as physiology is an essential factor in the development of the human race. Pathologists will, I know, agree with me that a conviction of the essential unity of physiology and pathology lay at the foundation of the pathological revolution which Virchow effected.

[2] With this result Dr. Ballantyne—who may be said to be the chief British authority on pathology in its antenatal aspects—in the main concurs. He even goes so far as to assert (*Manual of Antenatal Pathology*, 1902, p. 35) that natural birth in its effects on the child may almost be regarded as a pathological process; "it is very certain that the same amount of distortion of parts, occurring at a later period of life, would be termed pathological."

[3] *Handbuch der pathologischen Anatomie*, 1812, vol. i. p. 9.

No disease is anything more than an exaggeration or disproportion or disharmony of normal phenomena."[1] The notion that disease and health are distinct principles or entities, Bernard regarded as a sort of idea belonging to the medical lumber room. These conceptions have been brilliantly developed in the work of recent pathologists.[2]

And if it is argued that a mathematician cannot be supposed familiar with the principles of pathology, it must be replied that Mr. Pearson has here entered a field that touches the very essence of these principles, and, further, that the principle in question is so simple and elementary that it may already be said to have entered general culture. I take up the latest volume of Nietzsche's works,[3]—written more than ten years ago, though only now published,—and read: "The value of all morbid conditions is that they show us in magnified form certain conditions that are normal, but in the normal condition not easily visible. *Health* and *Disease* are not essentially different, as the old physicians and some modern practitioners have believed. To regard them as distinct principles struggling for the living organism is foolish nonsense and chatter."

On the whole, then, there is no reason for rejecting abnormalities when we are considering the relative variational tendencies of men and women. To the mathematical mind— Professor Pearson forces us to admit—it is possible to conceive that the laws of pathology may reverse the laws of physiology, but such a conception the biologist regards as absurd.

More than this must, however, be said. Not only can we not leave anomalies out of account in dealing with this question, but it is precisely the anomalies which furnish us with the most reliable evidence. The word "abnormality" is apt to mislead, and Professor Pearson somewhat prejudices the matter in unscientific ears by insisting on its use. It is not a scientific term ; the so-called anomaly is not abnormal in the sense that it is morbid ; it is only exceptional. It merely indicates the extreme swings of a pendulum whose more frequent oscillations are popularly regarded as "normal." What is commonly termed an "anomaly" might really be regarded as the "variation" *par excellence*.

Such an assertion would be by no means arbitrary. It does

---

[1] Claude Bernard, *Leçons sur la chaleur animale* (19th Lesson), 1875.

[2] To those who may wish to gain an attractive insight into modern conceptions of pathology—according to which disease is a relative term and its study a branch of biology—I would recommend Professor Woods Hutchinson's highly suggestive *Studies in Human and Comparative Pathology* (1901).

[3] *Der Wille zur Macht*, Werke, Bd. xv.

in fact correspond with the usage of most of the writers who have investigated this matter until the present day, and it is possible to justify such usage. If—to return to the image of the pendulum—we wish to find out whether the male or female pendulum swings farthest, we must so far as possible let them swing freely; the more they are restrained by external forces the less the significance of the results we reach. Now the congenital "anomalies" are precisely the kind of variation that most nearly corresponds to the free swing of the pendulum. It is true that there is no absolute distinction between the initial energy and the subsequent modifying influences, but it is equally true that if we wish to measure and compare the aboriginal energies of the male and female organisms, we must so far as possible disregard these characters which are very considerably influenced by late modifying forces.

Professor Pearson has, however, chosen, as a final and crucial test of the variational tendency in men and women, the single point of difference in size, chiefly in adults. That is to say, he has selected, as a final and unimpeachable test, one of the most fragile of distinctions, a distinction that has been exposed to a life-time of modifying influences.

Even if we admit that size at birth constitutes a sound test— and this cannot be admitted without qualification, as we shall soon see—it is evident that the comparative variation of the sexes in this respect is liable to be affected by environmental circumstances as age increases. The influences of life differently affecting and exercising the two sexes, the influence of death probably exerting an unequal selective influence—both alike must be allowed for if this kind of evidence is to be regarded as a test of the first rank of importance.[1] Otherwise we are not dealing with the incidence of variations at all, but with the elimination of variations — an altogether different matter. Professor Pearson himself gradually awakes to a realisation of this fact as he proceeds with his task, and remarks at last that he strongly suspects that the slightly greater variability of woman which his results show is mainly due to a relatively less severe struggle for existence! Probably he is right, but if so his whole argument falls to the ground. The question of the organic variational tendencies of men and women remains untouched; we have been introduced instead to a problem in selection. So true is it that, as Bacon said, the half of know-ledge lies in asking the right question.

We are bound to suppose that when Professor Pearson set

---

[1] It is scarcely necessary to remind the reader that the influences of the environment are limited by inherited aptitude. This limitation is very clearly pointed out by Galton, *Hereditary Genius* (2nd ed.), pp. 12-14, 40.

out he intended to use the term "variation" in the same sense as his predecessors had used it,—for otherwise his results could not validly be opposed to theirs,—but it would appear that as he went on, by an unconscious process of auto-suggestion, he insensibly glided into a familiar field.

It may seem unnecessary to pursue Professor Pearson any further. It is sufficiently clear that the inquiry he has carried out, however valuable it may be in other respects, has no decisive bearing on the question he undertook to answer, and can have no very damaging effect on the writers he attacks. But there is considerable interest in driving the point of the discussion still further home.

It may be agreed that since differences in size are probably affected by the influences of life and death to a considerable extent, and perhaps unequally eliminated in the two sexes, they do not form a reliable guide to the sexual incidence of variations. But, it may be argued, this cannot affect measurements made at birth, and we must therefore accept the validity of those of Professor Pearson's measurements which concern the infant at birth. Here, however, we encounter a fact which is of the first importance in its bearing on our subject : the elimination of variations in size has already begun at birth, and there is reason to suppose that that elimination unequally affects males and females. This was duly allowed for in *Man and Woman*, but there is no hint of it throughout Professor Pearson's long paper. He does not dispute this influence, nor does he realise that until he has disputed it his conclusions cannot be brought to bear against mine. Professor Pearson's earlier statistical excursions into the biological field were chiefly concerned with crabs ; in passing from crabs to human beings he failed to allow for the fact that human beings do not come into the world under the same conditions. This failure—pardonable as it is in one not at home in the obstetrical field—has profoundly affected the validity of his cherished criterion of sex variability, in so far as it is used against his predecessors.

Every child who is born into the world undergoes a severe ordeal due largely to the limited elasticity of the bony pelvic ring through which it has to pass. Probably as a result of this, a certain proportion perish as they enter the world or very shortly after. Among the number thus eliminated there appears to be a very considerable proportion of the largest infants. It is doubtless because male infants tend to be larger than female infants that males suffer most at and shortly after birth. This appears to be the rule everywhere.[1]

---

[1] For the exact proportion of male to female still-born children in most civilised countries, see *e.g.* Ploss, *Das Weib*, 7th edition, 1901, vol. i. p. 336.

So far as I am aware, the first attempt to explain this matter scientifically was made in 1786 by an English doctor named Clarke, physician to the Lying-in Hospital at Dublin.[1] By weighing and measuring 120 new-born infants of both sexes he found that there was a marked tendency for the males to be larger than the females. "Hence appears," as he is pleased to put it, "the merciful dispensations of Providence towards the female sex, for when deviations from the medium standard occur it is remarkable that they are much more frequently below than above this standard." He considered that the greater mortality of males at and shortly after birth is largely due to the injuries to the head occurring at birth, but also that, since the males are larger and therefore make from the first a larger demand on the nutritive capacity of the mother, they are more likely to suffer from any defect of the mother in this respect. The problem and its possible and probable explanations were thus clearly stated more than a century ago.

As often happens with pioneers, Clarke's little paper was forgotten, and for more than half a century, although a number of workers brought extensive contributions of new data, their attitude was frequently illogical or one-sided, and the progress of scientific knowledge was not great. In 1844 Simpson published a well-known study which brought together a mass of evidence bearing more or less on the question before us.[2] He showed that in male births the mothers suffered excessively as well as the infants ; he refused to admit that the greater mortality of males at and shortly after birth could be due to any other cause than the generally recognised larger size of the male head (mainly on the ground that fœtal deaths up to birth are fairly apportioned to the two sexes),[3] and concluded that the greater size of the male head is the cause of a vast annual mortality. A number of later obstetrical inquirers furnished additional contributions to the matter, at one point or another, though not always agreeing that so great a mortality could be

[1] Joseph Clarke, "Observations on some Causes of the Excess of the Mortality of Males above that of Females," *Philosophical Transactions*, 1786. It may be said here that the very first attempt to weigh and measure infants accurately had only been made not so many years previously, by Roederer, in 1753.

[2] J. Y. Simpson, "On the Sex of the Child as a Cause of Difficulty and Danger in Human Parturition," *Obstetric Memoirs*, vol. i. pp. 394 *et seq.*

[3] On this point subsequent investigators have not always confirmed Simpson, some, indeed, finding an enormous preponderance of males among prematurely expelled fœtuses. See *e.g.* Rauber's valuable work, *Der Ueberschuss an Knabengeburten und seine Biologische Bedeutung*, 1900, pp. 140-144.

due to a difference of size which seemed so small.[1]   One authority, indeed, roundly declared that the belief in the larger size of the male head was merely "a popular prejudice"; this led to fresh measurements, and in this field Stadtfeldt of Copenhagen received credit which really belonged to Clarke of Dublin. Veit showed that even at equal weights more boys than girls die at birth, but, on the other hand, according to Pfannkuch's results, even at equal weights boys' heads are larger than girls'.[2]   In any case it certainly seemed probable that the larger size of the male child's head was an important factor in this mortality, and when at length the question began to attract the attention of statistical anthropologists this conclusion was confirmed.   The Anthropometric Committee of the British Association, presided over by Mr. Francis Galton, in its final report in 1883 stated its belief that "it would appear that the physical (and most probably the mental) proportions of a race, and their uniformity within certain limits, are largely dependent on the size of the female pelvis, which acts as a gauge, as it were, of the race, and eliminates the largest infants, especially those with large heads (and presumably more brains), by preventing their survival at birth."[3]

It must be added, however, that no direct and final demonstration has been brought forward of the tendency to the elimination of the males (or even infants independently of sex) of the greatest weight or those having the largest heads.   For this we require to compare male and female stillborn infants at full term, with those who are born living and which subsequently survived for at least a week (a longer period would be more desirable but difficult to secure).   Such measurements are not to be found in medical literature, so far as I can discover ; at the most we find averages, which are meaningless from the present point of view.[4]   I applied to obstetrical and

---

[1] They usually relied on averages which are here of little significance. Thus Olshausen measured the diameter of 1000 skulls and found the average very minutely greater in the boys.   We should expect this if males are more variable than females ; we need to know the number of cases for each different degree of size.

[2] *Arch. f. Gynäk.*, Bd. iv. p. 297.

[3] It is of some interest to point out that while it is probable that the pressure of the pelvic ring thus tends to eliminate the largest males, on the other hand, so far as psychic and nervous character are concerned, there is reason to suppose that this pressure sometimes exerts a life-long influence in increasing male variation.   See *e.g.* Sir J. Crichton-Browne, *West Riding Asylum Reports*, vol. i., 1871.

[4] It is noteworthy, however, that Boyd's data (*Phil. Trans.*, 1861) showed that the still-born male infant at full term is relatively larger compared to the still-born female infant than is the living male infant compared to the living female infant.   The size of the males is reduced to a greater extent by the difficulties of birth than is the size of the females.

anatomical authorities in various countries and received a number of interesting letters and data, including series of entries from the registers of maternity hospitals. But none of the series so far received contains a sufficient number of still-born children. So far as they go, they are confirmatory of the belief that it is more especially the large children that are eliminated by the selection of birth. The largest series (with 60 stillborn male babies and 50 stillborn females), for which I am indebted to Dr. C. M. Green, of the Boston Lying-in Hospital, shows that among the stillborn of either sex the range of variation is greater than among the living of the same sex, the absolute range of variation being not only greater as compared with the living babies of the same sex, but there being a greater piling up at each end in the case of the stillborn. The data do not suffice to indicate that there is a greater mortality of the largest sized males than of the largest sized females, when we compare the stillborn with the living of the same sex and weight. Another series, more elaborate in its details but still smaller in number as regards the stillborn—for which I am indebted to Professor Whitridge Williams, of John Hopkins' Hospital—leads to a similarly incomplete conclusion.[1]

There is, however, another test which, while it can by no means be put forward as having any statistical validity, yet furnishes a highly significant indication in this matter. Just as on the psychic side certain very rare individuals appear in the world whose intellectual capacity enormously excels that of their fellows, so, corresponding to "genius," we have on the physical side certain equally rare individuals who at birth enormously excel their fellows in physical size, while yet re-maining normal and well proportioned. Now, we may ask, do these individuals possessing congenital physical "genius" resemble persons of psychic genius in being more often male than female? Ordinary statistics are not here available, for these cases are so rare that they very seldom fall into an ordinary series. Smellie found one child weighing over 13 pounds in 8000 cases; in France, a child of 12 pounds was only found in 20,000 cases.[2] As a child of even 9 pounds is

[1] It seems unnecessary to deal with this point more in detail here, not only because of the lack of sufficient data at present, but because the establishment of this point is by no means necessary for the defence of my position against Professor Pearson's attack.

[2] It must also be said that (as in the case of psychic genius) it is among the well-to-do classes that these very large infants are most usually found, not only because the parents tend to be larger among these classes, but because, as has lately been shown (see *e.g.* Bachi-mont, *Documents pour servir à l'Histoire de la Puériculture intra-utérine*, Thèse de Paris, 1898), other things being equal, women who rest during pregnancy tend to have larger children.

generally considered large, it is clear that when we get beyond
13 pounds we reach a point at which the average difference
between males and females is trifling, so that there is almost as
great a chance of females as of males reaching the extremely
large weights. The only practicable way of obtaining information concerning these cases lay in collecting the scattered
records. I have collected all that I can find in medical
journals of standing, chiefly English, during the past half
century, being aided by the references in Neale's *Medical
Digest*. I have only noted the cases that appear to have been
healthy and well developed and weighed over 13 pounds at
birth. One unexpected difficulty I encountered : in many
cases, even when numerous measurements were given, no
reference was made to sex. While such cases were necessarily
rejected, I may say that I think it probable that most, and
perhaps all, of these rejected cases were males ; this was so in
the only case in which, by writing to the medical reporter
immediately on publication, I was able to repair the omission ;
the medical mind seems to share in some degree the instinctive
conviction that the typical human being is a male, and that in
the case of males it is unnecessary to make any reference to
sex. My cases were thus reduced to 21. Of these there were
only 3 females to 18 males. The females all died at birth, as
well as about half the males. However rough this method of
estimation may be, it is highly improbable that any more
methodical inquiry on children of this size would entirely
reverse so large a preponderance of males.[1]

Such a result, it will be seen, while it amply confirms the
conclusion that even in size the male shows the greater variational tendency, cannot be considered as absolute proof that
there exists a selection at birth which in its operation tends to
the destruction of the larger male children either at the moment of
birth or during the succeeding days and weeks, though it renders
such selection probable. This element of doubt, however, by no
means renders Professor Pearson's attack on my position any
stronger. It is sufficient to show that for more than a century
past evidence has accumulated which indicates that the group
of data on which Professor Pearson solely and absolutely relies
for the foundation of his argument is modified by an influence
which renders it tainted for such a purpose. In view of this
circumstance, and of the fact that I had rejected this group of

[1] I have since met with a discussion of this question from the obstetrical standpoint (H. Dubois, *Les Gros Enfants au Point de vue Obsté-
rical*, Thèse de Paris, 1897) which independently confirms my results.
At weights of over 7000 grms. Dubois found nine boys to three girls.
Among only moderately large infants there was no such excess of males;
but of the three heaviest babies of all only one was a girl, and she was
the least heavy of the three.

evidence on these grounds, the *onus probandi* clearly rested with Professor Pearson. In other words, he had to show either that male children are not larger than female children at birth, or else that large children do not suffer more than smaller children in passing through the maternal pelvis. The fact that Professor Pearson gives no indication that he had realised the necessity of this preliminary step is sufficient proof that he was not adequately equipped for the task he has undertaken.

We now come to a point which is not the less interesting for being entirely hidden from Mr. Pearson. It has been seen that the selection exercised by the pelvis to the detriment of the larger male children is not absolutely proved. But if for the moment we assume that it exists, what are the phenomena that we should expect to find, as regards size, among the survivors? Obviously, a more or less diminished sexual difference during life, *with a maximum of sexual difference immediately after birth*.[1] Now this is exactly what Professor Pearson found! " Summing up in general our conclusions for weight," he states, " it would appear that, except at birth, man is not more variable than woman." The very great significance of this exception, as affecting any argument on these premises brought against the position maintained in *Man and Woman*, he undoubtedly failed to see. Still the exception evidently puzzled him. He accumulated series of data on the subject, some of them very extensive. But the conclusion remained on the whole unaffected. Thus we see that our author, in all innocence, supplies a valuable piece of proof in favour of that very position which he imagines that he is upsetting! If this is the way that the axe is to be laid to the root of "pseudo-scientific superstitions " they will certainly continue to flourish exceedingly.[2]

[1] In a large number of infants who have survived birth, death follows later as a result of the processes of birth. In children dying at or soon after birth, as a result of undue pressure, hemorrhages or congestions are nearly always found in the internal organs, but they are not of necessity immediately fatal. It is well known that the number of deaths in infancy is everywhere very large. In England and Wales a fifth of all deaths registered occur within the first year of life. During the first three months of life the excess of mortality among males is 26 per cent. (*Registrar General's Report for 1896*). In Italy, where careful statistical methods are adopted, it is found (1897) that nearly a sixth of the infants born within a year die in the first month of life. With reference to the unduly large proportion of boys among these infantile deaths, see *e.g.* Rauber, *Der Ueberschuss an Knabengeburten*, pp. 153-159.

[2] In proof that it does so flourish, notwithstanding Professor Pearson's ponderous attack, it may suffice to give one instance. Professor Schwalbe, certainly one of the greatest among living anatomists and the most searching of investigators into human varia-

We have now reached the climax of Professor Pearson's argument. It is from this giddy height that he surveys with contempt those foolish persons who still believe that the variational tendency is greater in men than in women, and nothing further remains to be said. If, instead of hastening to execute a war-dance on what he imagined was the body of a prostrate foe, Professor Pearson had pointed out, as he would have been quite warranted in doing, that his conclusions, so far as they rested on a definite basis of fact, confirmed the thesis maintained by Darwin and more fully enforced in *Man and Woman*, his position would have been unimpeachable. If, again, he had refrained altogether from attempting to interpret his own data, —a task for which, it is obvious, he was singularly ill-prepared, —and had put them forth simply as a study in natural selection,—which is what they really are,—his position would, again, have been altogether justifiable. But as the matter stands he has enmeshed himself in a tangle of misapprehensions, confusions, and errors from which it must be very difficult to extricate him.

It may be well to summarise briefly the main points set forth in the foregoing pages.

1. In opposition to the doctrine of Darwin, more fully set forth in my *Man and Woman*, that the variational tendency is, on the whole, more marked in men than in women, Professor Pearson resolved to show that this is one of "the worst of the pseudo-scientific superstitions."

2. Unfortunately, however, it never occurred to him to define what he meant by "variation," nor to ascertain what the writers whom he was opposing meant by the term.[1] A very little consideration shows that a typical variation, in what may fairly be called its classic sense, is a congenital organic character *on which selection works*, while, as understood by Professor Pearson, though without definite statement, a typical variation is a character—of almost any kind, occurring at any period of life—*produced by selection*. "To the biometrician," Professor Pearson has recently stated, "variation is a quantity determined by the class or group without reference to its ancestry." That

tion, after briefly summarising his own observations on this point, concludes :—" In general I come with Havelock Ellis to the result that women vary within a narrower range than men " (Presidential address, German Anatomical Society, *Verhandl. Anat. Gesell.*, 1898). It is indeed difficult (I do not say impossible) to find any authorities who come to any other result.

[1] It is somewhat unusual, Professor Pearson has remarked in another controversial paper (*Biometrika*, April 1902, p. 323), "in a discussion to give entirely different meanings to the terms originally used, and leave your adversary to find out with what significance you may be using them." It seems to occur sometimes, however.

is to say, it need not be organic or congenital, and it must usually be modified, and sometimes entirely produced, by its environment. This definition may be better than the more classical conception of a variation. But it is certainly very different. To suppose that conclusions reached concerning this kind of variation can be used to overthrow conclusions reached concerning the other kind is obviously unreasonable.

3. Having silently adopted this conception of a variation, Professor Pearson proceeds to inquire what "different degrees of variability are secondary sexual characters" and not "characteristics which are themselves characteristics of sex"; and is hereby led into various eccentricities of assertion which it is unnecessary to recapitulate. "Secondary sexual characters" remain, in his hands, like variation, undefined.

4. All "abnormalities" are added to the material rejected as unsuitable for investigation, on the ground that they are "pathological." It has been easy to show that this notion cannot be maintained, and that in his pious horror of "pseudo-scientific superstitions" Professor Pearson here lays himself open to retort. Anomalies are not pathological, except in the sense of Virchow, who regarded pathology as simply the science of anomalies. Moreover, scientific pathologists do not admit that even disease can be regarded as involving any new or different laws. Morbid as well as normal phenomena alike furnish proper material, if intelligently used, for the investigation of this question.

5. Professor Pearson decides that differences in size furnish the best measure of the variability of the sexes. In reaching this decision he makes no reference to the fact that the probabilities accumulated during a century tended to discredit this group of evidence for the purposes he had in view.

6. If, however, we put aside those probabilities which tend to render this evidence tainted, so far as the object of Professor Pearson's special argument is concerned, we still find that the results he reaches are precisely the results we should expect if the position he assails is sound. That is to say that at birth, before the results of the assumed selective action of the pelvis have yet been fully shown, there is greater variability of the males, so far as size is concerned, while later, as a result of that selection, there is a tendency to equality in sexual variability.

7. The net outcome of Professor Pearson's paper is thus found to be a confirmation of that very doctrine of the greater variational tendency of the male which he set out to prove to be "either a dogma or a superstition."

It may be as well to state, finally, that nothing I have said can be construed as an attempt to disparage those "biometrical" methods of advancing biology of which Professor Pearson is to-day the most brilliant and conspicuous champion. I am not competent to judge of the mathematical validity of such methods, but so far as I am able to follow them I gladly recognise that they constitute a very valuable instrument for biological progress. I say nothing against the instrument: I merely point out that, on this occasion, the results obtained by its application have been wrongly interpreted.[1]

[1] "A recent criticism by Mr. Havelock Ellis of my view that there is no preponderating variability of man over woman seems to need no reply" (we read in *Biometrika*, vol. ii., 1903, p. 372), "for the author does not appear to understand what weight is to be given to scientific evidence as compared with vague generalities." No one can realise more clearly than I do that the evidence I have had before me in discussing this question was very imperfect. It was, however, less imperfect than the evidence which enabled Darwin to reach a conclusion in the matter which is still accepted by most persons qualified to judge. Professor Pearson has introduced more exact methods of dealing with biological data, and for this we owe him a debt of gratitude. But it is necessary to point out, once more, that a scientific method is, strictly, an *instrument*. Its value depends upon the user. Professor Pearson possesses a statistical instrument of great precision, but the best instrument in the world will not enable a man to select his facts rightly or to interpret them correctly. I have shown (as specifically as I am able) that in attacking my position Professor Pearson has applied his method to the wrong facts, that he has, moreover, wrongly interpreted his own results, and that he has, further, fallen into many extraordinary errors by the way. Now, as he retires from the assault, he is content to say, in effect: "But then, you see, my methods were so scientific!" If that reply were adequate to the occasion it would constitute a serious criticism of scientific methods. It remains an instructive self-criticism.

INDEX OF AUTHORS.

INDEX OF SUBJECTS.

———◆———

THE WALTER SCOTT PUBLISHING CO., LIMITED, NEWCASTLE-ON-TYNE.